I first started teaching United States Air Force Test Pilot School (USAF TPS) students about "Pitot-Statics and the Standard Atmosphere" in the fall of 1997 (Class 97B). After teaching this course six times, the student feedback was quite clear that the textbook provided was difficult to understand for a first time student and left much to be desired. This was the same textbook that I had used as a student in the fall of 1989 (Class 89B) and had been in use for many years before that.

To ease my workload in teaching the course, in 2000 I requested permission to write a new Pitot-Statics textbook, with the goal of making it easier to understand and of filling in the holes of understanding left in the previous textbook, such as the source of the many seemingly bizarre equations. This textbook had the desired effect of reducing my teaching workload by giving the students a better reference. As my understanding of the subject increased over the years, I have incorporated that new understanding into improvements in the textbook in hopes of making that understanding more easily accessible for future flight testers.

In 2017, I became aware of interest in this textbook from organizations such as the Society of Flight Test Engineers (SFTE) and the Department of Aeronautics (DFAN) at the United States Air Force Academy. Realizing the lack of comprehensive references on Pitot-Statics available outside of Test Pilot Schools or aerospace company proprietary documents, USAF TPS began the long process to peer review this textbook and approve it for public release.

The reader is encouraged to also obtain a copy of *Pitot-Static Systems: Class Notes* from the United States Naval Test Pilot School (USNTPS) (Ref 1), approved for public release in 2019. The USNTPS textbook is not redundant with this textbook, following a more "operational" approach to doing flight tests with less emphasis on the mathematics. It also includes techniques used on aircraft not tested at the Air Force Test Center, such as helicopters. Rather than further increase the size of this textbook by repeating information only covered in the USNTPS textbook, the reader is simply encouraged to procure a copy of each.

Russell E. Erb

Summary of Changes

Fourth Edition
    Initial public release.

Table of Contents

Chapter 1. Why Study Pitot-Statics? 1
    Textbook Structure 2

Chapter 2. Standard Atmosphere 3
    Why Do I Need a Standard Atmosphere? 3
    Creating the Standard Atmosphere 3
    Measuring the Atmosphere 4
    Equation of State 4
    Pressure and Altitude 4
    Geopotential Altitude and the Constant g 6
    Geopotential Altitude 6
    Standard Atmosphere Assumptions 7
        Dry Air 7
        Air Acts as a Perfect Gas 8
        Constant Acceleration of Gravity 8
        Measured Temperature Variation 8
    Let's Do It! 9
    Isothermal Regions 9
    Gradient Regions 10
    Temperature, Pressure, and Density Ratios 11
    Putting the Numbers in the Equations 11
        Troposphere 13
        Stratosphere 13
    Standard Atmosphere History 14

Chapter 3. Altitude Measurement 19
    So How High Are We? 19
    The Altimeter 22
    Why Is It Called the Kollsman Window? 22
    How Much Does the Kollsman Window Setting Change the Altitude Displayed? 26
    Altimeter Settings and ATC 26
    Pressure Contour Levels 27
    Density Altitude—Finding Density for Non-Standard Conditions 29
    Measuring Rate of Climb 30

Chapter 4. Airspeed Measurement 33
    So How Fast Are We Flying? 33
    True Airspeed 34
    Equivalent Airspeed 34
    Calibrated Airspeed 35
    Time for the Nestea Plunge 37
    Differential Pressure (Compressible q) 38
    Effects of Temperature and Pressure on Airspeed 39
    Converting Airspeeds, Airspeed Method 40
    Supersonic Considerations 44
    Mach Number Revisited 45
    Converting Airspeeds, Mach Method 47
    Measuring Airspeed 50
    Air Data Sensors 52
    Airspeed Indicator Construction 55
    Mach Meter Construction 56
    Henri Pitot and His Tube 57

Ernst Mach and His Number 58

Chapter 5. Temperature Measurement 59
The You Can't Get There From Here 59
Determining the Temperature Recovery Factor 61
Variable Temperature Recovery Factor 62

Chapter 6. Air Data System Errors...63
Tell Me Again Why I Should Care 63
Instrument Error..63
System Errors...65
        Lag...65
        Dynamic Imbalance 68
        Leaks..69
How Does This Static Pressure Compensation Thing Work?....................66
Position Error 69
        Total Pressure Position Error 69
        Static Pressure Position Error 70
        Static Port Locations 71
Reducing Static Pressure Errors..72
        Supersonic Pitot-Static Tubes 72
        Compensated Pitot-Static Tubes..72
        Separate Static Source Compensation 73
        Effects of Non-Flush Static Ports 74
        Reducing Errors From Sideslip..75
        Cabin Static/Alternate Static Source...75
Position Error Terminology 75
Applying Instrument and Position Corrections 76
Position Error Ratio and Pressure Coefficient 77
Presenting Position Corrections 79
Variations in Position Corrections 80
A Word of Caution...83
Pitot Statics Gross Buffoonery 84

Chapter 7. Altitude Comparison Flight Test Techniques 85
The Big Picture 85
Tower Fly-By..85
Pace..91
Trailing Cone/Trailing Bomb...92
Survey 96
Ground Calibration 100

Chapter 8. Airspeed Comparison Flight Test Techniques.......................101
The Big Assumptions...101
Ground Speed Course 101
Using GPS as a Truth Source 103
All Altitude Speed Course 103
Horseshoe GPS Method 105
Cloverleaf..106
Turn Regression 108

Chapter 9. Data Reduction 111
Tower Fly-By Data Reduction 111
Pace Data Reduction 115
Trailing Cone/Bomb Data Reduction..121
Survey Data Reduction 124

Speed Course Data Reduction...130
All Altitude Speed Course Data Reduction...135
Horseshoe GPS Data Reduction..140
Cloverleaf Data Reduction (Vector Method)...146
Cloverleaf Data Reduction (Matrix Inversion Method)...154
Turn Regression Data Reduction 162
Calculating Position Corrections from the Position Error Ratio 170

Appendix A. Standard Atmosphere Heavy Math Section 179
Equation of State...179
Hydrostatic Equation...180
Geopotential Altitude..181
Radius of the Earth..183
Calculating the Standard Atmosphere...183
Isothermal Regions 184
Gradient Regions 185
Temperature, Pressure, and Density Ratios 188
Troposphere Equations 188
Stratosphere Equations..189
Comparing Water Vapor Density to Air Density...189
Calculating Density of Humid Air 190
Temperature Variations with Altitude...193
Tropospheric Cooling 194
Stratospheric Heating...196
Mesospheric Cooling 200
Thermospheric Heating...201
Isothermal Regions 202

Appendix B. Altitude Measurement Heavy Math Section 205
Pressure Altitude 205
Density Altitude 205
Kollsman Window Shift...206
Pressure Contour Shift With Temperature 207
Calculating Non-Standard Density 208

Appendix C. Airspeed, Mach, and Temperature Measurement Heavy Math Section 209
Dynamic Pressure 209
True Airspeed Equation 209
Equivalent Airspeed...215
Calibrated Airspeed..216
Differential Pressure Ratios 217
Continuity Between Subsonic and Supersonic Pressures...222
Finding Mach from Calibrated Airspeed and Pressure Altitude 223
Computing f Factor and ΔV_c...227
Mach Is Mach 231
Differential Pressure and Dynamic Pressure...232
Temperature Recovery Factor..237
Variable Temperature Recovery Factor 238

Appendix D. Pitot-Static System Errors Heavy Math Section 241
Position Errors 241
Finding Position Error Corrections 242
Finding Position Error From a Measured Altitude Position Correction....................242
Finding Position Error From a Measured Airspeed Position Correction 243
Finding Position Error From a Measured Mach Position Correction.........................244
Finding Altitude Position Correction From Position Error 245

Finding Airspeed Position Correction From Position Error..246
Finding Mach Position Correction From Position Error 248
Applying Instrument and Position Corrections 252
Position Error Ratio and Pressure Coefficient 252
Position Error Ratio and Coefficient Variations 253
Altitude Correction Variation With Altitude 255
Finding Position Error From a Measured Altitude Position Correction, Taylor Series ..256
Finding Position Error From a Measured Airspeed Position Correction, Taylor Series .261
Finding Position Error From a Measured Mach Position Correction, Taylor Series 269
Finding Altitude Position Correction From Position Error, Taylor Series....................275
Finding Airspeed Position Correction From Position Error, Taylor Series...................275
Finding Mach Position Correction From Position Error, Taylor Series.......................277

Appendix E. Cloverleaf FTT Data Reduction Heavy Math Section 279
Vector Method 279
Alternate Matrix Inversion Method..282

Appendix F. Finding Distances and Directions From Latitudes and Longitudes 287
Spherical Trigonometry 287
Basic Relationships..288
Distance Between Two Points 288
Direction to Another Point 290

Appendix G. Weather Balloon Heavy Math Section..291
Weather Balloons and Radiosondes 291
Wait A Minute! You Don't Measure Pressure? 292
Error Analysis 299

Appendix H. Turn Regression Heavy Math Section 301
Regression of Turn Data 301
Modifications for Higher Load Factors..304

Appendix I. Soaring Weather and Air Data 307
Dry Adiabatic Lapse Rate 307
Dry Adiabatic Expansion 310
Atmospheric Stability 311
Frost Formation..314
Skew-T/Log-P Diagram..316
Is It a Good Soaring Day?...322
Total Energy as a Guide to Atmospheric Motion..324
Venturi Total Energy Probes...326
Tube Total Energy Probes...328
So What Exactly Is Going On Here? 330

Appendix J. Example Pitot-Static Sensor Installations 333

Appendix K. Pitot-Statics Glossary..395

References 401

Chapter 1

Why Study Pitot-Statics?

Virtually every flying task depends in some way on knowing the aircraft altitude, airspeed, Mach number, or air temperature. These parameters are collectively known as "air data."

Performance testing is concerned with answering questions like "How fast? How high? How far?" These questions would need airspeed and altitude information to address. Handling qualities testing is primarily concerned with how the airplane feels to the pilot, but how the airplane feels to the pilot is strongly driven by dynamic pressure, which is again determined by knowing airspeed and altitude. Advanced flight control systems require air data for scheduling gains. Many systems depend on air data. Navigation systems need airspeed to determine winds, and weapon delivery systems need airspeed and altitude to calculate release parameters. Any sort of operational testing is going to require measurements of air data to properly define tactics and write instructional manuals.

Because virtually every flight test needs air data, good air data is needed from the beginning of a flight test program. If the aircraft is new, externally modified, or the air data system has been modified, a calibration of the air data system will probably be one of the first flight tests accomplished. This could be done as early as the first flight. On the first flight of the B-2 in 1989, airspeed and altitude readings were compared with those of the safety chase F-16.

But what's all this about calibration? Don't we know by now how to make an airspeed indicator or altimeter well enough that we don't have to individually calibrate each one? Well, yes, we do, but that's not the primary issue here. An airplane flies because it is designed to disturb the air in such a way as to create a pressure differential that will offset the aircraft's weight and produce forces and moments for maneuvering. It is very difficult to measure the undisturbed freestream values of temperature, ambient pressure, and total pressure on the airplane because the entire airplane is disturbing the airflow. Without these disturbances the airplane would not fly, but with them we cannot measure exactly the data we need. That's where the calibration comes in. By good design, we can minimize the size of the errors in reading air data, and then by calibration we can determine the size of the remaining errors to correct our measurements to our best estimate of the "real" answer.

Typically flight test air data systems are not production representative. The desire in flight test is to get the best possible air data with a simple system. Using a simple system reduces the amount of errors that are introduced by the system, such as software programming errors. Note that in flight test the "best possible air data" is concerned with getting precise data, whether or not they are unbiased. If the air data are precise (repeatable) with a known error, then the corrected data can be computed to high accuracy once the calibration is known. The known errors can be worked into the test point definition to ensure data are recorded at the desired conditions. If the air data are unbiased (correct mean value) but not precise (large scatter), then there is no method to reduce the data uncertainty. Design tradeoffs may result in production air data sensors being located in less than optimal locations, but most contemporary air data systems use some form of compensation, such as a Central Air Data Computer (CADC), to apply corrections before the data are presented to the flight crew.

This course is about air data systems, but is typically referred to as "Pitot-Statics" because Pitot-static systems are the most common air data systems and the primary type that will be discussed. TPS students typically think that this is a tough course. I suspect that's primarily because it is mostly new material. Most undergraduate and graduate college programs do not typically teach this material. The concepts are not that difficult, but understanding and discussion does require use of math at a higher level than you probably remember off the top of your head. Unfortunately, the resulting equations are not simple like F = ma. They end up being fairly complex, but they do work and they actually do model the real world results.

Textbook Structure

The design of this text book intentionally departs from the norm for the specific reason of arranging the information in the hope of accelerating understanding. Many textbooks are written in such a way that they make perfect sense if you already know the material, but not if you don't. Since I don't have a board of PhDs to get this approved by, I'm trying to avoid the problem that General Jimmy Doolittle had with his doctoral dissertation (Ref 2):

> I submitted a draft of the dissertation to my advisors and it was rejected. At first they said it wasn't erudite enough. This was disappointing and when I pressed for more information, was told that it needed more mathematical calculations to fit the actual flight results…I wanted the paper to be read and understood by the average pilot, not by an aeronautical engineer….
>
> As far as I'm concerned, the master's thesis was far more significant. I felt at the time that they wanted a doctoral dissertation to be so abstract that few people could understand it….

For subjects such as this one where mathematics are important to the understanding of the concepts, many textbooks include the derivation and development of the mathematics right in the middle of the running text. I have found that this slows down the reading and makes understanding more difficult. In this book, the derivation and development of the equations has been moved to appendices referenced from the text. However, since knowing where these equations come from and knowing the involved assumptions are still important, the derivations are covered in gross detail, avoiding as much as possible statements such as "and after a few steps" (that always seemed to be 30 steps that I couldn't figure out).

Likewise, the data reduction is explained in gross detail in the concept of calculation, actual equations, and results from example data.

Every effort has been made to ensure that any equation has only one equation number associated with it. These numbers are assigned in numerical order in the appendix in which they were derived. When used in the text, the equation retains the same equation number. The first letter of the equation number is the appendix from whence it came. This allows easy cross-reference to determine where any particular equation came from.

Explanations of the many available Flight Test Techniques (FTTs) are included, covering not only those that will be practiced in the USAF TPS curriculum, but also other methods used for other purposes or at other flight test centers. In Chapter 9, the data reduction section for each FTT is written to stand alone for ease of reference. Thus, they may seem repetitious if multiple sections are read at the same time.

Appendix J includes pictures of Pitot-static installations on many different aircraft for comparison. Appendix K is a glossary of all the symbols used in this text, useful for decoding all of the subscripts.

Lastly, please help us improve this text. We don't know what was difficult to understand unless you tell us. It all makes sense to us, but then again, we already know the material. Please let us know what parts of the text you had trouble with and why you didn't understand it if you can.

Chapter 2

Standard Atmosphere

Why Do I Need a Standard Atmosphere?

The atmosphere is a large, non-uniform, constantly changing mass. Part of it is heated by the sun, both directly and from terrestrial radiation. Another part of the atmosphere is on the shaded side of the earth and cools off by radiating heat into space. Because the atmosphere rotates with the earth, the portion that is being heated or cooled is constantly changing. Because the size of the atmosphere is so large compared to the rate at which thermal changes can flow through it (i.e. typical wind speeds), the atmosphere never reaches equilibrium. This is the basis for changing weather, which makes life far more interesting than if the atmosphere was one homogeneous mass.

Even so, engineers need a model of an "average" atmosphere. This requirement shows up both in the design phase and the flight test phase. In the design phase, if you want to build an altimeter to determine altitude based on the air pressure, then you'll need a model for how pressure changes with altitude. If you are trying to design an aircraft to fly at 30,000 feet at Mach 0.88, you'll need to know the density at that altitude to calculate your engine performance. You'll need to know the temperature to determine what true airspeed corresponds to that Mach number.

In the flight test arena, we need a way to compare results from different test locations or even different conditions at the same location. It is well known that an airplane will perform better at low altitude than at high altitude. Likewise, an airplane will perform better on a cold day than a hot day. So how do we compare the performance of an airplane in Florida (near sea level) in January with the same airplane in Colorado Springs (above 6,000 feet) in August? More importantly, how do we take that information and tell the operator in the field what performance to expect at his planned flight condition?

The answer is to define a standard atmosphere, which is a model of the atmosphere on a "standard day." We will then take our flight test results from a non-standard day and calculate what the results would have been if the same test was done on a standard day. These standardized results would then be used to increase sample size for improved statistical significance, to compare the performance of one airplane to another, to evaluate performance against specifications or guarantees, and to validate models that would be used to produce the flight manual performance charts. (Note: The methods for accomplishing this data standardization will not be covered in this textbook.)

Creating the Standard Atmosphere

The primary data we need for our model (or representation) of the atmosphere is to know how temperature (T), pressure (P), and density (ρ) vary with altitude. That is, I need to be able to determine the values of these three parameters at any specified altitude. Many standard altitude tables list other parameters besides these three, but any other parameters, such as speed of sound or kinematic viscosity, can be calculated from knowing temperature, pressure, and density.

Since we have three unknowns we are looking for (T, P, ρ), the mathematicians tell us that we need three equations. Well, if we had equations like T = f(h), P = f(h), and ρ = f(h), not only would our job be easy—it would be done! These are the types of equations that we are trying to find. So, what do we do now?

Measuring the Atmosphere

Another option would be just to measure the values of temperature, pressure, and density with altitude and fit equations to those data. Unfortunately, temperature, pressure, and density are not independent functions of altitude. That is, if one value changes at a particular location, it will change the other two. However, this method will work well for one variable. The temperature profile with altitude is essentially independent of the pressure (though not the other way 'round), and temperature and pressure will define density. Therefore, we will measure the temperature distribution with altitude and fit an equation to those data as one of our three equations.

Equation of State

Another equation that we have at our disposal is the Equation of State, also known as the Perfect Gas Law or the Ideal Gas Law. You may have first seen this equation in Chemistry class expressed as

$$PV = NRT \qquad\qquad (A1)$$

where

        P = Pressure
        V = Volume
        N = Number of molecules (moles)
        R = Gas Constant
        T = Temperature

Well, that was fine for chemists, but aero engineers aren't too interested in counting molecules, and it's tough to build a molecule counter. However, a given number of air molecules are going to have a certain mass, so the Equation of State can be re-written (with a different constant) as

$$PV = mRT \qquad\qquad (A2)$$

where m = mass.

That's closer, but still not the parameters we were looking for. Well, mass divided by volume is density, which is something that we're looking for. Hence, the Equation of State becomes

$$P = \rho RT \qquad\qquad (A3)$$

This is the version of the Equation of State most useful for our analysis. This equation is valid for a perfect gas, which is one in which intermolecular forces are negligible. This is a valid assumption for air at the temperatures and pressures that we will be dealing with.

The Equation of State is useful to us because it characterizes the relationship between the three parameters. However, it doesn't relate any of them to altitude.

So far, we have an equation that relates temperature to altitude, and an equation that relates temperature, pressure, and density to each other. We still need a third equation to characterize the atmosphere.

Pressure and Altitude

How about the relationship between pressure and altitude? First, let's look at why the air is under pressure. Figure 2.1 shows a column of bricks with interspersed weightless scales. The top scale shows a weight of zero bricks, since there are no bricks above it. The next scale shows three bricks, since there are three bricks above it. The next scale has eight bricks above it, plus the three bricks above the previous scale, so it shows a weight of 11 bricks. Likewise, the bottom scale shows a weight of 19 bricks because there is a total of 19 bricks above it.

What do all of these bricks have to do with air pressure? I want a standard atmosphere, not a retaining wall. Well, remember that air has weight—not a lot of weight, but weight nonetheless. A square foot of beach sand on the Eglin beach at sea level on a standard day has 2116 pounds of air above it. That is, if we took all of the air in a square column one foot on a side from the surface to outer space and weighed it, it would have a net weight of 2116 pounds. The weight of all of this air is pressing down on our square foot of beach sand, creating a pressure of 2116 psf. If we only looked at a column one inch on a side, it would contain 14.7 pounds of air, for a pressure of 14.7 psi. That number sound familiar?

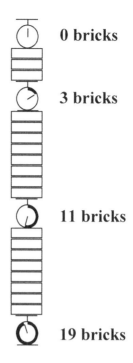

0 bricks

3 bricks

11 bricks

19 bricks

Now if we took a balloon up to 10,000 feet and held out a square foot of cardboard, the pressure on the cardboard would be 1456 psf, because there is only 1456 pounds of air above it. The air pressure is determined by the weight of the air above a point of interest. So how can we hold up the cardboard with that much weight on it? The air below the cardboard is pressurized to the same pressure by the weight of the air above it, so there is no net pressure force on the cardboard. (Okay, there is an ever so small

Figure 2.1. Column o' Bricks

difference in pressure because of the thickness of the cardboard and buoyancy effects, but these are extremely small compared to the weight of the cardboard, so we ignore them.)

This idea of an increase in pressure as altitude decreases is developed in Appendix A. Our result shows that pressure is related to altitude by the differential equation known as the Hydrostatic Equation

$$dP = -\rho\, g\, dh \qquad\qquad (A15)$$

where

P = pressure
ρ = density
g = acceleration of gravity
h = altitude (geometric)

This equation assumes that the fluid (liquid or gas) is at rest, such that there are no shear forces between fluid elements.

So all we need to do now to find the pressure change with altitude is to integrate this equation

$$\int_0^P dP = \int_0^h -\rho g\, dh \qquad\qquad (A16)$$

No problem, right? Not so fast, Moosebreath! We've got a minor problem here. First of all, we already agreed that density is a function of altitude, and we don't know what that function is yet, so it might be a little difficult to integrate a function we don't know. If that's not bad enough, talk to your friendly local astro major. She'll tell you that the acceleration of gravity changes with altitude too! Ooo, boy! So whadda we do now? Hmmm…

Geopotential Altitude and the Constant g

We'll deal with the density later by a neat mathematical trick. But first, let's talk about that non-constant acceleration of gravity. Our good buddy of yore Sir Isaac Newton told us that for a single body problem, the acceleration of gravity varies as

$$g = g_{SL} \left(\frac{R_{e_{SL}}}{R_{e_{SL}} + h} \right)^2$$ (A18)

where

g_{SL} = acceleration of gravity at sea level
$R_{e_{SL}}$ = radius of the earth

Why a single body problem? Because the mass, and thus the gravitational acceleration, of the air is negligible when compared to the earth.

Yes, the acceleration of gravity does vary with altitude, but let's take off our scientist hat and put on our engineering hat for a moment. How big is this effect?

First of all, the difference between the acceleration of gravity at sea level and the local acceleration of gravity at altitude grows larger the higher we go. But what are our altitudes of interest? In this textbook we will only concern ourselves with the Troposphere and Stratosphere. Here at the Flight Test Center, we rarely fly above 40,000 feet. So what is the acceleration of gravity at 40,000 feet? Using the values

g_{SL} = 32.1741 ft/sec^2 (adopted primary constant, 1962 US Standard Atmosphere, Ref 3)

$R_{e_{SL}}$ = 20,902,808.99 ft (radius of the earth at mean sea level at 34.9 degrees latitude, WGS-84 spheroid)

we get

$g_{40,000\,ft}$ = 32.051 ft/sec^2

Is this a problem? The difference is a whopping 0.382 percent, far less than one percent. That's not much, but we can use a math trick to deal with the change.

Geopotential Altitude

We can make g constant by shifting the change with altitude into a different concept of altitude. The hydrostatic equation,

$$dP = -\rho\, g\, dh$$ (A15)

is valid for a variable acceleration of gravity, that is, the real world case. If we are going to change the way that g changes with altitude (i.e. make it not change), then we have to make a reciprocal change in another parameter in the equation so that both sides will stay equal. The best candidate for this is the way we measure altitude. We will define a new type of altitude which we will call Geopotential Altitude (H), which refers to the distance that a given unit of energy (a potential) will lift a given unit of mass (Ref 4). Geopotential altitude is defined by the equation

$$g\, dh = g_{SL}\, dH$$ (A17)

Thus, any change in g will be offset by a reciprocal change in geopotential altitude. Based on this equation, we can substitute into the hydrostatic equation and get

$$dP = -\rho\, g_{SL}\, dH \qquad (A30)$$

We will use this equation to help define our standard atmosphere in terms of geopotential altitude. As will be seen later, this not only makes the math easier, it makes the math possible. Though our standard atmosphere will be calculated in geopotential altitude, it is not difficult to then convert those values to the values at geometric altitude. The physical length of geopotential units is not constant but increases at higher elevations because the acceleration of gravity decreases (same energy will raise the same mass farther because gravity's attraction (weight) is less). As shown in Appendix A, geopotential altitude and geometric altitude are related by

$$H = \left(\frac{R_{e_{SL}}}{R_{e_{SL}} + h} \right) h \qquad (A29)$$

What is the magnitude of this difference?

Let's look again at our case of flying at 40,000 feet geometric altitude on a standard day. Plugging 40,000 feet into Equation A29 yields a geopotential altitude of 39,924 feet, a difference of 76 feet and a 0.191 percent error. Small enough for most of our efforts. Besides, we will see later that for most flight testing, we will be more interested in yet another kind of altitude than geopotential or geometric.

Equation A29 also gives us the way to get the standard atmosphere values for geometric altitudes. If we want to know the temperature, pressure, and density on a standard day at 40,000 geometric feet, we use Equation A29 to calculate the corresponding geopotential altitude (39,924 feet). We would then calculate the temperature, pressure, and density at 39,924 geopotential feet, which will be the values for 40,000 geometric feet.

Standard Atmosphere Assumptions

We've already touched on some of the assumptions required to calculate the standard atmosphere, but let's bring them all together in one place.

Dry Air

This is, of course, not true. Flight testers at Eglin are frequently reminded that humidity exists, like every time they go outside. Some humidity will always exist, although in many locations it will be very small. As shown in Appendix A, water vapor has about 62 percent the density of dry air, meaning that a mixture of dry air and water vapor will have an overall lower density than dry air at the same pressure and temperature. Here in the desert environment of Edwards AFB, the relative humidity is typically around 53 percent in the morning to 25 percent in the afternoon. The difference between the actual moist air density and the dry air density at the same pressure and temperature will be around 1 percent at these conditions. At 100° F and 100 percent humidity, the error can be as much as 7 percent. At higher altitudes, especially above the clouds, humidity will drop off significantly.

Interestingly, in humid environments, the amount of lift and drag created by the wings, propellers, and other surfaces depends on the moist air density, the density of the air and water vapor mixture. However, reciprocating engine power depends only on the density remaining if the water vapor were taken away (density at the same temperature and pressure reduced by the partial pressure of water vapor), since the engine performance really depends on the amount of oxygen available. Jet performance is somewhere in between, since the combustion depends on oxygen available, but the mass flow to create thrust depends on the moist air density.

So if there is error involved with assuming dry air, why not assume moist air? As you may have already thought, allowing moisture into the question significantly complicates the analysis for very little gain. For our purposes, it would greatly complicate using the Equation of State, since air and water vapor have different gas constants (R), and their mixture would have yet another gas constant, which would depend on the humidity. So rather than have a standard atmosphere that changes with humidity, the defining body of the standard atmosphere decided that the air would be assumed dry.

Air Acts as a Perfect Gas

As alluded to before in our search for equations, we will assume that air acts as a perfect gas, which is to say that it obeys the Equation of State ($P = \rho R T$). R is defined as M/R^*, where M is the mean molecular weight of air and R^* is the universal gas constant. M is assumed to be constant up to an altitude of approximately 90 kilometers (295,000 feet), above which M changes because of increasing dissociation and diffusive separation.

Constant Acceleration of Gravity

As mentioned earlier, we will assume that the acceleration of gravity is fixed at its sea level value. As a result, the standard atmosphere will be defined in geopotential altitude.

Measured Temperature Variation

We said that we would measure the temperature profile to define one of our needed equations. Years of measurements from weather balloons, airplanes, and later sounding rockets were used to come up with a profile, shown in Figure 2.2. This profile is made up of altitude bands with temperature defined as varying linearly with altitude throughout the band. In some bands the temperature is constant for all altitudes within the band.

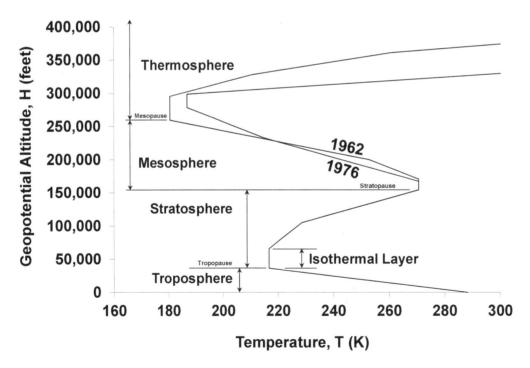

Figure 2.2. Temperature Profile, 1962 and 1976 US Standard Atmosphere (Ref 3 and 5)

The troposphere is heated from below by the surface of the earth, which is warmed by solar radiation. The air at higher altitude is cooler as it is farther away from the heat source. The stratosphere is warmed by the interaction of ultraviolet radiation with oxygen and ozone in the ozone layer. The mesosphere above the stratosphere cools with altitude as carbon dioxide absorbs and radiates infrared energy into space. The altitude bands that are a transition between the cooling and warming zones are modeled as isothermal regions, which is a simple model that is sufficiently representative of the transitions in these regions. More details of these heating and cooling processes are covered in Appendix A.

Let's Do It!

Finally we have all of the equations and assumptions we need to generate the standard atmosphere. To review, we have three unknowns (temperature, pressure, and density) so we need three equations. Our three equations are

1. The Equation of State
2. The Hydrostatic Equation
3. A Temperature Profile with Altitude

We also needed four assumptions.

1. Dry Air
2. Perfect Gas (covered in the Equation of State)
3. Constant Acceleration of Gravity
4. Linear or Constant Temperature Profile (covered in the measured temperature profile)

Armed with this information, let's hop to it. Let's see, where were we? Oh, yes—we were trying to integrate the Hydrostatic Equation when we ran up against the problem that density and the acceleration of gravity were both functions of altitude. Well, we solved our problem with gravity, but what about density? Somebody many years ago found a neat mathematical trick that will address our problem. If you flash back to algebra class (assuming that's not too frightening), you may recall that if we divide an equation by an equation, the result is still an equation.

With that obscure thought in mind, let's divide the Hydrostatic Equation by the Equation of State to get

$$\frac{dP}{P} = \frac{-\rho g_{SL} dH}{\rho RT} \qquad (A32)$$

If we divide out the density (my algebra teacher would never let us say "cancel") we get

$$\frac{dP}{P} = -\frac{g_{SL}}{RT} dH \qquad (A33)$$

Now we have an expression that we can actually integrate. g_{SL} and R are constants, and we'll know how T varies with altitude.

Isothermal Regions

Iso-what? Isothermal—it means constant temperature. We have two types of regions that we need to integrate Equation A33 in, regions where the temperature doesn't change (isothermal regions) and regions where the temperature changes linearly with altitude (gradient regions). We'll look at the isothermal regions first since the math is easier.

For isothermal regions, the relationship of temperature with altitude is simply

$$T = \text{constant} \tag{A34}$$

Betcha saw that one coming, eh? With that established, we will integrate Equation A33 starting at the base altitude (bottom of the altitude band, designated by subscript B) to the altitude of interest (no subscript). When we do that, we get

$$\frac{P}{P_B} = e^{-\left(\frac{g_{SL}}{RT_B}\right)(H-H_B)} \tag{A41}$$

Using this relationship with the Equation of State we can get the density variation as

$$\frac{\rho}{\rho_B} = e^{-\left(\frac{g_{SL}}{RT_B}\right)(H-H_B)} \tag{A44}$$

Gradient Regions

For the gradient regions we have a different relationship between temperature and altitude. We call this relationship the temperature lapse rate and define it as

$$L = \frac{dT}{dH} = \text{constant} \tag{A45}$$

Integrating this equation from the base altitude to the altitude of interest results in an expression for temperature.

$$\frac{T}{T_B} = 1 + \frac{L}{T_B}(H - H_B) \tag{A51}$$

Using Equation A45 to define the variation of temperature with altitude, we can again integrate our magic pressure equation

$$\frac{dP}{P} = -\frac{g_{SL}}{RT} dH \tag{A33}$$

to get

$$\frac{P}{P_B} = \left(1 + \frac{L}{T_B}(H - H_B)\right)^{\frac{-g_{SL}}{RL}} \tag{A63}$$

Again, returning to the equation of state, we find the density variation with altitude to be

$$\frac{\rho}{\rho_B} = \left(1 + \frac{L}{T_B}(H - H_B)\right)^{\frac{-g_{SL}}{RL}-1} \tag{A68}$$

It is interesting to note that for gradient regions, the density variation is exactly the same as the pressure variation except that it is raised to an exponent exactly 1 less.

Temperature, Pressure, and Density Ratios

You may have noticed by now that all of the equations we have derived are ratios of the parameter of interest to the value of that parameter at some base altitude. By far, the most popular values to use in the denominator are the values of temperature, pressure, and density at sea level on a standard day. So popular, in fact, that such ratios are given special symbols. The temperature ratio is labeled theta, the pressure ratio is labeled delta, the density ratio is labeled sigma, and are defined as such:

$$\theta = \frac{T}{T_{SL}} \qquad (A69)$$

$$\delta = \frac{P}{P_{SL}} \qquad (A70)$$

$$\sigma = \frac{\rho}{\rho_{SL}} \qquad (A71)$$

You might as well learn these now, because they will continue to pop up throughout your flight test career. As we calculate the actual values for the standard atmosphere, we will be calculating these ratios. Many equations tend to work better using these ratios instead of the values alone. Best of all, when using ratios you don't have to worry as much about keeping your units straight.

Putting the Numbers in the Equations

Having the equations is great, but unless we have values for the constants, they're not very useful. Reference 3 describes the 1962 US Standard Atmosphere as "idealized middle-latitude year-round mean conditions for the range of solar activity that occurs between sunspot minimum and sunspot maximum." Further digging implies that "middle-latitude" is taken as 45°. While this may seem well north of Edwards AFB, it is basically the latitude of Salem, Oregon, Minneapolis, Minnesota, Bangor, Maine, Southern France, Northern Italy, the north tip of Japan, and well south of England. When you consider this, the "average" sea level temperature of 59° F doesn't seem that unreasonable.

Table 2.1 shows the adopted primary constants for the 1962 and 1976 US Standard Atmospheres.

Table 2.1
Adopted Primary Constants, 1962 and 1976 US Standard Atmospheres (Ref 3 and 5)

Symbol	Parameter	Value
T_{SL}	Sea Level Temperature	15° C, 59°F, 288.15K
P_{SL}	Sea Level Pressure	2116.22 lb/ft^2
ρ_{SL}	Sea Level Density	0.076474 lb/ft^3 0.00237688 slug/ft^3
g_{SL}	Sea Level Acceleration of Gravity	32.1741 ft/sec^2
γ	Ratio of Specific Heats	1.40
R^*	Universal Gas Constant	1545.31 ft-lb/(lb-mol)-°R
M	Air Molecular Weight	28.9644 lbm/(lb-mol)
R	Specific Gas Constant (Air)	3089.8 ft-lb/slug-K 1716.6 ft-lb/slug-°R

Tables 2.2 and 2.3 and Figure 2.2 show the temperature profile as defined for the 1962 and 1976 US Standard Atmospheres. Note that altitudes for the Standard Atmosphere are defined in

geopotential altitude (H) up to 88.743 km (1962) or 84.8520 km (1976), and in geometric altitude (h) above these altitudes. These changes happen because the perfect gas assumption starts to break down because of increasing dissociation and diffusive separation.

Table 2.2
Temperature Profile, US Standard Atmosphere, 1962 (Ref 3)

Altitude, H km	Temperature, T K	Gradient, L K/km	Altitude, H ft	Gradient, L K/1000 ft	
0.000	288.15		0.00		
		-6.5		-1.9812	Troposphere
11.000	216.65		36,089.24		
		0.0		0.0	Stratosphere
20.000	216.65		65,616.8		
		+1.0		+0.3048	
32.000	228.65		104,986.9		
		+2.8		+0.85344	
47.000	270.62		154,199.5		
		0.0		0.0	Mesosphere
52.000	270.65		170,603.7		
		-2.0		-0.6096	
61.000	252.65		200,131.2		
		-4.0		-1.2192	
79.000	180.65		259,186.4		
		0.0		0.0	Thermosphere
88.743	180.65		291,151.6		
		0.0		0.0	
90 (h)	180.65		295,275.6		
		+3		+0.9144	
100 (h)	210.65		328,084.0		
		+5		+1.524	
110 (h)	260.65		360,892.4		
		+10		+3.048	
120 (h)	360.65		393,700.8		

Table 2.3
Temperature Profile, US Standard Atmosphere, 1976 (Ref 5)

Altitude, H km	Temperature, T K	Gradient, L K/km	Altitude, H ft	Gradient, L K/1000 ft	
0.000	288.15		0.00		
		-6.5		-1.9812	Troposphere
11.000	216.65		36,089.24		
		0.0		0.0	Stratosphere
20.000	216.65		65,616.8		
		+1.0		+0.3048	
32.000	228.65		104,986.9		
		+2.8		+0.85344	
47.000	270.65		154,199.5		
		0.0		0.0	Mesosphere
51.000	270.65		167,322.8		
		-2.8		-0.85344	
71.000	214.65		232,939.6		
		-2.0		-0.6096	
84.8520	186.95		278,385.8		
		0.0		0.0	Thermosphere
86 (h)	186.95		282,152.2		
		0.0		0.0	
91 (h)	186.95		298,556.4		
		12.0		3.6576	
110 (h)	414.95		360,892.4		

Troposphere

The troposphere is defined for an altitude band from –5 kilometers to 11 kilometers (-16,404.2 feet to 36,089.24 feet). The base altitude is mean sea level (0 geopotential feet). The base values for temperature, pressure, and density are given in Table 1. Note that the lapse rate, L, for the troposphere is –1.9812 K/1000 feet. This matches with the old pilot's rule of thumb that temperature decreases with altitude at the rate of 2° C per thousand feet.

Why –5 Kilometers?

It would not be unreasonable to ask why the standard atmosphere is defined all the way down to 5 kilometers below sea level. After all, the lowest point on earth is the Dead Sea, which has an elevation of –408 meters (-1339 feet), so it's doubtful that anyone would be aviating any lower than that.

One possible explanation arises when considering density altitude. Assume you are in Nome, Alaska, and the temperature is –90° C (-130° F). If we assume a sea level pressure, the resulting density altitude would be –16,341 feet. To allow for these temperature extremes, the standard atmosphere had to be defined to that low of an altitude.

After inserting our constants, we get

$$\theta = 1 - 6.87559 \times 10^{-6}\, H \tag{A78}$$

$$\delta = (1 - 6.87559 \times 10^{-6}\, H)^{5.2559} \tag{A79}$$

$$\sigma = (1 - 6.87559 \times 10^{-6}\, H)^{4.2559} \tag{A80}$$

Note that the units of the constant 6.87559×10^{-6} are per foot (/ft).

Stratosphere

The stratosphere includes an isothermal altitude band from 11 kilometers to 20 kilometers (36,089.24 feet to 65,616.8 feet), and an increasing temperature altitude band from 20 kilometers up to the stratopause at 47 kilometers. This textbook is primarily concerned with airplanes, which mostly fly below 65,000 feet. Therefore, we will only evaluate the isothermal portion of the stratosphere.

Of course, in the isothermal region there is no temperature lapse rate. The base altitude is 11 kilometers. The base values for temperature, pressure, and density come from the troposphere calculations at 11 kilometers, and are

$$T_B = 216.65 \text{ K} \quad \theta_B = 0.751865 \tag{A81}$$

$$P_B = 472.679 \text{ lb/ft}^2 \quad \delta_B = 0.223360 \tag{A82}$$

$$\rho_B = 0.0007061 \text{ slug/ft}^3 \quad \sigma_B = 0.297075 \tag{A83}$$

Our equations for isothermal regions are written as ratios of the parameter to its value at the base altitude. However, it is more useful to have ratios of the parameter to the sea level value. Note that

$$\theta = \frac{T}{T_{SL}} = \frac{T_B}{T_{SL}} \frac{T}{T_B} = \theta_B \frac{T}{T_B} \tag{A84}$$

Applying this concept and inserting our constants, we get

$$\boxed{\theta = 0.751865}$$ (A86)

$$\boxed{\delta = 0.223360 \ e^{(-4.80637 \times 10^{-5} \ (H - 36089.24))}}$$ (A87)

$$\boxed{\sigma = 0.297075 \ e^{(-4.80637 \times 10^{-5} \ (H - 36089.24))}}$$ (A88)

Note that the units of the constant 4.80637×10^{-5} are per foot (/ft).

Standard Atmosphere History

During the Revolutionary War, George Washington and the Continental Army had very little interest in the properties of the atmosphere above them. Shortly thereafter, though, with the start of ballooning in 1783 there was a sudden requirement amongst scientists to understand the properties of the atmosphere at altitudes more than a few feet above the ground. Even so, engineers did not have a compelling need for this type of information until the advent of heavier than air flight. Since flight performance is so dependent on air density, pressure and temperature, it was essentially impossible to do any sort of engineering design on aircraft without a model of the atmosphere. Furthermore, this model of the atmosphere should be agreed upon throughout the world if there was any hope of being able to communicate and compare engineering designs with any sort of validity. Thus the requirement for a standard atmosphere was born.

So where do you go to get data on the atmosphere? Hmmm, the Weather Bureau would seem like a good place to start. In 1915, the Chief of the U.S. Weather Bureau was C.F. Marvin, who also happened to be the chairman of an NACA subcommittee to investigate and report upon the existing status of atmospheric data and knowledge. Their report, "Preliminary Report on the Problem of the Atmosphere in Relation to Aeronautics" (NACA Report No. 4, 1915), stated

> The Weather Bureau is already in possession of an immense amount of data concerning atmospheric conditions, including wind movements at the earth's surface. This information is no doubt of distinct value to aeronautical operations, but it needs to be collected and put in form to meet the requirements of aviation.

And thus many scientists and engineers went to work studying the atmosphere. In 1920 A. Toussaint, director of the Aerodynamic Laboratory at Saint-Cyr-l'Ecole, France, suggested a relationship for temperature with altitude. He expressed this as

$$T = 15 - 0.0065H$$

where T was in degrees Celsius and H was the geopotential altitude in meters. If we convert meters to feet we get

$$T = 15 - 0.0019812H$$

which, if you check back a few sections (Tables 2.2 and 2.3), is still the temperature relationship used for the troposphere. Of course, in 1920 Toussaint had no reason to know about the stratosphere or any of those other –ospheres.

Toussaint's formula was formally adopted by France and Italy with the Draft of Inter-Allied Agreement on Law Adopted for the Decrease of Temperature with Increase of Altitude, issued by the Ministere de la Guerre, Aeronautique Militaire, Section Technique, in March 1920. England bought in the next year, and the United States shortly after that. Eighteen years after the Wright Brothers' first successful powered flight, on 17 December 1921 NACA adopted Toussaint's formula for airplane performance testing, saying "The subcommittee on aerodynamics recommends that for the sake of uniform practice in different countries that Toussaint's formula be adopted in determining the standard atmosphere up to 10 km (33,000 ft)...."

Toussaint's formula was supported by data from NACA Report No. 147, "Standard Atmosphere," by Willis Ray Gregg in 1922. This report cited data from free-flight tests at McCook Field in Dayton, Ohio, Langley Field in Hampton, Virginia, and Washington D.C. Additionally, artillery data from Aberdeen, Maryland and Dahlgren, Virginia were used. Finally, sounding balloon observations were used from Fort Omaha, Nebraska and St. Louis, Missouri. With all of these data, Gregg compiled the results shown in Table 2.4.

Table 2.4
Evaluation of Toussaint's Formula

Altitude (meters)	Mean Annual Temperature in United States (K)	Temperature from Toussaint's Formula (K)	Difference (K)
0	284.5	288	3.5
1,000	281.0	281.5	0.5
2,000	277.0	275.0	-2
5,000	260.0	255.5	-4.5
10,000	228.5	223.0	-5.5

Thus, Toussaint's formula was a reasonable model for reality while maintaining a simple mathematical form. This was Gregg's point, and he didn't go much farther in developing a standard atmosphere for engineering use.

Not wanting to let a thing like this slide, in 1925 Walter S. Diehl produced NACA Report No. TR 218 "Standard Atmosphere." This report included the first practical tables for aeronautical use. The tables were presented in English and Metric units, with data every 100 feet up to 32,000 feet, and every 200 feet up to 65,000 feet. Considering that the aircraft of the time were the same vintage as the Spirit of St Louis, these data were more than sufficient. Diehl used Toussaint's Formula for temperature up to 10,769 meters (35,331 feet), and then a constant temperature of -55°C up to 65,000 feet. Pressure and density were calculated in the same manner as described in this chapter.

Diehl's standard atmosphere was sufficient for a while, but started to be limited as aircraft continued to fly higher and higher. In the 1940s rockets such as the German V-2 and sounding rockets made it apparent that it was not sufficient to just continue the stratosphere model up to higher altitudes. With the development of intercontinental ballistic missiles and later space flight, a requirement arose to characterize the upper atmosphere. In 1954 the International Civil Aviation Organization (ICAO) published the *Manual of the ICAO Standard Atmosphere*. In 1953 the United States Committee on Extension to the Standard Atmosphere (COESA) was formed, and in 1958 published *U.S. Extension to the ICAO Standard Atmosphere—Tables and Data to 300 Standard Geopotential Kilometers*. This was followed by the Air Research Development Center (ARDC) 1959 Standard Atmosphere. For the lower 20 kilometers there were very few changes over the years, as shown in this comparison of Diehl's 1925 atmosphere with the ARDC 1959 atmosphere.

Table 2.5
Comparison of 1925 and 1959 Standard Atmospheres

Altitude (meters)	Temperature Diehl, 1925 (K)	Temperature ARDC, 1959 (K)	Difference (K)
0	288	288.16	0.16
1,000	281.5	281.66	0.16
2,000	275.0	275.16	0.16
5,000	255.5	255.69	0.19
10,000	223.0	223.26	0.26
10,800	218.0	218.03	0.03
11,100	218.0	216.66	-1.34
20,000	218.0	216.66	-1.34

As with so many things in America, everything was hunky-dory on the Standard Atmosphere front until two words: Sput-nik. Besides upsetting almost everything in the fabric of American culture, analysis of the orbital periods of Sputnik I indicated that densities at the upper altitudes were in error by more than an order of magnitude. COESA came together again in January 1960 to consider how the standard atmosphere needed to be revised. They couldn't analyze the data from Russian satellites closely because the Soviets for some unknown reason would not release the aerodynamic configuration of their satellites. Besides that, the Russian satellite data only covered the lower altitude range of satellite orbits. Data from United States satellites were used for extreme altitude data, along with high-altitude balloons and sounding rockets. Additionally, observations at satellite altitudes were included to understand the effects of solar activity and position. From these data, the *U.S. Standard Atmosphere, 1962* was published. This atmosphere matched the ICAO atmosphere up to 20 kilometers. It was unusual in that it included a more complicated gravity model than previous atmospheres, which had used the R^2 model presented in this text. The result was that the relationship between geopotential and geometric altitude were slightly different than for other standard atmospheres.

At high altitudes, it becomes more difficult to measure the air properties. Density is the primary atmospheric property measured at high altitudes, presumably by measuring the effects of air loads on rockets and satellites. However, it is necessary to define the atmosphere in terms of temperature for continuity with the lower altitudes. At these altitudes, it is necessary to differentiate between molecular-scale temperature and kinetic temperature. The difference between these temperatures arises because the mean molecular weight of air changes at extreme altitudes. The molecular-scale temperature is the defining property, but the kinetic temperature is what would be measured without compensating for the change in molecular weight. These temperatures are identical up to 90 kilometers.

The *U.S. Standard Atmosphere, 1962* agreed in general with but differed in detail from the Committee on Space Research (COSPAR) International Reference Atmosphere (CIRA) 1961, and the CIRA 1961 did not agree with the ICAO Standard Atmosphere. The *U.S. Standard Atmosphere,1962* provided detail and more parameters than did CIRA 1961, and included refinements in matching data that were not possible in the earlier COSPAR atmosphere.

While the *U.S. Standard Atmosphere, 1962* provided a good model of the atmosphere for engineering and design work, it was not very good for operational use, precisely because it was a single representation of the atmosphere for mid-latitude year-round mean conditions. This was not very useful for calculating re-entry trajectories or ephemeris predictions for low altitude orbits. At the behest of the U.S. space program, in 1966 supplements were released to the U.S. Standard Atmosphere, 1962 for conditions other than the mid-latitude mean. Tables were published that were representative of winter and summer conditions for various latitudes. Tables for the surface to 120 kilometers were keyed to seasonal and latitudinal variations. Tables for 120 to 1000 kilometers were keyed to solar and geomagnetic activity and solar angle.

During the 11 year solar cycle following the publication of the U.S. Standard Atmosphere, 1962, additional data were collected by rockets and satellites above 50 kilometers. With this increased knowledge of the upper atmosphere, the U.S. Standard Atmosphere, 1976 was published. Both the 1962 and 1976 U.S. Standard Atmospheres were identical to the ICAO Standard Atmosphere as revised in 1964 up to 32 kilometers, and the 1973 International Standards Organization (ISO) Standard Atmosphere up to 50 kilometers. The U.S. Standard Atmosphere, 1976 reverted back to the R^2 gravity model. The U.S. Standard Atmosphere, 1962 attempted to depict idealized middle-latitude year-round mean conditions for the range of solar activity that occurs between sunspot minimum and sunspot maximum, but subsequent observations showed mean conditions of solar activity were considerably lower. The World Meteorological Organizations's (WMO) definition of a standard atmosphere was accepted by COESA and is as follows:

> ...A hypothetical vertical distribution of atmospheric temperature, pressure and density which, by international agreement, is roughly representative of year-round, mid-latitude conditions. Typical usages are as a basis for pressure altimeter calibrations, aircraft performance calculations, aircraft and rocket design, ballistic tables, and meteorological diagrams. The air is assumed to obey the perfect gas law and hydrostatic equation which, taken together, relate temperature, pressure and density with geopotential. Only one standard atmosphere should be specified at a particular time and this standard atmosphere must not be subjected to amendment except at intervals of many years.

COESA added to this definition

> This atmosphere shall also be considered to rotate with the earth, and be an average over the diurnal cycle, semi-annual variation, and the range of conditions from active to quiet geomagnetic, and active to quiet sunspot conditions. Above the turbopause (about 110 km) generalized forms of the hydrostatic equations apply.

In the past, the Flight Test Center primarily used the U.S. Standard Atmosphere, 1962, though it has now mostly changed over to using the U.S. Standard Atmosphere, 1976. As mentioned earlier, for the altitudes of interest for most aircraft, the change has been immaterial, since the variations are in the upper atmosphere.

Chapter 3

Altitude Measurement

So How High Are We?

Before answering this question, we have to ask another question, namely "What do you mean by 'high'?" This isn't some sort of political verbal maneuvering, but a necessary question.

There are at least four different types of "altitude" that we will deal with: geometric (or tapeline), geopotential, pressure, and density.

Geometric Altitude is the one that you would probably first think of. Oddly enough, it is one of the less useful definitions of altitude for use in flight test. Geometric altitude is an actual distance (measured in units like feet or meters (or metres if you prefer)) above some datum plane. The two most popular datums (data?) are Mean Sea Level (expressed as feet MSL) and local ground elevation (expressed as feet AGL (Above Ground Level)). This type of altitude is also referred to as tapeline altitude, meaning that it is the distance you would read if you could lower a tape measure from your aircraft down to the datum plane.

Geopotential Altitude is an oddball altitude that we have already discussed. Geopotential altitude is measured in geopotential feet, which can be defined as the distance required to raise one pound-mass to increase its potential energy by one foot-pound force. Clear as Mississippi mud, right? Another way to look at it is what we get when we assume a constant acceleration of gravity with altitude. In reality, the acceleration of gravity (g) decreases with increasing altitude and the length of a geometric foot (h) remains constant. Because we insist on being able to solve our equations, we created a fictitious altitude defined such that the acceleration of gravity remains constant (g_{SL}) and the length of a geopotential foot (H) varies as required such that the following equation is satisfied:

$$g \, dh = g_{SL} \, dH \qquad \qquad (A17)$$

Pressure Altitude is a different animal altogether. (CHORUS: Pressure altitude is a different animal...) Feet of pressure altitude is another unit of pressure, just like pounds per square foot, newtons per square meter, or inches of mercury. The conversion is defined by the standard atmosphere. That is, for a pressure of interest, pressure altitude is the geopotential altitude that this pressure would occur at on a standard day. For example, a pressure of 1,456 pounds per square foot corresponds to a pressure altitude of 10,000 feet.

Whoa! How'd you figure that out? One method is to use the standard atmosphere tables. Look down the column of pressures until you find 1,456 psf, then read across to see what altitude that occurs at.

By equation, we know the pressure ratio, δ, given by

$$\delta = \frac{P}{P_{SL}} \qquad \qquad (A70)$$

The relationship between pressure and geopotential altitude is defined by the standard atmosphere equations

$$\delta = (1 - 6.87559 \times 10^{-6} \, H)^{5.2559} \qquad (H \le 36089.24 \text{ feet}) \quad (A79)$$

$$\delta = 0.223360 \, e^{(-4.80637 \times 10^{-5} \, (H - 36089.24))} \qquad (H > 36089.24 \text{ feet}) \quad (A87)$$

Since we have said that pressure altitude is equal to the geopotential altitude corresponding to the pressure of interest, we can simply "replace" the geopotential altitude "H" with a pressure altitude "H_c" to get

$$\delta = (1 - 6.87559 \times 10^{-6} \, H_c)^{5.2559} \qquad (H_c \le 36089.24 \text{ feet}) \quad (B1)$$

$$\delta = 0.223360 \, e^{(-4.80637 \times 10^{-5} \, (H_c - 36089.24))} \qquad (H_c > 36089.24 \text{ feet}) \quad (B2)$$

These equations will give us the pressure ratio corresponding to any pressure altitude of interest, REGARDLESS if it is a standard day or not. The difference on a non-standard day is that the pressure altitude will exist at a numerically different geopotential altitude. We can deal with that, because the airplane flies based on the pressure and temperature of the air (i.e. density) where it is, not based on how far it is above the rocks below. MSL and AGL altitudes are important for considerations such as obstacle clearance, but pressure (or pressure altitude) and temperature determine the aerodynamics that the airplane abides by.

If we already know the pressure, we can find the corresponding pressure altitude by inverting Equations B1 and B2 to give

$$H_c = \frac{1 - \sqrt[5.2559]{\delta}}{6.87559 \times 10^{-6}} \qquad (H_c \le 36089.24 \text{ feet}) \quad (B3)$$

$$H_c = \frac{\ln\left(\frac{\delta}{0.223360}\right)}{-4.80637 \times 10^{-5}} + 36089.24 \qquad (H_c > 36089.24 \text{ feet}) \quad (B4)$$

Note that the relationship between pressure and pressure altitude is monotonic. Every pressure (or pressure ratio) corresponds to a unique pressure altitude. Every pressure altitude corresponds to a unique pressure.

Pressure altitude is probably the most important type of altitude in flight test. Pressure altitude can be measured directly with an altimeter. In fact, an altimeter is a pressure gauge that measures absolute pressure and reports the result in units of feet pressure altitude. Except for test points defined in relation to the ground (such as weapons deliveries), most test points will be defined in terms of pressure altitude.

Pressure altitude at a particular elevation, such as at an airport, will change by small amounts as low pressure and high pressure weather systems are present. These are the same factors that cause a local barometer reading to change with time. Typically pressure altitudes at Edwards AFB (elevation 2303 feet) will vary from 2000 feet to 2400 feet.

Pressure altitude is also important to understanding physiological effects. Breathing depends on the difference between the partial pressures of oxygen and carbon dioxide in the air and in the blood stream. Hypoxia arises when the difference between the partial pressures is too small. The pressure of the air, which directly relates to the partial pressures of oxygen and carbon dioxide, can be expressed in terms of pressure altitude, giving a convenient measure that can be directly read in the cockpit. This cabin pressure altitude can then be easily interpreted by the aircrew for determination of physiological needs, such as supplemental oxygen.

Density Altitude is defined just like pressure altitude if you substitute the word "density" for the word "pressure." That is, the density altitude is the geopotential altitude in the standard atmosphere that the density of interest would occur at. For a given density, the density altitude can be determined by finding that density in the standard atmosphere table, then looking across to find the corresponding altitude. If we know the density ratio, σ, given by

$$\sigma = \frac{\rho}{\rho_{SL}} \tag{A71}$$

The relationship between density and geopotential altitude is defined by the standard atmosphere equations

$$\sigma = (1 - 6.87559 \times 10^{-6}\, H)^{4.2559} \qquad (H \le 36089.24 \text{ feet}) \tag{A80}$$

$$\sigma = 0.297075\, e^{(-4.80637 \times 10^{-5}\, (H - 36089.24))} \qquad (H > 36089.24 \text{ feet}) \tag{A88}$$

Since we have said that density altitude is equal to the geopotential altitude corresponding to the density of interest, we can simply "replace" the geopotential altitude "H" with a density altitude "H_ρ" to get

$$\sigma = (1 - 6.87559 \times 10^{-6}\, H_\rho)^{4.2559} \qquad (H_\rho \le 36089.24 \text{ feet}) \tag{B5}$$

$$\sigma = 0.297075\, e^{(-4.80637 \times 10^{-5}\, (H_\rho - 36089.24))} \qquad (H_\rho > 36089.24 \text{ feet}) \tag{B6}$$

These equations will give us the density ratio corresponding to any density altitude of interest, regardless if it is a standard day or not. The difference on a non-standard day is that the density altitude will exist at a numerically different geopotential altitude. (Is this beginning to sound repetitious?)

If we already know the density, we can find the corresponding density altitude by inverting Equations B5 and B6 to give

$$H_\rho = \frac{1 - \sqrt[4.2559]{\sigma}}{6.87559 \times 10^{-6}} \qquad (H_\rho \le 36089.24 \text{ feet}) \tag{B7}$$

$$H_\rho = \frac{\ln\left(\dfrac{\sigma}{0.297075}\right)}{-4.80637 \times 10^{-5}} + 36089.24 \qquad (H_\rho > 36089.24 \text{ feet}) \tag{B8}$$

Note that the relationship between density and density altitude is monotonic. Every density (or density ratio) corresponds to a unique density altitude. Every density altitude corresponds to a unique density.

Density altitude is an important number for describing aircraft performance. Many factors in aircraft performance, such as engine thrust, can be described as a first order approximation to vary with density. Thus, if the local density altitude is 5000 feet, the thrust of the engine can be expected to be about the same as would be seen at 5000 feet elevation on a standard day. However, density is not very useful in the cockpit because we generally do not have a method to measure density directly. Thus, we measure pressure (with the altimeter) to get a pressure altitude, and measure the temperature to determine the density during post-flight processing.

Since density altitude is affected both by pressure and temperature, the density altitude can vary by large amounts at a given elevation. Assuming standard pressure at Edwards AFB (elevation 2303), at a temperature of 105° F the density altitude would be 5655 feet. At a temperature of 20° F the density altitude would be 196 feet.

The Altimeter

The altimeter is merely an absolute pressure gauge. However, instead of reporting pressure in units like pounds per square foot, it reports pressure in units of feet pressure altitude. The conversion between the sensed pressure and feet pressure altitude is as defined by the standard altitude.

A mechanical altimeter, as shown in Figure 3.1, consists of a sealed case connected by a tube to the static port. Inside the case is a sealed bellows which expands and contracts as the pressure changes. This movement is translated through a clockwork mechanism to the pointer on the face of the instrument, which indicates the pressure in units of pressure altitude.

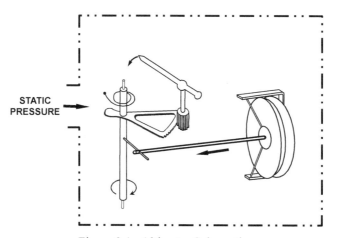

Figure 3.1. Altimeter Schematic

Virtually all sensitive altimeters are equipped with a knob that allows setting the local sea level barometric pressure in a small window commonly referred to as the "Kollsman Window." If this reading is set to 29.92, then the altimeter will directly read pressure altitude.

For most performance and flying qualities testing, one of the first steps on each mission is to set the altimeter to 29.92 so that it will read pressure altitude. This is because we are not interested in our actual distance above the ground, but rather in testing at certain atmospheric properties. Testing at pressure altitudes lets us know what the air pressure is.

However, just setting the altimeter to 29.92 will not necessarily cause it to read pressure altitude. Many aircraft

Why Is It Called the Kollsman Window?

Back in the days of early instrument flight when Jimmy Doolittle was trying to develop blind flying, altimeters were not adjustable and not very sensitive. Climbing from sea level to 20,000 feet sent one pointer around the face of the altimeter one time instead of twenty. You might have been able to read one to the nearest 500 feet. Doolittle needed a altimeter readable to at least 20 feet of altitude.

Mr. Kollsman worked for Bendix, a manufacturer of instruments, and he and Doolittle went to Switzerland to work with Swiss watchmakers to increase the sensitivity of an altimeter. While they were successful, solving one problem caused another—now the altimeter was sensitive enough to change significantly with local barometric changes. Kollsman designed the system to compensate for barometric changes, and the indicator window was named in his honor.

have devices, such as an air data computer (ADC) that electrically drive the altimeter. This allows corrections to be applied to the sensed static pressure to compensate for the position error, resulting in a more accurate altitude presented to the pilot. More accurate, that is, if the position error model in the air data computer is correct. In flight test, a position error model may not exist yet (since this is what air data calibration testing is supposed to determine) or it may be known to be wrong, such as when the Pitot-static system has been modified, such as by installing a nose boom.

In the T-38C, the altitude shown on the Primary Flight Display (PFD) is always compensated by the ADC. The standby altimeter only receives uncompensated static pressure. Because the T-38C uses a compensated Pitot-static tube (covered in Chapter 6), there is normally little difference between altitudes on the PFD and standby altimeter. Some TPS T-38Cs are modified with a flight test nose boom, and the ADC is modified with the appropriate position error compensation. In these aircraft, a large difference in the altitudes on the PFD and standby altimeter will be seen in certain flight conditions.

Some aircraft provide a method to defeat the static pressure compensation. In the F-16, the round dial altimeter is compensated in the "RESET" mode and uncompensated in the "PNEU" (pneumatic) mode (altitude as shown in the Head Up Display (HUD) is always compensated and not affected by the position of the RESET/PNEU switch). In the uncompensated mode, static pressure is fed directly from the static ports to the altimeter. While these modes were probably installed as a backup mode in case the air data computer failed, they have the additional benefit of allowing flight testers to defeat position error compensation while trying to determine what the position error actually is.

Some other aircraft, such as the F-15 or T-38C, use only an electrically driven altimeter. In this case, there is no option available to defeat the ADC inputs. Even so, it is not unreasonable to do Pitot-static calibrations on such an aircraft. The effects of the ADC inputs would be to change the shape of the perceived position error. To update the ADC would require adding the new correction to the correction in the ADC at the time of the testing.

So what happens when I turn that knob to something other than 29.92? Internally, the knob rotates the internal mechanism of the altimeter to move the needles to the new indication. Mathematically, the knob is adding a bias to shift the relationship between the pressure altitude measured and the geopotential altitude indicated, as shown in Figure 3.2. When set to 29.92, this bias is zero. The purpose of this adjustment is to allow a pressure altimeter give a reasonable indication of geopotential altitude.

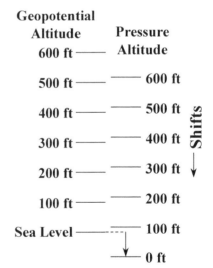

Figure 3.2. Kollsman Window set to 29.82 Shift

Consider the case of an airfield where the barometer reading is 29.82 inches of mercury. Now this does not mean that the ambient air pressure at the airfield is 29.82 inches. In fact, if you were to set up a mercury barometer (which reads absolute pressure) on the numbers of Runway 5R at Edwards (elevation 2303 feet MSL), the pressure reading would be 27.42 inches of mercury. How's that work? The barometer reading that you get from the weather shop is the sea level pressure that would give you the current local pressure at your elevation, assuming a standard sea level temperature and a standard temperature lapse rate.

It was so nice of Mr. Kollsman to provide us a window in our altimeters to adjust for non-standard day conditions. If only it really did. It turns out that while adjusting the altimeter reduces the errors in reading altitude on non-standard days, it does not eliminate them. To understand this, let's look at some notional non-standard days.

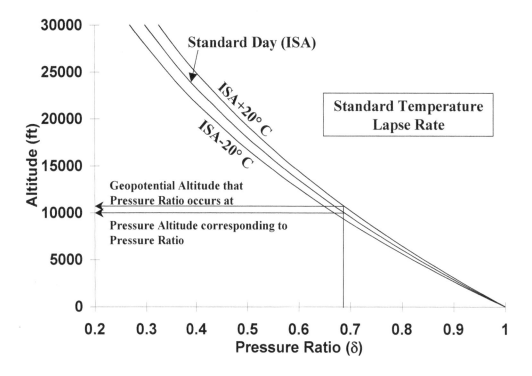

Figure 3.3. Pressure and Altitude Relationships on Non-Standard Days

Figure 3.3 shows the relationship of pressure ratio (δ) to geopotential altitude on a standard day, a day with a temperature 20° C hotter than standard, and a day with a temperature 20° C colder than standard. We could also call the x-axis Pressure, which would just change the scale on the axis. Looking at equation A63 for the troposphere

$$\frac{P}{P_B} = \left(1 + \frac{L}{T_B}\left(H - H_B\right)\right)^{\frac{-g_{SL}}{RL}} \tag{A63}$$

we see that the only variables which would change the result of this equation in Figure 3.3 are the sea level temperature (T_B) and the temperature lapse rate (L). Experience has shown that the temperature lapse rate stays reasonably constant at approximately 2° C per 1000 feet from day to day. Look at the temperatures aloft on most any day's weather report and you will see that this is generally true. Therefore, assuming a standard temperature lapse rate and no temperature inversions, the real driver in changing the pressure profile is the temperature at sea level (or what the temperature would be at sea level extrapolated down from the current elevation).

As seen from the lines shown on Figure 3.3, the pressure ratio of 0.6877 corresponds to a pressure altitude of 10,000 feet. This can be seen from the Standard Day (ISA) curve. On a standard day, the pressure ratio (and pressure) corresponding to 10,000 feet pressure altitude occurs at a geopotential altitude of 10,000 feet. However, if the temperature is 20° C above standard temperature, the pressure ratio (and pressure) corresponding to 10,000 feet pressure altitude now occurs at a geopotential altitude of 10,688 feet. Note that the change in the shape of the curve is not a direct vertical shift, but rather more of a rotation around $\delta = 1$ and sea level.

"But wait a minute, Moosebreath!" you think, being the sharp TPS student that you are. "You just said a few paragraphs back that changing the setting in the Kollsman window shifts the curve vertically (adds a bias to the displayed altitude for the pressure measured). How can those two match up?" Congratulations, Grasshopper. You are becoming wise in the ways of altimetry.

Of course, the answer is, "It depends." If the reason for the non-standard pressure is simply a high or low pressure system in the area with standard temperature and standard temperature lapse rate, then the altimeter can accurately model the altitude. However, if the difference is because the temperature in non-standard, then we have the conditions shown in Figure 3.4.

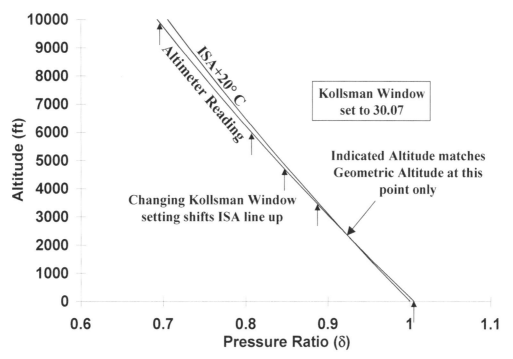

Figure 3.4. Altimeter Adjustments for Non-Standard Days

Figure 3.4 shows a notional non-standard day with the actual sea level pressure at 29.92 and the temperature at sea level 20° C above standard (standard lapse rate). At the elevation of Edwards (2303 feet), an altimeter setting of 30.07 makes a perfect altimeter indicate 2303 feet. However, because these two lines have different slopes, the indicated altitude only matches the geopotential altitude at one point (in this case, 2303 feet). How do we live with this error? Easily—all altimeters will have the same error, so altitude separation between airplanes is preserved.

Generally the altimeter setting will be given such that indicated altitude and geopotential altitude match at the field elevation. For instrument flight, near the ground is the location where this match is most critical.

Another interesting point hinted at by Figure 3.4 is that because the two lines diverge, for the same atmospheric conditions, the altimeter setting at a higher elevation airport will be higher than the altimeter setting at a lower elevation airport. This is because the altimeter cannot adjust itself for differences caused by non-standard temperatures. Operationally we have developed flight procedures and rules that work around this limitation.

How Much Does the Kollsman Window Setting Change the Altitude Displayed?

Ask this question of any pilot who has recently taken an FAA Knowledge Test and they will tell you "One inch of mercury per 1000 feet." Not bad as a rule of thumb, but hardly accurate enough for flight test data or building an altimeter.

Remember that the number in the Kollsman window is the pressure at sea level which would make your altimeter read field elevation at the current pressure (or pressure altitude), assuming standard sea level temperature and standard temperature lapse rate. Hence, we can figure out what the pressure ratio at sea level would be. For example, let's assume

$$\text{Altimeter Setting} = 29.82 \tag{B9}$$

$$\delta_{\text{sea level}} = \frac{\text{Altimeter Setting}}{P_{SL}} \tag{B10}$$

$$\delta_{\text{sea level}} = \frac{29.82}{29.92} \tag{B11}$$

$$\delta_{\text{sea level}} = 0.9967 \tag{B12}$$

Then by using Equation B3 we can find the amount of the shift.

$$H_c = \frac{1 - {}^{5.2559}\sqrt{\delta}}{6.87559 \times 10^{-6}} \tag{B3}$$

$$H_c = \frac{1 - {}^{5.2559}\sqrt{0.9967}}{6.87559 \times 10^{-6}} \tag{B13}$$

$$H_c = 93 \text{ feet} \tag{B14}$$

Altimeter Settings and ATC

Ever wonder why when you're talking to ATC, each time you get handed off to a new controller, the first thing he or she does is to tell you what the altimeter setting is at some nearby airport that you weren't planning to go to? Ever wonder why they think this is so important?

When you consider that your Mode C encoded altitude is pressure altitude, how does ATC ensure ground clearance if all they are receiving is pressure altitude? For that matter, why do they always know what altitude you are seeing on your altimeter, even though you're not set to 29.92?

As told to me by Pat Fagan, air traffic controller at Los Angeles center (ZLA):

"The radar screen that we look at is broken up by the computer into a grid, called sort boxes. The computer assigns data to a sort box, based on the computer program. One sort box may be assigned Boron as its main source for radar data, while the one next to it may be assigned Paso Robles. It is my understanding that the altimeters work the same way. A sort box may be assigned the Bakersfield altimeter, and the computer knows what the altimeter setting is for Bakersfield and automatically compensates for pressure altitude for us so that we see the same thing as the pilot. "

So for our example, an altimeter setting of 29.82 means a pressure altitude of 93 feet at a geopotential altitude of sea level (0 feet). Since 29.82 is less than 29.92, we would expect a positive pressure altitude for the lower pressure, so that checks.

How does this relate to what is displayed on our altimeter? Under these conditions, if an altimeter at sea level (geopotential altitude) is set to 29.92 (to read pressure altitude), it would indicate 93 feet of altitude. Turning the Kollsman window from a pressure of 29.92 DOWN to 29.82 would change the indicated altitude from 93 feet DOWN to 0 feet. So raising the pressure reading in the Kollsman window raises the indicated altitude, and lowering the pressure reading lowers the indicated altitude. This is the size of the shift up and down.

NOTE: This method can also be used to correct your altitude data if you ever inadvertently forget to set 29.92 on your altimeter before taking data. Just be sure to note what the altimeter setting was.

This raises the question of just how accurate is the Pilot's Rule of Thumb. The highest altimeter setting possible on most altimeters is 31.00. At this setting, the equations above show a shift of -984 feet. The rule of thumb calculates a shift of –1080 feet, for an error of 96 feet, or about 10 percent. This is an extreme example—generally the error will be much smaller.

Pressure Contour Levels

As temperature changes, the geopotential altitude that a particular pressure altitude occurs at changes. This is hinted at in Figure 3.3, but can also be seen by reviewing the Equation of State

$$P = \rho RT \qquad\qquad\qquad (A3)$$

For an air mass at constant pressure, if the temperature increases, the density must decrease. With a fixed mass of air, this means that the volume must increase.

This also happens on the macro scale of the atmosphere. As the air increases in temperature, it expands, and pushes the geopotential altitude that a particular pressure (and hence pressure altitude) occurs at higher. If we drew a line (or surface) connecting all of the points of equal pressure (a pressure contour), this line would move up in areas of localized heating. Figure 3.5 is a notional drawing of this effect. Likewise, if the air is cooled, the pressure contours will move down.

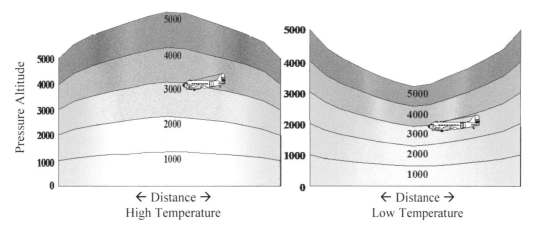

Figure 3.5. Pressure Contour Movement with Temperature

This expansion and contraction of the pressure contours has two major implications: the geopotential distance between the contours change, and their height above the ground changes.

The first implication affects the way we do flight test. One example comes in climb testing. We measure climb rate by recording the time to climb between two pressure altitudes, because our altitude instrument, the altimeter, measures pressure. Imagine doing climb testing on a hot day from 5000 to 6000 feet pressure altitude. You think you are measuring the time to climb 1000 feet, but on this day the 5000 foot pressure altitude contour and the 6000 foot pressure altitude contour are 1075 geopotential feet apart. Because climbing is an exercise in gaining potential energy, the amount of potential energy to be gained is dependent on geopotential feet, not on pressure altitude feet. Therefore, the climb will take longer because more geopotential altitude must be gained. To determine the climb rate on a standard day, this error brought on by a deficiency in our altitude measurement system must be accounted for. For small altitude changes (less than 3000 feet or so), this error can be corrected by the following relationship between geopotential altitude (H) and pressure altitude (H$_c$):

$$\Delta H = \frac{T_{test}}{T_{std}} \Delta H_c \qquad\qquad (B23)$$

where

T_{test} = Temperature measured at median altitude
T_{std} = Standard day temperature for median altitude

The second implication can affect our methods of operation. As the temperatures get colder, the pressure contours get closer to the ground. "High to Low, look out below" is a time-honored pilot catch phrase that sends a warning for going into either lower temperature or lower barometric pressure areas. This warning becomes especially important when operating close to terra firma, such as on approaches. As discussed around Figure 3.4, with a field altimeter setting in the Kollsman window, the indicated altitude and the geopotential altitude only match at one point, usually field elevation. That works fine for the touchdown point, but other AGL altitudes are important on an instrument approach. If the temperature is hotter than standard, there isn't a problem, because you are higher above the obstructions than you think. However, when it is colder than standard, your airplane will be closer to the obstructions than you think. DOD addresses this in the Flight Information Handbook (Ref 6), excerpted here:

3. Temperature Error

a. Pressure altimeters are calibrated to indicate true altitudes under International Standard Atmosphere (ISA) conditions. Any deviation from these standard conditions will result in an erroneous reading on the altimeter. This error becomes important when considering obstacle clearances in temperatures lower than standard since the aircraft's altitude is below the figure indicated by the altimeter.

b. The error is proportional to the difference [*sic, actually the ratio (Equation B23), not the difference*] between actual and ISA temperature and the height of the aircraft above the altimeter setting source. Height above altimeter source is considered to be published HAT [*height above touchdown*] or HAA [*height above airport*] for the approach. The amount of error is approximately 4 feet per thousand feet for each degree Celsius of difference.

c. Corrections will only be made for Decision Heights (DHs), Minimum Descent Altitudes (MDAs), and other altitudes inside, but not including, the Final Approach Fix (FAF). The same correction made to DHs and MDAs can be applied to other altitudes inside the FAF.

This text is then followed by a table with inputs of Airport Temperature and AGL altitudes. The table appears to be loosely based on Equation B23 assuming a sea level elevation with the values rounded up to a convenient multiple of 10 feet. A sea level elevation is the worst case, since the standard temperature is the greatest value above the temperature listed. The resulting corrections are thus conservative (more than needed) at higher elevations, and it greatly simplifies the chart by not introducing elevation as an independent variable.

Density Altitude—Finding Density for Non-Standard Conditions

Density altitude can be a powerful first-order predictor of aircraft performance. Additionally, air density is a required parameter for many data reduction calculations. So how do we determine density? Aircraft are typically not equipped with a density-ometer.

If we look at the Equation of State again,

$$P = \rho RT \tag{A3}$$

we see that we should be able to calculate density if temperature and pressure are known, since R is a known constant. Air temperature can be measured with various types of thermometers and corrected for Mach effects (see later section). Pressure can be determined from pressure altitude. By using the temperature and pressure ratios, we can even determine the density without having to remember the value of R.

Using the ambient air temperature, find the temperature ratio for the test condition.

$$\theta = \frac{T}{T_{SL}} \tag{A69}$$

Then determine the pressure ratio from the pressure altitude.

$$\delta = (1 - 6.87559 \times 10^{-6}\, H_c)^{5.2559} \qquad (H_c \leq 36089.24 \text{ feet}) \tag{B1}$$

$$\delta = 0.223360\, e^{(-4.80637 \times 10^{-5}\,(H_c - 36089.24))} \qquad (H_c > 36089.24 \text{ feet}) \tag{B2}$$

With these two ratios, the density ratio can be determined.

$$\sigma = \frac{\delta}{\theta} \tag{B26}$$

If necessary, the density can then be found from the definition of the density ratio.

$$\rho = \sigma\, \rho_{SL} \tag{B27}$$

Density altitude can be calculated from the density ratio.

$$H_\rho = \frac{1 - \sqrt[4.2559]{\sigma}}{6.87559 \times 10^{-6}} \qquad (H_\rho \leq 36089.24 \text{ feet}) \tag{B7}$$

$$H_\rho = \frac{\ln\left(\frac{\sigma}{0.297075}\right)}{-4.80637 \times 10^{-5}} + 36089.24 \qquad (H_\rho > 36089.24 \text{ feet}) \tag{B8}$$

The pressure ratio is found from the pressure altitude using the standard atmosphere relationships because pressure altitude is defined by the standard atmosphere. **Do not fall in the trap of finding the temperature ratio by the standard atmosphere formulas or by a standard atmosphere table with the pressure altitude.** Doing so will give the temperature ratio for a standard day, not the test day temperature ratio. This will also result in finding the standard day density, not the test day density. It is the non-standard temperature ratio that results in the non-standard density.

Measuring Rate of Climb

Measuring rate of climb is similar to measuring altitude, except that instead of measuring the pressure, we need to measure the rate of change of the pressure. A mechanical rate of climb indicator, also known as a Vertical Speed Indicator (VSI) or Vertical Velocity Indicator (VVI) is connected to the static ports to sense static pressure. It is constructed similar to an airspeed indicator with a single bellows, but static pressure is fed to the inside of the bellows and also into the case, as shown in Figure 3.6. The feed into the case is through a restricted orifice (highbrow talk for little bitty hole), which, oddly enough, restricts the flow. Static pressure can therefore feed in and out of the bellows freely, but changes slowly in the case. The resulting difference in pressure as the static pressure is changing deflects the bellows and moves the needle. In steady state conditions, the pressure inside the bellows and the pressure inside the case will equalize and the instrument will indicate zero climb.

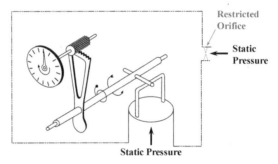

Figure 3.6. Vertical Velocity Indicator Schematic

Because of the principles used to measure the change in static pressure, the indication on the instrument will always lag behind changes in the actual rate of climb (i.e. vertical acceleration). It takes a finite time to build up a sufficient difference in pressure to cause an indication. The lag in the instrument depends on the size of the orifice.

If the orifice is very small, the instrument will react quickly to changes in pressure from the steady state, but will take a very long time to return to zero once steady state conditions are achieved. The pilot would see this as an overly sensitive and noisy indicator that would be likely to falsely report climbs and descents in level flight.

If the orifice is larger, the instrument will require much larger changes in pressure to react, but would achieve level flight indication more quickly. The pilot would see this as a sluggish and insensitive indicator that would not indicate small changes in climb or descent angle, and would not be useful as a trend instrument.

The best compromise solution for most aircraft seems to be a design with about a 9 second lag. Another design that has been developed for transport type aircraft is the so called "instantaneous" VVI. This system introduces a mechanical lead filter by adding a mass onto the bellows. In a vertical acceleration, such as pulling into a climb, the acceleration of the mass causes a force that deflects the bellows in the proper direction to give the initial climb or dive indication until the difference in pressure can build up. Presumably this allows opening the orifice size to allow the indicator to reach a level flight indication quicker. The result can be an indicator that is useful for a transport application where most flying is straight ahead and turns are gentle. Such a device would not be acceptable for aircraft that do a lot of maneuvering, because the instrument cannot tell the difference between vertical acceleration (relative to the earth) and normal acceleration (relative to the airplane). Thus, flying a level turn would show a false rate of climb because of the effect of the mass on the bellows.

Of course, in an air data computer equipped aircraft, rate of climb can be mathematically calculated from changes in static pressure with time. However, this type of differentiation tends to create a lot of high frequency noise, which must be damped out by a low pass filter, which again adds lag in the system. As a result, even rate of climb calculated in an air data computer will still have a noticeable lag in the indication.

Gliders require indication of rate of climb on the order of ±1000 feet per minute, unlike powered aircraft that typically indicate between ±2000 and ±6000 feet per minute. To achieve this level of sensitivity, a different design is used. Figure 3.7 shows a cutaway drawing of a variometer.

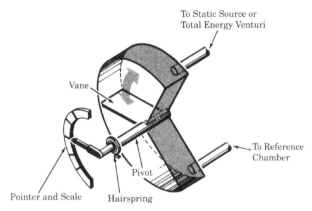

Figure 3.7. Variometer Schematic

One side of the variometer is connected to that static port or a "total energy probe" (described in Appendix I) and the other side is connected to a reference chamber, which is a sealed container holding a volume of air. As the aircraft climbs, static pressure is reduced, and air flows out of the reference chamber, through the variometer, and out the static port. As the air passes through the variometer, it flows past a vane and creates a force on that vane, which deflects a needle against a light spring. As the aircraft descends, air flows from the static port, through the variometer, and into the reference chamber. The size of the reference chamber will affect the response of the variometer, similar to the size of the orifice in the VVI. A large chamber will provide a lot of airflow, such that the variometer will be more sensitive, but will take longer to stabilize. A small chamber will result in an insensitive variometer which will stabilize quickly. Because of the very small pressure gradients being measured, the variometer tends to be more sensitive than a VVI and also more noisy in its indication.

Chapter 4

Airspeed Measurement

So How Fast Are We Flying?

Now that we've figured out how high we are, we next ask "How fast are we flying?" Much like answering the altitude question, the airspeed question is not that simple either. The answer is different depending on what you really want to know.

Your first question might be to support the question of "When will we get to our destination?" In this case, a navigation question, you are interested in your speed relative to the ground. This type of speed is called **Ground Speed**.

However, we also know that if we have a large headwind, it will take a lot longer to get where we're going. But the airplane doesn't fly based on how fast it is traversing the ground. In fact, the airplane has no idea how fast the ground is moving beneath it. All the airplane knows is how fast it is flying through the air mass around it. How fast that air mass is moving relative to the ground (wind speed) is mostly immaterial to how the airplane flies. The speed of the airplane through the air mass (or the speed of the air mass past the airplane) is called **True Airspeed**.

Of all the speeds that we will be discussing, only **Ground Speed** and **True Airspeed** are actually "speeds." That is, these are the only two speeds that can be characterized as the movement of some particle over a distance in a measured period of time. All of the other speeds discussed will be engineering constructs created because they have some useful characteristics in making the flying task or data analysis easier.

During many piloting tasks, the pilot is called upon to control his angle of attack. For a given configuration, an aircraft will always stall at the same angle of attack (the "critical" angle of attack), regardless of weight, load factor, altitude, or temperature. Maximum range will occur at a particular angle of attack. Likewise for maximum endurance or best glide. The landing approach is flown at a particular angle of attack, a certain fraction of the critical angle of attack. While some aircraft have angle of attack indicators, many do not. In these aircraft, airspeed has been used as a measure of angle of attack, but the airspeed corresponding to an angle of attack depends on weight, load factor, altitude, and temperature. If true airspeed were used for this purpose, a new airspeed would have to be computed for each approach as conditions changed. If we use something called **Equivalent Airspeed**, then the altitude and temperature (read: density) effects are accounted for, such that at a given weight and load factor, each angle of attack corresponds to a unique equivalent airspeed. Additionally, airspeed limits, such as gear extension or flap extension, which are really functions of dynamic pressure, are constant if expressed in equivalent airspeed.

Equivalent airspeed in many ways would be the best for the piloting task, but it is still difficult to measure with a mechanical pressure gauge. While we may have air data computers and electric instruments today, Bill Gates was born a little too late to sell a PC to the Wright Brothers. Aviators tend to be a conservative lot, in their flying operations at least if not their politics. That is, pilots like new airplanes to fly like the airplanes they've been flying. As a result, we still do a lot of things because "That's the way we've always done it," which is not necessarily a bad thing. In some cases, trying to change something to a "better way" might require a large change in the flying infrastructure that is not economically viable. What does all of this have to do with airspeed? Well, it turns out that if we make a small change to our definition of equivalent airspeed, we get something we call **Calibrated Airspeed** which is reasonably close (but not exact) to equivalent airspeed to give us many of the advantages of equivalent airspeed, but in a form much easier to build a mechanical gauge to measure. Because the gauge is easier to build, it is simpler, and thus cheaper and more reliable. That's the way it's been done in the past, and that's the way it will be done for the foreseeable future.

True Airspeed

From Bernoulli's Equation, we can get a fairly simple expression for airspeed for incompressible flow. However, it is not even worth looking at because we deal with many airplanes that fly at speeds significantly above the incompressible region. Since the compressible flow equations work equally well at incompressible speeds, we'll just jump straight to the compressible equations.

As shown in gross detail in Appendix C, starting with the first law of thermodynamics, the energy equation, the speed of sound and Mach Number (coming up in a later section), we can derive a velocity equation for an ideal gas in isentropic flow, which is the nice, "simple" relationship given by

$$V_t = \sqrt{\left(\frac{1}{\rho_a}\right)\frac{2\gamma}{\gamma-1}P_a\left(\left(\frac{P_T - P_a}{P_a}+1\right)^{\frac{\gamma-1}{\gamma}}-1\right)} \tag{C47}$$

Using $\gamma = 1.4$ for air

$$V_t = \sqrt{\left(\frac{1}{\rho_a}\right)7P_a\left(\left(\frac{P_T - P_a}{P_a}+1\right)^{\frac{2}{7}}-1\right)} \tag{C48}$$

There are three variables in this equation: Total Pressure (P_T), Ambient Pressure (P_a), and ambient density (ρ_a). We can measure total pressure from the Pitot tube, and ambient pressure (or at least a reasonable approximation) from the static ports, but what about the density? Density is not easily measured, and presumably we could measure ambient pressure and temperature to find density, but it is not easy. Mechanical true airspeed gauges have been built, and can still be seen in older C-130s and B-52s. These gauges had two pressure inputs and a temperature input, and were notoriously inaccurate. While a quick reading within 10 to 20 knots may be good enough for navigation purposes, it is way too much error for flight test purposes. Besides that, the complexity increased costs and degraded reliability.

So what would be the advantages of knowing true airspeed? About the biggest benefit is that true airspeed combined with winds can be used to find ground speed for navigation. In these days with ubiquitous GPS and INS in many aircraft, ground speed can be better determined with these devices.

Equivalent Airspeed

As mentioned earlier, the major problem in measuring true airspeed comes from measuring density. Additionally, true airspeed is not very useful to the pilot because the relationship between true airspeed and angle of attack varies with density. So, we say, why not just remove the dependence of airspeed on density? We can do that by replacing the ambient density (ρ_a) with a constant sea level density (ρ_{SL}). By choosing sea level density, equivalent airspeed and true airspeed are equal at sea level. The equivalent airspeed equation becomes

$$V_e = \sqrt{\left(\frac{1}{\rho_{SL}}\right)7P_a\left(\left(\frac{P_T - P_a}{P_a} + 1\right)^{\frac{2}{7}} - 1\right)} \tag{C49}$$

In addition to the benefits mentioned above to the piloting task, equivalent airspeed is very useful in conditions where a particular dynamic pressure is of interest, because each equivalent airspeed corresponds to a unique dynamic pressure, given by

$$q = \frac{\rho V_t^2}{2} = \frac{\rho_{SL} V_e^2}{2} \tag{C59}$$

Because the sea level density is a constant, the equivalent airspeed is the only variable on the right hand side, so each value of dynamic pressure corresponds to one value of equivalent airspeed, regardless of temperature or pressure altitude.

Equivalent airspeed has a lot of advantages and seems very attractive for our purposes, but it still has drawbacks for implementation in a mechanical instrument. A differential bellows could be used to measure the differential pressure ($P_T - P_a$), but a second bellows would be required to independently measure ambient pressure (P_a). Like a true airspeed gauge, the resulting instrument would be rather complex, costly, and not very reliable. I have never seen an example of a mechanical equivalent airspeed gauge.

To get equivalent airspeed from true airspeed

$$V_e = V_t \sqrt{\sigma} \tag{C53}$$

Calibrated Airspeed

Again, looking back in history, engineers were looking for a way to build a simple, reliable airspeed indicator. The concept of equivalent airspeed promised a lot of benefits, but still required measuring the differential pressure and the ambient pressure independently. But what if we just ignored the effect of ambient pressure? If we replace the ambient pressure with a constant sea level pressure, we create a new airspeed concept which we call "Calibrated Airspeed." Calibrated airspeed is given by

$$V_c = \sqrt{\left(\frac{1}{\rho_{SL}}\right)7P_{SL}\left(\left(\frac{P_T - P_a}{P_{SL}} + 1\right)^{\frac{2}{7}} - 1\right)} \tag{C65}$$

For low airspeeds and low altitudes, calibrated airspeed is very close to equivalent airspeed, and thus retains many of the benefits of equivalent airspeed with regards to stall speeds, approach speeds, limit speeds and such. Thus, we can produce a device very close to an equivalent airspeed gauge, yet build it with a single bellows. The only variable in Equation C65 is the differential pressure ($P_T - P_a$), so only one differential pressure sensor (bellows) is required. We will see later that calibrated airspeed also has some very useful properties with respect to Mach number.

But how can we convert between equivalent airspeed and calibrated airspeed and back again? Well, because the ambient pressure was changed to sea level pressure in two places from Equation C49 to Equation C65, there is not a simple, straightforward mathematical conversion as we saw between true airspeed and equivalent airspeed. Therefore, we again go back in history to the days of slide rules and before when complex mathematical equations were accomplished by use of tables and graphs. That way, we can do the calculations once (in our case, we can use a spreadsheet), and then refer to the table or graph after that.

Since we're brute forcing the equation, we can do it in either of two ways—by multiplication or addition. Hence, we use the "f factor" as

$$V_e = f\, V_c$$

where f is defined as

$$f = \frac{V_e}{V_c} \tag{C134}$$

Similarly, if we choose to convert by addition, we have

$$V_e = V_c + \Delta V_c$$

where ΔV_c is defined as

$$\Delta V_c = V_e - V_c \tag{C135}$$

Well, that was simple enough. If only. So how do we calculate the f factor or ΔV_c? Looking again at Equation C65, we can solve this equation for the differential pressure ($P_T - P_a$). If we choose a calibrated airspeed, we can calculate the corresponding differential pressure. If we then select a pressure altitude, we can calculate the ambient pressure (P_a). Using the differential pressure and the ambient pressure, we can then calculate the equivalent airspeed using Equation C49. Having now both the calibrated airspeed and the equivalent airspeed, we can divide them to get the f factor (Table 4.1) or subtract them to find ΔV_c.

Table 4.1
f Factors

Pressure Altitude (ft)	Calibrated Airspeed (knots)		
	100	200	300
Sea Level	1.000	1.000	1.000
10,000	0.999	0.995	0.989
20,000	0.997	0.987	0.973
30,000	0.993	0.975	0.950
40,000	0.988	0.957	0.916
50,000	0.979	0.930	0.871

A more complete table of f factors is shown in Appendix C, along with a table of ΔV_c and charts of each.

You may have had a flight instructor in the past who drilled into your head that stall speeds, approach speeds, flap and gear limits, or whatever were constant in terms of calibrated airspeed, at least at a particular gross weight. Or you may have seen it written as "indicated" airspeed, which is the same as calibrated airspeed if there are no instrument or position errors (more on that later). Questions on this topic even appear on the FAA ~~written~~ knowledge tests. If the FAA says it's true, it must be true, right? Well, not quite.

We established a few pages ago that these speeds were constant in terms of equivalent airspeed, because each equivalent airspeed corresponded to a unique dynamic pressure, regardless of altitude or temperature. We have also established that calibrated airspeed and equivalent airspeed are not the same. So what's the deal?

Well, when do you really care about stall speeds and approach speeds? When you're slow and generally close to the ground. Well, let's assume you're landing your T-38 at Leadville, Colorado, the highest airport in the contiguous 48 states. (Of course, you might not think that a good idea since the elevation is 9927 feet and the runway is only 6400 x 75 feet.) Let's assume that your approach speed today is 200 knots calibrated airspeed (KCAS). Looking at Table 6, the f factor at 200 KCAS and 10,000 feet pressure altitude is 0.995. Running through the highly complex math, that gives us an equivalent airspeed of 199 knots equivalent airspeed (KEAS). This is such a small difference, even at this extreme condition, that it just isn't worth worrying about. This error is also probably smaller than other errors present in the airspeed system. Hence, for ease of training, we say that the performance speeds are constant with calibrated airspeed. While not absolutely true, it is true within acceptable tolerances.

In the common parlance, the f factor has been referred to, albeit incorrectly, as the "compressibility correction." If we look back at the definition of compressible flow, we find that compressibility refers to a condition where the density is not constant. However, the differences between equivalent airspeed and calibrated airspeed arise because of differences between ambient pressure and sea level pressure. Thus, the f factor is a **pressure** correction, not a **density** correction.

So why the confusion? My suspicion is that the need to apply the f factor was not significant until airplanes were flying fast enough and high enough that the airflow had to be considered compressible. This was the region where compressibility effects, such as transonic drag rise and Mach tuck became an issue, so someone incorrectly concluded that the airspeed correction must be a compressibility effect too. There's no benefit in trying to correct everyone now, but as professional testers and engineers we should understand that the f factor represents the results of changing the pressure value that we use in our equations.

Time for the Nestea Plunge

Having trouble relating the various airspeeds? Take a look at Figure 4.1.

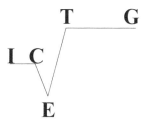

Figure 4.1. Airspeed ICE-T

This handy graphic shows the relative magnitudes of the different types of airspeed. We draw a radical (square root sign) and label the corners as shown, where

I	Indicated
C	Calibrated
E	Equivalent
T	True
G	Ground

The conversion from indicated to calibrated airspeed is the addition of instrument and position corrections (to be introduced later), which are generally small and don't change the magnitude very much. To get from calibrated to equivalent airspeed we multiply by the f factor, which is almost always less than one, so the magnitude of the equivalent airspeed will be less than the magnitude of the calibrated airspeed. To get true airspeed, we divide the equivalent airspeed by the square root of the density ratio. Since we are dividing by the square root of a number less than one, the magnitude of the true airspeed will be greater than the magnitude of the equivalent airspeed. Also, it turns out that typically the true airspeed will have a higher magnitude than the calibrated airspeed as well. To calculate ground speed, we add the winds to the true airspeed, which may increase or decrease the magnitude.

These generalizations will hold true for most cases, unless you're doing something odd like flying fast below sea level in Death Valley on a really cold day. Of course, if you're doing that, the Ops Officer wants to see you about scheduling your Flight Evaluation Board to review your gross poor flight discipline.

Figure 4.1 can also help you remember how to do the conversions. For instance, you know that to calculate the equivalent airspeed from calibrated airspeed, you need to multiply or divide by the f factor, but can't remember which. Looking at the figure, you know that the equivalent airspeed needs to be less than the calibrated airspeed. Because you also remember that the f factor is less than one, you can reason that you need to multiply the calibrated airspeed by the f factor to get a smaller number. Easier done than wildly flipping pages through this book.

Differential Pressure (Compressible q)

From incompressible flow, we had from Bernoulli's Equation

$$P_T = P_a + \frac{\rho V_t^2}{2} \tag{C1}$$

We could rearrange this to

$$P_T - P_a = \frac{\rho V_t^2}{2} \tag{C2}$$

From this concept came the definition of dynamic pressure, q, as

$$q = \frac{\rho V_t^2}{2} \tag{C3}$$

For our purposes, and through most engineering disciplines, this is the definition of dynamic pressure. In this equation, the density is the freestream density, or the density of the air far enough ahead of the aircraft to be unaffected by the aircraft.

This works fine at low speeds, but at higher speeds the density is no longer constant. For Equation C1 to remain true, the density in the equation must be allowed to change to that actually seen at the Pitot and static ports, which will be higher than the freestream density. Rather than mess with that, we will leave the definition of dynamic pressure alone and define the differential pressure as

$$q_c = P_T - P_a \qquad \text{(subsonic)} \tag{C66}$$

The relationship between dynamic pressure and differential pressure is given by

$$q_c = q\left(1 + \frac{M^2}{4} + \frac{M^4}{40} + \frac{M^6}{1600} + ...\right) \tag{C184}$$

At low Mach numbers, these two pressures are essentially equal, but diverge at higher Mach numbers. The real benefit to defining "q_c" is that it is shorter to write than "$P_T - P_a$".

Effects of Temperature and Pressure on Airspeed

By looking at how temperature and pressure affect airspeed, we can get some guidance about optimum altitudes to fly at. For purposes of this discussion, we will assume that the differential pressure, q_c, remains constant, so that the pressures, and thus forces, seen by the airplane remain constant.

Calibrated airspeed is solely a function of q_c, as seen in Equation C65

$$V_c = \sqrt{\left(\frac{1}{\rho_{SL}}\right)7P_{SL}\left(\left(\frac{P_T - P_a}{P_{SL}} + 1\right)^{\frac{2}{7}} - 1\right)} \qquad (C65)$$

Thus, at a constant q_c, the calibrated airspeed will always be the same. In fact, every value of calibrated airspeed corresponds to a unique value of q_c. Changes in pressure and temperature will not affect calibrated airspeed under these conditions.

Equivalent airspeed, given by

$$V_e = \sqrt{\left(\frac{1}{\rho_{SL}}\right)7P_a\left(\left(\frac{P_T - P_a}{P_a} + 1\right)^{\frac{2}{7}} - 1\right)} \qquad (C49)$$

does not have a temperature dependence, because density has been set to the sea level standard value. The pressure dependence is not obvious from inspecting the equation, but if we look at the f factor table (Table 6) at a constant calibrated airspeed (constant q_c), we see that as the pressure altitude increases (decreasing pressure) the equivalent airspeed also decreases.

True airspeed, given by

$$V_t = \sqrt{\left(\frac{1}{\rho_a}\right)7P_a\left(\left(\frac{P_T - P_a}{P_a} + 1\right)^{\frac{2}{7}} - 1\right)} \qquad (C48)$$

has the same pressure dependence as equivalent airspeed, plus a pressure and temperature dependence through the density term. Thus, for a constant q_c and constant pressure altitude, if temperature decreases, density increases, and true airspeed decreases. For a constant q_c and constant temperature (such as in the stratosphere), as pressure altitude increases, true airspeed increases for the same reasons as equivalent airspeed. Additionally, we know from the standard atmosphere model that we can expect density to decrease with an increase in altitude, which will lead to a higher true airspeed.

That's nice as a mathematical exercise, but what does it mean to us? Consider the case of the airliner in cruise. Any airplane will cruise best at a particular angle of attack. For a given weight in level flight, this angle of attack will occur at a particular equivalent airspeed. Since a given angle of attack will result in a particular drag coefficient, the equivalent airspeed gives a unique dynamic pressure, and the reference area is a constant, the drag for this condition will be the same regardless of what altitude we fly at.

In the cruise condition, thrust required is roughly equal to drag. For jet engines, the fuel flow is roughly proportional to thrust. So for this condition, if the drag is the same regardless of altitude, the fuel flow will be the same regardless of altitude.

As altitude increases, the true airspeed corresponding to a given equivalent airspeed increases. So if my fuel flow is constant with regards to equivalent airspeed and altitude, I should want to fly at a high altitude to get a high true airspeed. Because the true airspeed is higher, the time to reach the destination will be less. Because the time is less at a constant fuel flow, the total amount of fuel burned will be less. Customers are happy because the trip takes less time, and management is happy because operating costs are reduced.

Of course, there is a limit to the savings possible, primarily driven by the fuel required to climb to altitude. A reasonable rule of thumb is that the time to climb should be no more than 15 percent of the entire flight time.

Converting Airspeeds, Airspeed Method

While calibrated airspeed is convenient for the piloting task, it is not very useful for the navigation task or mission planning, such as determining time on target. We need to be able to change between the different types of airspeed to accomplish our mission.

Let's start with a calibrated airspeed and calculate true airspeed and Mach. In the process, we'll also determine our equivalent airspeed. For example, let's say we're flying with "Narco" and "Hojo" in the KC-135 to France on your class field trip. Currently our flight conditions are

Calibrated Airspeed (V_c):   300 knots calibrated airspeed (KCAS)
Altitude: FL 300
Ambient Air Temperature (T_a):   -30 °C

Our first step is to convert calibrated airspeed into equivalent airspeed. We have a choice of two equally effective methods. The first is to use the f factor (multiplication method). The f-factor can be found in Table C1 or Figure C1. From Equation C134

$$V_e = f\,V_c$$

$$f = 0.950$$

$$V_e = 285 \text{ knots equivalent airspeed (KEAS)}$$

Similarly, if we choose to convert by addition, we have from Equation C133

$$V_e = V_c + \Delta V_c$$

$$\Delta V_c = -15 \text{ knots}$$

$$V_e = 285 \text{ KEAS}$$

Next we can calculate true airspeed, but first we need the density ratio. To find the density ratio, we need the temperature and pressure ratios. The temperature ratio is straightforward, given by

$$\theta = \frac{T}{T_{SL}} \qquad\qquad (A69)$$

Remembering to convert Celsius to Kelvin, we get

$$\theta = \frac{-30 + 273.15}{288.15}$$

$$\theta = 0.84383$$

To find the pressure ratio, we need the pressure altitude. Remember that in the flight levels (above 18,000 feet MSL), we fly with the altimeter set to 29.92. Thus, FL 300 is 30,000 feet pressure altitude. The pressure ratio at this altitude is given by

$$\delta = (1 - 6.87559 \times 10^{-6}\, H_c)^{5.2559} \qquad (H_c \le 36089.24 \text{ feet}) \quad (B1)$$

$$\delta = 0.29696$$

Now we can calculate the density ratio

$$\sigma = \frac{\delta}{\theta} \qquad\qquad (B26)$$

$$\sigma = 0.35192$$

Finally, the true airspeed is given by

$$V_t = \frac{V_e}{\sqrt{\sigma}} \qquad\qquad (C54)$$

$$V_t = 480 \text{ knots true airspeed (KTAS)}$$

To find the Mach number, we first need the speed of sound, given by

$$a = \sqrt{\gamma R T_a} \qquad\qquad (C31)$$

Again, remembering to convert to Kelvin, we get

$$a = \left(\frac{3600\, \frac{sec}{hour}}{6076\, \frac{ft}{nm}} \right) \sqrt{ (1.4)\left(3089.8\, \frac{ft\text{-}lb}{slug\text{-}K} \right)(-30^\circ C + 273.15) }$$

$$a = 607.2 \text{ knots}$$

So Mach number would be

$$M = \frac{V_t}{a} \qquad\qquad (C33)$$

$$M = \frac{480 \text{ knots}}{607.2 \text{ knots}}$$

$$M = 0.79$$

Now let's change the scenario and go the other way. Let's imagine that you have a test point at the following conditions:

Pressure Altitude: 16,000 feet
Mach number: 0.80
Ambient Air Temperature: -5 °C

What calibrated airspeed would you expect to need to fly to get these conditions? Again, we need to find the speed of sound.

$$a = \sqrt{\gamma R T_a} \qquad \text{(C31)}$$

Remembering to convert to Kelvin, we get

$$a = \left(\frac{3600 \frac{\text{sec}}{\text{hour}}}{6076 \frac{\text{ft}}{\text{nm}}}\right) \sqrt{(1.4)\left(3089.8 \frac{\text{ft - lb}}{\text{slug - K}}\right)\left(-5°C + 273.15\right)}$$

$$a = 637.7 \text{ knots}$$

The true airspeed is found from the Mach number

$$V_t = Ma \qquad \text{(C60)}$$

$$V_t = (0.80)(637.7 \text{ knots})$$

$$V_t = 510 \text{ KTAS}$$

To find the equivalent airspeed, we need the density ratio, which we find from the temperature and pressure altitude.

$$\theta = \frac{T}{T_{SL}} \qquad \text{(A69)}$$

Remembering to convert Celsius to Kelvin, we get

$$\theta = \frac{-5 + 273.15}{288.15}$$

$$\theta = 0.93059$$

$$\delta = (1 - 6.87559 \times 10^{-6} \text{ H}_c)^{5.2559} \qquad (H_c \leq 36089.24 \text{ feet}) \quad \text{(B1)}$$

$$\delta = (1 - 6.87559 \times 10^{-6} / \text{feet} (16,000 \text{ feet}))^{5.2559}$$

$$\delta = 0.54197$$

Now we can calculate the density ratio

$$\sigma = \frac{\delta}{\theta} \tag{B26}$$

$$\sigma = \frac{0.54197}{0.93059}$$

$$\sigma = 0.58239$$

The equivalent airspeed is given by

$$V_e = V_t \sqrt{\sigma} \tag{C53}$$

$$V_e = 510 \text{ KTAS}\sqrt{0.58239}$$

$$V_e = 389 \text{ KEAS}$$

Next, we need to find the f factor or ΔV_c to calculate calibrated airspeed. From Equation C134

$$V_c = \frac{V_e}{f}$$

While a table of f factors could be produced in terms of equivalent airspeed, generally f factor is presented in terms of calibrated airspeed and pressure altitude. Thus we can approach this problem with a small iteration technique. We know from our ICE-T discussion that calibrated airspeed should generally be greater than equivalent airspeed. We also know that the f factor will be close to one, so the calibrated airspeed will be close to the equivalent airspeed. Therefore, let's pick the f factor from the table closest to our pressure altitude and equivalent airspeed. Without interpolating, there will be some error, but if the error is on the order of a knot it won't matter for this problem because we can't read the airspeed indicator that precisely anyway. Selecting 15,000 feet pressure altitude and 400 KCAS we get

$$f = 0.9706$$

$$V_c = \frac{389 \text{ KEAS}}{0.9706}$$

$$V_c = 401 \text{ KCAS}$$

Looking at the table again, would you have picked an f-factor any different based on 16,000 feet pressure altitude and 401 KCAS? Probably not. The exact answer would be an f factor of 0.9677 and a calibrated airspeed of 402.6 KCAS, but the answer above would be close enough for mission planning.

Using the ΔV_c method, we would enter the table for ΔV_c using the same logic at 15,000 feet pressure altitude and 400 KCAS and get

$$\Delta V_c = -11.75 \text{ knots}$$

$$V_c = V_e - \Delta V_c$$

$$V_c = 389 \text{ KEAS} - (-11.75 \text{ knots})$$

$$V_c = 401 \text{ KCAS}$$

Same assumptions, same result. Good to see it still works out that way.

Supersonic Considerations

For supersonic flow, the equations discussed so far (true airspeed, equivalent airspeed, calibrated airspeed) are still valid from a theoretical point of view. From a practical point of view, they cease to be useful above Mach 1 because it is no longer possible to directly measure the freestream total pressure. In subsonic flight, the differential pressure divided by the ambient pressure is given by

$$\frac{P_T - P_a}{P_a} = \left(1 + 0.2M^2\right)^{7/2} - 1 \qquad (M < 1) \qquad (C69)$$

The parameter on the left of Equation C69 is significant because it appears in the center of the equivalent airspeed equation.

As discussed in Reference 7, in supersonic flow a normal shock will form in front of the Pitot tube. Because a shock wave is a huge producer of entropy, the air will lose energy passing through the shock wave, with the result being that the total pressure immediately behind the shock wave (sensed by the Pitot tube) is less than the freestream total pressure. However, all is not lost! One of the convenient properties of a normal shock wave is that if we know the properties of the flow downstream of the shock wave, we can determine the properties of the flow upstream of the shock wave. That is, if we measure the total pressure behind a normal shock wave (P_T'), we can calculate the total pressure in front of the shock wave (P_T) with no other required data. With some mathemagic, we can relate what we actually measure to the freestream Mach number in something known as "The Rayleigh Supersonic Pitot Tube Formula."

$$\frac{P_T' - P_a}{P_a} = \frac{166.921M^7}{\left(7M^2 - 1\right)^{5/2}} - 1 \qquad (M > 1) \qquad (C103)$$

Note that this equation does not represent a change in the relationship between freestream pressures and airspeed. This equation shows that what we are able to measure aboard the aircraft changes, and thus we have to change the relationship we use to determine what we're really interested in.

Note that for supersonic flow, the definition of differential pressure is changed slightly. It is still the difference in the pressures being sensed by the airspeed indicator, but in relation to the flow field parameters we have

$$q_c = P_T' - P_a \qquad (\text{supersonic}) \qquad (C96)$$

To see the effect of this loss of total pressure, let's change slightly what we're looking at. Rather than use the ratio from the center of the equivalent airspeed equation, we'll use the ratio from the center of the calibrated airspeed equation. This has the benefit of removing an altitude dependence so that it is easier to see the effects of just the shock wave. As shown in Appendix C, these equations are

$$\frac{q_c}{P_{SL}} = \left[1 + 0.2\left(\frac{V_c}{a_{SL}}\right)^2 \right]^{\frac{7}{2}} - 1 \qquad (V_c < a_{SL}) \quad (C106)$$

$$\frac{q_c}{P_{SL}} = \frac{166.921\left(\dfrac{V_c}{a_{SL}}\right)^7}{\left(7\left(\dfrac{V_c}{a_{SL}}\right)^2 - 1\right)^{\frac{5}{2}}} - 1 \qquad (V_c > a_{SL}) \quad (C107)$$

The selection of the equation to use is now based on the value of calibrated airspeed with respect to the speed of sound at sea level.

These two equations are plotted in Figure 4.2.

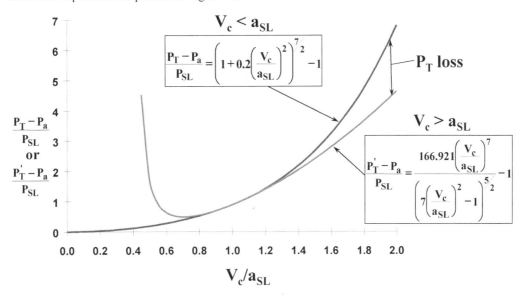

Figure 4.2. Subsonic and Supersonic Airspeed Relationships at Sea Level

The difference between the lines above $V_c/a_{SL} = 1$ represents the total pressure loss ($P_T - P'_T$) through the normal shock wave.

These two lines are continuous at $V_c/a_{SL} = 1$. This is shown in Appendix C as the values of both equations are equal and the values of their derivatives are equal at $V_c/a_{SL} = 1$.

Mach Number Revisited

Mach number is a big player in compressible aerodynamics, and it is still a very useful term in air data systems, even at incompressible (low) airspeeds. To review, Mach number is the ratio of the true airspeed and the local speed of sound. The local speed of sound is given by

$$a = \sqrt{\gamma R T_a} \qquad (C31)$$

and the Mach number is given by

$$M = \frac{V_t}{a} \tag{C33}$$

Mach number has a lot of useful properties and many concepts are more easily expressed in terms of Mach number instead of airspeed. Study of Appendix C will show that much of the airspeed theory was developed using Mach number. Perhaps one of the most convenient properties of Mach number is that which is summarized in the flight test axiom

Mach is Mach!

So you're thinking "Huh?" Allow me to elucidate (+5 points, correct use of elucidate in a sentence). As shown in Appendix C, for any given test point, the Mach number at test day conditions will be the same as the Mach number on a standard day, because the corresponding true airspeed and speed of sound both vary with the square root of temperature, such that their ratio (Mach number) remains the same.

In general, when standardizing for non-standard atmospheric properties, we are looking for the conditions on a standard day that would result in the same lift and drag coefficients as seen at the test day conditions. Another way to say this would be that we are looking for the conditions on a standard day that would result in the same angle of attack as seen at the test day conditions. Normally we keep the pressure altitude the same between the test day conditions and the standard day conditions. For the same gross weight, the same amount of lift and drag will be required to do the same maneuver. Therefore, if the lift and drag forces remain constant, the lift and drag coefficients remain constant, and the reference area remains constant, then the dynamic pressure must also remain constant. At a set pressure altitude, as the temperature changes, the density of the air changes. To keep the dynamic pressure constant, the true airspeed must change. As it turns out, because of the temperature change, the speed of sound changes proportionally to the true airspeed, with the end result being that the Mach number does not change.

Another way to look at this is to consider the expression for dynamic pressure in terms of Mach

$$q = \frac{\gamma}{2} P_a M^2 \tag{C64}$$

From this expression, we can see that for dynamic pressure to remain constant at a constant pressure altitude, Mach number must remain constant.

Another interesting property of Mach number is found in the words of Lt Col Charlie Longnecker (and many other Pitot-static instructors) back in 1989:

"Mach is not a function of temperature"

Say what? Just look back at Equations C31 and C33 and it is very clear that Mach number changes with temperature. The point would actually be better stated as "Mach number can be calculated without an explicit reference to temperature." How do we do that? Simple. Bury the temperature effects in some other parameter.

Appendix C shows that for subsonic conditions, we can derive an equation for Mach number with inputs of calibrated airspeed and pressure ratio (from pressure altitude).

$$M = \sqrt{5\left[\left[\left(\frac{1}{\delta}\left\{\left[1+0.2\left(\frac{V_c}{a_{SL}}\right)^2\right]^{7/2}-1\right\}+1\right)^{2/7}-1\right]\right]} \qquad (M < 1) \quad (C118)$$

So where do the temperature effects show up in this equation? For a **constant true airspeed and pressure altitude**, the corresponding Mach number will change as the temperature changes. Higher temperatures, higher speed of sound, lower Mach number. A higher temperature will also reduce the air density, which will decrease the equivalent airspeed corresponding to the true airspeed. The corresponding calibrated airspeed will also decrease (the f factor will increase slightly, but far less than the equivalent airspeed decreased). Thus, the result of the temperature increase at a constant true airspeed and pressure altitude is a reduction in calibrated airspeed. Looking at Equation C118, this will reduce the Mach number as expected.

Alternatively, if Mach number is held constant at a constant pressure altitude, the resulting calibrated airspeed will not change as the temperature changes. A given Mach number corresponds to a given differential pressure to ambient pressure ratio (($P_T - P_a)/P_a$ – see Equation C68). For a constant pressure altitude, the ambient pressure is constant, therefore the differential pressure will be constant for this scenario. A constant differential pressure corresponds to a constant calibrated airspeed. So what does change? As the temperature changes, the true airspeed varies with the square root of the temperature. However, because the speed of sound also varies with the square root of the temperature, the ratio of true airspeed and the speed of sound (i.e. the Mach number) does not change. Hence for a given pressure altitude, a given Mach number will result in the same calibrated airspeed regardless of temperature. However, that same Mach number will occur at different true airspeeds as the temperature changes.

Therefore, even though Mach number can be calculated without a temperature measurement, any changes in Mach number caused by changes in temperature will be accounted for by the corresponding change in calibrated airspeed.

For supersonic flow, an explicit equation for Mach number in terms of calibrated airspeed and pressure ratio cannot be derived because of the behaviour of pressures through the shock wave. However, a method is shown shortly for how Mach can be calculated using an iterative process. Additionally, because the correspondence between calibrated airspeeds and pressure altitude with Mach number is unique, tables and graphs can be produced to show this relationship as well.

Converting Airspeeds, Mach Method

Mach number can also be determined from calibrated airspeed and pressure altitude. This has the advantage of being able to make the conversion without knowing temperature. Additionally, this method can be used to find true airspeed if temperature is known. The advantage of using this method to find true airspeed, at least for the subsonic case, is that this method can be programmed into a computer program or spreadsheet without needing a table look up routine for the f factor or ΔV_c.

For the subsonic case, the method is straightforward. From the pressure altitude, calculate the pressure ratio.

$$\delta = (1 - 6.87559 \times 10^{-6} \, H_c)^{5.2559} \qquad (H_c \leq 36089.24 \text{ feet}) \quad (B1)$$

$$\delta = 0.223360 \, e^{(-4.80637 \times 10^{-5} \, (H_c - 36089.24))} \qquad (H_c > 36089.24 \text{ feet}) \quad (B2)$$

Using the subsonic Mach meter equation, find Mach Number.

$$M = \sqrt{5 \left[\left(\frac{1}{\delta} \left\{ \left[1 + 0.2 \left(\frac{V_c}{a_{SL}} \right)^2 \right]^{7/2} - 1 \right\} + 1 \right)^{2/7} - 1 \right]} \qquad (M < 1) \quad (C118)$$

Equation C118 is valid only for Mach numbers less than 1. If the result of Equation C118 is greater than 1, the answer is invalid and must be calculated using the supersonic method. That is, assuming that the reason you got an answer greater than 1 was not just because you punched it into the calculator wrong. If $V_c > a_{SL}$ in your favorite units system, then Equation C118 will definitely be invalid. However, it is possible to have a calibrated airspeed less than a_{SL} (661.48 knots) that is supersonic because of the pressure altitude. So what do we do?

To understand the problem, let's look at what is going on in Equation C118. If you look at the middle of Equation C118, you will find the right hand side of Equation C106. So we are using calibrated airspeed to find q_c/P_{SL}. This ratio has a one-to-one correspondence to calibrated airspeed. The definition of calibrated airspeed can be summarized as calibrated airspeed works exactly like true airspeed at sea level on a standard day. So even if the aircraft is supersonic, if the differential pressure seen at the airspeed indicator corresponds to 600 knots, it will still indicate 600 knots, whether a shock wave was involved or not. The equations for calibrated airspeed only change for supersonic effects at a_{SL}, because as far as the airspeed indicator is concerned, the only altitude it knows is sea level.

However, next the value of q_c/P_{SL} is divided by the pressure ratio. This introduces the effects of altitude and changes the ratio to q_c/P_a, as seen in

$$\frac{q_c}{P_a} = \frac{q_c}{P_{SL}} \frac{1}{\delta} \qquad (C109)$$

This will typically result in $q_c/P_a > q_c/P_{SL}$. There is a one-to-one correspondence between q_c/P_a and Mach Number. If $q_c/P_a > 0.89293$, then $M > 1$. So if $V_c < a_{SL}$, then q_c/P_{SL} calculated by Equation C106 will be less than 0.89293. However, dividing q_c/P_{SL} by the pressure ratio may result in a q_c/P_a that is greater than 0.89293, indicating a supersonic condition. This requires use of the supersonic equations.

Hence, for supersonic conditions, first find q_c/P_{SL} using the appropriate equation based on the value of calibrated airspeed.

$$\frac{q_c}{P_{SL}} = \left(1 + 0.2\left(\frac{V_c}{a_{SL}}\right)^2\right)^{7/2} - 1 \qquad (V_c < a_{SL}) \quad (C106)$$

$$\frac{q_c}{P_{SL}} = \frac{166.921\left(\dfrac{V_c}{a_{SL}}\right)^7}{\left(7\left(\dfrac{V_c}{a_{SL}}\right)^2 - 1\right)^{5/2}} - 1 \qquad (V_c > a_{SL}) \quad (C107)$$

Next, find q_c/P_a by

$$\frac{q_c}{P_a} = \frac{q_c}{P_{SL}}\frac{1}{\delta} \qquad (C109)$$

If the resulting value of q_c/P_a is less than 0.89293, go back and use Equation C118 like you should have in the first place. If q_c/P_a is greater than 0.89293, then the aircraft is supersonic and Mach number must be found by using

$$M = 0.881284\sqrt{\left(\frac{q_c}{P_a}+1\right)\left(1 - \frac{1}{7M^2}\right)^{5/2}} \qquad (M > 1 \text{ or } q_c/P_a > 0.89293) \quad (C124)$$

Of course, the sharper ones in the class immediately recognize that Equation C124 is not explicit in Mach number. Therefore, it must either be solved by iteration or by reference to a table of values (for those of you still sporting slide rules). Equation C124 can be solved by functional iteration. That is, start with an estimate of Mach number. Use it to calculate a new Mach number. Use this result in Equation C124 to calculate another Mach number. Continue until the result converges with the input.

In either case, to find true airspeed, use the ambient temperature to calculate the speed of sound

$$a = \sqrt{\gamma R T_a} \qquad (C31)$$

and then find the true airspeed by

$$V_t = Ma \qquad (C60)$$

To go the other direction, let's start with Mach number and pressure altitude and find calibrated airspeed. From the pressure altitude, calculate the pressure ratio.

$$\delta = (1 - 6.87559\text{x}10^{-6}\, H_c)^{5.2559} \qquad (H_c \leq 36089.24 \text{ feet}) \quad (B1)$$

$$\delta = 0.223360\, e^{(-4.80637\text{x}10^{-5}\,(H_c - 36089.24))} \qquad (H_c > 36089.24 \text{ feet}) \quad (B2)$$

For the subsonic case (M < 1), the calibrated airspeed can then be calculated directly by

$$V_c = a_{SL}\sqrt{5\left[\left(\delta\left\{\left[1+0.2M^2\right]^{7/2}-1\right\}+1\right)^{2/7}-1\right]} \qquad (M<1) \quad (C129)$$

For the supersonic case, first calculate q_c/P_a by

$$\frac{q_c}{P_a} = \frac{166.921M^7}{\left(7M^2-1\right)^{5/2}}-1 \qquad (M>1) \quad (C102)$$

This will result in a $q_c/P_a > 0.89293$. Next calculate q_c/P_{SL} by

$$\frac{q_c}{P_{SL}} = \frac{q_c}{P_a}\delta \qquad (C110)$$

If the resulting value of q_c/P_{SL} is less than 0.89293, calculate V_c by

$$V_c = a_{SL}\sqrt{5\left(\left(\frac{q_c}{P_{SL}}+1\right)^{2/7}-1\right)} \qquad (C126)$$

If the resulting value of q_c/P_{SL} is greater than 0.89293, calculate V_c by iterating on

$$V_c = a_{SL}\,0.881284\sqrt{\left(\frac{q_c}{P_{SL}}+1\right)\left(1-\frac{1}{7\left(\frac{V_c}{a_{SL}}\right)^2}\right)^{5/2}} \qquad \left(\frac{q_c}{P_{SL}}>0.89293\right) \quad (C131)$$

Measuring Airspeed

Over the years, many different methods have been tried for measuring airspeed, with varying degrees of success.

When the Wright Brothers made their first flight in 1903, their airspeed measuring device was more of a Data Acquisition System than an airspeed indicator. They fitted their aircraft with a Richard anemometer and a stop watch that could be started and stopped with a single lever at the beginning and end of the flight. The anemometer was made by Richard in Paris, purchased by Octave Chanute, and given to the Wrights as a gift in April 1903 (Figure 4.3). As the air spun the vanes, a shaft moved the pointer on the lower dial. This dial indicated in "metres" (French spelling) how far the device had passed through the air mass, which presumably was resettable to zero prior to each trial. This distance was differentiated to airspeed post flight by dividing by the number of seconds shown on the stop watch in the middle. (Ref 8)

Figure 4.3. Richard
anemometer and stopwatch

During the era of biplanes, a common method of sensing airspeed was listening to the pitch of the vibrating rigging wires. Very effective from an open cockpit to detect changes in airspeed, but not very effective for getting measured values for flight testing. Also a difficult method to use when rigging wires are not present on the aircraft.

Another straight forward method for slow airplanes was to put a flat plate perpendicular to the airstream on a spring (see Figure 4.4). The amount that the plate blew back indicated the airspeed. This is somewhat effective over low airspeed ranges, but its precision is questionable.   After the plate has blown back sufficiently, say about 60 degrees, any further increase in airspeed would cause little additional movement. The resolution of this device is relatively fixed. A stronger spring could be used to measure to a higher airspeed, but the number of increments that could be measured would remain the same.

In the laboratory, manometers can be used very effectively to measure pressure differences and thus compute airspeed, such as in a wind tunnel. Unfortunately, manometers would be rather large and ungainly for use in the cockpit. Additionally, the calibration would change with load factor, and a

Figure 4.4. Flat Plate and Spring Airspeed Indicator

manometer would be essentially useless (and messy) at negative load factors.

The APN-147 Doppler Radar, once used in C-130, RC-135A, C-141, and other aircraft, "transmits two fan-shaped beams continuously, one forward and the other to the rear. The receiver samples alternate pairs of forward and rear beams (Janus mode), obtaining a resultant Doppler shift frequency proportional to the groundspeed. The antenna is maintained parallel to the track of the aircraft by rotating in azimuth to cancel lateral Doppler shift frequencies. The angular displacement with respect to the center-line of the aircraft is drift angle and is displayed on the Groundspeed and Drift Angle Indicator." (Ref 9)

An Inertial Navigation System (INS) or Global Positioning System (GPS) can also give a measurement of ground speed. While ground speed is useful for navigation, it does not account for the wind and is thus not very usable for the piloting task. However, it may be available as a backup if the airspeed system(s) should malfunction.

One moderately successful system at low speeds was a venturi mounted on the exterior of the aircraft. Air flow accelerates into the throat of the venturi, lowering the pressure in the throat. By measuring the ambient pressure and comparing it to the pressure in the throat the airspeed can be determined. However, this method starts to break down when the flow through the venturi becomes compressible (about Mach 0.3 through the throat), which will be a much lower freestream Mach number. In practice, the venturi becomes impractical above about 100 knots. Even if compressible flow equations were developed for the venturi, at some Mach number well below Mach 1 the flow at the throat would reach Mach 1 and the flow would be choked, and the venturi would not show any change at any higher airspeeds. Of course, there's also that minor detail that venturis hanging out in the airstream create additional drag.

A technique useful in the laboratory or wind tunnel for measuring airspeed is hot wire anemometry, where a short length of wire is heated by an electrical current. When placed in a flow field, the passing air convectively cools the wire. The electrical resistance of the wire depends on its temperature, and its temperature depends on the velocity of air past the wire. By measuring the current flowing through the wire, the airspeed can be determined. The main advantage to hot wires is a very high bandwidth, that is rapid changes in velocity can be detected.

This is useful when studying phenomena such as turbulence. The main disadvantage of hot wire anemometry is the fragile nature of the sensor. Hot wires are frequently broken in laboratory conditions, and this is considered normal. Such a sensor could not be expected to hold up in operational usage under varying conditions.

By far, the most useful method for determining airspeed over large speed ranges is the Pitot-static system. This system measures total pressure and ambient pressure (or some combination thereof) and determines airspeed and altitude from these pressures.

Air Data Sensors

The Pitot-static theory discussed heretofore has been based on the idea that we can measure freestream total pressure and ambient pressure. In the simplest sense, to measure total pressure, we just need an open-ended tube pointed into the airstream (parallel to the flow) to measure total pressure. To measure ambient pressure, we need an open ended tube pointed perpendicular to the flow. In this direction, the tube would not pick up any of the additional pressure from the velocity of the flow.

One method for mounting these ports is to use a Pitot tube for total pressure and mount a flush port on the side of the fuselage to measure ambient pressure. This installation is common in low speed aircraft, including the Cessna 172, C-12, and C-130, though it is also used on the B-52, which is hardly a low speed aircraft. The location of the port on the side of the fuselage is important to reducing errors in sensing ambient pressure. The location is usually determined experimentally by trying several locations and picking the one with the least error over the aircraft's angle of attack and speed range. While this is fine for production aircraft where many will be built, it is not practical for one-off designs or limited production runs.

Another option is to use two tubes, both pointed into the airstream. One is open at the end and is used to sense total pressure. The other tube is closed at the end and senses ambient pressure through holes in the side of the tube. This type of setup has been used on aircraft such as the Bellanca Scout and Schweizer SGS 2-33 glider. If the tubes are concentric, with the total pressure tube inside the ambient pressure tube, the sensor is called a Pitot-static tube. Pitot-static tubes are very common on high-speed aircraft, and have also been used on low speed aircraft as well.

Using simple tubes as the air data sensors can lead to problems, primarily with water ingestion. Water in the air data tubes can lead to all sorts of erroneous readings. If a slug of water gets caught in a vertical (or at least slanted) portion of the air data tube, the weight of the water will cause the pressure in the tube to change as the water is pulled down by gravity or acceleration while still sealing the tube. As an extra bonus, this error will vary as the load factor changes.

Many production Pitot or Pitot-static probes are designed to protect the air data tubes from water ingestion. Some techniques for rejecting water can be seen in Figure 4.5 in the design of the "Shark Fin" AN5816 Pitot-Static Probe. Ram air enters through the Pitot port on the right side of the diagram. The first water separator is a baffle in front of the first total pressure line. The total pressure air can get around the baffle, but large rain drops bounce off the baffle and fall to the bottom of the chamber, where the water exits out a small drain hole, aided by the total pressure. Any moisture that makes it past the baffle travels to a Moisture Trap, where it tends to fall to the floor and continue out the rear drain hole. The Total Pressure Line is a standpipe in the Moisture Trap, which senses the dry air pressure about one inch higher.

Now you may wonder, how does this probe properly measure total pressure if the air does not come to a complete stop because of the drain holes allowing it to pass through? First of all, the drain holes are very small compared to the Pitot port, so there is very little airflow velocity through the moisture trap. Second, the air does come to a complete stop, and therefore reach full total pressure, at the top end of the Total Pressure Line that leads to the instruments, since the remainder of this line is sealed.

The ambient air pressure enters through static ports on the top and bottom of the probe. Any moisture trapped in the static pressure chamber will drain out the lower static port. The Static Pressure Line is another standpipe to sense the dry air pressure from the top of the chamber.

Electric heaters are installed to prevent blockage by ice accumulation.

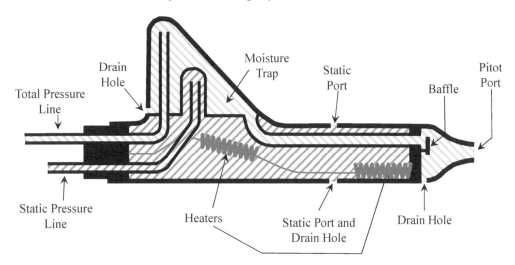

Figure 4.5. AN5816 Pitot Static Probe

Another common Pitot-static probe is the L-Shaped Pitot-Static Probe, as shown in Figure 4.6. Water ingestion is minimized in a similar way. Water entering the Pitot port will drain through the provided drain hole. Any water making its way into the first total pressure line will be stopped by the baffle on the second total pressure line and remain in the moisture trap, eventually draining back down the first total pressure line. Water in the static pressure chamber will drain out the lower static port.

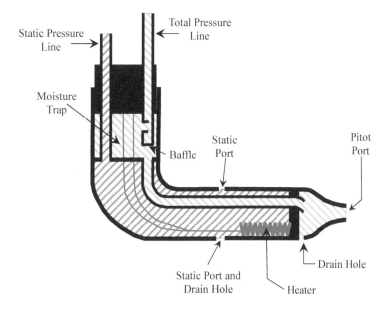

Figure 4.6. L-shaped Pitot Static Probe

For flight test use, a Pitot-static tube will frequently be mounted on a nose boom in front of the aircraft. This boom is also frequently used to mount vanes for measuring angle of attack and sideslip. At the AFTC, this setup is typically referred to as a Yaw-Angle of attack-Pitot-Static (YAPS) head.

Modifying an aircraft with a YAPS boom does have one undesirable effect—the YAPS boom will have a different correction curve than the production Pitot-static system. While the YAPS boom may cause a bias in the static pressure corrections, the benefit is usually a more precise (repeatable) measurement. How this difference is handled depends on the installation. For AFTC F-16s modified with a YAPS boom, "When this boom is installed, the source error correction (SEC) in the Central Air Data Computer (CADC) is bypassed by connecting CADC connector J105 pin 35 (SEC Bypass Engage) to aircraft ground. The SEC in the CADC is used only with the production pitot-static boom, which has a different static pressure (Ps) position error than the flight test boom. With the SEC bypassed, all air data parameters that are a function of Ps will be affected by the flight test boom position error." (Ref 10) Some T-38Cs modified with a YAPS boom are equipped with an air data computer that allows selection of multiple correction curves. Some of these aircraft have been equipped with correction curves specifically derived for the YAPS boom configuration. In AFTC DAS modified C-12s, the YAPS boom Pitot and static pressures are only connected to the DAS. The pilot and copilot Primary Flight Displays (PFD) remain connected to the production Pitot tubes and static ports.

Another way to get flow angularity data is to use a multiple hole probe. One hole in the center is used like a normal Pitot tube to measure total pressure. Behind the center hole the probe is shaped like a cone with ports on the surface of the cone. The F-117 probe is similar to the five hole probe, except that instead of a cone it uses four facets with a hole in the center of each.

Consider the five hole probe. Ports above and below the Pitot port are used to determine the angle of attack. When the probe is placed at an angle of attack to the airstream, the port on the bottom of the probe is more aligned with the airstream and thus picks up more of the total pressure rise. The port on the top of the probe is less aligned (more perpendicular) with the airstream and thus picks up less of the total pressure rise. The difference in pressure between the top and bottom port is related to the angle of attack. Similarly, the ports on either side of the Pitot port can be used to measure sideslip. For ambient pressure, a separate set of ports are used, either farther back on the probe or on the fuselage.

Taking the multiple hole idea one step farther would be multiple flush ports on the exterior of the aircraft. This system is used on the B-2. Booms and tubes tend to have a large radar cross section, and there is no point making an aircraft stealthy if the Pitot boom grossly magnifies the radar cross section. Using multiple ports can result in a stealthy design, but it will require a computer to interpret the pressures. How the pressures are to be interpreted would need to be worked out either experimentally (wind tunnel, flight test) or analytically (computational fluid dynamics).

For flight test work, some specialized sensors are sometimes used. One concern is that at high angles of attack the error in sensing total pressure increases as the Pitot tube becomes less aligned with the airstream. One seemingly obvious answer to this would be to mount the Pitot tube on a horizontal pivot and add some stabilizing fins to keep it aligned with the flow. While we're at it, we pivot it vertically so that it will remain aligned in sideslip. The result is a swivel probe, as shown in Figure 4.7. The added complexity is not

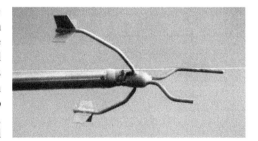

Figure 4.7. Swivel Probe

justified for operational flying, but may be useful in flight test. The probe will need to be sufficiently stable that it doesn't oscillate constantly in flight and thus corrupt the readings. If used at high speeds, the possibility of flutter in the probe should be investigated.

Another approach to improve total pressure sensing is to place the Pitot tube in a larger tube. This setup is referred to as a Kiel probe, as shown in Figure 4.8. The outer tube helps the flow to turn more in line with the sensing tube. A Kiel probe was used on the C-17 for high angle of attack testing as the total pressure truth source. According to the manufacturer of the probe, the Kiel probe had zero total pressure loss at flow angles of up to 58 degrees. Thus, for most conditions, the Kiel probe will accomplish the same results as the swivel probe but with less complexity.

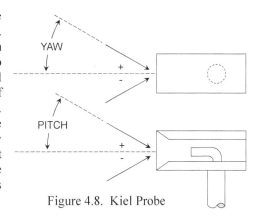

Figure 4.8. Kiel Probe

To more accurately measure the ambient pressure in flight test, a trailing cone or trailing bomb system may be used. In this system, a long tube is trailed behind the aircraft to pick up ambient pressure from outside of the flow field of the aircraft. The specifics of this system will be further described in the flight test techniques section.

Airspeed Indicator Construction

The airspeed indicator is a differential pressure gauge. However, instead of reporting differential pressure in units like pounds per square foot, it reports pressure in units of calibrated airspeed in knots, miles per hour, or kilometers per hour. Airspeed indicators marked in furlongs per fortnight (0.00032328 knots, about one centimeter per minute) are rare. The conversion between the sensed pressure and airspeed is as defined by the calibrated airspeed equation.

$$V_c = \sqrt{\left(\frac{1}{\rho_{SL}}\right)7P_{SL}\left(\left(\frac{P_T - P_a}{P_{SL}}+1\right)^{\frac{2}{7}}-1\right)} \qquad (C65)$$

Per this equation, the airspeed indicator senses the differential pressure $P_T - P_a$ and displays the corresponding calibrated airspeed. We know this equation is valid up to a calibrated airspeed equal to the speed of sound at sea level (661.48 knots). It is conceivable that an instrument could be built that would follow the supersonic relationship (Equation C131) above 661.48 knots. In practice, aircraft that have performance sufficient for this to be an issue have typically had an air data computer to interpret the pressures, solving the problem in software instead of mechanical gears. The airspeed indicator is then driven electrically or is a readout from the air data computer.

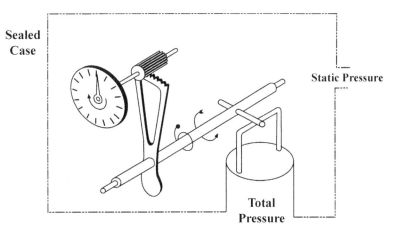

Figure 4.9. Airspeed Indicator Schematic

A mechanical airspeed indicator, as shown in Figure 4.9, consists of a sealed case connected by one tube to the Pitot tube and one tube to the static port. The total pressure is fed to the inside of a bellows, and the static pressure is fed into the case. The difference in these pressures causes the bellows to expand and contract as the differential pressure changes. This movement is translated through a clockwork mechanism to the pointer on the face of the instrument, which indicates the pressure differential in units of airspeed.

Mach Meter Construction

The Mach meter is a combination absolute and differential pressure gauge. The conversion between the sensed pressures and Mach number is as defined by the Mach meter equation.

$$M = \sqrt{5\left(\left(\frac{q_c}{P_a} + 1\right)^{2/7} - 1\right)} \quad (M < 1 \text{ or } q_c/P_a < 0.89293) \quad (C117)$$

Per this equation, the Mach meter senses the differential pressure q_c and ambient pressure P_a and displays the corresponding Mach number. We know this equation is valid up to sonic speed (M = 1). For supersonic Mach numbers, the supersonic relationship (Equation C124) would be used. In practice, most supersonic aircraft have an air data computer to interpret the pressures, solving the problem in software instead of mechanical gears. The Mach meter is then driven electrically or is a readout from the air data computer. The T-38A is supersonic and does not have an air data computer. I suspect the Mach meter in the T-38 does not change to the supersonic equation above Mach 1, since with a maximum Mach of about 1.2 M any error arising from only using Equation C117 would be very small.

A mechanical Mach meter, as shown in Figure 4.10, consists of a sealed case connected by one tube to the Pitot tube and one tube to the static port. The total pressure is fed to the inside of a bellows, and the static pressure is fed into the case. The difference in these pressures causes this bellows to expand and contract as the differential pressure changes. An additional bellows is sealed and reacts to the ambient pressure changes. The movements of these two bellows are mixed together according to Equation C117 through a clockwork mechanism to the pointer on the face of the instrument, which indicates the result in units of Mach number.

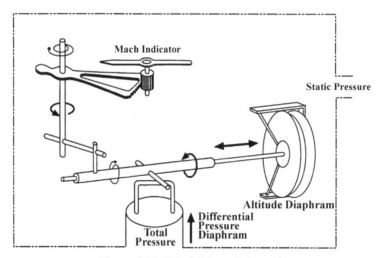

Figure 4.10. Mach Meter Schematic

Because of the two bellows system and the complexity involved, the mechanical Mach meter has a lower accuracy and reliability that the airspeed indicator and altimeter. They are also more difficult to calibrate. Although they are amazingly good considering these drawbacks, there are some considerations to remember when using a mechanical Mach meter in flight test. Mechanical Mach meters can be used for reference in flight to fly a maneuver, but a more accurate Mach number can be calculated post flight using the airspeed and altitude recorded during the maneuver. For airplanes using air data computers, this issue may be moot. For instance, in the F-16, the air data computer measures total pressure and ambient pressure and uses these pressures to digitally calculate altitude, airspeed, and Mach number, which are then projected on the HUD. In this case, if you recorded the airspeed and altitude from the HUD and calculated the Mach number, you'd better get the same value that was in the HUD or somebody's making a mistake!

Henri Pitot and His Tube

Henri Pitot (Figure 4.11) was born in Aramon, France on 3 May 1695. Like many eventual great thinkers, as a boy he intensely disliked academic studies. However, while serving briefly in the French military, he purchased a geometry text and spent the next three years studying mathematics and astronomy. He moved to Paris in 1718, and became an assistant in the chemistry laboratory of the Royal Academy of Sciences in 1723. He did well enough to get himself elected to the Academy in 1724.

Figure 4.11. Henri Pitot

Pitot became interested in hydraulics, mostly in the flow of water in rivers and canals. At the time, the prevailing method of measuring flow velocity was by observing flotsam on the surface, but that only told the velocity on the surface. A prevailing theory of the time stated that flow velocity at a given depth was proportional to the mass above it, and thus flow velocity increased with depth. Pitot devised his measurement technique by using one tube oriented into the flow and a second tube perpendicular to the flow. He used this device to measure the flow of the Seine River between two piers of a bridge in 1732. The results were presented to the Royal Academy on 12 November 1732, ~~right after the Veterans Day holiday~~. His results showed that the flow velocity decreased as depth increased, in keeping with modern boundary layer theory, which would be developed by Ludwig Prandtl in the early 1900s.

Pitot's tube was not the overnight success story that might be expected. In fact, it fell into disfavor in the engineering community, mostly because of other investigators using it improperly. Many tried using just the total pressure tube, not understanding the importance of the static pressure tube. Various shapes for the opening, rather than just a simple tube, were used, which led to erroneous results.

While Pitot tubes are introduced to young aeronautical engineering students as an obvious outgrowth of Bernoulli's equation, Pitot had no rational theory to explain its use. He invented the Pitot-static tube in 1732, six years before Daniel Bernoulli published *Hydrodynamica* and well before Euler developed the theory into what we commonly refer to as Bernoulli's Equation. Pitot simply used intuition and empirical results to determine that the pressure differential was proportional to the square of the flow velocity. The Pitot tube would not be linked to the Bernoulli equation until 1913, when John Airey presented the results of experiments at the University of Michigan.

Strangely enough, Airey used the Pitot tube for measuring velocity in liquids, making no mention of its use in airplanes or wind tunnels. The first practical airspeed indicator was driven by a venturi tube on an aircraft by French Captain A. Eteve in January 1911. Later in 1911, British engineers at the Royal Aircraft Establishment (RAE) at Farnborough used a Pitot tube on an airplane for the first time. One of the first tasks of the newly formed NACA in 1915 was to investigate reliable airspeed meters. NACA Report No. 2 developed the theory for the Pitot tube in compressible flow.

Henri Pitot retired to his birthplace, dying in Aramon on 27 December 1771. (Ref 11)

Ernst Mach and His Number

Figure 4.12. Ernst Mach

Ernst Mach (Figure 4.12) was born 18 February 1838 at Turas, Moravia (then part of the Austrian Empire, now part of the Czech Republic). His studies were widely varied, leading American philosopher William James to refer to him as a man who knew "everything about everything."

Surprisingly, even though his name is forever associated with supersonic flow, it was a rather small part of his research. He was the first to capture a photograph of shock waves (Figure 4.13) around a supersonic bullet in 1887. He used the shadowgraph method to get the shot. This was very impressive since he managed split-second timing without the benefit of vacuum tubes, much less solid state electronics.

Mach was also the first researcher of the basic characteristics of supersonic flow. He recognized the importance of the ratio of the velocity to the speed of sound, and noted that there was discontinuity in flow behaviour when this ratio changed from less than one to greater than one. However, he did not go so far as to name this ratio after himself. It was Swiss engineer Jakob Ackeret who referred to this ratio as "Mach number" in 1929 during a lecture in Zurich. "Mach number" did not reach the English literature until 1932. (Ref 11)

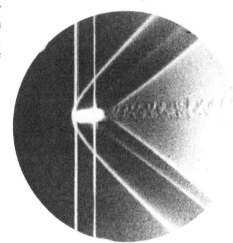

Figure 4.13. Mach's photograph of supersonic bullet

Chapter 5

Temperature Measurement

You Can't Get There From Here

You would think that measuring air temperature would be easy enough. Weather Guessers do it all of the time. Your mother could even do it (you never would listen to her and put your coat on, would you?). Even so, pilots just can't seem to handle it, because

IT IS IMPOSSIBLE TO MEASURE AMBIENT AIR TEMPERATURE IN FLIGHT!

Now before you get all excited and tell me that your flight engineer or copilot would read the outside air temperature to you all of the time, realize that the key word in that statement is "ambient," namely, the temperature of the air at rest. The second key word (in importance, not in order) is "measure." I didn't say we couldn't determine the ambient air temperature, just that we can't measure it directly.

"So why not, oh purveyor of Pitot-static wisdom?" you may be asking. The problem arises because the air is in motion (or the airplane is in motion). The airplane disturbs the air as it passes through it, and a temperature measuring transducer may or may not have a stagnation point associated with it. In any case, the end result is that the measured temperature is going to be the ambient temperature, plus some amount of total temperature rise.

This can easily be understood for probes that stick out in the airstream. The probe will have a stagnation point, just like a wing or fuselage, where the air molecules are brought to a stop relative to the probe. This causes a rise in pressure (total pressure) and also a rise in temperature. If the air is brought to a stop adiabatically, then the relationship of the total temperature to the ambient temperature is given by

$$\frac{T_T}{T_a} = \left(1 + \frac{\gamma - 1}{2} M^2\right)$$

(C34)

So why not just make the temperature probes flush like we do to measure static pressure? The temperature probes on the MC-130H are flush probes on either side of the fuselage near the nose gear well, and these probes still see 80 percent of the total temperature rise over the ambient temperature (the flight manual claims it to be 90 percent, but flight testing has shown it to be closer to 80 percent). Why? Because the nose of the fuselage is disturbing the air.

Equation C34 shows us what happens if the air is brought to a stop adiabatically. However, a temperature probe with a finite diameter may see the full total temperature at the stagnation point, but lower temperatures at other locations on the probe. Because of this temperature difference, some of the heat energy will be conducted away from the stagnation point to other parts of the probe. Additionally, the higher temperature will cause some of the heat energy to be lost to the surroundings as radiation. Hence, the process is not adiabatic and the output temperature may be less than the actual total temperature. This effect is dealt with in the traditional engineering manner, namely by the insertion of a fudge factor. In this case we call it the Temperature Recovery Factor (K_t), and the resulting equation looks like (using $\gamma = 1.4$ for air)

$$\frac{T_{ic}}{T_a} = 1 + 0.2 K_t M^2$$

(C186)

For a well-designed probe, such as used for flight test or air data on some aircraft (such as the F-15 and F-16), the temperature recovery factor will be very close to 1, in a range of 0.90 to 0.99. Typical light aircraft systems (such as seen on a Cessna 172 or a C-12) tend to have temperature recovery factors closer to 0.8 or even 0.7.

Note, however, that for Equation C186 to work, the temperatures must be expressed in an absolute temperature scale, such as Kelvin or Rankine. In fact, the sooner you shed those childhood notions of temperature in Fahrenheit or Celsius and just do all of your engineering in Kelvin or Rankine, the better off you'll be. Of course, your family will think you've flipped when you start saying "Man, I'm freezing! It's only 273 degrees out here!

When talking about airspeed, we had to choose which equation to used, based on if we were in subsonic or supersonic flow, or at a calibrated airspeed greater than or less than the speed of sound as sea level. Well, here comes a well-deserved break. The only assumption we had to make to get Equation C34, and thus Equation C186, was that the flow was adiabatic. Isentropic flow was not required. We learned in Compressible Aero that flow through a shock was adiabatic, even if it was very entropic. As such, the Total Temperature did not change passing through a shock wave. Hence, Equation C34, and thus Equation C186, are valid for subsonic and supersonic flow.

Figure 5.1 shows a cutaway of a typical total temperature probe.

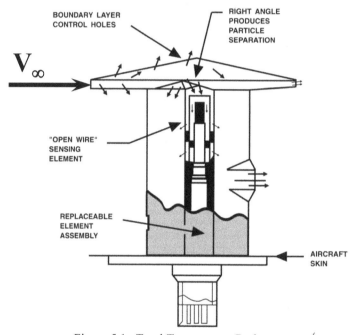

Figure 5.1. Total Temperature Probe

In this probe, the air enters the top section of the probe. The boundary layer is reduced through holes in the walls. Part of the airstream is turned through 90 degrees, effectively bringing it to a stop relative to the airplane. The remainder of the airstream exits the back of the probe. This 90 degree turn also acts as an inertial separator, since dirt, water drops, and other contaminants cannot make the turn and continue out the rear, thus protecting the temperature sensor. The air that was turned 90 degrees passes over a temperature sensing element and then exits through the rear of the strut portion of the probe. Because the air is slowed in a controlled fashion, this type of probe has a higher temperature recovery factor than a simple rod placed in the airstream.

Determining the Temperature Recovery Factor

To determine the temperature recovery factor (K_t), we first collect data for indicated temperature, ambient temperature, and Mach number. This is usually done in conjunction with the position error flight test techniques (FTTs), using a source separate from the test system to determine the ambient temperature. Then, using Equation C194, we plot the parameter (T_{ic}/T_a -1) as the "y" parameter and the parameter ($M^2/5$) as the "x" parameter to produce a plot as shown in Figure 5.2.

$$\frac{T_{ic}}{T_a} - 1 = K_t \frac{M^2}{5} + \text{bias}$$
(C194)

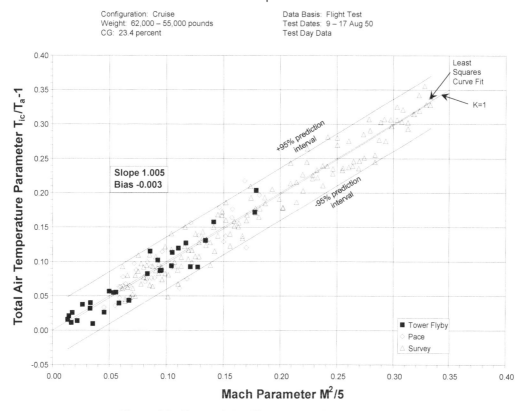

Figure 5.2. Determining Temperature Recovery Factor

These points should fit to a straight line. The slope of this line will be the Temperature Recovery Factor (K_t). In Figure 5.2, the particular uncertainty of the data points lead to a least squares curve fit with a slope of 1.005. However, since there is no additional source of heat energy (such as a probe heater) in this system, physics tells us that the temperature recovery factor (in this case) should be no more than 1.0. Therefore, a proper data analysis of these data would return a $K_t = 1.0$. Figure 5.2 also shows a reference line (K=1) to show an ideal temperature recovery for comparison.

Theoretically, this line should pass through the origin, but uncertainty in measurements or instrument errors in the temperature probe will occasionally lead to a slight bias, or non-zero intercept. This bias should be very small if it does exist.

Variable Temperature Recovery Factor

The previous discussion assumed that the Temperature Recovery Factor (K_t) was a constant. Equation C186 came about by inserting a fudge factor in Equation C34. This method has been shown to work well for subsonic flow, but may not be effective for supersonic flow with certain types of total temperature probes.

The higher quality total temperature probes (something more sophisticated than a simple rod in the airstream) typically depend on some sort of internal flow through passages. While the Total Temperature (T_T) in supersonic flow does not change through the shock wave, at supersonic speeds the temperature recovery characteristics of the probe may change, due to factors such as choked flow through the probe passages.

To address this, an alternate recovery correction (η) can be defined as

$$\eta = \frac{T_T - T_{ic}}{T_T} \qquad\qquad (C196)$$

In this approach, η is typically variable for subsonic Mach numbers and constant for supersonic Mach numbers. Values for η should be available from the probe manufacturer.

To find ambient temperature, the total temperature is calculated first.

$$T_T = \frac{T_{ic}}{1 - \eta} \qquad\qquad (C197)$$

Then the ambient temperature is calculated by

$$T_a = \frac{T_T}{1 + 0.2M^2} \qquad\qquad (C198)$$

Note that there is no recovery factor in Equation C198 because that effect was taken care of by calculating the actual total temperature.

Chapter 6

Air Data System Errors

Tell Me Again Why I Should Care...

So far we've spent a lot of time discussing the standard atmosphere and how Pitot-static systems work. But flight test professionals like ourselves are not tasked with designing these systems, so what is our role in this testing?

The role of the flight tester in Pitot-static systems arises because any uncompensated Pitot-static system will have errors in it. Period. Dot. It's just the nature of the beast. Operational aircrew need to know what the right answers are, so flight testers measure and characterize the errors. This information is then either given to the aircrew directly as corrections to be applied to the instrument readings, or is incorporated into a computer system to correct the air data before it is displayed to the aircrew.

There are three major sources of errors in a Pitot-static system: instrument errors, system errors, and position (or installation) errors. Each type of error must be handled differently.

Instrument Error

Mechanical instruments (altimeter, airspeed indicator, Mach meter) are designed to be fed a pressure or pressures and display an output value corresponding to the input pressures according to a defined equation. Several problems can get in the way of accomplishing this goal.

The simplest problem could arise from the markings on the face of the instrument. If the lines and numbers are not painted in the right position per the design of the instrument, the resulting readings referencing those lines and numbers will have errors. This is generally not a problem with quality instruments as normally used in aircraft. Some instruments will be installed with a witness mark on the frame and glass of the instrument. If this witness mark is broken (doesn't line up), then the face has been moved relative to where the internal mechanism thinks it is, and that instrument should be repaired.

Other errors come from the internal mechanisms. These errors could come from reactions to magnetic fields, temperature changes (expansion or contraction of parts), or even errors arising from the design of the gauge not perfectly realizing the intended equation. These errors can be reduced in magnitude by good design.

The biggest contributor to instrument error is hysteresis arising from internal friction. This causes the instrument to lag behind the correct reading as the property being measured is changing. For instance, in a climb an altimeter will show a lower than actual altitude. In a descent, the altimeter will show a higher than actual altitude. While friction can be reduced through design, it cannot be eliminated.

To calibrate an altimeter, the altimeter is fed a known pressure, and the reading on the dial is compared to the calculated altitude for that pressure. To check for hysteresis, readings are recorded first as the altitude is increased and then as the altitude is decreased. Because of hysteresis, the altitude read while decreasing altitude will be higher than the altitude read while increasing altitude for the same input pressure. Typically the hysteresis values for altimeters will be around 20 feet or less, possibly increasing at higher altitudes. Figure 6.1 shows the results of a calibration of a typical altimeter.

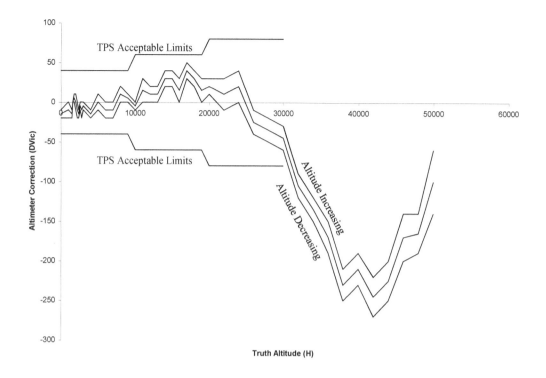

Figure 6.1. Example Altimeter Instrument Correction Curve

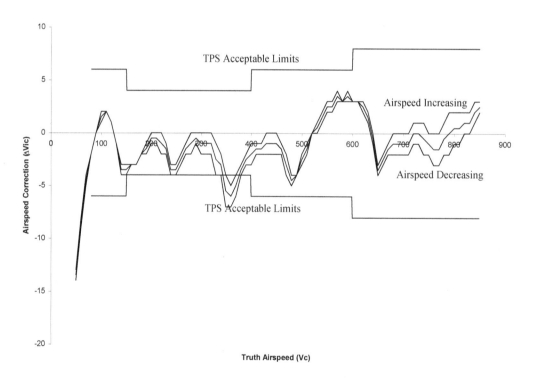

Figure 6.2. Example Airspeed Indicator Instrument Correction Curve

So if the instrument correction is different depending on whether the altitude is increasing or decreasing, which one do we use? For simplicity's sake, in general we assume that we do not know the direction of the last change of altitude, so we use the average of the up and down value as our instrument correction. The sharper ones in the class will immediately recognize that this leaves some residual error. That's true, and generally we accept that. In the above example, the residual error would be 20 feet at most generally, which is acceptably small for most cases.

Airspeed indicators and Mach meters are calibrated in the same fashion, feeding known pressures and comparing the instrument readings to the calculated values. Figure 6.2 shows the results of a calibration of a typical airspeed indicator.

As mechanical gauges wear, the calibrations will change, requiring periodic recalibration. Back when TPS aircraft primarily used calibrated mechanical flight instruments, the airspeed indicators and altimeters were changed out annually and the calibrations were checked on the aircraft six months after installation.

Electrical measurement systems don't have to worry about friction, but have a different set of errors to be considered. A pressure transducer's relationship between input pressure and output value can slowly change with time, which is usually referred to as "drift." Variations in input voltage to the system may cause changes in the output voltage, although well designed systems are tolerant of a wide range of input voltages without a change in the output. Errors may arise from variations or improper settings of amplifiers or signal conditioning equipment. If analog signals are converted to digital measurements, then some errors may come from the analog to digital conversion. While theoretically it would be possible to calibrate each item in the system, it is typically easier and most defensible to perform an "end to end" calibration. For instance, a known pressure would be applied to the static port and the resulting altitude value would be recorded at the final system output and compared to the calculated altitude. Thus, all of the separate calibrations would be combined into one overall system calibration.

Data Acquisition Systems (DAS) are a form of electrical measurement systems. The engineering units output from a DAS are typically presented as "instrument corrected" values. The DAS data as actually recorded on the recording media are in "counts", that is, a raw number value output by the sensor in "units" that are convenient to the range of that sensor. In post-flight processing, these "counts" are converted to engineering units through a calibration routine specific to that parameter on that DAS. Running this calibration routine is equivalent to applying instrument corrections, such that the output data are considered "instrument corrected" values. These calibration routines are determined by running "end to end" calibrations where possible. When not possible, simulated values are input to the system as close to the sensor as possible.

System Errors

Lag

Because the Pitot-static system has a non-zero volume, the system will exhibit a time delay between a change in pressure at the ports and a change in reading on the face of the instrument. Looking at the equation of state (Equation A3), if we assume nearly constant temperature, then for the pressure to change inside the static system, the air density must change as well. If the volume of the system doesn't change, then the mass of the air must change. For an increase in pressure, more molecules must move into the static system. If we allow an increase in volume for the bellows to expand, then even more molecules must move into the static system. These molecules require a finite amount of time to move in and out of the static port. If the port is small or otherwise restricted, then the required amount of time will increase. Of course, the length of time involved is generally small, on the order of seconds or fractions of seconds.

Lag is increased by factors that slow down this movement in molecules. These factors include:

Pressure drop in the tubing due to viscous friction—as long as the air is moving through the tube, there will be a pressure loss from friction, because the tubing walls have a boundary layer. If the input pressure stabilizes, the pressure in the tube will eventually stabilize at the input pressure as the air stops moving.

Inertia of the air mass in the tubing—it takes time to accelerate a mass to a velocity, and the air has to move to change pressure.

Instrument inertia and viscous and kinetic friction—once the pressure gets to the instrument, the instrument takes time to react.

The finite speed of pressure propagation (acoustic lag)—a pressure change can travel no faster than the local speed of sound.

Reference 12 has a more detailed discussion of lag, but states "A detailed mathematical treatment of the response of such a system would be difficult." It goes on to say that "it is generally not possible to assume that the overall lag error correction can be made with a precision of more than 80 percent." For stabilized flight test techniques, lag is generally not an issue and can be safely ignored. It can be an issue for quasi-steady flight test techniques, with the effect of lag increasing as the rate of energy change (altitude or airspeed) increases.

Lag can be reduced by increasing the size of the tubing, which reduces the effect of friction in the tubes by moving the walls away from more of the air in the tube. For this to be effective, the size of the ports must also be increased. Since a change in pressure will cause a finite flow rate through the port, if the port size is unchanged, the increase in volume from the larger tubes can actually increase the lag because of the increase in volume.

Shortening the tubes (moving the ports closer to the instruments) can also reduce lag by reducing the volume of the system.

For an operational example of the effects of lag, consider an F-4 on a dive bombing pass. Early F-4s had the Pitot-static tube mounted on the vertical fin, which made for very long tubes to the instruments. Later F-4s moved the Pitot-static tube to the nose of the radome, which presumably shortened the required tubing somewhat. To reduce the impact of static pressure lag, the F-4 was equipped with a static pressure compensator (SPC).

How Does This Static Pressure Compensation Thing Work?

Air Data Computers (ADC) were introduced during the Century Series fighters as air data (airspeed, Mach number, altitude) were required to actuate systems such as inlet ramps or adjust gains in the flight control system. In current aircraft, the ADC takes inputs from the pressure sensors and outputs electrical signals or bus words to send the corrected air data values to where they are needed. The F-4 ADC took a little different approach. While it did have electrical outputs, the ADC output air at the "corrected" pressures to standard mechanical altimeters, airspeed indicators, and Mach meters in the cockpits. From NAVAIR 01-245FDB-1: "One of the functions of the ADC is to supply all systems requiring static pressure inputs with a static pressure which has been corrected for static source position error. This correction is accomplished through the static pressure compensator. When operating normally, the compensator utilizes static air pressure as a balancing force only. The corrected static pressure output is actually auxiliary equipment air, corrected for the static source error as dictated by the instantaneous flight situation. If a malfunction occurs in the compensator, a fail safe solenoid is deenergized allowing static pressure from the static source to be routed directly to all systems requiring static pressure inputs. With a malfunction, overall accuracy suffers, but no system dependent on static pressure becomes inoperative." Rather than having redundant ADCs (probably space and cost prohibitive), the fail safe mode was simply to turn off the static pressure compensation and plumb static pressure air directly to the instruments.

Consider a dive bombing pass at 400 knots true airspeed (KTAS) and a 45 degree dive angle. From Figure 6.3, with the SPC operative, we see that the altimeter will be reading 92 feet higher than the actual altitude. For the same conditions, with the SPC inoperative (Figure 6.4), the altimeter will be reading 1,120 feet higher than the actual altitude. If the bomb release altitude is anywhere close to the ground, this would introduce significant errors to the bombing solution, not to mention possibly endangering the aircraft and crew!

Reference 13 discusses some methods for measuring altimeter lag, though these tests have not commonly been done recently. One method is to use a calibrated aircraft to lay a smoke trail at a specified altitude. The test aircraft dives at the smoke trail at a predetermined airspeed and dive angle. As the test aircraft passes through the smoke trail, the indicated airspeed, altitude, and dive angle are recorded. The difference between the calibrated altitude of the smoke aircraft and the instrument corrected altitude of the test aircraft is the measurement of the lag.

TO IF-4E-1

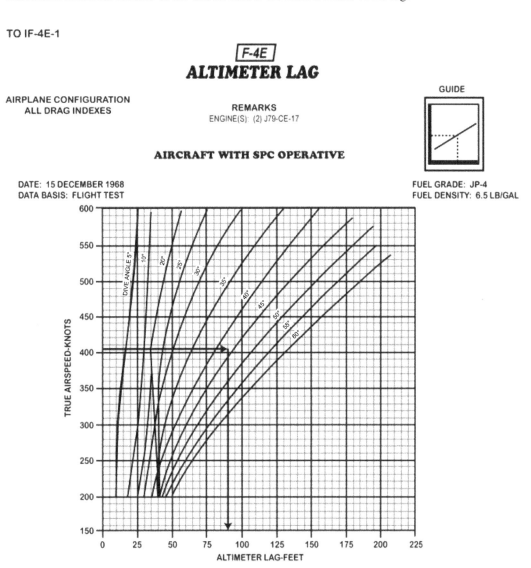

Figure 6.3. F-4E Altimeter Lag, Static Pressure Compensator Operative

F-4E

ALTIMETER LAG

GUIDE

AIRPLANE CONFIGURATION
ALL DRAG INDEXES

REMARKS
ENGINE(S): (2) J79-CE-17

AIRCRAFT WITH SPC INOPERATIVE

DATE: 15 DECEMBER 1968
DATA BASIS: FLIGHT TEST

FUEL GRADE: JP-4
FUEL DENSITY: 6.5 LB/GAL

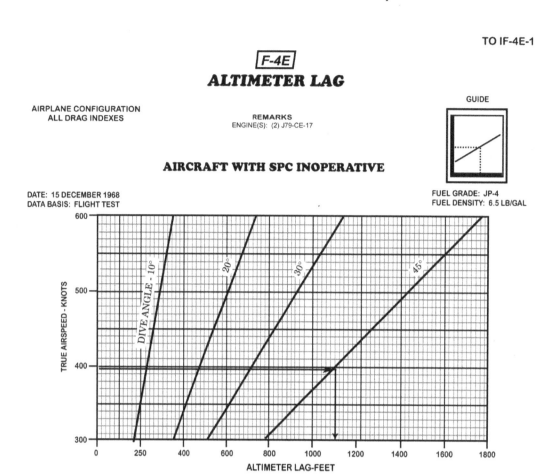

Figure 6.4. F-4E Altimeter Lag, Static Pressure Compensator Inoperative

The second method described in Reference 13 uses a tracking radar, although Wide Area Augmentation System (WAAS) or Differential GPS would be suitable today. If the test aircraft has already been calibrated for steady state position corrections then no additional calibrated aircraft is required. Similar to the survey method discussed in the next chapter, the aircraft flies at an airspeed where corrections are known at the altitude of interest and an altitude above and an altitude below. These runs correlate the pressure altitude with geometric altitude at the time of the test. The test aircraft then dives through the altitude of interest. The lag is then determined by taking the aircraft's geometric altitude (from GPS), finding the corresponding pressure altitude (from the survey) and comparing that to the instrument corrected altitude.

Dynamic Imbalance

An error can also be introduced into a Pitot-static system if the lag time constants for the total pressure side and the static pressure side are significantly different. While this will not affect the altimeter or the Vertical Velocity Indicator (VVI), it will affect the airspeed indicator and any other instruments that use differential pressure. It is likely that the static pressure system has a longer lag time constant than the total pressure system, since the static pressure system has more volume because more instruments are connected to it. In a climb at a constant calibrated airspeed, the static pressure and total pressure are both decreasing, but their difference, q_c, remains constant. If the static pressure system has more lag than the total pressure system, the static pressure system will be supplying a higher pressure (lower altitude) than truth to the airspeed indicator. The differential pressure will thus be less and the airspeed indicator will read a lower than truth airspeed. Like lag, this problem will occur only when the ambient or total pressure is changing.

Dynamic imbalance errors are a function of the design of the Pitot-static system, and thus can be characterized by testing but cannot be changed without changing the system.

Leaks

Leaks in a Pitot-static system will also give erroneous readings. A leak in the total pressure system would result in a lower pressure reaching the instruments, as the pressure in the tube leaked to the presumably lower pressure in the cabin. This would result in an airspeed reading lower than truth. In a pressurized cabin, it is possible that the error would be in the opposite direction if the cabin pressure was higher than the outside total pressure.

A leak in the static system would produce erroneous altitude and airspeed readings. The direction of the error would depend on the relative values of the static pressure and cabin pressure.

Errors from leaks can be eliminated by maintenance. FAA regulations require that the Pitot-static system be checked for leaks every two years if flying under Instrument Flight Rules (IFR) (14CFR §91.411(a)(1)).

Prior to performance testing and especially Pitot-static calibrations, it is highly recommended to do a leak check on the Pitot-static system of the test aircraft. With the proper test equipment (TTU-205 or similar), this leak check can also serve as an end-to-end test for instrument errors.

Position Error

The objective of the air data system is to measure the freestream values of total and ambient pressure and use these pressures to determine altitude, airspeed, and Mach number. The sensors (ports) that sense these pressures are necessarily located on the airframe. **The problem with trying to measure these pressures in the flow field of the airplane is that the whole point of the design of the airplane is to disturb the freestream flow in such a way that produces lift.** Thus, if the location of the ports were randomly selected, they would very likely end up in a location where the local pressures do not represent the freestream pressure. Because the pressures measured do not match the freestream pressures, but are interpreted by the instruments as freestream pressures, there is an error in the results known as position error. This is also called installation error, since it arises from the way the air data system is installed on the aircraft.

Total Pressure Position Error

For minimal error, the total pressure port (Pitot tube) should be aligned with the local velocity. We know that the tube will sense total pressure if aligned with the flow and will sense ambient pressure if perpendicular to the flow. From this, we can see that the error in the total pressure reading should increase as the angle of attack between the probe and flow field increases. However, the relationship between total pressure error and angle of attack is far from linear, and is typically close to zero error in the normal flight range of angle of attack. As such, **the error in reading total pressure is generally assumed to be negligible**.

Of course, it is possible for a Pitot tube to have significant errors. The design of the probe can affect how quickly errors grow with angle of attack. The location of the Pitot tube makes a big difference on the existence of errors. Ideally the Pitot tube would be installed to see an undisturbed airstream. Some of the locations for a Pitot tube which would cause large errors would be:

- Behind a propeller – the local velocity of the slipstream would be higher than the freestream, so the sensed total pressure would be higher than the "correct" total pressure. Another way to consider it is that the purpose of the propeller is to produce thrust by increasing the total pressure of the slipstream.

- In the boundary layer – the boundary layer exists because the friction with the surface removes energy from the flow, and when energy is removed, total pressure drops. This can also be seen as the velocity of the air in the boundary layer is reduced, so the sensed airspeed would be less. Pitot tubes which are not mounted on booms are typically mounted on struts that move the Pitot tube well outside of the boundary layer.

- In the wing wake – the wing wake is the remains of the boundary layer formed as the air passed over the wing. Because the boundary layer had energy losses (total pressure losses), the wake behind the wing will also have less velocity and less total pressure than the freestream air.

- In localized supersonic flow – a normal shock wave will form in front of the Pitot tube, causing a total pressure loss. The airspeed indicator will interpret this reduced total pressure as an airspeed lower than the correct airspeed.

- Behind an oblique shock wave – a Pitot tube will naturally have a normal shock wave in front of it in supersonic flow. This is acceptable because the flow behind a normal shock wave is subsonic (so no other shock waves will form), and the total pressure loss through the shock wave is solely a function of Mach number. Therefore, it is possible to compensate for this loss and determine the Mach number in front of the shock wave based on the pressures behind the shock wave. However, behind an oblique shock wave, the flow is still supersonic, albeit slower than freestream, and the total pressure loss through the oblique shock wave depends on the freestream Mach number and the turning angle. Therefore, the Rayleigh supersonic Pitot tube formula is insufficient to account for all of the total pressure loss. Sometimes, other considerations will force a Pitot tube to be placed behind an oblique shock wave. On the F-15, to leave an unobstructed view for the radar, the Pitot tubes were placed on the fuselage behind the radome. The corrections for the oblique shock waves are made through a more complex calibration in the air data computer and displayed by an electrically driven instrument.

The statement that total pressure error is negligible is based on the assumption that the Pitot tube is in undisturbed flow. An example of when this assumption breaks down can be found in many gliders. If the Pitot tube is buried in the nose of the glider or is very close to the vertical fin, then the airflow to the Pitot tube is disturbed during large sideslips. Glider sideslips at normal operational speeds can indicate airspeeds around zero knots (or some other obviously incorrect airspeed), caused by large pressure errors at the Pitot tube.

Another example can be found in the B-52 flight manual, which states "Significant Mach position errors exist at airspeeds above Mach 0.81 indicated due to the EVS pod installation. The pods create a region of localized supersonic flow in the vicinity of the Pitot tube. This results in sensing a lower pressure and causes the airspeed and Mach indicating systems to read low. Therefore, the aircraft will not be flown at speeds greater than 0.84 Mach indicated to prevent exceeding the limiting Mach of 0.91 true." Because the error comes from the flow in the vicinity of the Pitot tube, this means that the error is a total pressure error. While charts are provided for the Mach correction above 0.81 Mach number, the correction changes greatly with gross weight and with altitude, so the instruments are generally considered unreliable in these flight conditions. Flight tests requiring weapon releases at maximum Mach number (above 0.81 M) were flown in formation with an F-16 pace aircraft to avoid inadvertently exceeding the B-52's maximum Mach number.

Because of large vertical velocity components, helicopters and V/STOL aircraft may have challenges locating a Pitot probe for total pressure measurements related to horizontal speeds, particularly at low horizontal speeds.

Static Pressure Position Error

The freestream total pressure can be sensed fairly accurately in many locations, regardless of whether the flow has been accelerated or not, by creating a stagnation point. However, the local ambient pressure depends on the local velocity, and decreases as the velocity increases. This is the basic principle used to create lift. However, to measure the freestream ambient pressure, the port needs to be located at a point where the local velocity is equal to the freestream velocity. While these points exist on and around the aircraft, they move as the flow field changes with changes in angle of attack, Mach number, and Reynolds number. Thus, all of the physics which help us make an airplane fly also work against us when trying to measure the ambient pressure.

Therefore, errors in sensing ambient pressure are pretty much unavoidable. About the best a designer can do is to choose a location for the static ports where the errors are minimized. Because the errors in reading ambient pressure are significant, we give the sensed pressure a different name—static pressure. **Because total pressure errors are generally negligible compared to the errors in static pressure, position error is assumed to arise only from static pressure errors.**

Static Port Locations

For subsonic aircraft, static ports are frequently located on the fuselage. Some general aviation aircraft locate the static port on the side of the fuselage just aft of the cowling. Another popular location is on the aft fuselage between the wing and tail. The static ports on the C-12 are located on the side of the fuselage just forward of the tail. C-130 static ports are located on the fuselage both in front and aft of the wing. The drawback of mounting static ports on the fuselage is the effort required to find a suitable location for the static port. Many times this is done through trial and error, either in the wind tunnel or in flight test. This is suitable for production aircraft, since once a suitable location has been found it should work for all models of that aircraft. However, for one-off or prototype aircraft, this level of effort may not be desirable.

Subsonic static ports can also be located on probes, as shown in Figure 6.5. These probes look similar to Pitot tubes, but have the front end sealed and holes drilled in the side of the tube. The probe may cause additional drag and is more likely to be bumped or otherwise damaged, but may produce better results than a randomly placed fuselage port. The primary consideration is that the probe be located in an area assumed to have undisturbed flow. An example of this type of probe can be found on the Schweitzer SGS 2-33 glider.

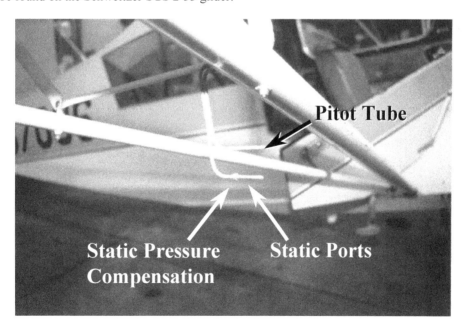

Figure 6.5. Separate Pitot and Static Probes

So if the static ports can be located on a probe, why not locate them on the side of the Pitot probe? This is actually the preferred method for high speed aircraft (and will work on subsonic aircraft as well). The resulting probe is referred to as a Pitot-static probe. Pitot-static probes can be found on the T-38 and F-16, along with many other aircraft. For flight test work, a Pitot-static probe is frequently mounted on a long nose boom well in front of the aircraft's flow field, and frequently has vanes mounted for measuring angle of attack and sideslip. At Edwards this is usually referred to as a YAPS boom, from Yaw, Angle of attack, Pitot, Static.

Reference 14 has an excellent discussion of Pitot and static port placement in Chapter 3.

Reducing Static Pressure Errors

Supersonic Pitot-Static Tubes

Placing the static ports on the Pitot tube has another benefit in supersonic flight if the Pitot-static tube is mounted on the nose of the aircraft or otherwise ahead of any other shock waves caused by the aircraft. Because flow disturbances cannot propagate upstream in supersonic flow, any position error at the static ports is caused only by the Pitot probe in front of the ports. Thus, the position errors tend to be smaller because they are not affected by the entire aircraft.

Wind tunnel and other testing many years ago (probably documented in some NACA reports I haven't found yet) determined an optimal design for supersonic Pitot-static tubes. One such design is shown in Figure 6.6. The probe has a constant diameter with a total pressure port at the tip. The static ports are located eight to ten times the diameter of the probe back from the tip. You may have noticed when we derived the airspeed equations for supersonic flow, we accounted for the loss of total pressure through the normal shock wave in front of the total pressure port. However, we know that ambient pressure increases through a shock wave, yet we did not account for that effect. Why not, you ask? Because the flow is not constrained and the surface does not continue to turn the flow, the higher pressure air behind the shock wave immediately expands until its pressure drops back to ambient pressure. Testing has shown that by locating the static ports eight to ten diameters behind the tip, the air has sufficient time to expand back to ambient pressure, such that the sensed pressure is a good representation of the ambient pressure.

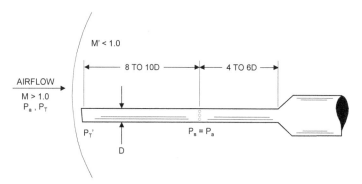

Figure 6.6. Supersonic Pitot-Static Probe Design

Figure 6.6 also stipulates that the static ports be at least four to six diameters ahead of any shoulder or increased diameter. This distance keeps the static ports ahead of any shock waves caused by the shoulder. While presumably this distance could be longer, it would be limited by the structural strength of the Pitot-static tube.

Compensated Pitot-Static Tubes

In subsonic flight, nose mounted Pitot-static tubes tend to have positive position corrections because of the high pressure area around the nose of the aircraft. How do we know that?

Consider the leading edge of a wing. The leading edge will have a stagnation point where the local ambient pressure is equal to the total pressure. It follows that for some area around the stagnation point the local ambient pressure will be above the freestream ambient pressure but below the total pressure. Since the static ports on the nose mounted Pitot-static tube will be in this higher pressure "bow wave", they will sense a higher than ambient pressure. A higher pressure at the static port will cause the altimeter to read lower than truth and the airspeed indicator to read lower than truth.

So why not use our friend Bernoulli to help out here? If we accelerate a flow, the local ambient pressure will decrease. So if I decrease the pressure from a pressure that is too high, in theory I can get the local ambient pressure back to the correct value, right? Such is the theory behind the compensated Pitot-static tube. As shown in Figure 6.7, the diameter of the exterior of the probe increases from the front, which accelerates the airflow just like the upper surface of the wing. This reduces the local ambient pressure back to a value close to the freestream ambient pressure.

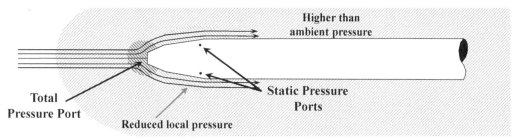

Figure 6.7. Compensated Pitot-Static Tube

By this method, position errors can be reduced to almost zero at Mach numbers below the critical Mach number. Once shock waves start to form in front of the aircraft nose, the high pressure area caused by the aircraft nose goes away, but the compensating effect of the increasing diameter of the Pitot-static tube remains. Therefore, position errors at supersonic speeds tend to increase with increasing Mach number. Additionally, these position errors typically do not generalize well, and tend to be altitude dependent. That is, the position error cannot be characterized by a single curve as is typically possible with uncompensated Pitot-static probes.

During the XB-70 test program, air data calibrations were accomplished both with a compensated Pitot-static probe and with an uncompensated Pitot-static probe. The Mach correction as shown in Figure 6.8 is reproduced from *NASA TN D-6827 Flight Calibration of Compensated and Uncompensated Pitot-Static Airspeed Probes and Application of the Probes to Supersonic Cruise Vehicles* (Ref 15). In the subsonic regime, the compensated probe had smaller corrections. However, supersonically the corrections grew in magnitude with Mach number, whereas the corrections for the uncompensated probe remained much closer to zero.

Separate Static Source Compensation

Another way to compensate for position errors is to place an obstruction to the flow in the vicinity of the static ports. If the static ports are located on a probe, this can be done by placing a collar around the probe, as shown in Figures 6.5 and 6.9.

If the collar is located just behind the static ports, the static ports will see a higher pressure because of the local high pressure area just in front of the collar, similar to the high pressure area in front of the aircraft nose as discussed earlier. This high pressure would reduce altimeter and airspeed readings. If the collar is located ahead of the static ports, the separation behind the collar will cause an area of pressure below the ambient air pressure. This lower pressure would increase the altimeter and airspeed readings. The amount of the compensation can be adjusted by moving the collar relative to the static ports.

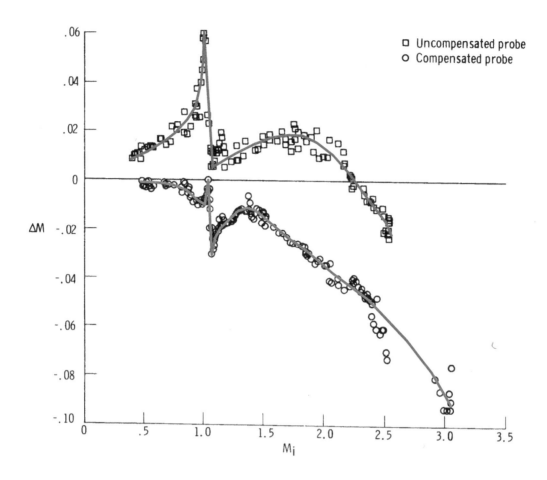

Figure 13. Variation of Mach number position error with Mach number for the two pitot-static probes used on the XB-70. S_1/S_2 configuration.

Figure 6.8. XB-70 data from NASA TN D-6827 (Ref 15)

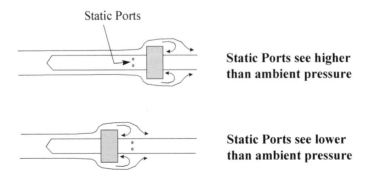

Figure 6.9. Static Pressure Compensation

Effects of Non-Flush Static Ports

Generally fuselage mounted static ports are constructed to be flush with the skin. If the material around the static port protrudes into the airstream, as shown in Figure 6.10, the forward lip will accelerate the flow, much like the forward portion of a wing. This can result in a lower pressure being sensed at the static port. While it would seem that this would be a design to be avoided, this technique can be used for compensation.

Figure 6.10. Non-Flush Static Port Installation (side view)

Reducing Errors From Sideslip

The static port is designed for the direction of flow to be perpendicular to the axis of the opening. If the flow is not perpendicular, then there will be some component of the velocity aligned with the opening, and thus the static port will pick up a portion of the total pressure. This could occur with a static port mounted on the side of the fuselage flying with a non-zero sideslip angle. The accepted solution to this problem is to mount static ports on both sides of the fuselage. The static port on the upwind side will see a higher than ambient pressure, but the static port on the downwind side will see a lower than ambient pressure. These two ports are connected by a tube, that is, they are "manifolded" together. The difference in pressure at the two static ports will cause air to flow through this tube from the high pressure side to the low pressure side. This tube is connected to the instrument static tube with a tee. Because the air is moving through the manifold tube, the additional total pressure seen at the upwind static port is maintained as velocity energy (dynamic pressure), such that the static pressure sensed at the tee is a good approximation of the freestream ambient pressure.

Cabin Static/Alternate Static Source

Sometimes non-pressurized aircraft are built with the static pressure fittings of the instruments just left open to the air in the cockpit. This may be done in an effort to simplify the system or by someone who doesn't know any better. The problem arises because the local ambient pressure in the cockpit is not the same as the freestream ambient pressure. If you've ever rolled down a window in your car while driving and felt your ears pop with the pressure change, then you get the idea. Thus, the airspeed and altimeter corrections can be changed by opening a window, turning on the heater, changing angle of attack, or any number of other unrelated operations. Good Pitot-static data require an external static port.

However, venting the static pressure lines into the cabin is suitable as a back-up method. For an unpressurized aircraft in icing conditions, if the primary static ports ice over, an alternate static source valve can be opened, venting the static system into the cabin. While this will introduce some errors as mentioned above, these errors would be far less than the errors caused by iced over static ports. In pressurized aircraft, the alternate static source valve is plumbed to a second set of static ports.

One day while flying my Bearhawk at 118 KIAS and 6480 feet pressure altitude, I opened the alternate static source valve which vented the static system into the cockpit. The indicated airspeed immediately jumped to 131 KIAS and the altitude jumped to 6690 feet. That was a 13 knot jump and a 210 feet increase in altitude, all due to induced static system errors.

Position Error Teminology

Yikes! More subscripts! Relax…it only gets worse…

Table 6.1 shows the important pressures when talking about position error.

Table 6.1
Position Error Terminology

P_a	Freestream Ambient Pressure
P_s	Static Pressure as measured at the static port
ΔP_p	Error in reading ambient pressure ($P_s - P_a$)
q_c	Differential Pressure or "Compressible q" ($P_T - P_a$)
q_{cic}	Sensed Differential Pressure ($P_T - P_s$)

Note that I can measure P_s and q_{cic}. We use these as approximations of P_a and q_c.

Applying Instrument and Position Corrections

Once the instrument and position corrections are known, they are applied simply by adding them on in the correct order. The instrument corrected reading (subscript ic) is the sum of the indicated reading (subscript i) and the instrument correction (Δ and subscript ic). In equation form,

$$H_{ic} = H_i + \Delta H_{ic} \tag{D66}$$

$$V_{ic} = V_i + \Delta V_{ic} \tag{D67}$$

$$M_{ic} = M_i + \Delta M_{ic} \tag{D68}$$

As discussed earlier, this step is not usually required with DAS data, as the post-flight conversion to engineering units is equivalent to this step.

The position corrected reading (subscript pc) then is the sum of the instrument corrected reading (subscript ic) and the position correction (Δ and subscript pc). In equation form,

$$H_{pc} = H_{ic} + \Delta H_{pc} \tag{D69}$$

$$V_{pc} = V_{ic} + \Delta V_{pc} \tag{D70}$$

$$M_{pc} = M_{ic} + \Delta M_{pc} \tag{D71}$$

Using the subscript pc implies that the value shown was measured and corrected for instrument and position errors. Note the following equivalencies:

$$H_c = H_{pc} + \text{residual errors} \tag{D72}$$

$$V_c = V_{pc} + \text{residual errors} \tag{D73}$$

$$M = M_{pc} + \text{residual errors} \tag{D74}$$

The residual errors can come from many sources. One known source is hysteresis in mechanical instruments. Selecting the middle value between calibrations for going up and calibrations for going down left some residual errors. Position corrections are a mean value drawn through data scatter. That data scatter or dispersion (variance to the statistician) represents residual errors. Because uncertainty exists in all our measurements (at least we think it does), we can never account for all of the residual error. Our best bet is to use the best techniques we can to minimize the size of the residual errors.

H_c, V_c, and M are typically thought of as "truth" values. These are either the conditions we are aiming for (such as those called out in a test plan) or the output values of some FTT truth source. H_{pc}, V_{pc}, and M_{pc} are considered values measured in flight test which have been corrected for all known errors. The values (subscript "pc") are considered our "best estimates" of the truth values. We call them "best estimates" rather than the truth values because we know there is uncertainty because of the residual errors. If the uncertainty has been quantified, the estimate can be expressed with a "plus or minus" value of uncertainty. Otherwise, the residual errors are assumed zero and the measured and corrected values are used for the remainder of any data reduction.

Position Error Ratio and Pressure Coefficient

As aviators and flight testers, we talk about position error in terms of ΔH_{pc}, ΔV_{pc}, and ΔM_{pc}, because these values are in units that we can understand. However, the real issue at hand is the inability of the static port to correctly sense the ambient pressure. Thus, position error is, strictly speaking, a pressure difference, which we represent as ΔP_p. However, saying that the position error is "0.02 pound per square inch" is not very useful for the piloting task, whereas just about any pilot can understand the phrase "the airspeed indicator at these conditions reads 2 knots low." The calculation of ΔH_{pc}, ΔV_{pc}, and ΔM_{pc} puts the position error into units that pilots and engineers can understand.

When we assume the total pressure error is zero, then all of the position error arises from the error in the static pressure, which is the difference between the measured static pressure and the ambient pressure (ΔP_p). However, ΔP_p by itself is not a very useful number. For instance, a 1 psi pressure error would be a relatively small error if the ambient pressure was 14 psi, but the same 1 psi pressure error would be a relatively large error if the ambient pressure was only 5 psi. Therefore, it would seem reasonable to consider the magnitude of the pressure error relative to the ambient pressure. However, it would be easier to use something that we can measure that is related to the ambient pressure, namely the static pressure. Hence we introduce the Position Error Ratio, $\Delta P_p/P_s$. By dividing (normalizing) the pressure error by the static pressure, we get a value that for a given angle of attack and Mach number remains reasonably constant with altitude changes. We will also see that we can write equations that express ΔH_{pc}, ΔV_{pc}, and ΔM_{pc} as functions of $\Delta P_p/P_s$.

While $\Delta P_p/P_s$ gives a value that is relatively insensitive to altitude changes, it does vary widely with airspeed changes. It would be convenient to have a similar value that was relatively insensitive to airspeed changes as well, at least through the subsonic region. Let us assume for a minute (we'll justify this a few paragraphs from now) that $\Delta P_p/P_s$ grows as a function of the square of the Mach number (M_{ic}^2). This is reasonable, since we know that pressures in the flow field, such as dynamic and total pressures, vary as functions of true airspeed squared (V_t^2) or Mach number squared (M^2). Figure 6.11 shows a notional shape of a $\Delta P_p/P_s$ curve as a function of M_{ic}^2.

Since $\Delta P_p/P_s$ varies as a function of M_{ic}^2, to flatten this curve out we need to multiply by another value that is a function of $1/M_{ic}^2$. A suitable value would be the reciprocal of q_{cic}/P_s, and we know that q_{cic}/P_s is strictly a function of M_{ic}^2, as seen here:

$$\frac{q_{cic}}{P_s} = \left(1 + 0.2M_{ic}^2\right)^{7/2} - 1 \qquad\qquad (M_{ic} < 1) \quad (D76)$$

$$\frac{q_{cic}}{P_s} = \frac{166.921M_{ic}^7}{\left(7M_{ic}^2 - 1\right)^{5/2}} - 1 \qquad\qquad (M_{ic} > 1) \quad (D77)$$

The shape of the $1/(q_{cic}/P_s)$ curve is also shown in Figure 6.11.

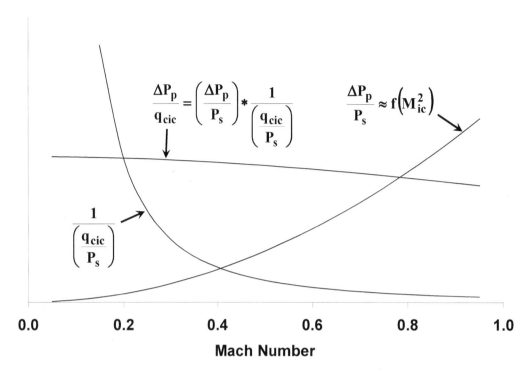

Figure 6.11. Notional Shapes for Position Error Curves (relative magnitudes adjusted for clarity)

We can form a new parameter, the Position Error Pressure Coefficient, $\Delta P_p/q_{cic}$, defined by

$$\frac{\Delta P_p}{q_{cic}} = \frac{\dfrac{\Delta P_p}{P_s}}{\dfrac{q_{cic}}{P_s}} \qquad \text{(From D75)}$$

As shown in Figure 6.11, $\Delta P_p/q_{cic}$ is reasonably constant with airspeed or Mach number, at least much more so than $\Delta P_p/P_s$ was. Because test results from actual aircraft frequently show values of $\Delta P_p/q_{cic}$ that are reasonably constant with Mach number, we can accept our initial assumption that $\Delta P_p/P_s$ is roughly a function of Mach number squared (M_{ic}^2).

Thus, in $\Delta P_p/q_{cic}$ we have an expression for position error that is relatively insensitive to altitude and Mach number, at least in subsonic flight. Please note that in just a minute we will say that $\Delta P_p/q_{cic}$ is a function of angle of attack and Mach number. The point here is that the variation of $\Delta P_p/q_{cic}$ with Mach number in the subsonic realm is small, at least in comparison with the variation of $\Delta P_p/P_s$.

As shown in Appendix D, $\Delta P_p/P_s$ and $\Delta P_p/q_{cic}$ are both functions of angle of attack and Mach number.

$$\frac{P_s - P_a}{P_s} = \frac{\Delta P_p}{P_s} = f_3(\alpha, M_{ic}) \qquad \text{(D80)}$$

$$\frac{\Delta P_p}{q_{cic}} = f_4(\alpha, M_{ic}) \qquad \text{(D81)}$$

Since $\Delta P_p/P_s$ and $\Delta P_p/q_{cic}$ are functions of the same inputs, they are both valid representations of the position error information contained in ΔP_p.

The value of $\Delta P_p/P_s$ can be somewhat problematic, since it involves small differences of large numbers, which the mathematicians in the group tell us can be overly sensitive. For example, consider this case

$$H_c = 3189 \text{ feet}$$

$$\Delta H_{pc} = +42.7 \text{ feet}$$

$$P_a = 1883 \text{ lb/ft}^2$$

$$P_s = 1886 \text{ lb/ft}^2$$

$$\frac{\Delta P_p}{P_s} = 0.00159$$

Now consider a change of 1 lb/ft^2 in the measurement of static pressure, giving

$$P_a = 1883 \text{ lb/ft}^2$$

$$P_s = 1885 \text{ lb/ft}^2$$

$$\frac{\Delta P_p}{P_s} = 0.00106$$

So a change in the fourth significant digit of the static pressure results in a change in the second significant digit of $\Delta P_p/P_s$. This would indicate a caution about too much truncation while calculating $\Delta P_p/P_s$.

Presenting Position Corrections

Earlier we stated "Because total pressure errors are generally negligible compared to the errors in static pressure, position error is assumed to arise only from static pressure errors." The static pressure error is represented as ΔP_p. Based on this statement, all of our position corrections, including altitude position correction (ΔH_{pc}), airspeed position correction (ΔV_{pc}), and Mach position correction (ΔM_{pc}), are directly related to the static pressure error (ΔP_p). Expressing this idea in mathematical language,

$$\Delta H_{pc} = f\left(\frac{\Delta P_p}{P_s}\right) \qquad \Delta V_{pc} = f\left(\frac{\Delta P_p}{P_s}\right) \qquad \Delta M_{pc} = f\left(\frac{\Delta P_p}{P_s}\right)$$

These position corrections could also be expressed as functions of $\Delta P_p/q_{cic}$. Because the three "pilot friendly" position corrections are all functions of $\Delta P_p/P_s$, it seems reasonable to present position correction in one uniform plot of $\Delta P_p/P_s$. This idea is shown graphically in Figure 6.12.

Figure 6.12 shows to find position correction data, a Flight Test Technique (FTT), as covered in Chapters 7 and 8, would be flown, which would result in measured values for either ΔH_{pc}, ΔV_{pc}, or ΔM_{pc}. Using the appropriate data reduction scheme in Chapter 9, these values would be reduced to values of $\Delta P_p/P_s$. The primary representation would then be a plot of $\Delta P_p/P_s$ against instrument corrected Mach number (M_{ic}) or possibly instrument corrected airspeed (V_{ic}). An equivalent presentation could be done using $\Delta P_p/q_{cic}$ in place of $\Delta P_p/P_s$ if desired.

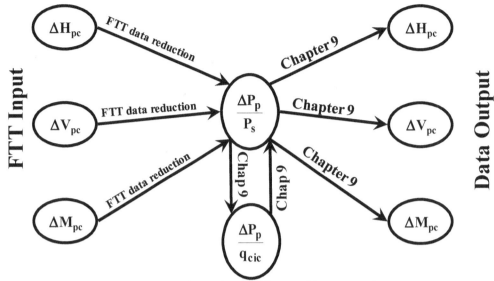

Figure 6.12. Reducing and Expanding Position Correction Data
(Chapter 9 refers to "Calculating Position Corrections From the Position Error Ratio")

Once the position corrections have been reduced to their most basic form as $\Delta P_p/P_s$ they can then be expanded to create plots for altitude, airspeed, and Mach position correction, also plotted against instrument corrected Mach number or instrument corrected airspeed.

Variations in Position Corrections

Because the position error is caused by the flow field around the aircraft, the position error and resulting position corrections will be affected by the same variables that affect the flow field. By dimensional analysis, we can see that the factors that cause pressure changes in the flow field can be represented by shape, angle of attack (α), angle of sideslip (β), Mach number (M), Reynolds number (R_e), and the Prandtl number (P_r). Of these factors, "it can be shown" (see Appendix D) that the most significant factors are angle of attack and Mach number, or in mathematical notation

$$\frac{\Delta P_p}{q_{cic}} = f_4(\alpha, M_{ic}) \tag{D81}$$

With additional derivation, we can represent the angle of attack in other terms to give

$$\frac{\Delta P_p}{q_{cic}} = f_8(M_{ic}, \frac{nW}{\delta_{ic}}) \tag{D90}$$

Note that the assumptions used in Appendix D to get to this point do not include factors such as compensated Pitot-static tubes or non-optimal locations. **In general, the following discussion will apply only to subsonic aircraft with uncompensated Pitot-static systems or high-speed aircraft with nose mounted uncompensated Pitot-static systems.** Thus, there are airplanes, such as the F-15, which will not follow these generalizations.

Angle of attack is going to have the largest variations at low speeds when dynamic pressure is low. Additionally, maneuvering at low speeds will require larger changes to angle of attack to get the desired load factors. Increasing weight will require a higher angle of attack for the same load factor, and changes in altitude will change the dynamic pressure, again requiring a change in angle of attack. The changes in the position error ratio or coefficient caused by angle of attack will be seen at low Mach numbers. At high Mach numbers the angle of attack changes are small and the result collapses to a single line. This behaviour is shown in notional fashion in Figure 6.13.

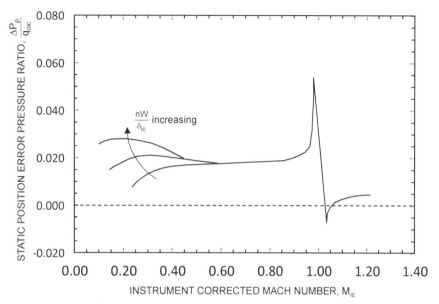

Figure 6.13. Position Error Coefficient Variations

At Mach numbers from the transonic range and higher, the Mach effects, such as compressibility and shock waves, start to affect the position error. As shown in Figure 6.13, the position error coefficient starts to grow in the transonic region as the shock waves approach the static ports. Around Mach 1.0 the shock wave passes the static ports and the position error coefficient reduces, possibly even changing sign, then stabilizes at a small value as Mach number continues to increase.

Because the altitude position correction (ΔH_{pc}), airspeed position correction (ΔV_{pc}), and Mach position correction (ΔM_{pc}) are positive functions of $\Delta P_p/P_s$, and thus $\Delta P_p/q_{cic}$, these corrections will have shapes similar to Figure 6.13 when plotted against Mach number.

If we look at the position error with respect to airspeed, we will see a similar behaviour. As shown in Appendix D, at low Mach numbers the position error coefficient is primarily a function of angle of attack, which can also be represented by

$$\frac{\Delta P_p}{q_{cic}} = f_9 \left(\frac{nW}{V_{ic}^2} \right) \tag{D95}$$

so variations due to angle of attack will be represented by varying values of nW. The altitude effects (δ_{ic}) seen when plotting against Mach number are accounted for by the relationship between true airspeed and calibrated airspeed. This behaviour is shown in notional fashion in Figure 6.14.

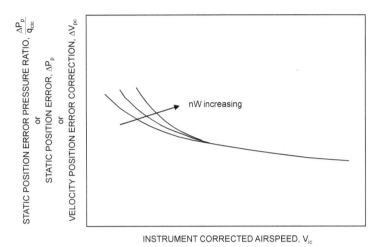

Figure 6.14. Variations in Position Error with Angle of Attack

The position error coefficient will still have the same behaviour as the Mach number increases into the transonic region and beyond, but it will look different if we plot against airspeed. The spike at Mach 1 moves as altitude increases because the calibrated airspeed corresponding to Mach 1 changes, as shown in Figure 6.15.

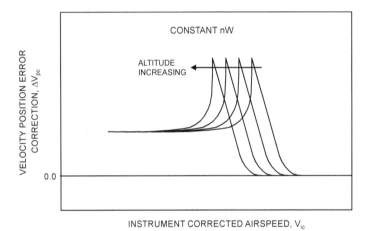

Figure 6.15. Variations in Position Error with Mach Number

The altitude position correction shows an additional change with altitude. At the higher Mach numbers where angle of attack effects are small, Appendix D shows that for small perturbations

$$\Delta H_{pc} = \frac{RT}{g_{SL}} \frac{\Delta P_p}{P_s} \tag{D102}$$

For a given position error ratio at a given Mach number, the only variable on the right hand side of Equation D102 is temperature. Thus, as altitude increases, temperature decreases, and thus the altitude position correction decreases, as shown in Figure 6.16.

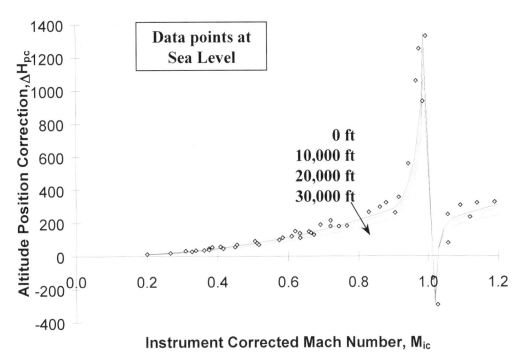

Figure 6.16. Altitude Effects on Altitude Position Correction

A Word of Caution

The preceding analysis has assumed that the total pressure error was zero and that the Pitot-static system was uncompensated. Do not expect that real world Pitot-static data will necessarily follow this pattern. The point is that the corrections can vary with altitude, Mach number, and angle of attack.

Sometimes Pitot-static data cannot be generalized, as shown in Figure 6.17. In the case shown, ΔH_{pc} changes sign with increasing altitude, a behaviour that is not accounted for in any of the equations we have used. As we will see, the methods we have for predicting position corrections at a different altitude calculate the corrections at the new altitude for the same Mach number as at the original altitude. There is no accounting for any angle of attack effects. The assumption is that at "operational" Mach numbers the change in angle of attack caused by changing altitudes will be negligible. Behaviour as shown in Figure 6.17 would be most likely caused by changes in angle of attack as altitude changes.

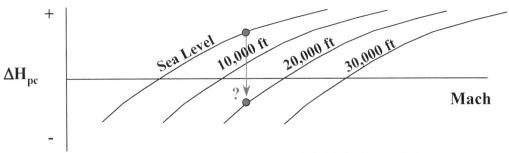

Figure 6.17. Position Correction Data Not Suitable for Extrapolation

Pitot Statics Gross Buffoonery

A favorite topic of discussion centers around failure states of the Pitot-static system. Primarily this involves what happens if one of the ports is plugged. This could arise from buffoonery, such as failure to remove tape covering the static ports after washing or failing to take the cover off of the Pitot tube. Another conceivable problem would be if a port was plugged with ice while flying in icing conditions.

If the Pitot tube was blocked, the airspeed indicator and Mach meter would be affected, since they are connected to the total pressure system. The altimeter and VVI would not be affected since they are only connected to the static pressure system. During takeoff or a level acceleration, the total pressure would not increase as expected, while the static pressure would remain relatively constant. As such, the differential pressure (q_c) would stay the same, the readings on the airspeed indicator and Mach meter would not change as the aircraft accelerated.

In a climb with the Pitot tube blocked, the total pressure would remain constant while the static pressure decreased. The differential pressure would increase as the climb progressed, resulting in a constantly increasing indication on the airspeed indicator and Mach meter. This has caused accidents in the past, where a pilot would keep increasing pitch attitude in a climb trying to slow back to climb speed as shown on the airspeed indicator, resulting eventually in losing so much real airspeed that the aircraft stalled. In a similar fashion, a blocked Pitot tube in a descent would cause a constantly decreasing indication on the airspeed indicator and Mach meter.

On a TPS flight in the past, an F-16 flying on a Monday morning was indicating about 60 knots when the airplane was flying somewhere around 250 knots as shown by the INS ground speed. After landing, a large amount of dirt was found in the nose Pitot tube, which had apparently blown in there over the weekend. This had caused a partial blockage of the Pitot tube, allowing only part of the total pressure to get through. The F-16 Pitot-static system uses three separate sources for total pressure, two of which are located in the nose boom and one is located on a separate probe on the side of the fuselage aft of the radome. If the air data computer sees one reading that does not agree with the other two and the other two agree, the first is thrown out. In this case, two total pressure readings were bad, but they were bad by about the same amount. Hence, the air data computer selected the "bad" total pressure as the "good" total pressure.

If the static port is blocked, it affects all of the air data instruments. During takeoff or a level acceleration, the ambient pressure remains effectively constant, so no apparent errors would appear in the readings on the altimeter, airspeed indicator, Mach meter, or VVI. In a constant airspeed climb or descent, the static pressure would stay the same because of the blockage, such that the altimeter and VVI readings would not change. In a climb, the total pressure, which is an increment above the ambient pressure, decreases because the ambient pressure decreases. Since the static pressure does not change because of the blockage, the differential pressure decreases, resulting in decreasing indications on the airspeed indicator and Mach meter. Likewise, the indicated airspeed and Mach number would increase in a constant airspeed descent.

Chapter 7

Altitude Comparison Flight Test Techniques

The Big Picture

Students always want to see the "Big Picture." Mike Machat's mural "The Golden Age of Flight Test" at the AFTC Flight Test Museum is a pretty big picture. However, it has very little to do with calibrating air data systems.

If we can measure an altitude error, an airspeed error, or a Mach error, we can calculate the Position Error Ratio. But how do we measure these errors? We need to be able to compare the cockpit (or DAS) readings to an independent truth source. The difference will be the error we need. The point of each of the Flight Test Techniques (FTTs) we will discuss is to provide that truth data source.

Tower Fly-By

Concept

One of the most time-honored FTTs is the Tower Fly-by. Pilots like it because it is a license to fly very fast very low to the ground. Public Affairs likes it because it makes good TV. Air Data engineers like it because it is very simple in concept and thus more likely to get accurate data.

The Tower Fly-by is an altitude comparison technique, and the truth altitude of the test aircraft is determined through use of similar triangles. This is shown in Figure 7.1.

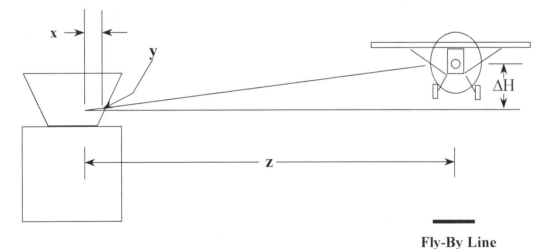

Figure 7.1. Tower Fly-by Concept

As the airplane flies past the tower, an observer looks through an eyepiece and notes the position of the aircraft on a grid. Figure 7.2 shows the eyepiece and grid at the Edwards Fly-by tower.

Figure 7.2. Edwards Fly-By Tower Grid and Eyepiece

The distance from the eyepiece to the grid is known, and the interval between the grid lines is known. The distance from the eyepiece to the aircraft is known because the pilot flies directly over a reference line, such as the centerline of the runway. Using the ratio of distances (similar triangles), the geometric height of the aircraft above the eyepiece and zero line of the grid can be determined. This geometric difference is converted to a difference in pressure altitude using temperature and added to the measured pressure altitude of the tower. This gives the truth altitude that is compared to the cockpit readings.

Each pass yields one datum at one airspeed. Thus, multiple passes are required to determine the correction curve over the airspeed range of the aircraft. The test aircraft must fly low enough to be visible in the grid, with the best accuracy at the zero line of the grid, and decreasing accuracy as altitude increases. The lower limit on altitude is set by safety considerations (typically 50 feet for fighter type aircraft and 100 feet for large aircraft) or by avoiding ground effect. Maintaining an altitude above the ground of at least one wingspan is generally sufficient to avoid corrupting the data due to ground effect.

Figure 7.3 shows the change in induced drag caused by the ground inhibiting downwash from the wing (Ref 16). This change is presented as a function of altitude above the ground. This curve can be interpreted as the effect of the ground on the flow field around the aircraft. At an altitude equal to one wingspan, the downwash intensity is 99.6 percent of its value well away from the ground. This is considered good enough to ignore the effects of ground effect.

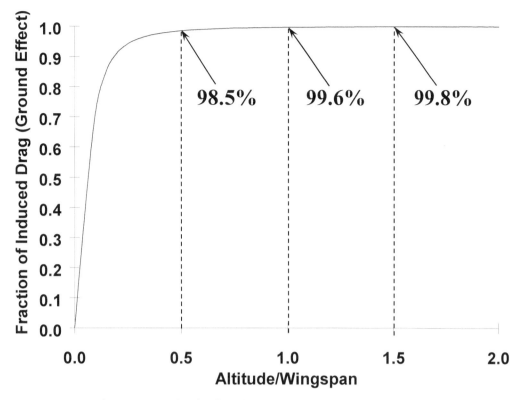

Figure 7.3. Reduction in Induced Drag caused by Ground Effect

Data Requirements

On the aircraft, the critical parameter is indicated altitude (H_i) as the aircraft passes the tower. The altimeter should be set to read pressure altitude (29.92 in the Kollsman window).

Next in importance is the indicated airspeed (V_i). Indicated airspeed is used to locate the calculated altitude position correction (ΔH_{pc}) on the graph of ΔH_{pc} vs. V_{ic}. Indicated temperature should be recorded if determining the temperature recovery factor (K_t) is an objective. Record weight to check for Angle of Attack effects. Record the configuration to determine any dependence of position error on aircraft configuration. Many flight manuals show that the correction curve will change when the landing gear or flaps are deployed.

In the tower, record the grid reading of the aircraft as it goes by. Then record the pressure altitude of the zero line of the grid. Record the ambient air temperature (be sure to record it in the shade). In the case where the aircraft is large enough to fill a significant portion of the grid, the reading should be made at the point on the aircraft where the altitude transducer (usually the altimeter) that is being read in the cockpit is located. See the Trailing Cone/Trailing Bomb section for an explanation of this reasoning. Alternatively, read the grid at an easily definable location on the aircraft that has a known location relative to the altitude transducer. Making this transformation may require measurement or estimation of the aircraft angle of attack.

When introduced to the tower fly-by, almost everyone has the same idea—wouldn't it be better to record the aircraft's position on the grid photographically? Recent developments have made this less impractical than in the past. The preferred method for collecting tower fly-by data is still to make the grid reading by Mk I eyeball (Mk I Mod 1 if wearing corrective lenses).

There are two primary problems with using a camera to record tower fly-by data: timing and depth of field. At high speeds, the test aircraft will be in the grid for little more than one second. While some film cameras will take a picture immediately upon pressing the shutter release, auto focus cameras typically delay taking a picture for more than a second while focusing. There are ways to compensate for these delays, but the risk of missing the picture (taking a picture of the grid with no airplane), and thus missing the data is significant. There are those who would then offer that the timing problem could be solved by using a video camera. In the past, the resolution of video images was significantly less than that of still images.

The second problem would be with depth of field. When properly positioned in the Edwards Fly-By tower, the camera would be 3.666 feet from the grid but 1379 feet from the aircraft. Typically the grid will be in the near field of view for the camera while the aircraft will be in the far field of view, essentially at infinity. Unless the camera has a very long depth of field, either the grid or the aircraft (or both) will be out of focus. Auto focus cameras tend to focus on the grid, not at infinity.

Reference 13 discusses use of a Polaroid camera in the Edwards Fly-By tower. To solve the depth of field problem, this camera used a lens aperture set at f/4.5 with a "pin-hole" diaphragm which gave an effective aperture of f/90. This is extremely high, as typical camera lenses can only be stopped down to about f/16. To work with this small of a hole, the film used was ISO (formerly ASA) 3200, and a typical exposure time was 1/125 second. The mount for this Polaroid camera still exists, as does the camera. However, the Polaroid company no longer produces the required film. Reference 13 goes on to say "The camera data are considered to be supplemental information and should not be obtained in lieu of peep sight readings."

Tests with GoPro video cameras have shown promising results. The aperture is f/2.8, but according to some Internet sources, because the lens is small and wide angle, the resulting depth of field is approximately 8 inches to infinity. The focus is fixed. With a camera resolution of 1920x1080, test shots showed the grid and aircraft to be sufficiently in focus to make a reasonable reading of the grid (Figure 7.4). The frame rate is sufficiently high that 600 knot passes show at least 5 frames of the aircraft in view.

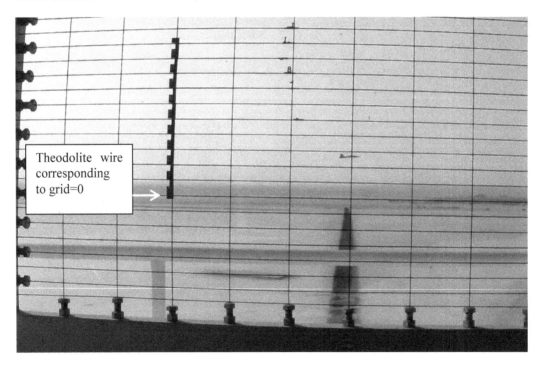

Figure 7.4. Sample frame capture from GoPro video camera

If, understanding these limitations, a camera is used to record tower fly-by data, the camera must be positioned with the entry aperture (front lens) at the same distance from the grid and at the same level as the eyepiece. It is highly recommended that the data be collected manually by eyeball with the camera used as a backup.

Benefits

The primary benefit of the Tower Fly-By Flight Test Technique is its simplicity. Because of its simplicity and traceability of the "calibrations" (distances, level setup, etc), it is considered the most accurate of all of our air data system calibration techniques. While many test programs will use other calibration techniques to collect the majority of the air data system calibration data, they will typically also collect tower fly-by data to confirm the data collected by other means. If you ever hear someone say that "Tower Fly-by is such an old technique. Nobody uses that anymore.", you can tell them that even the F-22 was flying tower fly-bys in 2001.

Drawbacks

Obviously, the Tower Fly-by Flight Test Technique requires some sort of equipment, including a grid and an eyepiece. This does not have to be in a purpose-built tower; in fact, it does not need to be in a tower at all. A grid could be positioned on the ground in such a place that it can look up far enough to see the aircraft. However, the more the aircraft is above the level of the grid, the more the data is degraded by angle measurement errors.

Because the test aircraft must be stable in level flight when passing the tower, this technique requires a large, unobstructed area for the run-in and departure.

High speed flight close to the ground raises the operational risk. Of course, this is the very reason that this FTT is a favorite with pilots.

The Tower Fly-by FTT can only collect data at low altitudes and essentially only at one altitude. This is not very useful for determining the position errors at high altitudes, but it is very useful for comparing to other methods, such as pace, which can collect data at other altitudes. Because of the low altitude and proximity of other structures, tower fly-by tests are generally limited to subsonic speeds only.

Finally, like any other altitude comparison technique, the accuracy of an airspeed position correction (ΔV_{pc}) calculated from an altitude position correction (ΔH_{pc}) degrades at lower speeds. In a sensitivity analysis, at low speeds the error in the calculated static pressure caused by an error in measuring the altitude position correction (ΔH_{pc}) is on the same order of magnitude as the differential pressure, q_{cic}. This is because at low speeds the total pressure is only slightly more than the static pressure. The error in static pressure makes a significant error in the differential pressure, thus causing a large error in the calculated airspeed position correction (ΔV_{pc}). At high speeds the same error in static pressure is two orders of magnitude less than the differential pressure because the total pressure is so much larger. Thus the error caused in calculating the airspeed position correction is much smaller. Figure 7.5 shows the error in calculating the airspeed position correction caused by a 31.4 feet error in the altitude position correction.

31.4 feet (1 division) error in ΔH$_{pc}$

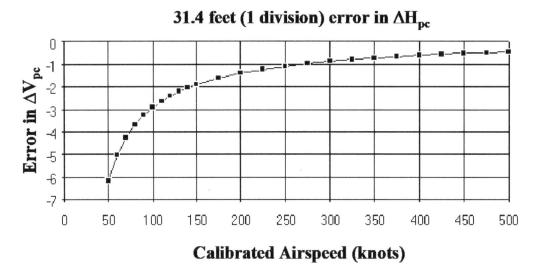

Figure 7.5. Resulting error in ΔV_{pc} from an error in ΔH_{pc}

Tower Fly-By Variations

The U.S. Naval Test Pilot School uses a variation on the Tower Fly-By FTT. Instead of flying over a line on the ground to determine the distance from the eyepiece to the test aircraft, a photograph is taken and stadiametric ranging is used to determine the test aircraft's height above the tower.

The test aircraft is flown over one of several locations, including the St. Marys river just offshore from Webster Field, offshore of Point Lookout, or over the runways at Pax River. The aircraft is optically tracked from the theodolite tower to obtain a photo similar to that shown in Figure 7.6. As described earlier, at the designated point where the photo is taken, the aircrew record the cockpit readings or mark the DAS. Tower personnel record the pressure altitude and temperature at the tower. (Ref 1)

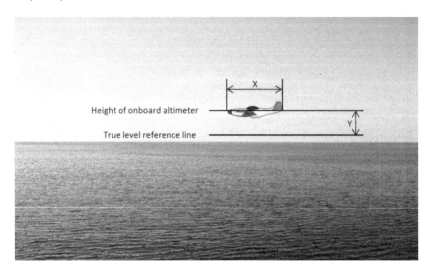

Figure 7.6. Stadiametric Tower Fly-By Photograph (Ref 1)

The actual length of the test aircraft, $L_{aircraft}$, is used to scale the distances in the photograph. The height of the aircraft above the tower, $h_{aircraft\ above\ tower}$, is determined from

$$h_{aircraft\ above\ tower} = \frac{L_{aircraft}}{X} Y$$

where X is the scaled length of the aircraft and Y is the scaled height of the aircraft above a marker showing the local level of the camera. The height above the tower is equivalent to the height above the tower determined by reading the grid. The remainder of the data reduction is identical to that shown for the Tower Fly-By FTT.

It is important that the photograph be taken very close to the point of closest approach, when the camera is looking perpendicular to the longitudinal axis of the aircraft. Otherwise the visible length of the airplane will be foreshortened. For example, a photograph taken 15 degrees from perpendicular would introduce a 3.4 percent error in measuring the length of the aircraft.

It is also important that the camera be tested for lens distortion before being used for data collection.

Another variation that was successfully used at Hurlburt Field FL to do calibrations on a C-130 used the radar altimeter to provide the "height above tower". The aircraft was flown in level flight low over a runway. A runway is not required, but it is important that a wide, flat surface is used to ensure the radar altitude returned is actually off of the desired location. A reasonably low altitude should be used such that the temperature can be assumed to be constant from the ground to the aircraft's altitude. Ground observers are required to record the pressure altitude of the ground and the air temperature as the aircraft flies overhead. At the same time, the aircrew would record the cockpit readings or mark the DAS. At a minimum, the cockpit readings would include indicated altitude, indicated airspeed, and radar altitude. The radar altitude is equivalent to the height above the tower determined by reading the grid. The remainder of the data reduction is identical to that shown for the Tower Fly-By FTT.

In a further variation of the radar altimeter technique, a differentially corrected GPS altitude above a known location has been used in place of the radar altimeter reading. The temperature and pressure altitude of the known location is recorded as the aircraft flies over.

Pace

Concept

Probably the most obvious (knowing how dangerous it is to use the word obvious in an instructional text) method to check the airspeed and altitude calibrations on a test aircraft would be to fly it in formation with an aircraft known to have a good airspeed and altitude calibration. This method, known as "pace" as in flying with a pace aircraft, does work very well, just as it would seem. This is, of course, considering that the minor requirement to have a "calibrated" aircraft can be met.

If the test aircraft and pace aircraft are sufficiently compatible, they may be flown in formation. The altitudes and airspeeds read at each point can be compared directly to find the altitude and airspeed position corrections. In this method, pace is both an altitude and an airspeed comparison technique. It is important to understand that in this case "flying at the same altitude" must be interpreted as "flying with the static pressure transducers of both aircraft at the same altitude". While this shouldn't be a problem when using similar aircraft, such as two F-16s, it can be a very real problem in a case such as pacing a C-17 with an F-16. Because the altitude sensed is the altitude of the pressure transducer, it is important that the non-lead airplane adjust altitude until both aircraft's pressure transducers are at the same altitude. If necessary to fly to some other reference point, then the difference in altitude of the transducers must be accounted for.

If the aircraft are not compatible in speed range, such as a C-12 and an F-16, a different form of the pace method can be used. The slower aircraft flies at the desired airspeed, and the faster aircraft flies past the slower aircraft while keeping the slower aircraft visually on the horizon. This results in the faster aircraft passing the slower aircraft at the same altitude. The altitude in each cockpit is read as the aircraft pass. In this case, the method is only an altitude comparison method.

Data Requirements

Data should be recorded in both cockpits (test aircraft and pace aircraft) simultaneously. This is usually accomplished by one person calling "Ready, ready, read" over the radio to the other aircraft. In each aircraft, record altitude, airspeed, and temperature (if calibrating the temperature system). Record the weight and configuration to determine any angle of attack or configuration effects.

Benefits

The Pace FTT is a simple, quick, and easy method to collect position correction data across the test aircraft's altitude and airspeed range. For this reason, the Pace FTT is a popular method of calibrating air data systems at the Air Force Test Center. As of 2015, the Center has F-16s modified to serve as pace aircraft. However, because the precision pressure transducers used for the pace instrumentation are not as robust as the operational pressure transducers, the pace instrumentation trays are normally not installed in the aircraft. One to two days are required to reinstall the pace instrumentation.

The Pace FTT can also be used to get a quick check of calibrations on the first flight of an aircraft by comparing the test aircraft to the safety chase aircraft. While the safety chase aircraft may not be as finely calibrated as a mission specific pace aircraft, it should be well within operational tolerances, and could thus be used to identify any gross errors. The B-2 used a very non-traditional air data system, and on the first flight of the first B-2, the air data system was checked against the F-16 chase to confirm that it was operating as designed.

Drawbacks

One of the first questions that pops to mind when trying to set up a pace FTT is "How do I calibrate the pace aircraft?" This is especially true if another calibrated aircraft is not readily available. To answer the question, the pace aircraft must be calibrated by other means. The Tower Fly-by FTT can be used to calibrate the altitude system at low altitude, and trailing cone or survey FTTs can be used at higher altitudes. The cloverleaf FTT can be used to calibrate the airspeed system.

Because of possible problems with shock wave interactions, the pace FTT is generally limited to subsonic speeds. Other FTTs, such as the survey FTT, are used for supersonic calibrations.

Trailing Cone/Trailing Bomb

Concept

Errors in measuring ambient pressure (position errors) arise because of trying to measure ambient air pressure on the surface of the aircraft which has disturbed the air pressure in its effort to fly. So what if we trailed a long tube out the back of the aircraft that could pick up the ambient air pressure outside the flow field of the aircraft? This is exactly what the trailing cone and trailing bomb methods attempt to do.

The trailing bomb is a bomb-like aerodynamic shape connected to the end of a tube that would hang down below the aircraft. This shape has static pressure ports around its perimeter as shown in Figure 7.7. The sensed pressure is fed back to the aircraft through the connecting tube. A trailing bomb may also be equipped with a Pitot tube with a separate connecting tube to allow measurement of airspeed as well as altitude.

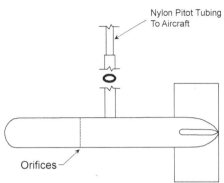

Figure 7.7. Trailing Bomb

In the trailing cone system, the ambient pressure is sensed through the tube itself. Typically the section with the orifices is a metal tube. The remaining tubing is the same diameter as the metal tube and made of a flexible material. Behind the metal tube is another section of flexible tubing which is sealed at some point and carries a stabilizing cone. The stabilizing cone will typically have large holes in it to improve its stability. The sole purpose of the cone is to stabilize the tubing in flight. The general setup of the trailing cone system is shown in Figure 7.8.

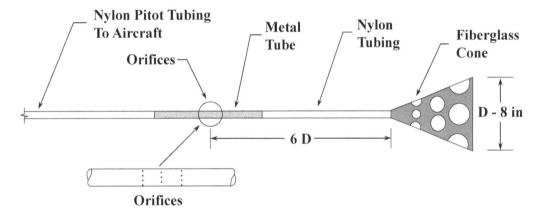

Figure 7.8. Trailing Cone

Trailing cones intended for use at high speed are frequently constructed with a cable inside the tubing from the anchor point to the cone attachment point so that the drag loads are not borne by the tubing.

The trailing cone or trailing bomb tubing is connected to a pressure transducer in the airplane. This transducer can be an absolute pressure transducer, such as an electrical transducer or a mechanical altimeter. In this case, the transducer would read the truth pressure altitude. Alternatively, the tubing would be connected to one side of a differential pressure transducer, with the aircraft static pressure being connected to the other side. In this case, the transducer would read the position error (ΔP_p) directly.

Students are frequently surprised that it is not necessary to know the position of the trailing cone or bomb relative to the aircraft. The beauty of this method is that gravity affects the air molecules inside the tube just like it does those outside the tube. Therefore, the hydrostatic equation

(Equation A15) still applies inside the tubing. That is, the pressure inside the tubing decreases with increasing altitude, just like the pressure does outside the tubing. The result of this change in pressure is that the pressure altitude read on the transducer is the pressure altitude where that transducer is located. Therefore, we want that transducer on board the aircraft and at a known location. If the transducer was located at the cone end of the system, then it would be necessary to know the location of the cone and the temperature profile between the transducer and the aircraft. If tubing is used to connect the sensed pressure to the transducer aboard the aircraft, the physics of the system works all of that out for us.

So several paragraphs ago I said that the trailing cone or trailing bomb system senses ambient air pressure from outside the aircraft's flow field. How do we know when it is outside the flow field? How do we know when the tube is long enough? If the tubing length can be changed in flight, the proper length can be determined by a simple experiment. Fly the aircraft at a constant indicated altitude and constant airspeed. Reel out the tubing to some length. Allow everything to stabilize and record the aircraft indicated altitude and the trailing cone/bomb indicated altitude. Reel the tubing out some more, and record the indicated altitudes again. Repeat until the difference between the indicated altitudes remains constant as more tubing is reeled out, as shown in Figure 7.9. Any length beyond the length where the difference stopped changing will be an acceptable length.

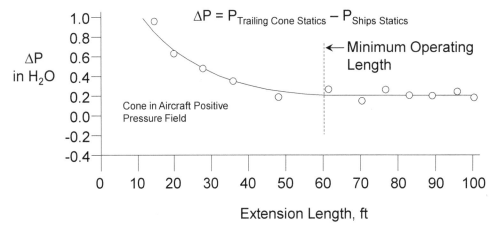

Figure 7.9. Determining Trailing Cone Tubing Length

Historical data can give some idea of an expected tubing length, as shown in Figure 7.10 (Ref 17). The required tubing length, as determined empirically by multiple programs, seems to be a loose function of wingspan. This seems reasonable, since the size of the disturbed flow field is somewhat determined by wingspan.

Note that longer is not always better. Tests with an F-16 determined that an optimum tubing length was around 60 feet. This is longer than the nominal envelope would show. However, tests with tubing lengths up to 100 feet showed an increased tendency to oscillations in the tubing. (Ref 18)

Frequently the trailing cone pressure transducer cannot be collocated with the aircraft static pressure transducer. In an F-16 installation, the pressure transducer was placed at the top of the vertical fin above the rudder where a Radar Warning Receiver antenna normally resides. In this case it is necessary to know the relative positions of the two pressure transducers so that their difference in altitude can be accounted for. In the F-16 case, the trailing cone transducer was so far behind the aircraft static pressure transducer that it was necessary to record the aircraft pitch angle so that the relative vertical positions could be calculated.

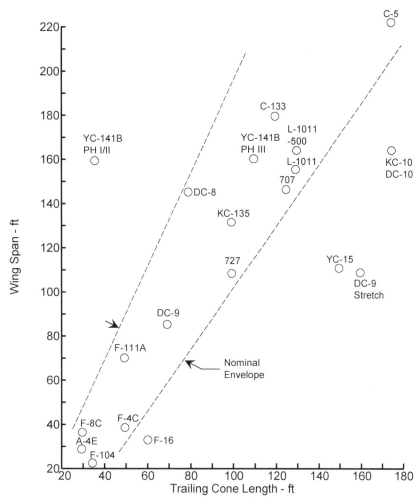

Figure 7.10. Determining Fin-Mounted Trailing Cone Tubing Length (Ref 17)

Data Requirements

For each test point, record the indicated altitude, indicated airspeed, and trailing cone/bomb altitude. Altitude should be stable when data is recorded.

Benefits

Both the trailing bomb and trailing cone systems give an undisturbed static pressure reading, and are a truth source aboard the test aircraft (i.e. moves around with the test aircraft, is not tied to a ground station or another aircraft). Trailing bombs have been fitted with Pitot tubes in addition to the static ports, giving both a truth altitude and a truth airspeed. A trailing bomb can also be very useful in helicopter testing. In this case, the bomb can be hung well below the helicopter, below where the rotor wake has dissipated to give airspeed and altitude information at low speeds.

Drawbacks

The trailing bomb system needs to be calibrated prior to use. This can generally be done in a wind tunnel to develop a calibration curve against Mach number.   Theoretically the trailing cone system has zero position error, although some contractors have been known to calibrate them in wind tunnels. Tower Flyby testing with aircraft equipped with a trailing cone has indicated some small position errors in the trailing cone system (Ref 18). Since both trailing cones and trailing bombs have holes all around the circumference, it would seem that any angle of attack would result in air passing in one side and out the other, thus relieving any total pressure buildup.

The tube has a large volume compared to the size of the holes for sensing the pressure. As a result, a noticeable lag can happen when changing altitude quickly. A lot of molecules have to move in or out of the tube to change the pressure in the tube, and when the holes are small, they create a restriction to the flow. Thus, a trailing cone/bomb system would probably not be suitable for use during steep climbs or descents. The best data will be collected when the altitude is constant.

The trailing bomb has an upper speed limit of approximately 200 knots. It is intended to hang below the test aircraft. Around 200 knots the bomb would be more behind the aircraft rather than below it because of its aerodynamic drag. Because of the way the tube pulling the bomb is attached, it will become unstable and start to thrash around the sky. The trailing cone was developed to use the same principle at higher speeds. In terms of stability, the trailing cone does not necessarily have an upper speed limit. However, at high speeds the dynamic pressure may collapse the cone, requiring a stronger cone or a smaller cone be used.

As generally used, the trailing cone/bomb system requires a recovery system, which usually includes a large reel to hold the tubing. For transport type aircraft, finding such space is usually not a problem, but generally is a problem in small aircraft such as fighters. If space for a recovery system is not available, the alternative is to lay out the trailing cone/bomb next to the aircraft on the runway prior to takeoff. The tubing drags along the runway during takeoff and could be damaged. Additionally, the system can be whipped into the air and smash onto the runway because of dirty airflow behind the aircraft. For aircraft that can open a window or door in flight, an alternative is to have a crewmember pass the tubing out the window after takeoff. This method has been used in gliders with good success over the years.

The trailing cone/bomb only provides ambient pressure information and thus cannot be used to calibrate temperature sensors.

Survey

Concept

To calibrate our altimeter, we need to know what the truth pressure altitude is at our current location. The basis of the survey method is to determine our position in space by one method, commonly referred to as Time-Space-Position-Information, or TSPI. Then, using a separate method, we determine the relationship of pressure altitude and geometric altitude at the time of the test. Knowing the geometric altitude at the time of the test, the corresponding pressure altitude can be determined.

TSPI

Thanks to advances in technology, the TSPI portion of this technique is actually the easy part. "Back in the day" this TSPI was typically done by FPS-16 tracking radars. These radars were initially developed for tracking missiles, and were used to track the launches of Explorer 1 and Vanguard 1 in 1958. They were also used for tracking for spacecraft as well. The radar worked best when used in conjunction with a radar transponder. The radar was capable of azimuth and elevation angular errors of less than 0.1 milliradian and range errors of less than 15 feet. These radars worked very well for their stated mission, but as demand for their services decreased, the cost of operation rapidly grew until they were very uneconomical.

It is possible to use other TSPI methods, such as Cinetheodolites (also called Phototheodolites), which have movie cameras that record azimuth and elevation angles to a target. A minimum of three cinetheodolites are required to get thee dimensional position information. Compared to radar, these are fairly short range (30 km), so the measureable volume is rather limited for aircraft testing. Again, demand for this method has reduced over the years to where the cost of operation grew rapidly.

The technology that has really eclipsed other forms of TSPI is (of course) GPS, or more specifically Differential GPS or WAAS GPS. The specification for WAAS accuracy in the vertical direction is 7.6 meters (about 25 feet). Demonstrated accuracy is actually much better, on the order of 1.5 meters (about 5 feet). This should be within the size of errors that we are trying to measure. Cost is virtually a non-issue, since a suitable GPS is probably already installed in the aircraft for other purposes. If not, suitable handheld GPS units are available at low cost (at least in airplane terms).

Pressure Altitude Map

The second half of a survey method is to obtain the current relationship between pressure altitude and geometric altitude. Several approaches to finding this relationship have been used.

The simplest and relatively cheapest approach is to launch a weather balloon. This will probably need to be explicitly requested for your test, since there are probably no regular weather balloon launches near your test location or at the time of your test. In 2015 the closest regularly scheduled weather observation balloon launches to Edwards AFB are at Vandenberg AFB and San Diego, both about 130 nautical miles away. The weather office at Edwards AFB has the capability to launch balloons—of course, your project will pay for it.

The balloon itself is just a transport mechanism for the Radiosonde ("sonde" is French and German for probe) which has the actual instrumentation in it. Modern day radiosondes carry a GPS unit to determine geometric altitude and wind direction and speed. Air data are measured by a temperature sensor and a humidity sensor. A radio transmitter telemeters the data back to a ground station.

"Wait a minute, Moosebreath! I thought we needed to know pressure altitude. You obviously forgot to mention the pressure sensor!" Actually, no I didn't. There is no pressure sensor on a typical radiosonde. Seems odd, huh? A radiosonde measures geometric altitude, temperature, and humidity. Pressure is found knowing the pressure at the launch elevation (measured by a separate instrument) and then integrating temperature with altitude to find pressure, in a method very similar to how we derived the standard atmosphere. It is even necessary to convert geometric altitudes into geopotential altitudes. The biggest wrinkle to that is when modeling the real world we can no longer assume dry air. The humidity, also measured, must be considered, which complicates the calculations a bit. This process is covered in gross detail in Appendix G.

So why not use a pressure sensor? Some designs of radiosondes can use a pressure sensor. Besides the additional cost on what is essentially a one-time use disposable unit, there is a question of accuracy for the pressure sensor because of the range of pressures involved. At sea level, standard day, atmospheric pressure is 1013 millibars (the weatherman's preferred unit). In the stratosphere, pressures drop below 100 millibars, or 10 per cent of the sea level value. It is difficult to build a single sensor that will measure accurately over an order of magnitude change. Tests have shown that the temperature integration method actually produces more accurate pressures at high altitudes than using a pressure sensor.

While the weather balloon provides a relationship between pressure altitude and geometric altitude, strictly speaking it only provides that information at one location. With proper considerations, this is still acceptable.

Another method that was used back in the days of radar tracking and is still viable is to use a "calibrated aircraft". Calibration is not required throughout the flight envelope, but just at the airspeed (and to a lesser extent, altitude) that the aircraft will be flying. This aircraft flies a similar ground track to that flown by the aircraft to be calibrated. It records pressure altitude and geometric altitude though the test corridor. Depending on the method used, ambient air temperature may also be required. If possible, record position (latitude, longitude) as well. Unlike the weather balloon, this method provides the pressure altitude/geometric altitude relationship over a line, not just a point. This may reduce uncertainty over the weather balloon method, but only if the calibration of the aircraft has the same uncertainty (or less) as the weather balloon.

The test aircraft can be used as the "calibrated aircraft" if the altitude calibration is confidently known for at least one airspeed. This calibration could come from some other method, such as a Tower Flyby or Turn Regression (described in the Airspeed Comparison section).

When expensive radar tracking was used, the calibrated aircraft would generally make one calibration pass. This approach required measuring ambient air temperature, because temperature was required to convert the geometric altitude difference between the calibration altitude and test aircraft altitude into a pressure altitude difference. This requirement also encourages flying the calibration runs at low Mach numbers because the effects of uncertainty in the temperature measurement are minimized.

Another approach which eliminates the need for a temperature measurement is to fly two calibration runs, one slightly above the test altitude, and one slightly below the test altitude. This allows a linear interpolation of the pressure altitude based on the geometric altitudes alone. This is also possible with weather balloon data, as data should be available above and below the test altitude.

To take it one step further, if you are concerned with time-varying conditions, it is possible to fly calibration runs before and after the test run and build an interpolation model with time as a variable. In practice, when testing in appropriate conditions this is probably not necessary.

So what are "appropriate conditions"? Especially when using weather balloon data, we need to assume that the relationship between pressure altitude and geometric altitude doesn't change over the distance between where the weather balloon was and where the test aircraft was. On a weather map this would be represented by isobars that are far apart. Figure 7.11 shows isobars from the day the image was captured and a notional representation of R-2508. As shown, the pressure change between plotted isobars is four millibars. The pressure altitude change between isobars would be 109 feet at sea level, and 147 feet at 10,000 feet pressure altitude. On the day as depicted, assuming that the weather balloon and test aircraft were within 20 to 30 miles of each other the error due to distance would be sufficiently small.

Another quick indication as to the suitability of conditions is to check the wind speed at the test altitude. Every Private Pilot ground school course teaches that when the isobars are close together (high pressure gradient with distance) the wind speed is high. If the isobars are far apart (low pressure gradient with distance—what we want) the wind speed will be low. Storms or fronts in the area will make the atmosphere unstable. Also check the winds aloft forecast for any wind shears (sudden changes of direction or speed) or non-linear temperature gradients near the test altitude. Any of these will cause data quality problems.

Test Aircraft Profile

The test aircraft flies "near" where the pressure survey was conducted, recording indicated altitude and geometric altitude, and possibly position. The efficiency of this method comes from the ability to collect data for multiple airspeeds in quick succession. Thus, typically the test aircraft will slowly accelerate level through the test corridor, collecting data continuously across the entire airspeed range. Accelerations should be slow to minimize effects of Pitot-static lag.

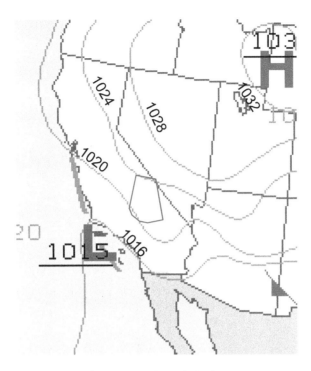

Figure 7.11. Sample Isobars

Alternatively, data can be collected while decelerating at a constant altitude. By climbing to a higher altitude and then accelerating in a dive to the test altitude, calibrations can be obtained for speeds higher than the maximum sustainable level flight speed.

Data Requirements

For a weather balloon or a calibrated aircraft, geometric altitude and pressure altitude are required. For the calibrated aircraft, if only one calibration altitude is mapped, then ambient air temperature must be recorded. If two calibration altitudes are mapped (immediately below and above the test altitude) ambient air temperature is not required for calibrating altitude. Uncertainty can possibly be reduced by recording the position (latitude, longitude) of each reading by the calibrated aircraft. Ambient air temperature is required if calibrating temperature on the test aircraft.

For the test aircraft, geometric and indicated pressure altitude is required. Position (latitude, longitude) are desired for evaluating uncertainty. Indicated air temperature is required if calibrating temperature on the test aircraft.

If Air Data and Position Data are not recorded on the same data stream, then time will need to be recorded in each stream for data correlation.

Benefits

While the survey method may seem more complicated or difficult to understand than other methods, it is useful for high altitude calibrations. It is one of the few methods that can be used for supersonic calibrations. It is also efficient since one pass can calibrate throughout the airspeed range for a particular altitude.

Drawbacks

Because the passes are flown asynchronously, winds aloft can introduce errors by moving the air mass around. To minimize this error, the pressure altitude survey and the test run should be done with as little delay between them as possible.

Errors are introduced by the tracking equipment (radar or GPS). The tracking system should have a significantly smaller uncertainty than the altitude errors being measured.

Ground Calibration

Sometimes it is useful to characterize position errors at airspeeds below flight speeds, such as seen during takeoff or landing roll. Noseboom equipped aircraft, which typically have positive corrections, exhibit the somewhat entertaining characteristic of indicated altitudes that descend below the runway during the takeoff roll. Errors in airspeed can affect rotation speeds and thus takeoff distance.

Fighter aircraft can have significant difference in position errors with different store configurations, which can affect calculating takeoff speeds.

Multi-engine aircraft need to have well defined position errors below takeoff airspeed and in ground effect so that accurate values can be known for ground minimum control speed (V_{mcg}), critical engine failure speed, as well as rotation and initial climb speed can be presented to the pilot.

Calculating these corrections can be as simple as assuming the runway is flat and using the pressure altitude recorded while stationary (M = 0) as the truth value. Data quality can be improved if the slope of the runway is known and included in the calculation.

A more extensive discussion of calibration methods for use in ground effect can be found in 412TW-TIH-16-02 *Determining Pitot-Static Position Error Corrections In-Ground Effect* (Ref 19).

Chapter 8

Airspeed Comparison Flight Test Techniques

The Big Assumptions

All airspeed comparison (or Mach comparison) methods share two assumptions. The first is that **an accurate measurement of ambient temperature** is available. This may require getting the temperature system calibrated, or iterative solutions as the temperature system is calibrated.

The second assumption is a big one and is tough to control. All of these methods assume that the **wind velocity throughout the maneuvers is constant**. That is, the wind direction does not change, and the wind speed does not change. Wind gusts, gradients, or changes will degrade the data quality. Frequently you will hear that these FTTs should be done in calm winds or early in the morning. The reasoning behind this is that if the wind is calm or very light, the size of any gusts or gradients will also be very small. Theoretically these FTTs could be accomplished in any steady wind condition. In practice, it just doesn't work out that way.

Ground Speed Course

Concept

If the Tower Fly-by FTT is the Father of all Air Data System Calibration FTTs, then the Ground Speed Course is the Granddaddy. This method was in use long before the Tower Fly-by. Quite simply, the aircraft is flown over two points on the ground a known distance apart, timing how long it takes to fly between them. Of course, some considerations have to be made for wind.

The aircraft is flown over a known distance close to the ground as shown in Figure 8.1. This distance can be a runway, two roads, or any other prominent landmarks a known distance apart. To eliminate the effects of steady wind, the course is flown in opposite directions for each target airspeed. The average ground speed will equal the true airspeed if the wind is constant.

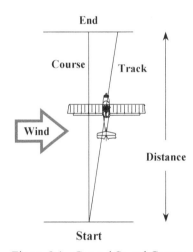

Figure 8.1. Ground Speed Course

To minimize any effects of non-steady winds, the preferred direction of the ground speed course is perpendicular to the wind. This way, any variations in the wind are mostly perpendicular to the airspeed measurement and cause minimal changes. If flown with a headwind/tailwind, any variations in the wind directly affect the airspeed measurement. Flying when winds are calm gives the best results. Winds over 10 knots will probably have enough variation to pollute the data beyond usability, because wind variations will be on the same order of magnitude as the errors being measured.

Because the airspeed is measured parallel to the centerline of the aircraft, the centerline of the aircraft must be held parallel to the course. Another way to say this is that the pilot flies the same heading as the course and allows the aircraft to blow downwind. This may be difficult for some pilots because they are used to crabbing to track parallel to ground paths such as runways. To see the reason for not crabbing, consider the vectors in Figure 8.2. If the aircraft is crabbed, the airspeed vector is not aligned with the ground course which is being used to measure ground speed. Consider how much the ground speed would be slowed in a crosswind on the order of the airspeed of the aircraft. When done properly, the additional ground speed caused by the wind is the component of ground speed perpendicular to the course. Because this speed is perpendicular to the course, it does not affect the component of ground speed measured in the direction of the course.

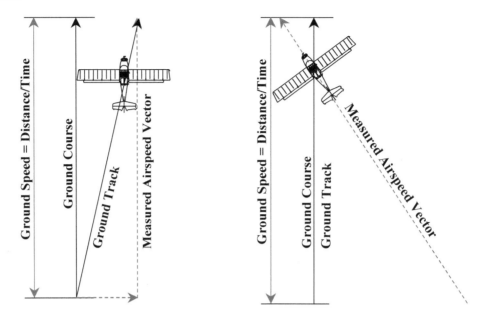

Figure 8.2. Not crabbing vs. crabbing on the Ground Speed Course

The headwind/tailwind component of wind (the component aligned with the ground speed course) is the only component of the wind that will affect the measured ground speed. Figure 8.3 shows how the measured ground speeds average out to equal the true airspeed for a constant wind.

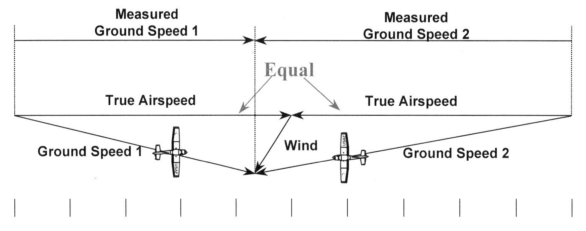

Figure 8.3. Measured ground speeds average out to equal true airspeed

Consider starting the course aligned with the course or on the downwind side of the course such that the course remains visible (rather than passing under the aircraft) for the entire run.

Each set of two passes at one airspeed results in one datum point. Like the Tower Fly-by, the speed course must be repeated at each desired airspeed throughout the airspeed envelope.

While flying lower to the ground will allow better timing, do not fly so low that ground effect becomes an issue. Maintain at least one wingspan or more of altitude above the ground. For improved timing accuracy, hold your head in the same position for each timing hack and call the hack as the line passes some visible part of the airplane. Another method useful on the Edwards Speed Course or when using roads is to call the hack when looking straight down the crossing line.

Note that the Ground Speed Course on the Edwards lakebed is marked in *statute* miles (5280 feet), not nautical miles. That should tell you something about how old this FTT is. Based on the Edwards range charts, the course is laid out on a 003-183 heading.

Data Requirements

The primary data include indicated altitude, indicated airspeed, indicated temperature, and time to fly the course in each direction. Secondary data would be weight (to investigate any angle of attack effects) and configuration (to investigate any configuration effects).

Benefits

The ground speed course is simple for low speed aircraft and does not require any special infrastructure. A suitable speed course can usually be made from existing items such as a runway or roads. Simplicity of the method should lead to good results.

Drawbacks

As mentioned earlier, non-gusty winds are a must, with the preference being for calm winds. Non-steady winds will pollute the data.

Because we are trying to measure errors in airspeed on the order of a few knots, the aim airspeed must be held very tightly, such as ±1 knot, with ±0 knots preferred.

Errors in timing directly lead to errors in the results. Even a one second total error in timing can lead to significant errors in the results. This effectively limits the applicability of this FTT to airspeeds of 200 knots or less.

Like the tower fly-by, this FTT requires flight low to the ground. The course lines available may not be perpendicular to the wind—in fact runways tend to be parallel with the wind. If using a runway as the course, steps must be taken to avoid traffic conflicts when flying down the runway the opposite direction of normal operations.

Using GPS as a Truth Source

When doing calibrations, unaugmented GPS position, especially on Coarse/Acquisition (C/A) code (civilian code), is generally not sufficiently accurate. However, the GPS ground speed is far more accurate, since it is derived from the Doppler shift of the signal, not from differentiating position. The specification accuracy of ground speed from C/A code is 0.10 meters per second, or 0.19 knots per second. Since this is smaller than the size of the errors we are trying to measure, we should be able to use GPS Ground Speed with good results.

All Altitude Speed Course

Concept

The All Altitude Speed Course was developed and tested in the HAVE PACER II test management project during USAF TPS Class 95A. This method compares the drift corrected GPS ground speed to the Pitot-static true airspeed.

Like the Ground Speed Course, the All Altitude Speed Course is flown perpendicular to the wind to minimize wind effects. The first challenge is to determine what the wind direction is at altitude. Of course, the weather-guessers will tell you what they think the wind direction is at your altitude of choice, but based on their record of predicting temperature and rain, you may just want to consider that a starting point.

A method of approximating the wind direction is shown in Figure 8.4.   A shallow constant airspeed turn is flown. Starting aligned with the expected wind direction is recommended but not required. Based on the calibrated airspeed and temperature, a true airspeed is calculated. A "whiz wheel" can be useful for this calculation. Note the heading on which the GPS Ground Speed matches the calculated true airspeed.   This will be the approximate crosswind heading. Check the ground speed on the reciprocal heading. Adjust the headings until the ground speeds in both directions are approximately equal (within a couple of knots).   The resulting heading will be within a few degrees of crosswind and sufficiently close to perpendicular to the wind for the purposes of this FTT.

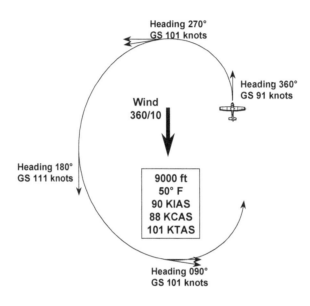

Figure 8.4. Determining wind direction at altitude

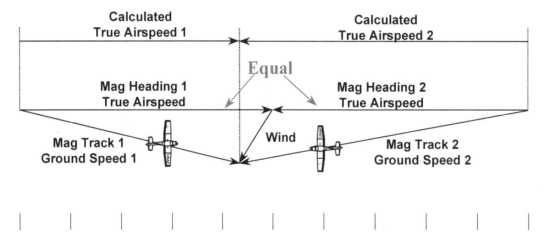

Figure 8.5. Calculated true airspeeds (drift corrected groundspeeds) average out to equal true airspeed

Once the crosswind heading has been determined, fly the aircraft at the aim airspeed and record data. Repeat on the reciprocal heading. Continue for each aim airspeed. Similar to the ground speed course, the average groundspeed measured will equal the true airspeed for constant wind, as shown in Figure 8.5.

Data Requirements

On each pass, record heading, indicated airspeed, indicated temperature, indicated altitude, GPS ground speed, and GPS track angle. Record data multiple times on one pass (every few seconds). Any variation in GPS ground speed or track angle may indicate wind gradients.

Benefits

As its name suggests, the All Altitude Speed Course can be done at any altitude, unlike the Ground Speed Course which is constrained to altitudes near the ground. The only special instrumentation required is a GPS receiver, which may already be installed in the aircraft. A C/A code receiver is sufficient for this FTT.

Drawbacks

The data reduction depends on knowing the drift angle, which is derived from the heading. Depending on the sophistication of the heading system, the compass may be one of the least accurate instruments in the cockpit.

Horseshoe GPS Method

Concept

This method was developed by the National Test Pilot School (NTPS) and uses a GPS ground speed measurement to calculate the truth source. The test aircraft is flown at a constant indicated airspeed on three orthogonal headings, as shown in Figure 8.6.

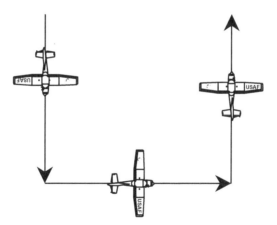

Figure 8.6. Horseshoe GPS method

The resulting wind triangles are shown in Figure 8.7.

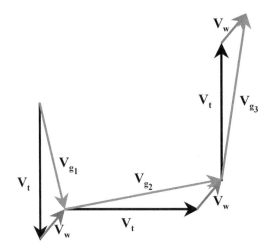

Figure 8.7. Three legged GPS method wind triangles

Data Requirements

On each leg, record indicated airspeed, indicated temperature, indicated altitude, and GPS ground speed.

Benefits

This FTT can be applied at any altitude and does not require determining the wind direction. In fact, the wind direction will be determined as an output of the data reduction.

Drawbacks

The data reduction assumes that the three headings flown are orthogonal (90 degrees apart) and both turns are to the left. Accurate and precise heading control is required for good data. However, the actual headings relative to the wind are not important.

Cloverleaf

Concept

The cloverleaf technique was developed at the Air Force Flight Test Center in the early 1970s as a method for calibrating airspeed at up and away altitudes. At that time, a tracking radar was used to measure the ground speed and track of the test aircraft. Because of the expense involved in operating the radar, use of this method was pretty much limited to calibrating the pace aircraft. With the advent of GPS, measuring ground speed and track becomes almost free, so this FTT has become more practical in latter years.

Note that this maneuver has nothing to do with the aerobatic maneuver of the same name that you learned in pilot training. A C-130 test plan calling for cloverleafs generated some humorous banter with the owning squadron who didn't understand the difference.

The test aircraft is flown at the aim altitude and airspeed on three headings approximately 120 degrees apart over the same location, as shown in Figure 8.8. This was the original vision for the technique, and provides the most mathematical independence between legs. However, the method has been done in other shapes, including triangles and squares. Care must be taken, for the constant wind assumption becomes very strained when legs are separated by 20 nautical miles because the aircraft is flying at high speeds.

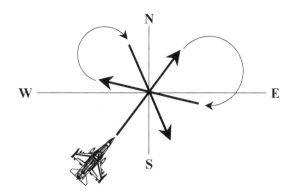

Figure 8.8. Cloverleaf flight path

True airspeed, wind direction and wind speed can be calculated by vector math. An alternate method is to calculate the true airspeed error, wind direction and wind speed by inverting a matrix of equations derived from the wind triangles. While that sounds scary, spreadsheets such as Excel and Matlab have functions which invert numerical matrices. A benefit of calculating the true airspeed error instead of the true airspeed is that small variations in indicated airspeed do not affect the result, if we assume that the airspeed position correction remains constant over that small variation of indicated airspeed.

The stability of the mathematical solution increases with increasing angle between the passes. While theoretically the solution could be found from three passes spaced in heading by five degrees, the result would have a large uncertainty. The least uncertainty comes from passes spaced by 120 degrees.

Data Requirements

On each pass, record indicated airspeed, indicated temperature, indicated altitude, GPS ground speed, and GPS track angle. If available, recording winds as reported by the aircraft systems can give insight to how constant the wind speed and direction is.

Benefits

Unlike the previous GPS methods, the headings do not need to be spaced by an exact amount. Each pass only needs to be sufficiently long for the GPS ground speed and track angle to stabilize. As with other GPS methods, this FTT can be done at any altitude.

A C/A code GPS is sufficiently accurate for this method. This would include a commercial handheld GPS.

Drawbacks

Like the Ground Speed Course or the Tower Fly-by, each set of three passes only results in one datum point (airspeed correction), so it can take a while to calibrate across the speed range. Additional uncertainty due to changes in wind direction and wind speed can arise if passes are widely separated in position or time.

Turn Regression

Concept

As mentioned earlier, all airspeed comparison methods must assume that wind direction and velocity are constant for all test passes in various directions. The uncertainty caused by this assumption has been minimized over the years by procedures such as flying in the early morning when light winds are common and by minimizing the time and space needed to complete a set of passes. These techniques have met with varying degrees of success.

All of the methods discussed previously are deterministic. That is, the data reduction returns a single value with no information about the uncertainty present in that value. A desirable change would be a method that would return a stochastic value, complete with statistics characterizing the uncertainty in that value. To accomplish this, many more than three measurements are required.

Reference 20 proposed "Orbis Matching", a method where the aircraft is flown in a level turn at constant airspeed and constant load factor for a full circle. True airspeed and heading are recorded, along with GPS ground speed and GPS ground track. Plotting the northerly component of air velocity against the easterly component of air velocity, both calculated from the true airspeed and heading, should result in a circle, centered around the origin. Plotting the northerly component of ground velocity against the easterly component of ground velocity, both calculated from the GPS ground speed and GPS ground track, results in a spiral path, distorted from a circle by the wind. The Orbis Matching method seeks to determine a wind speed and direction that will adjust this path back to a circle. Once the wind speed and direction are known, the error in true airspeed can be calculated.

As mentioned above, cloverleaf data can be analyzed by matrix inversion, which returns an error in true airspeed (as opposed to the true airspeed), which has the benefit of minimizing any uncertainty due to slightly varying airspeeds. Reference 21 built on the ideas of Orbis Matching and the Cloverleaf to provide stochastic values complete with confidence intervals about the solution coefficients.

In the Turn Regression technique, the aircraft is flown in a level turn at constant airspeed and constant load factor, as in the Orbis Matching technique. A complete full circle turn is required, as doing a partial turn leads to problems with data statistical independence. Data are continuously recorded by a DAS in a turn, or recorded by hand on multiple straight segments approximating a turn. Each data point is turned into a wind triangle. A linear regression is run on the collection of wind triangles, returning an estimate of the true airspeed error, wind direction, and wind speed. Additionally, the regression returns confidence bounds on each estimate, along with a p value to characterize the significance of the resulting model. The regression can be run in Excel, Matlab, or many other software packages.

Small confidence intervals will indicate small uncertainties and good data quality. Larger confidence intervals will bring into question the validity of the constant wind assumption for that group of test data, and can be a basis for rejecting those results. High sample rate data may need to be decimated to avoid problems with serial correlation. Data at 1 Hz has been shown to be sufficiently independent.

One hidden assumption in the original data reduction is that the measured heading is equal to the direction of the component of velocity in the North-East (horizontal) plane. For aircraft operating at cruise speeds and bank angles less than 30 degrees (load factors less than 1.15g), the angle of attack is sufficiently close to zero that this assumption is valid. Reference 22 showed that because heading is measured in the body axes and velocity is measured in the stability axes (assuming no sideslip), a significant difference arises between these vectors as the angle of attack becomes significantly non-zero. If the data reduction compares the direction of the heading vector and the ground track vector, then at load factors of 2g or greater the error in angular measurement is on the order of magnitude of the angle of attack itself. Reference 22 shows that this error can be greatly minimized by incorporating angle of attack and bank angle measurements into the data reduction.

Data Requirements

Record indicated airspeed, indicated temperature, indicated altitude, heading, GPS ground speed, and GPS track angle. Record continuously with a DAS, or record by hand on straight segments, turning slightly between segments to approximate a circle. If available, record angle of attack and bank angle, especially if turning at load factors of 2g or more.

Benefits

As discussed above, because the number of data points (equations) is far greater than the number of unknowns, stochastic methods can be used. The additional information from the large number of data points is used to give an indication as to the uncertainty present in the data. As with other GPS methods, this FTT can be done at any altitude.

A C/A code GPS is sufficiently accurate for this method. This would include a commercial handheld GPS.

Drawbacks

Like the Ground Speed Course or the Tower Fly-by, each turn only results in one datum point (airspeed correction), so it can take a while to calibrate across the speed range. References 23 and 24 cover an extension to this method, which by making some assumptions about the shape of the calibration curve, uses an accelerating or decelerating turn to calibrate most of the airspeed range in a single maneuver.

As stated in earlier chapters, the position error and corresponding corrections are functions of angle of attack and Mach number. Position corrections are usually presented for 1g flight. Collecting data in a turn does result in a higher angle of attack at a particular airspeed, which can change the results. Higher angles of attack also introduce data measurement problems. To minimize this uncertainty, it is recommended to keep load factors small, such as with bank angles no greater than 30 degrees. If higher load factors are required, angle of attack and bank angle should be measured. For aircraft appropriately equipped, these maneuvers could be flown with an autopilot using altitude hold.

Chapter 9

Data Reduction

NOTE: The section for each Flight Test Technique (FTT) is written to stand alone. Each section will progress from the collected data through finding the static port position error ratio ($\Delta P_p/P_s$). The final section will cover how to use the static port position ratio to calculate the altitude, airspeed, and Mach number position corrections.

Tower Fly-By Data Reduction

Overview

The tower fly-by FTT is an altitude comparison technique. The truth altitude of the aircraft is determined by triangulation from the tower, and then compared to the pressure altitude read in the cockpit or on a DAS. To find the altitude position correction (ΔH_{pc}), we will

        a. Find the geometric altitude of the aircraft relative to the tower
        b. Find the truth pressure altitude
        c. Correct cockpit readings for instrument errors
        d. Find the altitude position correction
        e. Find the static port position error ratio ($\Delta P_p/P_s$)

For purposes of this discussion, we will use the following example data:

Theodolite Pressure Altitude ($H_{c_{tower}}$)	2500 feet
Grid Reading	5.2
Tower Ambient Temperature (T_{test})	5 °C
Altimeter Instrument Correction (ΔH_{ic})	+15 feet
Airspeed Instrument Correction (ΔV_{ic})	-2.5 knots
Indicated Altitude (H_i)	2450 feet
Indicated Airspeed (V_i)	425 knots

Find the geometric altitude of the aircraft relative to the tower

The geometric altitude of the aircraft static pressure transducer relative to the tower is found by triangulation, as shown in Figure 9.1. Because this distance is relatively short (less than 600 feet), the geopotential altitude difference is assumed equal to the geometric altitude difference.

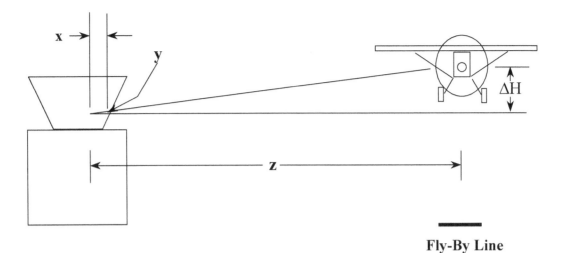

Fly-By Line

Figure 9.1. Tower Fly-By Geometry

For Figure 9.1,

  x   Eyepiece to Grid Distance
  y   Grid Division Height*Tower Grid Reading
  z   Eyepiece to Fly-By Line Distance

By similar triangles, we see that

$$\frac{\Delta H}{z} = \frac{y}{x}$$

or

$$\Delta H = \frac{z}{x} y$$

If we separate the Grid Division Height from the Tower Grid Reading, we can find a grid constant

$$\text{Grid Constant} = \left(\frac{\text{Eyepiece to Flyby Line Distance}}{\text{Eyepiece to Grid Distance}}\right)(\text{Grid Division Height})$$

For the Edwards Fly-by Tower, the grid constant is 31.4 feet/division. Therefore, the aircraft geometric altitude above the tower is given by

$$\Delta H = (\text{Grid Constant})(\text{Grid Reading})$$

$$\Delta H = \left(31.4\,\frac{\text{ft}}{\text{division}}\right)(5.2\ \text{divisions})$$

$$\Delta H = 163.28\ \text{feet}$$

Find the truth pressure altitude

To find the truth pressure altitude, we need to convert the geometric altitude above the tower to a pressure altitude above the tower. The relationship between geometric altitude and pressure altitude is dependent on the ratio of the test day temperature and the standard temperature for the pressure altitude

$$\Delta H = \frac{T_{test}}{T_{std}} \Delta H_c \qquad\qquad (B23)$$

T_{test} is measured at the fly-by tower. We find the standard temperature from the pressure altitude measured in the tower. (From Equations A69 and A78)

$$\frac{T_{std}}{T_{SL}} = (1 - 6.87559 \times 10^{-6} H_{c_{tower}})$$

$$T_{std} = (1 - 6.87559 \times 10^{-6} H_{c_{tower}}) T_{SL}$$

$$T_{std} = (1 - 6.87559 \times 10^{-6}/\text{feet } (2500 \text{ feet}))(288.15 \text{ K})$$

$$T_{std} = 283.2 \text{ K}$$

Rearranging Equation B23, we can get the pressure altitude difference between the aircraft and the tower

$$\Delta H_c = \frac{T_{std}}{T_{test}} \Delta H$$

$$\Delta H_c = \frac{283.2 \text{ K}}{(5°C + 273.15)} (163.28 \text{ feet})$$

$$\Delta H_c = 166 \text{ feet}$$

The truth pressure altitude of the aircraft is then this difference added to the tower pressure altitude.

$$H_c = H_{c_{tower}} + \Delta H_c$$

$$H_c = 2500 \text{ feet} + 166 \text{ feet}$$

$$H_c = 2666 \text{ feet}$$

Correct cockpit readings for instrument errors

The instrument corrected altitude and airspeed are calculated by adding the instrument corrections to the indicated values.

$$H_{ic} = H_i + \Delta H_{ic} \qquad\qquad (D66)$$

$$H_{ic} = 2450 \text{ feet} + (+15 \text{ feet})$$

$$H_{ic} = 2465 \text{ feet}$$

$$V_{ic} = V_i + \Delta V_{ic} \qquad\qquad (D67)$$

$$V_{ic} = 425 \text{ knots} + (-2.5 \text{ knots})$$

$$V_{ic} = 422.5 \text{ knots}$$

Find the altitude position correction

The altitude position correction is the difference between the instrument corrected altitude and the truth pressure altitude.

$$\Delta H_{pc} = H_c - H_{ic} \qquad\qquad (D5)$$

$$\Delta H_{pc} = 2666 \text{ feet} - 2465 \text{ feet}$$

$$\Delta H_{pc} = 201 \text{ feet}$$

Find the static port position error ratio ($\Delta P_p/P_s$)

The Position Error, or ΔP_p, is defined as

$$\Delta P_p = P_s - P_a \qquad\qquad (D1)$$

Therefore, we calculate the static and ambient pressures

$$P_s = P_{SL}(1 - 6.87559 \times 10^{-6} \, H_{ic})^{5.2559} \qquad (H_{ic} \leq 36089.24 \text{ feet}) \quad (D8)$$

$$P_s = (2116.22 \text{ lb/ft}^2)(1 - 6.87559 \times 10^{-6} \, (2465 \text{ feet}))^{5.2559}$$

$$P_s = 1934.38 \text{ lb/ft}^2$$

$$P_a = P_{SL}(1 - 6.87559 \times 10^{-6} \, H_c)^{5.2559} \qquad (H_c \leq 36089.24 \text{ feet}) \quad (D10)$$

$$P_a = (2116.22 \text{ lb/ft}^2)(1 - 6.87559 \times 10^{-6} \, (2666 \text{ feet}))^{5.2559}$$

$$P_a = 1920.13 \text{ lb/ft}^2$$

Then the static port position error ratio is

$$\frac{\Delta P_p}{P_s} = \frac{P_s - P_a}{P_s}$$

$$\frac{\Delta P_p}{P_s} = \frac{1934.38 \text{ lb}/\text{ft}^2 - 1920.13 \text{ lb}/\text{ft}^2}{1934.38 \text{ lb}/\text{ft}^2}$$

$$\frac{\Delta P_p}{P_s} = 0.0073667$$

Pace Data Reduction

Overview

The pace FTT is an altitude comparison technique, or a combination altitude and airspeed comparison technique. If the calibrated ("Pace") aircraft flies by the test aircraft at the same altitude, then it is an altitude comparison technique. If the calibrated aircraft and test aircraft fly in formation, then it is both an altitude and an airspeed comparison technique. The truth altitude and truth airspeed of the aircraft are determined from the instruments in the calibrated aircraft after correcting for instrument and position error. These values are compared to the indicated pressure altitude and indicated airspeed read in the test aircraft cockpit or on a DAS. To find the altitude position correction (ΔH_{pc}) and airspeed position correction (ΔV_{pc}), we will

      a. Find the position correction of the pace aircraft
      b. Find the instrument and position corrected ("truth") altitude and airspeed for the pace
aircraft
      c. Correct cockpit readings for instrument errors
      d. Find the altitude and airspeed position corrections
      e. Find the static port position error ratio ($\Delta P_p/P_s$)

For purposes of this discussion, we will use the following example data:

Pace coefficients	
C_0	54 feet
C_1	-324 feet
C_2	850 feet
C_3	0 feet
C_4	0 feet
Airspeed Position Correction ($\Delta V_{pc_{pace}}$)	+3 knots
Altimeter Instrument Correction ($\Delta H_{ic_{pace}}$)	+20 feet
Airspeed Instrument Correction ($\Delta V_{ic_{pace}}$)	-2 knots
Indicated Altitude ($H_{i_{pace}}$)	20,000 feet
Indicated Airspeed ($V_{i_{pace}}$)	280 knots
Test aircraft data	
Altimeter Instrument Correction ($\Delta H_{ic_{test}}$)	-15 feet
Airspeed Instrument Correction ($\Delta V_{ic_{test}}$)	+3 knots
Indicated Altitude ($H_{i_{test}}$)	20,010 feet
Indicated Airspeed ($V_{i_{test}}$)	275 knots

Find the position correction of the pace aircraft

Note: This step assumes that the position correction curve for the pace aircraft has been supplied as coefficients to a polynomial of the form

$$\Delta H_{pc_{pace}} = (C_0 + C_1 M_{ic_{pace}} + C_2 M_{ic_{pace}}^{\,2} + C_3 M_{ic_{pace}}^{\,3} + C_4 M_{ic_{pace}}^{\,4} + \ldots)\, \theta_{std_{test\ alt}}$$

Position error curves of this form were used in the past on AFFTC pace aircraft. A pace aircraft may be fitted with a computer system that automatically applies instrument and position corrections to the indicated values before displaying them to the crew. These values are H_{pc} and V_{pc}. If using a system like this, skip forward to "Correct cockpit readings for instrument errors."

The polynomial above assumes that the altitude position error is only a function of Mach number and temperature ratio. This assumes that the pace aircraft is at a sufficiently high airspeed that angle of attack effects are negligible and that the Pitot-static probe is uncompensated.

To calculate the altitude position error from the polynomial above, we first need the instrument corrected Mach number and standard day temperature ratio at the test altitude. We can calculate these from the instrument corrected altitude and instrument corrected airspeed.

The instrument corrected altitude and airspeed are calculated by adding the instrument corrections to the indicated values. From Equations D66 and D67,

$$H_{ic_{pace}} = H_{i_{pace}} + \Delta H_{ic_{pace}}$$

$$H_{ic_{pace}} = 20000 \text{ feet} + (+20 \text{ feet})$$

$$H_{ic_{pace}} = 20020 \text{ feet}$$

$$V_{ic_{pace}} = V_{i_{pace}} + \Delta V_{ic_{pace}}$$

$$V_{ic_{pace}} = 280 \text{ knots} + (-2 \text{ knots})$$

$$V_{ic_{pace}} = 278 \text{ knots}$$

From this we can get our best number for the standard day temperature ratio at the test altitude. If we were really picky, we could iterate after finding H_{pc}, but the difference would most likely be insignificant, i.e. within a foot or two. From Equation A78,

$$\theta_{std_{test alt}} = 1 - 6.87559 \times 10^{-6} \, H_{ic_{pace}}$$

$$\theta_{std_{test alt}} = 1 - 6.87559 \times 10^{-6}/\text{feet} \, (20020 \text{ feet})$$

$$\theta_{std_{test alt}} = 0.8623$$

To calculate instrument corrected Mach number ($M_{ic_{pace}}$), we need the instrument corrected pressure ratio ($\delta_{ic_{pace}}$) and instrument corrected airspeed ($V_{ic_{pace}}$). To calculate $\delta_{ic_{pace}}$ (from Equation A79)

$$\delta_{ic_{pace}} = (1 - 6.87559 \times 10^{-6} \, H_{ic_{pace}})^{5.2559}$$

$$\delta_{ic_{pace}} = (1 - 6.87559 \times 10^{-6}/\text{feet} \, (20020 \text{ feet}))^{5.2559}$$

$$\delta_{ic_{pace}} = 0.4592$$

So Mach number would be calculated by (from Equation C118)

$$M_{ic_{pace}} = \sqrt{5\left[\left(\frac{1}{\delta_{ic_{pace}}}\left\{\left[1+0.2\left(\frac{V_{ic_{pace}}}{a_{SL}}\right)^2\right]^{7/2}-1\right\}+1\right)^{2/7}-1\right]}$$

$$M_{ic_{pace}} = \sqrt{5\left[\left(\frac{1}{0.4592}\left\{\left[1+0.2\left(\frac{278\ knots}{661.48\ knots}\right)^2\right]^{7/2}-1\right\}+1\right)^{2/7}-1\right]}$$

$$M_{ic_{pace}} = 0.6058$$

Now we can calculate the altitude position correction.

$$\Delta H_{pc_{pace}} = (C_0 + C_1 M_{ic_{pace}} + C_2 M_{ic_{pace}}^2 + C_3 M_{ic_{pace}}^3 + C_4 M_{ic_{pace}}^4 + ...)\theta_{std_{test\ alt}}$$

$$\Delta H_{pc_{pace}} = (54\ feet + (-324\ feet)(0.6058) + (850\ feet)(0.6058)^2 + (0\ feet)(0.6058)^3 +$$
$$(0\ feet)(0.6058)^4 + ...)(0.8623)$$

$$\Delta H_{pc_{pace}} = 146\ feet$$

Find the instrument and position corrected ("truth") altitude and airspeed for the pace aircraft

So the instrument and position corrected altitude ("truth" altitude) is (from Equation D69)

$$H_{pc_{pace}} = H_{ic_{pace}} + \Delta H_{pc_{pace}}$$

$$H_{pc_{pace}} = 20020\ feet + (+146\ feet)$$

$$H_{pc_{pace}} = 20166\ feet$$

Note that if we took this altitude and recalculated $\theta_{std_{test\ alt}}$ we would get 0.8613, a difference of 0.1 percent, and would change the altitude position correction to 145.8 feet, or an error of less than a foot for using H_{ic} to calculate $\theta_{std_{test\ alt}}$ instead of iterating on the answer.

To calculate instrument and position corrected airspeed, the airspeed position correction would have to be provided or calculated from ΔH_{pc} assuming zero total pressure error. (From Equation D70)

$$V_{pc_{pace}} = V_{ic_{pace}} + \Delta V_{pc_{pace}}$$

$$V_{pc_{pace}} = 278 \text{ knots} + (+3 \text{ knots})$$

$$V_{pc_{pace}} = 281 \text{ KCAS}$$

Correct test aircraft cockpit readings for instrument errors

The instrument corrected altitude and airspeed are calculated by adding the instrument corrections to the indicated values. (From Equations D66 and D67)

$$H_{ic_{test}} = H_{i_{test}} + \Delta H_{ic_{test}}$$

$$H_{ic_{test}} = 20{,}010 \text{ feet} + (-15 \text{ feet})$$

$$H_{ic_{test}} = 19{,}995 \text{ feet}$$

$$V_{ic_{test}} = V_{i_{test}} + \Delta V_{ic_{test}}$$

$$V_{ic_{test}} = 275 \text{ knots} + (+3 \text{ knots})$$

$$V_{ic_{test}} = 278 \text{ knots}$$

Find the test day altitude and airspeed position corrections

The test day position corrections are the difference between the instrument corrected altitude and the truth pressure altitude. From Equation D5

$$\Delta H_{pc_{test}} = H_{pc_{pace}} - H_{ic_{test}}$$

$$\Delta H_{pc_{test}} = 20{,}166 \text{ feet} - 19{,}995 \text{ feet}$$

$$\Delta H_{pc_{test}} = 171 \text{ feet}$$

This assumes that the static pressure transducers for both aircraft are both at the same altitude. If there is a known difference in altitude, then that difference must be included when calculating $\Delta H_{pc_{test}}$.

From Equation D6

$$\Delta V_{pc_{test}} = V_{pc_{pace}} - V_{ic_{test}}$$

$$\Delta V_{pc_{test}} = 281 \text{ knots} - 278 \text{ knots}$$

$$\Delta V_{pc_{test}} = 3 \text{ knots}$$

Find the Position Error Ratio

The position error ratio can be calculated from the altitude position correction or the airspeed position correction. If the total pressure error is truly negligible, the results from both methods will be the same.

If we choose to start with the altitude position correction, we calculate the static and ambient pressures

$$P_s = P_{SL}(1 - 6.87559 \times 10^{-6} \, H_{ic_{test}})^{5.2559} \qquad (H_{ic_{test}} \leq 36089.24 \text{ feet}) \quad (D8)$$

$$P_s = (2116.22 \text{ lb/ft}^2)(1 - 6.87559 \times 10^{-6} \, (19{,}995 \text{ feet}))^{5.2559}$$

$$P_s = 972.70 \text{ lb/ft}^2$$

$$P_a = P_{SL}(1 - 6.87559 \times 10^{-6} \, H_{pc_{pace}})^{5.2559} \qquad (H_{pc_{pace}} \leq 36089.24 \text{ feet}) \quad (D10)$$

$$P_a = (2116.22 \text{ lb/ft}^2)(1 - 6.87559 \times 10^{-6} \, (20{,}166 \text{ feet}))^{5.2559}$$

$$P_a = 965.75 \text{ lb/ft}^2$$

Then the static port position error ratio is

$$\frac{\Delta P_p}{P_s} = \frac{P_s - P_a}{P_s}$$

$$\frac{\Delta P_p}{P_s} = \frac{972.70 \text{ lb/ft}^2 - 965.75 \text{ lb/ft}^2}{972.70 \text{ lb/ft}^2}$$

$$\frac{\Delta P_p}{P_s} = 0.007145$$

If we choose to start with the airspeed position correction, we calculate the following ratios, From Equation C106

$$\frac{q_c}{P_{SL}} = \left(1 + 0.2\left(\frac{V_{pc_{pace}}}{a_{SL}}\right)^2\right)^{7/2} - 1 \qquad (V_{c_{pace}} < a_{SL})$$

$$\frac{q_c}{P_{SL}} = \left(1 + 0.2\left(\frac{281 \text{ knots}}{661.48 \text{ knots}}\right)^2\right)^{7/2} - 1$$

$$\frac{q_c}{P_{SL}} = 0.13212$$

and from Equation D12

$$\frac{q_{cic}}{P_{SL}} = \left(1 + 0.2\left(\frac{V_{ic_{test}}}{a_{SL}}\right)^2\right)^{7/2} - 1 \qquad (V_{ic} < a_{SL})$$

$$\frac{q_{cic}}{P_{SL}} = \left(1 + 0.2\left(\frac{278 \text{ knots}}{661.48 \text{ knots}}\right)^2\right)^{7/2} - 1$$

$$\frac{q_{cic}}{P_{SL}} = 0.12919$$

Then

$$\Delta P_p = \left(\frac{q_c}{P_{SL}} - \frac{q_{cic}}{P_{SL}}\right)P_{SL} \qquad (D16)$$

$$\Delta P_p = (0.13212 - 0.12919)2116.22 \text{ lb} / \text{ft}^2$$

$$\Delta P_p = 6.2005 \text{ lb/ft}^2$$

$$\frac{\Delta P_p}{P_s} = \frac{6.2005 \text{ lb} / \text{ft}^2}{972.70 \text{ lb} / \text{ft}^2}$$

$$\frac{\Delta P_p}{P_s} = 0.0063745$$

While this value looks much different than the value determined from the altitude position correction, starting with the value determined from the altitude position correction and working backwards gives a $V_{ic_{test}}$ of 277.629 knots, which is only 0.370 knots different. Thus, it would be reasonable to say that this example does not show a significant total pressure error.

Trailing Cone/Bomb Data Reduction

Overview

The trailing cone or trailing bomb FTT is an altitude comparison technique. The truth altitude of the aircraft is determined by sampling the freestream ambient pressure from outside the flow field of the aircraft. To find the altitude position correction (ΔH_{pc}), we will

  a. Correct the trailing cone readings for instrument and position errors
  b. Correct cockpit readings for instrument errors
  c. Find the altitude position correction
  d. Find the static port position error ratio ($\Delta P_p/P_s$)

For purposes of this discussion, we will use the following example data:

Trailing Cone Altitude ($H_{i_{cone}}$)	10020 feet
Trailing Cone Altimeter Instrument Correction ($\Delta H_{ic_{cone}}$)	+25 feet
Trailing Cone Position Correction ($\Delta H_{pc_{cone}}$)	+0 feet
Altimeter Instrument Correction (ΔH_{ic})	+15 feet
Airspeed Instrument Correction (ΔV_{ic})	-2.5 knots
Indicated Altitude (H_i)	10000 feet
Indicated Airspeed (V_i)	425 knots

Correct the trailing cone readings for instrument and position errors

The truth pressure altitude is calculated by adding the instrument and position corrections to the indicated values. From Equations D66 and D69,

$$H_c = H_{i_{cone}} + \Delta H_{ic_{cone}} + \Delta H_{pc_{cone}}$$

$$H_c = 10020 \text{ feet} + (+25 \text{ feet}) + (+0 \text{ feet})$$

$$H_c = 10045 \text{ feet}$$

Correct cockpit readings for instrument errors

The instrument corrected altitude and airspeed are calculated by adding the instrument corrections to the indicated values.

$$H_{ic} = H_i + \Delta H_{ic} \qquad\qquad \text{(D66)}$$

$$H_{ic} = 10000 \text{ feet} + (+15 \text{ feet})$$

$$H_{ic} = 10015 \text{ feet}$$

$$V_{ic} = V_i + \Delta V_{ic} \qquad\qquad \text{(D67)}$$

$$V_{ic} = 425 \text{ knots} + (-2.5 \text{ knots})$$

$$V_{ic} = 422.5 \text{ knots}$$

Find the altitude position correction

The altitude position correction is the difference between the instrument corrected altitude and the truth pressure altitude.

$$\Delta H_{pc} = H_c - H_{ic} \qquad (D5)$$

$$\Delta H_{pc} = 10045 \text{ feet} - 10015 \text{ feet}$$

$$\Delta H_{pc} = 30 \text{ feet}$$

This assumes that the static pressure transducers for the aircraft and the trailing cone are both at the same altitude. If there is a known difference in altitude, then that difference must be included when calculating ΔH_{pc}.

Find the static port position error ratio ($\Delta P_p/P_s$)

The Position Error is the error in reading the ambient pressure (difference between static and ambient pressure), or ΔP_p, defined as

$$\Delta P_p = P_s - P_a \qquad (D1)$$

Therefore, we calculate the static and ambient pressures

$$P_s = P_{SL}(1 - 6.87559 \times 10^{-6} H_{ic})^{5.2559} \qquad (H_{ic} \leq 36089.24 \text{ feet}) \ (D8)$$

$$P_s = (2116.22 \text{ lb/ft}^2)(1 - 6.87559 \times 10^{-6} (10015 \text{ feet}))^{5.2559}$$

$$P_s = 1454.48 \text{ lb/ft}^2$$

$$P_a = P_{SL}(1 - 6.87559 \times 10^{-6} H_c)^{5.2559} \qquad (H_c \leq 36089.24 \text{ feet}) \ (D10)$$

$$P_a = (2116.22 \text{ lb/ft}^2)(1 - 6.87559 \times 10^{-6} (10045 \text{ feet}))^{5.2559}$$

$$P_a = 1452.79 \text{ lb/ft}^2$$

Then the position error ratio is

$$\frac{\Delta P_p}{P_s} = \frac{P_s - P_a}{P_s}$$

$$\frac{\Delta P_p}{P_s} = \frac{1454.48 \text{ lb/ft}^2 - 1452.79 \text{ lb/ft}^2}{1454.48 \text{ lb/ft}^2}$$

$$\frac{\Delta P_p}{P_s} = 0.0011619$$

Alternatively, if the trailing cone is connected to one side of a differential pressure sensor with the aircraft static system connected to the other side, then the sensor would read ΔP_p directly. For this example, it would read

$$\Delta P_p = 1.69 \text{ lb/ft}^2$$

To calculate the position error ratio, simply divide by the static pressure.

$$\frac{\Delta P_p}{P_s} = \frac{1.69 \text{ lb} / \text{ft}^2}{1454.48 \text{ lb} / \text{ft}^2}$$

$$\frac{\Delta P_p}{P_s} = 0.0011619$$

Survey Data Reduction

Overview

The survey FTT is an altitude comparison technique. The truth altitude of the aircraft is determined by comparing its geometric altitude to a pressure altitude map generated by a weather balloon or by the same or another aircraft. To find the altitude position correction (ΔH_{pc}), we will

     a. Determine the tapeline (geometric) altitude of the test aircraft
     b. Find the truth pressure altitude of the test aircraft
     c. Correct cockpit readings for instrument errors
     d. Find the altitude position correction
     e. Find the static port position error ratio ($\Delta P_p/P_s$)

Determine the tapeline (geometric) altitude of the test aircraft

For purposes of this discussion, we will use the following example data for the test aircraft:

Indicated Altitude ($H_{i_{test}}$)	19970 feet
Indicated Airspeed ($V_{i_{test}}$)	425 knots
Time	16:04:52
Altimeter Instrument Correction ($\Delta H_{ic_{test}}$)	-15 feet
Airspeed Instrument Correction ($\Delta V_{ic_{test}}$)	-2.5 knots

At the time 16:04:52, the TSPI data (radar or GPS) give a location of the aircraft and a tapeline altitude of

Tapeline Altitude (h_{test})	25132 feet

Find the truth pressure altitude of the test aircraft

Our method for finding the truth pressure altitude of the test aircraft depends on how the pressure altitude map was measured.

Weather Balloon

Weather balloon data will come with many columns of information, but the only two that we need for this analysis are the pressure and geometric altitude. For this example, assume we have these data

Pressure (mBar)	Geometric Altitude (feet)
463.4	25273
468.0	25011

Yes, those weather guessers love their millibars. That's great, but we need pressure altitude. All we need to know is that sea level pressure is 1013.25 millibars. Then we can find the pressure altitude

$$\delta = \frac{P}{P_{SL}} \tag{A70}$$

$$\delta = \frac{463.4 \text{ mBar}}{1013.25 \text{ mBar}}$$

$$\delta = 0.45734$$

$$H_c = \frac{1 - \sqrt[5.2559]{\delta}}{6.87559 \times 10^{-6}} \qquad (H_c \leq 36089.24 \text{ feet}) \quad (B3)$$

$$H_c = \frac{1 - \sqrt[5.2559]{0.45734}}{6.87559 \times 10^{-6}}$$

$$H_c = 20115 \text{ feet}$$

So our table of data would now read

Pressure (mBar)	Pressure Altitude (feet)	Geometric Altitude (feet)
463.4	20114	25273
468.0	19879	25011

To find the truth pressure altitude, we simply interpolate these data at the test aircraft geometric altitude (h_{test}) of 25132 feet

$$H_{c\,test} = \frac{(25132 - 25011)}{(25273 - 25011)}(20114 - 19879) + 19879$$

$$H_{c_{test}} = 19987 \text{ feet}$$

Calibrated Aircraft – Single Pass

To find the truth pressure altitude at a particular test aircraft airspeed, we want to consult the pressure altitude map at the positions closest to where the test aircraft was at that airspeed as it accelerated through the measurement corridor. To determine this location, find the test aircraft location (latitude, longitude) at the desired airspeed. Calculate the distance from this location to each location recorded by the calibrated aircraft. As shown in Appendix F, this distance between points calculated by

$$\cos (\text{Distance Angle}_{1-2}) = \sin (\text{Lat}_2) \sin (\text{Lat}_1) + \cos (\text{Lat}_2) \cos (\text{Lat}_1) \cos (\text{Long}_2 - \text{Long}_1) \tag{F7}$$

$$\text{Distance}_{1-2} = \frac{\text{Distance Angle}_{1-2}}{360 \text{ deg}} * 21600 \text{ nm} \tag{F8}$$

Equation F8 assumes the Distance Angle$_{1-2}$ is expressed in degrees. If this angle is calculated in radians (as many computer programs do) substitute "2π" for "360 deg" in the denominator.

Find the location that was at the minimum distance from the test aircraft location. For this example, assume these were your results.

Tapeline Altitude (h_{cal})	25202 feet
Time	15:59:32

Consulting the data recorded onboard the calibrated aircraft at 15:59:32

Indicated Altitude ($H_{i_{cal}}$)	20020 feet
Indicated Airspeed ($V_{i_{cal}}$)	300 knots
Indicated Temperature (T_i)	25 °C
Altimeter Instrument Correction ($\Delta H_{ic_{cal}}$)	-10 feet
Altimeter Position Correction ($\Delta H_{pc_{cal}}$)	+40 feet
Airspeed Instrument Correction ($\Delta V_{ic_{cal}}$)	-1.5 knots
Airspeed Position Correction ($\Delta V_{pc_{cal}}$)	+1 knots
Temperature Instrument Correction (ΔT_{ic})	+1 °C
Temperature Recovery Factor (K_t)	0.98

The difference in geometric (tapeline) altitude would be

$$\Delta h = h_{cal} - h_{test}$$

$$\Delta h = 25202 \text{ feet} - 25132 \text{ feet}$$

$$\Delta h = 70 \text{ feet}$$

For the calibrated aircraft, the instrument and position corrected altitude and airspeed are calculated by adding the instrument and position corrections to the indicated values. From Equations D66 and D69

$$H_{pc_{cal}} = H_{i_{cal}} + \Delta H_{ic_{cal}} + \Delta H_{pc_{cal}}$$

$$H_{pc_{cal}} = 20020 \text{ feet} + (-10 \text{ feet}) + (+40 \text{ feet})$$

$$H_{pc_{cal}} = 20050 \text{ feet}$$

and from Equations D67 and D70

$$V_{pc_{cal}} = V_{i_{cal}} + \Delta V_{ic_{cal}} + \Delta V_{pc_{cal}}$$

$$V_{pc_{cal}} = 300 \text{ knots} + (-1.5 \text{ knots}) + (+1 \text{ knot})$$

$$V_{pc_{cal}} = 299.5 \text{ knots}$$

To determine the temperature at the test altitude, we need the Mach number of the calibrated aircraft. From Equation A79

$$\delta = (1 - 6.87559 \times 10^{-6} \, H_{pc_{cal}})^{5.2559}$$

$$\delta = (1 - 6.87559 \times 10^{-6}/\text{feet} \, (20050 \text{ feet}))^{5.2559}$$

$$\delta = 0.45858$$

From Equation C118

$$M = \sqrt{5\left[\left(\frac{1}{\delta}\left\{\left[1+0.2\left(\frac{V_{pc_{cal}}}{a_{SL}}\right)^2\right]^{7/2}-1\right\}+1\right)^{2/7}-1\right]}$$

$$M = \sqrt{5\left[\left(\frac{1}{0.45858}\left\{\left[1+0.2\left(\frac{299.5 \text{ knots}}{661.48 \text{ knots}}\right)^2\right]^{7/2}-1\right\}+1\right)^{2/7}-1\right]}$$

$$M = .6509$$

To convert the tapeline altitude difference to a pressure altitude difference, we need to know the standard temperature and the ambient temperature at the test altitude.

For the standard temperature (from Equations A69 and A78)

$$T_{std} = (1 - 6.87559 \times 10^{-6} \, H_{pc_{cal}})T_{SL}$$

$$T_{std} = (1 - 6.87559 \times 10^{-6}/\text{feet} \, (20050 \text{ feet}))(288.15 \text{ K})$$

$$T_{std} = 248.42 \text{ K}$$

For the test temperature (from Equations C185 and C187)

$$T_a = \frac{T_i + \Delta T_{ic}}{1 + 0.2 K_t M^2}$$

$$T_a = \frac{25 + 1 + 273.15}{1 + 0.2(0.98)(0.6509)^2}$$

$$T_a = 276.21 \text{ K}$$

To convert the difference in tapeline altitude to a difference in pressure altitude (from Equation B23)

$$\Delta H_c = \frac{T_{std}}{T_a} \Delta h$$

$$\Delta H_c = \frac{248.42 \text{ K}}{276.25 \text{ K}} \left(70 \text{ feet}\right)$$

$$\Delta H_c = 62.9 \text{ feet}$$

The truth pressure altitude for the test aircraft can be found by subtracting the difference in pressure altitude from the pressure altitude of the calibrated aircraft.

$$H_{c_{test}} = H_{pc_{cal}} - \Delta H_c$$

$$H_{c_{test}} = 20050 \text{ feet} - 62.9 \text{ feet}$$

$$H_{c_{test}} = 19987 \text{ feet}$$

Calibrated Aircraft – Pass Above and Below Test Altitude

If pressure altitude map data were recorded above and below the test altitude, a linear regression model of pressure altitude can be calculated in terms of geometric altitude and position (or distance down track). This can be done in Excel, Matlab, or many other math packages. If pressure altitude map data were recorded above and below the test altitude, both before and after the test run, then the regression model could also be calculated in terms of time, though time will probably not be a strong factor if consideration was given to testing in stable weather conditions.

Alternatively, a table similar to the type used in the weather balloon analysis of pressure altitude and geometric altitude can be determined for each airspeed of the test aircraft. Using the latitude and longitude of the test aircraft at each airspeed of interest, use the method described above to find the closest point of the survey passes and their geometric and pressure altitudes. With these data, interpolate with the test aircraft geometric altitude to find the truth pressure altitude as described in the weather balloon section.

For less calculation, simply build a table of geometric versus pressure altitude for one location on the survey passes and use it for all test aircraft airspeeds. This will result in the same uncertainty with regards to location as in the weather balloon method.

Correct cockpit readings for instrument errors

For the test aircraft, the instrument corrected altitude and airspeed are calculated by adding the instrument corrections to the indicated values. From Equation D66

$$H_{ic_{test}} = H_{i_{test}} + \Delta H_{ic_{test}}$$

$$H_{ic_{test}} = 19970 \text{ feet} + (-15 \text{ feet})$$

$$H_{ic_{test}} = 19955 \text{ feet}$$

and from Equation D67

$$V_{ic_{test}} = V_{i_{test}} + \Delta V_{ic_{test}}$$

$$V_{ic_{test}} = 425 \text{ knots} + (-2.5 \text{ knots})$$

$$V_{ic_{test}} = 422.5 \text{ knots}$$

Find the altitude position correction

The altitude position correction is the difference between the instrument corrected altitude and the truth pressure altitude. From Equation D5

$$\Delta H_{pc_{test}} = H_{c_{test}} - H_{ic_{test}}$$

$$\Delta H_{pc_{test}} = 19987 \text{ feet} - 19955 \text{ feet}$$

$$\Delta H_{pc_{test}} = 32 \text{ feet}$$

Find the static port position error ratio ($\Delta P_p/P_s$)

The Position Error is the error in reading the ambient pressure (difference between static and ambient pressure), or ΔP_p, defined as

$$\Delta P_p = P_s - P_a \tag{D1}$$

Therefore, we calculate the static and ambient pressures

$$P_s = P_{SL}(1 - 6.87559\text{x}10^{-6}\ H_{ic_{test}})^{5.2559} \qquad (H_{ic} \leq 36089.24 \text{ feet}) \tag{D8}$$

$$P_s = (2116.22 \text{ lb/ft}^2)(1 - 6.87559\text{x}10^{-6}\ (19955 \text{ feet}))^{5.2559}$$

$$P_s = 974.33 \text{ lb/ft}^2$$

$$P_a = P_{SL}(1 - 6.87559\text{x}10^{-6}\ H_{c_{test}})^{5.2559} \qquad (H_c \leq 36089.24 \text{ feet}) \tag{D10}$$

$$P_a = (2116.22 \text{ lb/ft}^2)(1 - 6.87559\text{x}10^{-6}\ (19987 \text{ feet}))^{5.2559}$$

$$P_a = 973.02 \text{ lb/ft}^2$$

Then the position error ratio is

$$\frac{\Delta P_p}{P_s} = \frac{P_s - P_a}{P_s}$$

$$\frac{\Delta P_p}{P_s} = \frac{974.33 \text{ lb}/\text{ft}^2 - 973.02 \text{ lb}/\text{ft}^2}{974.33 \text{ lb}/\text{ft}^2}$$

$$\frac{\Delta P_p}{P_s} = 0.0013445$$

Speed Course Data Reduction

Overview

The speed course FTT is an airspeed comparison technique. The truth airspeed of the aircraft is determined from measurements of ground speed, and then compared to the airspeed read in the cockpit or on a DAS. Even though we refer to it as an airspeed comparison technique, the best way to reduce the data is to find the Mach position correction (ΔM_{pc}), because it does not have the altitude dependence that airspeed does. The basic process is

- a. Find the truth true airspeed
- b. Find the truth Mach number
- c. Correct cockpit readings for instrument errors
- d. Find the indicated Mach number
- e. Find the Mach position correction

If we assume the total pressure error is zero, we can

- f. Find the position error ratio ($\Delta P_p/P_s$)

For purposes of this discussion, we will use the following example data:

First Leg

Indicated Airspeed (V_i)	110 knots
Indicated Altitude (H_i)	2450 feet
Indicated Temperature (T_i)	15 °C
Time (t_1)	02:02.0
Distance (D_1)	5 sm

Second Leg

Indicated Airspeed (V_i)	110 knots
Indicated Altitude (H_i)	2400 feet
Indicated Temperature (T_i)	15 °C
Time (t_2)	02:13.0
Distance (D_2)	5 sm
Altimeter Instrument Correction (ΔH_{ic})	-20 feet
Airspeed Instrument Correction (ΔV_{ic})	+2 knots
Temperature Instrument Correction (ΔT_{ic})	-1°C (-1 K)
Temperature Recovery Factor (K_t)	0.8

Find the truth true airspeed

If we assume that wind direction and wind speed along the course are constant and the same for the runs in both directions, and that the indicated airspeed and indicated altitude are the same for both runs, then the true airspeed is the same for both runs and is equal to the average ground speed for both runs.

So why do we make a big deal about doing the speed course in low winds and perpendicular to the wind? It's that first assumption—that the wind is constant. Most of the time winds will be gusty to some extent and these gradients cannot be accounted for in the data reduction. By doing the speed course in low winds and perpendicular winds, the effects of these gusts are minimized.

So the Average Ground Speed and thus True Airspeed is given by

$$V_t = V_g = \frac{1}{2}\left(\frac{D_1}{t_1} + \frac{D_2}{t_2}\right)$$

$$V_t = \frac{1}{2}\left(\frac{5\,\text{sm}}{122\,\text{sec}} + \frac{5\,\text{sm}}{133\,\text{sec}}\right)\frac{3600\,\text{sec}}{\text{hr}}\frac{5280\,\text{ft}}{\text{sm}}\frac{\text{nm}}{6076\,\text{ft}}$$

$$V_t = 122.9 \text{ knots}$$

While not required for our data reduction, the headwind component can be calculated as a measure of data quality. Headwind is given by

$$\text{Headwind} = \frac{1}{2}\left|\frac{D_1}{t_1} - \frac{D_2}{t_2}\right|$$

$$\text{Headwind} = \frac{1}{2}\left|\frac{5\,\text{sm}}{122\,\text{sec}} - \frac{5\,\text{sm}}{133\,\text{sec}}\right|\frac{3600\,\text{sec}}{\text{hr}}\frac{5280\,\text{ft}}{\text{sm}}\frac{\text{nm}}{6076\,\text{ft}}$$

$$\text{Headwind} = 5.3 \text{ knots}$$

Find the truth Mach number

We can find the truth Mach number from the truth true airspeed, but we will need to know the local speed of sound at the test conditions. To find the local speed of sound, we need to know the temperature. Yes, we measured the temperature, but the indicated temperature needs to be corrected to ambient before we can use it.

Normally we correct for total temperature rise using Mach number, but that would be tough in this case because we're trying to determine the Mach number. There is an alternative method using true airspeed, which requires knowing the value of C_p for air. Various values for C_p are

$$C_p = 1005\frac{\text{m}^2}{\text{sec}^2\,\text{K}} = 3796\frac{\text{knots}^2}{\text{K}} = 5027\frac{\text{mph}^2}{\text{K}} = 10814\frac{\text{ft}^2}{\text{sec}^2\,\text{K}} = 0.24\frac{\text{BTU}}{\text{lbm}\,°\text{R}} = 186.72\frac{\text{ft lbf}}{\text{lbm}\,°\text{R}}$$

The ambient temperature is then given by (from Equations C185 and C191)

$$T_a = T_i + \Delta T_{ic} - \frac{K_t V_t^2}{2C_p}$$

$$T_a = (15°\text{C}) + (-1°\text{C}) - \frac{(0.8)(122.9 \text{ knots})^2}{2\left(3796\,\dfrac{\text{knots}^2}{\text{K}}\right)} + 273.15$$

$$T_a = 12.4 °\text{C} = 285.6 \text{ K}$$

The test temperature ratio is given by (from Equation A69)

$$\theta_{test} = \frac{T_a}{T_{sl}}$$

$$\theta_{test} = \frac{285.6 \text{ K}}{288.15 \text{ K}}$$

$$\theta_{test} = 0.9910$$

Now we can find the Mach number (from Equation C75)

$$M = \frac{V_t}{a_{SL}\sqrt{\theta_{test}}}$$

$$M = \frac{122.9 \text{ knots}}{661.48 \text{ knots}\sqrt{0.9910}}$$

$$M = 0.1866$$

Correct cockpit readings for instrument errors

The instrument corrected altitude and airspeed are calculated by adding the instrument corrections to the indicated values. If the indicated values of airspeed or altitude are not identical between runs, about the best that we can do is to average the two values.

$$H_{ic} = H_i + \Delta H_{ic} \tag{D66}$$

$$H_{ic} = 2425 \text{ feet} + (-20 \text{ feet})$$

$$H_{ic} = 2405 \text{ feet}$$

$$V_{ic} = V_i + \Delta V_{ic} \tag{D67}$$

$$V_{ic} = 110 \text{ knots} + (+2 \text{ knots})$$

$$V_{ic} = 112 \text{ knots}$$

Find the indicated Mach number

So our next step is to determine the indicated Mach number at the test conditions. We could jump straight to the Mach meter equation with calibrated airspeed and pressure altitude, but since we will need q_{cic}/P_{SL} later, we'll calculate that first. This is the value in the middle of the calibrated airspeed equation.

$$\frac{q_{cic}}{P_{SL}} = \left(1 + 0.2\left(\frac{V_{ic}}{a_{SL}}\right)^2\right)^{7/2} - 1 \qquad (V_{ic} < a_{SL}) \quad (D12)$$

$$\frac{q_{cic}}{P_{SL}} = \left(1 + 0.2\left(\frac{112 \text{ knots}}{661.48 \text{ knots}}\right)^2\right)^{3.5} - 1$$

$$\frac{q_{cic}}{P_{SL}} = 0.02021$$

Note that because this value was calculated using V_{ic}, this is the pressure ratio seen at the airspeed indicator, and thus contains the position error. This is why the value is q_{cic}/P_{SL} and not q_c/P_{SL}.

To find the Mach number we will need q_{cic}/P_s, and to find that we need q_{cic}/P_{SL} and δ_{ic}. We'll find δ_{ic} (which also contains the position error) seen by the altimeter from the instrument corrected altitude, H_{ic}. From Equation A79

$$\delta_{ic} = (1 - 6.87559 \times 10^{-6} \, H_{ic})^{5.2559}$$

$$\delta_{ic} = (1 - 6.87559 \times 10^{-6}/\text{feet} \, (2405 \text{ feet}))^{5.2559}$$

$$\delta_{ic} = 0.9161$$

We can now find q_{cic}/P_s

$$\frac{q_{cic}}{P_s} = \frac{q_{cic}}{P_{SL}} \frac{P_{SL}}{P_s} = \frac{q_{cic}}{P_{SL}} \frac{1}{\delta_{ic}}$$

$$\frac{q_{cic}}{P_s} = (0.02021)\frac{1}{0.9161}$$

$$\frac{q_{cic}}{P_s} = 0.02206$$

This is the number we find in the middle of the true airspeed and Mach equations. Now we can find the instrument corrected Mach number, M_{ic}, which is what a perfect Mach meter in the cockpit would have read. Note that because this Mach is calculated using numbers that contain the position error, it too contains the position error.

$$M_{ic} = \sqrt{5\left[\left(\frac{q_{cic}}{P_s} + 1\right)^{2/7} - 1\right]} \qquad \text{(D49)}$$

$$M_{ic} = \sqrt{5\left[(0.02206 + 1)^{2/7} - 1\right]}$$

$$M_{ic} = 0.1768$$

Find the Mach position correction

Now that we know the truth Mach number and the indicated Mach number, the Mach position correction can be found simply by subtracting.

$$\Delta M_{pc} = M - M_{ic} \tag{D7}$$

$$\Delta M_{pc} = 0.1866 - 0.1768$$

$$\Delta M_{pc} = 0.0098$$

Find the static port position error ratio ($\Delta P_p/P_s$)

From the truth Mach number, we calculate the ratio P_T/P_a

$$\frac{P_T}{P_a} = \left(1 + 0.2M^2\right)^{7/2} \qquad (M < 1) \quad (D17)$$

$$\frac{P_T}{P_a} = \left(1 + 0.2(0.1866)^2\right)^{7/2}$$

$$\frac{P_T}{P_a} = 1.02459$$

Doing the same for instrument corrected Mach number

$$\frac{P_T}{P_s} = \left(1 + 0.2M_{ic}^2\right)^{7/2} \qquad (M_{ic} < 1) \quad (D20)$$

$$\frac{P_T}{P_s} = \left(1 + 0.2(0.1768)^2\right)^{7/2}$$

$$\frac{P_T}{P_s} = 1.02205$$

The position error ratio can then be calculated directly from these ratios by

$$\frac{\Delta P_p}{P_s} = \left(\frac{1}{\dfrac{P_T}{P_s}} - \frac{1}{\dfrac{P_T}{P_a}}\right)\frac{P_T}{P_s} \tag{D23}$$

$$\frac{\Delta P_p}{P_s} = \left(\frac{1}{1.02205} - \frac{1}{1.02459}\right)1.02205$$

$$\frac{\Delta P_p}{P_s} = 0.0024790$$

All Altitude Speed Course Data Reduction

Overview

The All Altitude Speed Course FTT is an airspeed comparison technique. The truth airspeed of the aircraft is determined from measurements of ground speed and track angle, and then compared to the airspeed read in the cockpit or on a DAS. The basic process is

      a. Find the drift angle
      b. Find the adjusted truth true airspeed
      c. Find the truth Mach number
      d. Correct cockpit readings for instrument errors
      e. Find the indicated Mach number
      f. Find the truth Mach number
      g. Find the Mach position correction

If we assume the total pressure error is zero, we can

      h. Find the position error ratio ($\Delta P_p / P_s$)

For purposes of this discussion, we will use the following example data:

TABLE 9.1
Example Data

Magnetic Heading (deg)	Indicated Airspeed (knots)	GPS Track (deg)	GPS Ground Speed (knots)	Drift Angle (deg)	Ground Speed Component (knots)	Adjusted Ground Speed Component (knots)
First Leg						
185	50	177	69.7	-008	69.0	69.0
185	52	176	72.6	-009	71.7	69.7
185	49	175	69.1	-010	68.0	69.0
185	50	174	69.3	-011	68.0	68.0
185	50	175	70	-010	68.9	68.9
181	51	172	72.4	-009	71.5	70.5
180	51	172	71.6	-008	70.9	69.9
Second Leg						
005	50	020	72.2	015	69.7	69.7
004	50	019	71.3	015	68.8	68.8
006	50	019	71.2	013	69.3	69.3
005	50	020	71.1	015	68.6	68.6
005	50	019	74.1	014	71.8	71.8
004	51	020	73.9	016	71.0	70.0
005	50	020	73.0	015	70.5	70.5
001	51	018	72.4	017	69.2	68.2

First Leg

        Indicated Altitude (H_i)   9020 feet
        Indicated Temperature (T_i)   17.1 °C

Second Leg

        Indicated Altitude (H_i)   8980 feet
        Indicated Temperature (T_i)   17.1 °C

        Altimeter Instrument Correction (ΔH_{ic})   -20 feet
        Airspeed Instrument Correction (ΔV_{ic})   +0 knots
        Temperature Instrument Correction (ΔT_{ic})   -1°C (-1 K)
        Temperature Recovery Factor (K_t)   0.8

Find the drift angle

The drift angle is the difference between the heading and the track.

$$\text{Drift Angle} = \text{GPS Mag Track} - \text{Mag Heading}$$

Results are shown in Table 9.1.

Find the adjusted truth true airspeed

The ground speed component in the heading direction is calculated by

$$V = \text{GPS Ground Speed} * \cos(\text{Drift Angle})$$

Results are shown in Table 9.1.

Eventually we will average the ground speed components in each direction and compare them to the true airspeed derived from the aim airspeed (50 knots in this example). Note, however, that the indicated airspeed varied slightly from the aim airspeed. We will remove some of this error by subtracting a knot from the ground speed component for each knot the indicated airspeed exceeds the aim airspeed. Note that this assumes a change of one knot indicated airspeed is the same size as a knot of ground speed. While not exact, it is very close. The formula is

$$V_{adj} = V + (V_{aim} - V_i)$$

Results are shown in Table 9.1.

Averaging the adjusted ground speed components in the southerly direction gives 69.29 knots. Averaging the adjusted ground speed components in the northerly direction gives 69.61 knots. The average of these two numbers gives the adjusted truth true airspeed.

$$V_t = 69.5 \text{ knots}$$

Correct cockpit readings for instrument errors

The instrument corrected altitude and airspeed are calculated by adding the instrument corrections to the indicated values. If the indicated values of airspeed or altitude are not identical between runs, about the best that we can do is to average the two values.

$$H_{ic} = H_i + \Delta H_{ic} \qquad\qquad (D66)$$

$$H_{ic} = 9020 \text{ feet} + (-20 \text{ feet})$$

$$H_{ic} = 9000 \text{ feet}$$

$$V_{ic} = V_i + \Delta V_{ic} \qquad\qquad (D67)$$

$$V_{ic} = 50 \text{ knots} + (+0 \text{ knots})$$

$$V_{ic} = 50 \text{ knots}$$

Find the indicated Mach number

So our next step is to determine the indicated Mach number at the test conditions. From Equation A79

$$\delta_{ic} = (1 - 6.87559 \times 10^{-6}\, H_{ic})^{5.2559}$$

$$\delta_{ic} = (1 - 6.87559 \times 10^{-6}/\text{feet}\ (9000\ \text{feet}))^{5.2559}$$

$$\delta_{ic} = 0.71481$$

From Equation C118

$$M_{ic} = \sqrt{5\left[\left[\left(\frac{1}{\delta_{ic}}\left\{\left[1+0.2\left(\frac{V_{ic}}{a_{SL}}\right)^2\right]^{7/2}-1\right\}+1\right)^{2/7}-1\right]\right]}$$

$$M_{ic} = \sqrt{5\left[\left[\left(\frac{1}{0.71481}\left\{\left[1+0.2\left(\frac{50\ \text{knots}}{661.48\ \text{knots}}\right)^2\right]^{7/2}-1\right\}+1\right)^{2/7}-1\right]\right]}$$

$$M_{ic} = .08937$$

Find the truth Mach number

We can find the truth Mach number from the truth true airspeed, but we will need to know the local speed of sound at the test conditions. To find the local speed of sound, we need to know the temperature. Now that we know the truth true airspeed, we can use that to find the correct ambient temperature. We will use the alternative method, which requires knowing the value of C_p for air. Various values for C_p are

$$C_p = 1005 \frac{m^2}{sec^2 \, K} = 3796 \frac{knots^2}{K} = 5027 \frac{mph^2}{K} = 10814 \frac{ft^2}{sec^2 \, K} = 0.24 \frac{BTU}{lbm \, °R} = 186.72 \frac{ft \, lbf}{lbm \, °R}$$

The ambient temperature is then given by (from Equations C185 and C191)

$$T_a = T_i + \Delta T_{ic} - \frac{K_t V_t^2}{2C_p}$$

$$T_a = (17.1°C) + (-1°C) - \frac{(0.8)(69.5 \, knots)^2}{2\left(3796 \frac{knots^2}{K}\right)} + 273.15$$

$$T_a = 15.6 \, °C = 288.7 \, K$$

The test temperature ratio is given by (from Equation A69)

$$\theta_{test} = \frac{T_a}{T_{sl}}$$

$$\theta_{test} = \frac{288.7 \, K}{288.15 \, K}$$

$$\theta_{test} = 1.0019$$

Now we can find the truth Mach number (from Equation C75)

$$M = \frac{V_t}{a_{SL} \sqrt{\theta_{test}}}$$

$$M = \frac{69.5 \, knots}{661.48 \, knots \sqrt{1.0019}}$$

$$M = 0.1050$$

Find the Mach position correction

Now that we know the truth Mach number and the indicated Mach number, the Mach position correction can be found simply by subtracting.

$$\Delta M_{pc} = M - M_{ic} \tag{D7}$$

$$\Delta M_{pc} = 0.1050 - 0.08937$$

$$\Delta M_{pc} = 0.0156$$

Find the static port position error ratio ($\Delta P_p/P_s$)

From the truth Mach number, we calculate the ratio P_T/P_a

$$\frac{P_T}{P_a} = \left(1 + 0.2M^2\right)^{7/2} \qquad (M < 1) \tag{D17}$$

$$\frac{P_T}{P_a} = \left(1 + 0.2(0.1050)^2\right)^{7/2}$$

$$\frac{P_T}{P_a} = 1.0077$$

Doing the same for instrument corrected Mach number

$$\frac{P_T}{P_s} = \left(1 + 0.2M_{ic}^2\right)^{7/2} \qquad (M_{ic} < 1) \tag{D20}$$

$$\frac{P_T}{P_s} = \left(1 + 0.2(0.08937)^2\right)^{7/2}$$

$$\frac{P_T}{P_s} = 1.0056$$

The position error can then be calculated directly from these ratios by

$$\frac{\Delta P_p}{P_s} = \left(\frac{1}{\dfrac{P_T}{P_s}} - \frac{1}{\dfrac{P_T}{P_a}} \right) \frac{P_T}{P_s} \tag{D23}$$

$$\frac{\Delta P_p}{P_s} = \left(\frac{1}{1.0056} - \frac{1}{1.0077} \right) 1.0056$$

$$\frac{\Delta P_p}{P_s} = 0.0020840$$

Horseshoe GPS Data Reduction

Overview

The Horseshoe GPS FTT is an airspeed comparison technique. The truth airspeed of the aircraft is determined from measurements of ground speed on three orthogonal headings, and then compared to the airspeed read in the cockpit or on a DAS. **Note that the data reduction method presented here assumes left turns between legs.** The basic process is

- a. Find the wind direction
- b. Find the wind speed
- c. Find the true airspeed
- d. Correct cockpit readings for instrument errors
- e. Find the indicated Mach number
- f. Find the truth Mach number
- g. Find the Mach position correction

If we assume the total pressure error is zero, we can

- h. Find the position error ratio ($\Delta P_p/P_s$)

For purposes of this discussion, we will use the following example data:

First Leg

Indicated Airspeed (V_i)	175 knots
Indicated Altitude (H_i)	15000 feet
Indicated Temperature (T_i)	-15 °C
GPS Ground Speed	207.0 knots
Heading	40°

Second Leg

Indicated Airspeed (V_i)	175 knots
Indicated Altitude (H_i)	15000 feet
Indicated Temperature (T_i)	-15 °C
GPS Ground Speed	220.0 knots

Third Leg

Indicated Airspeed (V_i)	175 knots
Indicated Altitude (H_i)	15000 feet
Indicated Temperature (T_i)	-15 °C
GPS Ground Speed	226.0 knots

Altimeter Instrument Correction (ΔH_{ic})	-20 feet
Airspeed Instrument Correction (ΔV_{ic})	+2 knots
Temperature Instrument Correction (ΔT_{ic})	-1°C (-1 K)
Temperature Recovery Factor	0.95

Find the wind direction

The wind direction relative to the heading of the first leg is given by

$$\psi_{rel} = \tan^{-1}\left(\frac{-V_{g1}^2 + 2V_{g2}^2 - V_{g3}^2}{V_{g3}^2 - V_{g1}^2}\right)$$

$$\psi_{rel} = \tan^{-1}\left(\frac{-(207.0)^2 + 2(220.0)^2 - (226.0)^2}{(226.0)^2 - (207.0)^2}\right)$$

$$\psi_{rel} = 19.26°$$

To get the wind direction relative to North, add the initial heading

$$\psi = \psi_{rel} + \text{Leg 1 Heading}$$

$$\psi = 19.26° + 40°$$

$$\psi = 59.26°$$

Find the wind speed

The wind speed is given by the following equation. The plus or minus is selected so as to give a positive quantity within the outermost parentheses. It may be necessary to try both plus and minus and select the most reasonable answer.

$$V_w = \frac{1}{2}\left(V_{g3}^2 + V_{g1}^2 \pm \sqrt{\left(V_{g3}^2 + V_{g1}^2\right)^2 - \left(\frac{-V_{g1}^2 + 2V_{g2}^2 - V_{g3}^2}{\sin\psi_{rel}}\right)^2}\right)^{1/2}$$

$$V_w = \frac{1}{2}\left((226.0)^2 + (207.0)^2 - \sqrt{\left((226.0)^2 + (207.0)^2\right)^2 - \left(\frac{-(207.0)^2 + 2(220.0)^2 - (226.0)^2}{\sin(19.26°)}\right)^2}\right)^{1/2}$$

$$V_w = 10.07 \text{ knots}$$

Find the truth true airspeed

The truth true airspeed is given by

$$V_t = \sqrt{\frac{V_{g3}^2 + V_{g1}^2}{2} - V_w^2}$$

$$V_t = \sqrt{\frac{(226.0)^2 + (207.0)^2}{2} - (10.07)^2}$$

$$V_t = 216.5 \text{ knots}$$

Correct cockpit readings for instrument errors

The instrument corrected altitude and airspeed are calculated by adding the instrument corrections to the indicated values. If the indicated values of airspeed or altitude are not identical between runs, about the best that we can do is to average the three values.

$$H_{ic} = H_i + \Delta H_{ic} \tag{D66}$$

$$H_{ic} = 15000 \text{ feet} + (-20 \text{ feet})$$

$$H_{ic} = 14980 \text{ feet}$$

$$V_{ic} = V_i + \Delta V_{ic} \tag{D67}$$

$$V_{ic} = 175 \text{ knots} + (+2 \text{ knots})$$

$$V_{ic} = 177 \text{ knots}$$

Find the indicated Mach number

So our next step is to determine the indicated Mach number at the test conditions. From Equation A79

$$\delta_{ic} = (1 - 6.87559 \times 10^{-6} \, H_{ic})^{5.2559}$$

$$\delta_{ic} = (1 - 6.87559 \times 10^{-6}/\text{feet} \, (14980 \text{ feet}))^{5.2559}$$

$$\delta_{ic} = 0.56480$$

From Equation C118

$$M_{ic} = \sqrt{5\left[\left[\left(\frac{1}{\delta_{ic}}\left\{\left[1+0.2\left(\frac{V_{ic}}{a_{SL}}\right)^2\right]^{7/2}-1\right\}+1\right)^{2/7}-1\right]\right]}$$

$$M_{ic} = \sqrt{5\left[\left[\left(\frac{1}{0.56480}\left\{\left[1+0.2\left(\frac{177\text{ knots}}{661.48\text{ knots}}\right)^2\right]^{7/2}-1\right\}+1\right)^{2/7}-1\right]\right]}$$

$$M_{ic} = 0.35369$$

Find the truth Mach number

We can find the truth Mach number from the truth true airspeed, but we will need to know the local speed of sound at the test conditions. To find the local speed of sound, we need to know the temperature. Now that we know the truth true airspeed, we can use that to find the correct ambient temperature. We will use the alternative method, which requires knowing the value of C_p for air. Various values for C_p are

$$C_p = 1005\frac{m^2}{\sec^2 K} = 3796\frac{\text{knots}^2}{K} = 5027\frac{\text{mph}^2}{K} = 10814\frac{\text{ft}^2}{\sec^2 K} = 0.24\frac{\text{BTU}}{\text{lbm }^\circ R} = 186.72\frac{\text{ft lbf}}{\text{lbm }^\circ R}$$

The ambient temperature is then given by (from Equations C185 and C191)

$$T_a = T_i + \Delta T_{ic} - \frac{K_t V_t^2}{2C_p}$$

$$T_a = (-15^\circ C) + (-1^\circ C) - \frac{(0.95)(216.5\text{ knots})^2}{2\left(3796\frac{\text{knots}^2}{K}\right)} + 273.15$$

$$T_a = -21.9\ ^\circ C = 251.3\ K$$

The test temperature ratio is given by (from Equation A69)

$$\theta_{test} = \frac{T_a}{T_{SL}}$$

$$\theta_{test} = \frac{251.3\ K}{288.15\ K}$$

$$\theta_{test} = 0.87212$$

Now we can find the truth Mach number (from Equation C75)

$$M = \frac{V_t}{a_{SL}\sqrt{\theta_{test}}}$$

$$M = \frac{216.5 \text{ knots}}{661.48 \text{ knots}\sqrt{0.87212}}$$

$$M = 0.35047$$

Find the Mach position correction

Now that we know the truth Mach number and the indicated Mach number, the Mach position correction can be found simply by subtracting.

$$\Delta M_{pc} = M - M_{ic} \tag{D7}$$

$$\Delta M_{pc} = 0.35047 - 0.35369$$

$$\Delta M_{pc} = -0.00322$$

Find the static port position error ratio ($\Delta P_p/P_s$)

From the truth Mach number, we calculate the ratio P_T/P_a

$$\frac{P_T}{P_a} = \left(1 + 0.2M^2\right)^{7/2} \qquad (M < 1) \quad (D17)$$

$$\frac{P_T}{P_a} = \left(1 + 0.2(0.35047)^2\right)^{7/2}$$

$$\frac{P_T}{P_a} = 1.0887$$

Doing the same for instrument corrected Mach number

$$\frac{P_T}{P_s} = \left(1 + 0.2M_{ic}^2\right)^{7/2} \qquad (M_{ic} < 1) \quad (D20)$$

$$\frac{P_T}{P_s} = \left(1 + 0.2(0.35369)^2\right)^{7/2}$$

$$\frac{P_T}{P_s} = 1.0903$$

The position error can then be calculated directly from these ratios by

$$\frac{\Delta P_p}{P_s} = \left(\frac{1}{\dfrac{P_T}{P_s}} - \frac{1}{\dfrac{P_T}{P_a}}\right)\frac{P_T}{P_s} \tag{D23}$$

$$\frac{\Delta P_p}{P_s} = \left(\frac{1}{1.0903} - \frac{1}{1.0887}\right)1.0903$$

$$\frac{\Delta P_p}{P_s} = -0.0014696$$

Cloverleaf Data Reduction (Vector Method)

Overview

The preferred method for reducing cloverleaf data is to use the matrix inversion method (discussed later). The vector method requires more assumptions, specifically that the true airspeed on each leg must be identical. Variations in true airspeed between legs will lead to errors in the results. The vector method is included here for better understanding of the geometry involved. Three legs of data conceptually lead to three vectors (ground speed). A solution of three equal length vectors (true airspeed) is found which matches the endpoints of the ground speed vectors. The origin of these three vectors defines the wind vector, as shown in Figure 9.2.

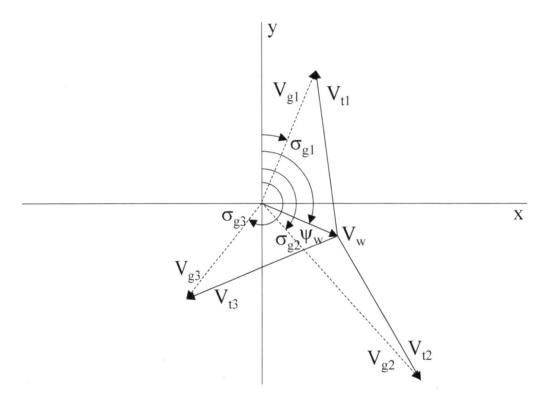

Figure 9.2. Wind triangles for three passes

The cloverleaf FTT is an airspeed comparison technique. The truth airspeed of the aircraft is determined from measurements of ground speed and track angle, and then compared to the airspeed read in the cockpit or on a DAS. The basic process is

  a. Correct cockpit readings for instrument errors
  b. Find the indicated Mach number
  c. Find the truth true airspeed and wind velocity
  d. Find the truth Mach number
  e. Find the Mach position correction

If we assume the total pressure error is zero, we can

  f. Find the position error ratio ($\Delta P_p/P_s$)

For purposes of this discussion, we will use the following example data:

First Leg

Indicated Airspeed (V_i)	130 knots
Indicated Altitude (H_i)	6000 feet
Indicated Temperature (T_i)	11 °C
GPS Ground Speed (V_g)	130.3 knots
GPS Ground Track (σ_g)	7°

Second Leg

Indicated Airspeed (V_i)	130 knots
Indicated Altitude (H_i)	6000 feet
Indicated Temperature (T_i)	11 °C
GPS Ground Speed (V_g)	153.8 knots
GPS Ground Track (σ_g)	114°

Third Leg

Indicated Airspeed (V_i)	130 knots
Indicated Altitude (H_i)	6000 feet
Indicated Temperature (T_i)	11 °C
GPS Ground Speed (V_g)	122.5 knots
GPS Ground Track (σ_g)	234°
Altimeter Instrument Correction (ΔH_{ic})	-20 feet
Airspeed Instrument Correction (ΔV_{ic})	+2 knots
Temperature Instrument Correction (ΔT_{ic})	-1°C (-1 K)
Temperature Recovery Factor (K_t)	1.0

Correct cockpit readings for instrument errors

The vector method assumes the true airspeed on each leg is identical. If the indicated values of airspeed or altitude are not identical between runs, about the best that we can do is to average the values.

The instrument corrected altitude, airspeed, and temperature are calculated by adding the instrument corrections to the indicated values.

$$H_{ic} = H_i + \Delta H_{ic} \tag{D66}$$

$$H_{ic} = 6000 \text{ feet} + (-20 \text{ feet})$$

$$H_{ic} = 5980 \text{ feet}$$

$$V_{ic} = V_i + \Delta V_{ic} \tag{D67}$$

$$V_{ic} = 130 \text{ knots} + (+2 \text{ knots})$$

$$V_{ic} = 132 \text{ knots}$$

$$T_{ic} = T_i + \Delta T_{ic} \qquad\qquad (C185)$$

$$T_{ic} = 11\ ^\circ C + (-1\ ^\circ C) + 273.15$$

$$T_{ic} = 283.15\ K$$

Find the indicated Mach number

So our next step is to determine the indicated Mach number at the test conditions. We could jump straight to the Mach meter equation with calibrated airspeed and pressure altitude, but since we will need q_{cic}/P_{SL} later, we'll calculate that first. This is the value in the middle of the calibrated airspeed equation.

$$\frac{q_{cic}}{P_{SL}} = \left(1 + 0.2\left(\frac{V_{ic}}{a_{SL}}\right)^2\right)^{7/2} - 1 \qquad (V_{ic} < a_{SL}) \quad (D12)$$

$$\frac{q_{cic}}{P_{SL}} = \left(1 + 0.2\left(\frac{132\ knots}{661.48\ knots}\right)^2\right)^{3.5} - 1$$

$$\frac{q_{cic}}{P_{SL}} = 0.028153$$

Note that because this value was calculated using V_{ic}, this is the pressure ratio seen at the airspeed indicator, and thus contains the position error. This is why the value is q_{cic}/P_{SL} and not q_c/P_{SL}.

To find the Mach number we will need q_{cic}/P_s, and to find that we need q_{cic}/P_{SL} and δ_{ic}. We'll find δ_{ic} (which also contains the position error) seen by the altimeter from the instrument corrected altitude, H_{ic}. From Equation A79

$$\delta_{ic} = (1 - 6.87559\times10^{-6}\ H_{ic})^{5.2559}$$

$$\delta_{ic} = (1 - 6.87559\times10^{-6}/feet\ (5980\ feet))^{5.2559}$$

$$\delta_{ic} = 0.80198$$

We can now find q_{cic}/P_s

$$\frac{q_{cic}}{P_s} = \frac{q_{cic}}{P_{SL}}\frac{P_{SL}}{P_s} = \frac{q_{cic}}{P_{SL}}\frac{1}{\delta_{ic}}$$

$$\frac{q_{cic}}{P_s} = (0.028153)\frac{1}{0.80198}$$

$$\frac{q_{cic}}{P_s} = 0.035104$$

This is the number we find in the middle of the true airspeed and Mach equations. Now we can find the instrument corrected Mach number, M_{ic}, which is what a perfect Mach meter in the cockpit would have read. Note that because this Mach is calculated using numbers that contain the position error, it too contains the position error.

$$M_{ic} = \sqrt{5\left[\left(\frac{q_{cic}}{P_s}+1\right)^{2/7}-1\right]}$$ (D49)

$$M_{ic} = \sqrt{5\left[(0.035104+1)^{2/7}-1\right]}$$

$$M_{ic} = 0.22256$$

Find the truth true airspeed and wind velocity

This step involves building the solution matrix. First we need to find the components of ground speed. For the first leg

$$V_{gx} = V_g \sin \sigma_g$$ (E1)

$$V_{gx1} = 130.3 \sin 7°$$

$$V_{gx1} = 15.88 \text{ knots}$$

$$V_{gy} = V_g \cos \sigma_g$$ (E2)

$$V_{gy1} = 130.3 \cos 7°$$

$$V_{gy1} = 129.33 \text{ knots}$$

$$V_{gx2} = 140.50 \text{ knots}$$

$$V_{gy2} = -62.56 \text{ knots}$$

$$V_{gx3} = -99.10 \text{ knots}$$

$$V_{gy3} = -72.00 \text{ knots}$$

Next we calculate the slope of the line segment between V_{g1} and V_{g2} and between V_{g1} and V_{g3}

$$\text{Slope} = \frac{V_{gy2} - V_{gy1}}{V_{gx2} - V_{gx1}}$$ (E3)

$$\text{Slope}_{1-2} = \frac{-62.56 - 129.33}{140.50 - 15.88}$$

$$\text{Slope}_{1-2} = -1.5398$$

$$\text{Slope}_{1-3} = 1.7510$$

Next we need the slope of the perpendicular bisector to these two line segments

$$\text{Slope}_{\perp} = -\frac{1}{\text{Slope}} \qquad (E4)$$

$$\text{Slope}_{\perp 1-2} = -\frac{1}{-1.5398}$$

$$\text{Slope}_{\perp 1-2} = 0.6494$$

$$\text{Slope}_{\perp 1-3} = -0.5711$$

The midpoints of the line segments are given by

$$\left(x_{\text{midpoint}}, y_{\text{midpoint}}\right) = \left(\frac{V_{gx1} + V_{gx2}}{2}, \frac{V_{gy1} + V_{gy2}}{2}\right) \qquad (E5)$$

$$\left(x_{\text{midpoint}1-2}, y_{\text{midpoint}1-2}\right) = \left(\frac{15.88 + 140.50}{2}, \frac{129.33 + -62.56}{2}\right)$$

$$(x_{\text{midpoint}1-2}, y_{\text{midpoint}1-2}) = (78.19, 33.385)$$

$$(x_{\text{midpoint}1-3}, y_{\text{midpoint}1-3}) = (-41.61, 28.665)$$

Now we can find the intercepts

$$\text{Intercept}_{\perp} = y_{\text{midpoint}} - \text{Slope}_{\perp}\left(x_{\text{midpoint}}\right) \qquad (E8)$$

$$\text{Intercept}_{\perp 1-2} = 33.385 - 0.6494\,(78.19)$$

$$\text{Intercept}_{\perp 1-2} = -17.39$$

$$\text{Intercept}_{\perp 1-3} = 4.90$$

Next is the component of the wind in the x direction

$$\frac{b_1 - b_2}{m_2 - m_1} = x \qquad (E13)$$

$$V_{wx} = \frac{-17.39 - 4.90}{-0.5711 - 0.6494}$$

$$V_{wx} = 18.26 \text{ knots}$$

This x value for the wind is then inserted in the equation for one of the perpendicular bisectors

$$y = mx + b \tag{E6}$$

$$V_{wy} = 0.6494\,(18.26) - 17.39$$

$$V_{wy} = -5.53 \text{ knots}$$

The true airspeed can then be calculated using

$$V_t = \sqrt{\left(V_{gx1} - V_{wx}\right)^2 + \left(V_{gy1} - V_{wy}\right)^2} \tag{E17}$$

$$V_t = \sqrt{\left(15.88 - 18.26\right)^2 + \left(129.33 - (-5.53)\right)^2}$$

$$V_t = 134.9 \text{ knots}$$

Find the Wind Vector

The wind vector would be found by

$$V_w = \sqrt{V_{wx}^2 + V_{wy}^2} \tag{E14}$$

$$V_w = \sqrt{\left(18.26\right)^2 + \left(-5.53\right)^2}$$

$$V_w = 19.08 \text{ knots}$$

$$\psi = \tan^{-1}\frac{V_{wx}}{V_{wy}} \tag{E15}$$

$$\psi = \tan^{-1}\frac{18.26}{-5.53}$$

$$\psi = 106.9 \text{ deg rees}$$

Two things to note about the calculation of the wind angle. The "y" and "x" coordinate seem to be reversed. This is because compass directions are defined differently than Cartesian coordinates. Rather than being defined counterclockwise from the horizontal (x) axis, directions are defined clockwise from the vertical (north, y) axis. Using the function ATAN2(V_{wy}, V_{wx}) in Excel will return the proper direction in the proper quadrant.

Secondly, this is the direction of the wind vector, i.e. where the wind is blowing to, not from. To match the traditional method of defining wind direction as the "from" direction, simply add 180 degrees to get 286.9 degrees.

Find the truth Mach number

We can find the truth Mach number from the truth true airspeed, but we will need to know the local speed of sound at the test conditions. To find the local speed of sound, we need to know the temperature. Now that we know the truth true airspeed, we can use that to find the correct ambient temperature. We will use the alternative method, which requires knowing the value of C_p for air. Various values for C_p are

$$C_p = 1005 \frac{m^2}{sec^2\,K} = 3796 \frac{knots^2}{K} = 5027 \frac{mph^2}{K} = 10814 \frac{ft^2}{sec^2\,K} = 0.24 \frac{BTU}{lbm\,°R} = 186.72 \frac{ft\,lbf}{lbm\,°R}$$

The ambient temperature is then given by (from Equations C185 and C191)

$$T_a = T_i + \Delta T_{ic} - \frac{K_t V_t^2}{2C_p}$$

$$T_a = (11°C) + (-1°C) - \frac{(1.0)(134.9\ knots)^2}{2\left(3796 \frac{knots^2}{K}\right)} + 273.15$$

$$T_a = 7.6\ °C = 280.7\ K$$

The test temperature ratio is given by (from Equation A69)

$$\theta_{test} = \frac{T_a}{T_{SL}}$$

$$\theta_{test} = \frac{280.7\ K}{288.15\ K}$$

$$\theta_{test} = 0.97415$$

Now we can find the truth Mach number (from Equation C75)

$$M = \frac{V_t}{a_{SL}\sqrt{\theta_{test}}}$$

$$M = \frac{134.9\ knots}{661.48\ knots\sqrt{0.97415}}$$

$$M = 0.2066$$

Find the Mach position correction

Now that we know the truth Mach number and the indicated Mach number, the Mach position correction can be found simply by subtracting.

$$\Delta M_{pc} = M - M_{ic} \tag{D7}$$

$$\Delta M_{pc} = 0.2066 - 0.22256$$

$$\Delta M_{pc} = -0.01596$$

Find the static port position error ratio ($\Delta P_p/P_s$)

From the truth Mach number, we calculate the ratio P_T/P_a

$$\frac{P_T}{P_a} = \left(1 + 0.2M^2\right)^{7\!/\!2} \qquad (M < 1) \quad (D17)$$

$$\frac{P_T}{P_a} = \left(1 + 0.2(0.2066)^2\right)^{7\!/\!2}$$

$$\frac{P_T}{P_a} = 1.03020$$

Doing the same for instrument corrected Mach number

$$\frac{P_T}{P_s} = \left(1 + 0.2M_{ic}^2\right)^{7\!/\!2} \qquad (M_{ic} < 1) \quad (D20)$$

$$\frac{P_T}{P_s} = \left(1 + 0.2(0.22256)^2\right)^{7\!/\!2}$$

$$\frac{P_T}{P_s} = 1.03510$$

The position error can then be calculated directly from these ratios by

$$\frac{\Delta P_p}{P_s} = \left(\frac{1}{\dfrac{P_T}{P_s}} - \frac{1}{\dfrac{P_T}{P_a}}\right)\frac{P_T}{P_s} \qquad (D23)$$

$$\frac{\Delta P_p}{P_s} = \left(\frac{1}{1.03510} - \frac{1}{1.03020}\right)1.03510$$

$$\frac{\Delta P_p}{P_s} = -0.0047563$$

Cloverleaf Data Reduction (Matrix Inversion Method)

The Matrix Inversion method is preferred for reducing cloverleaf data because it solves for the true airspeed correction instead of solving for the true airspeed. This may not sound like a big difference, but consider this. Assume that the airspeed position correction is essentially constant over a small range, say ±2 knots. As long as the true airspeed on each leg is "constant" within ±2 knots, this method will calculate the correct true airspeed correction. The result is that this method allows more uncertainty in the airspeed input without having a significant effect on the result. Our Test Pilots do their best to fly precisely, but even the best have small variations, which they will usually blame on the atmosphere. Even so, this data reduction method is tolerant of those small errors.

The basic process is

       a. Correct cockpit readings for instrument errors
       b. Find the indicated Mach number
       c. Find the indicated true airspeed
       d. Find the true airspeed error and wind velocity
       e. Find the Mach position correction

If we assume the total pressure error is zero, we can

       f. Find the position error ratio ($\Delta P_p / P_s$)

For purposes of this discussion, we will use the following example data (note these data are the same as for the Vector Method with slight variations in airspeed):

First Leg

Indicated Airspeed (V_i)	131 knots
Indicated Altitude (H_i)	6000 feet
Indicated Temperature (T_i)	11 °C
GPS Ground Speed (V_g)	131.3 knots
GPS Ground Track (σ_g)	7°

Second Leg

Indicated Airspeed (V_i)	130 knots
Indicated Altitude (H_i)	6000 feet
Indicated Temperature (T_i)	11 °C
GPS Ground Speed (V_g)	153.8 knots
GPS Ground Track (σ_g)	114°

Third Leg

Indicated Airspeed (V_i)	129 knots
Indicated Altitude (H_i)	6000 feet
Indicated Temperature (T_i)	11 °C
GPS Ground Speed (V_g)	121.5 knots
GPS Ground Track (σ_g)	234°
Altimeter Instrument Correction (ΔH_{ic})	-20 feet
Airspeed Instrument Correction (ΔV_{ic})	+2 knots
Temperature Instrument Correction (ΔT_{ic})	-1°C (-1 K)
Temperature Recovery Factor (K_t)	1.0

Correct cockpit readings for instrument errors

The instrument corrected altitude, airspeed, and temperature are calculated by adding the instrument corrections to the indicated values.

$$H_{ic} = H_i + \Delta H_{ic} \qquad\qquad \text{(D66)}$$

$$H_{ic1} = 6000 \text{ feet} + (-20 \text{ feet})$$

$$H_{ic1} = 5980 \text{ feet}$$
$$H_{ic2} = 5980 \text{ feet}$$
$$H_{ic3} = 5980 \text{ feet}$$

$$V_{ic} = V_i + \Delta V_{ic} \qquad\qquad \text{(D67)}$$

$$V_{ic1} = 131 \text{ knots} + (+2 \text{ knots})$$

$$V_{ic1} = 133 \text{ knots}$$
$$V_{ic2} = 132 \text{ knots}$$
$$V_{ic3} = 131 \text{ knots}$$

$$T_{ic} = T_i + \Delta T_{ic} \qquad\qquad \text{(C185)}$$

$$T_{ic1} = 11 \text{ °C} + (-1 \text{ °C}) + 273.15$$

$$T_{ic1} = 283.15 \text{ K}$$
$$T_{ic2} = 283.15 \text{ K}$$
$$T_{ic3} = 283.15 \text{ K}$$

Find the indicated Mach number

So our next step is to determine the indicated Mach number at the test conditions. We could jump straight to the Mach meter equation with calibrated airspeed and pressure altitude, but since we will need q_{cic}/P_{SL} later, we'll calculate that first. This is the value in the middle of the calibrated airspeed equation.

$$\frac{q_{cic}}{P_{SL}} = \left(1 + 0.2\left(\frac{V_{ic}}{a_{SL}}\right)^2\right)^{7/2} - 1 \qquad (V_{ic} < a_{SL}) \quad \text{(D12)}$$

$$\frac{q_{cic1}}{P_{SL}} = \left(1 + 0.2\left(\frac{133 \text{ knots}}{661.48 \text{ knots}}\right)^2\right)^{3.5} - 1$$

$$\frac{q_{cic1}}{P_{SL}} = 0.028586$$

$$\frac{q_{cic2}}{P_{SL}} = 0.028153$$

$$\frac{q_{cic3}}{P_{SL}} = 0.027724$$

Note that because this value was calculated using V_{ic}, this is the pressure ratio seen at the airspeed indicator, and thus contains the position error. This is why the value is q_{cic}/P_{SL} and not q_c/P_{SL}.

To find the Mach number we will need q_{cic}/P_s, and to find that we need q_{cic}/P_{SL} and δ_{ic}. We'll find δ_{ic} (which also contains the position error) seen by the altimeter from the instrument corrected altitude, H_{ic}. From Equation A79

$$\delta_{ic} = (1 - 6.87559 \times 10^{-6} \, H_{ic})^{5.2559}$$

$$\delta_{ic1} = (1 - 6.87559 \times 10^{-6}/\text{feet} \,\, (5980 \text{ feet}))^{5.2559}$$

$$\delta_{ic1} = 0.80198$$
$$\delta_{ic2} = 0.80198$$
$$\delta_{ic3} = 0.80198$$

We can now find q_{cic}/P_s

$$\frac{q_{cic}}{P_s} = \frac{q_{cic}}{P_{SL}} \frac{P_{SL}}{P_s} = \frac{q_{cic}}{P_{SL}} \frac{1}{\delta_{ic}}$$

$$\frac{q_{cic1}}{P_s} = (0.028586)\frac{1}{0.80198}$$

$$\frac{q_{cic1}}{P_s} = 0.035644$$

$$\frac{q_{cic2}}{P_s} = 0.035105$$

$$\frac{q_{cic3}}{P_s} = 0.034570$$

This is the number we find in the middle of the true airspeed and Mach equations. Now we can find the instrument corrected Mach number, M_{ic}, which is what a perfect Mach meter in the cockpit would have read. Note that because this Mach is calculated using numbers that contain the position error, it too contains the position error.

$$M_{ic} = \sqrt{5\left[\left(\frac{q_{cic}}{P_s}+1\right)^{2/7} - 1\right]} \tag{D49}$$

$$M_{ic1} = \sqrt{5\left[(0.035105 + 1)^{2/7} - 1\right]}$$

$$M_{ic1} = 0.22424$$
$$M_{ic2} = 0.22256$$
$$M_{ic3} = 0.22088$$

Find the Indicated True Airspeed

The Matrix Inversion Method requires knowing the indicated true airspeed, or the true airspeed calculated from the instrument corrected airspeed. To find the indicated true airspeed, we need to find the ambient temperature. Since we don't have the true Mach number, we will use the indicated Mach number as our best information. From Equation C187

$$T_{a_i} = \frac{T_{ic}}{1 + 0.2K_t M_{ic}^2}$$

$$T_{a_{i1}} = \frac{283.15}{1 + 0.2(1.0)(0.22424)^2}$$

$$T_{a_{i1}} = 280.33 \text{ K}$$
$$T_{a_{i2}} = 280.37 \text{ K}$$
$$T_{a_{i3}} = 280.41 \text{ K}$$

With this temperature we can calculate the indicated true airspeed (from Equations A69 and C76)

$$V_{t_i} = M_{ic} a_{SL} \sqrt{\theta}$$

$$V_{t_{i1}} = (0.22424)(661.48 \text{ knots})\sqrt{\frac{280.33K}{288.15K}}$$

$$V_{t_{i1}} = 146.30 \text{ knots}$$
$$V_{t_{i2}} = 145.21 \text{ knots}$$
$$V_{t_{i3}} = 144.13 \text{ knots}$$

Find the True Airspeed Correction and Wind Velocity

This step involves building the solution matrix. We need to find the components of ground speed.

$$V_{gx} = V_g \sin \sigma_g \qquad (E1)$$

$$V_{gx1} = 131.3 \sin 7°$$

$$V_{gx1} = 16.00 \text{ knots}$$

$$V_{gy} = V_g \cos \sigma_g \qquad (E2)$$

$$V_{gy1} = 131.3 \cos 7°$$

$$V_{gy1} = 130.32 \text{ knots}$$

$$V_{gx2} = 140.50 \text{ knots}$$

$$V_{gy2} = -62.56 \text{ knots}$$

$$V_{gx3} = -98.29 \text{ knots}$$

$$V_{gy3} = -71.41 \text{ knots}$$

The solution matrix is given by

$$\begin{bmatrix} 2V_{t_i1} + \Delta V_t & 2V_{gx1} - V_{wx} & 2V_{gy1} - V_{wy} \\ 2V_{t_i2} + \Delta V_t & 2V_{gx2} - V_{wx} & 2V_{gy2} - V_{wy} \\ 2V_{t_i3} + \Delta V_t & 2V_{gx3} - V_{wx} & 2V_{gy3} - V_{wy} \end{bmatrix} \begin{bmatrix} \Delta V_t \\ V_{wx} \\ V_{wy} \end{bmatrix} = \begin{bmatrix} V_{g1}^2 - V_{t_i1}^2 \\ V_{g2}^2 - V_{t_i2}^2 \\ V_{g3}^2 - V_{t_i3}^2 \end{bmatrix} \qquad (E36)$$

$$[A][x] = [C] \qquad (E37)$$

To start the calculations, we will assume

$$\begin{bmatrix} \Delta V_t \\ V_{wx} \\ V_{wy} \end{bmatrix} = \begin{bmatrix} 0 \\ 0 \\ 0 \end{bmatrix} \qquad (E39)$$

Calculating the numbers gives an initial matrix

$$\begin{bmatrix} 292.61 & 32.00 & 260.64 \\ 290.44 & 281.01 & -125.11 \\ 288.26 & -196.59 & -142.83 \end{bmatrix} \begin{bmatrix} \Delta V_t \\ V_{wx} \\ V_{wy} \end{bmatrix} = \begin{bmatrix} -4165.7 \\ 2565.8 \\ -6011.8 \end{bmatrix}$$

Using the MINVERSE function in Excel to invert this matrix and multiplying for a new solution

$$[x] = [A]^{-1}[C] \qquad (E38)$$

$$\begin{bmatrix} \Delta V_t \\ V_{wx} \\ V_{wy} \end{bmatrix} = \begin{bmatrix} 0.001182 & 0.000852 & 0.001411 \\ -0.0001 & 0.002135 & -0.00205 \\ 0.002522 & -0.00122 & -0.00133 \end{bmatrix} \begin{bmatrix} -4165.7 \\ 2565.8 \\ -6011.8 \end{bmatrix} = \begin{bmatrix} -11.2175 \\ 18.21988 \\ -5.62618 \end{bmatrix}$$

Using this new solution vector to recalculate the A matrix we have

$$\begin{bmatrix} 281.3942 & 13.78301 & 266.2688 \\ 279.2209 & 262.7867 & -119.486 \\ 277.0471 & -214.811 & -137.206 \end{bmatrix} \begin{bmatrix} \Delta V_t \\ V_{wx} \\ V_{wy} \end{bmatrix} = \begin{bmatrix} -4165.7 \\ 2565.818 \\ -6011.88 \end{bmatrix}$$

Using the MINVERSE function in Excel to invert this matrix and multiplying for a new solution

$$\begin{bmatrix} \Delta V_t \\ V_{wx} \\ V_{wy} \end{bmatrix} = \begin{bmatrix} 0.001172 & 0.00105 & 0.00136 \\ -0.0001 & 0.002134 & -0.00205 \\ 0.002522 & -0.00122 & -0.00133 \end{bmatrix} \begin{bmatrix} -4165.7 \\ 2565.818 \\ -6011.88 \end{bmatrix} = \begin{bmatrix} -10.3655 \\ 18.21626 \\ -5.63332 \end{bmatrix}$$

Repeating this iteration three more times gives a final solution vector

$$\begin{bmatrix} \Delta V_t \\ V_{wx} \\ V_{wy} \end{bmatrix} = \begin{bmatrix} -10.3329 \\ 18.21613 \\ -5.63359 \end{bmatrix}$$

From this we see that the true airspeed correction is –10.3 knots.

$$\Delta V_t = -10.3 \text{ knots}$$

Find the Wind Vector (Optional)

The wind vector would be found by

$$V_w = \sqrt{V_{wx}^2 + V_{wy}^2} \qquad (E14)$$

$$V_w = \sqrt{(18.21)^2 + (-5.63)^2}$$

$$V_w = 19.07 \text{ knots}$$

$$\psi = \tan^{-1} \frac{V_{wx}}{V_{wy}} \qquad (E15)$$

$$\psi = \tan^{-1} \frac{18.21}{-5.63}$$

$$\psi = 107.2 \text{ deg rees}$$

Two things to note about the calculation of the wind angle. The "y" and "x" coordinate seem to be reversed. This is because compass directions are defined differently than Cartesian coordinates. Rather than being defined counterclockwise from the horizontal (x) axis, directions are defined clockwise from the vertical (north, y) axis. Using the function ATAN2(V_{wy}, V_{wx}) in Excel will return the proper direction in the proper quadrant.

Secondly, this is the direction of the wind vector, i.e. where the wind is blowing to, not from. To match the traditional method of defining wind direction as the "from" direction, simply add 180 degrees to get 287.2 degrees.

Find the Mach Position Correction

We now know the true airspeed correction, but this is not the form that we normally use position corrections. We will convert this true airspeed correction into a Mach correction. To do this, we need to know the local speed of sound at the test conditions. To find the local speed of sound, we need to know the temperature. Using the true airspeed correction we can find the truth true airspeed, and use that to find the correct ambient temperature. We will use the alternative method, which requires knowing the value of C_p for air. Various values for C_p are

$$C_p = 1005 \frac{m^2}{\sec^2 K} = 3796 \frac{knots^2}{K} = 5027 \frac{mph^2}{K} = 10814 \frac{ft^2}{\sec^2 K} = 0.24 \frac{BTU}{lbm\,°R} = 186.72 \frac{ft\,lbf}{lbm\,°R}$$

The truth true airspeed would be

$$V_t = V_{t_i} + \Delta V_t$$

$$V_t = 145.2 \text{ knots} + (-10.3 \text{ knots})$$

$$V_t = 134.9 \text{ knots}$$

The ambient temperature is then given by (from Equations C185 and C191)

$$T_a = T_i + \Delta T_{ic} - \frac{K_t V_t^2}{2 C_p}$$

$$T_a = (11°C) + (-1°C) - \frac{(1.0)(134.9 \text{ knots})^2}{2\left(3796 \dfrac{\text{knots}^2}{K}\right)} + 273.15$$

$$T_a = 7.6 \text{ °C} = 280.6 \text{ K}$$

The test temperature ratio is given by (from Equation A69)

$$\theta_{test} = \frac{T_a}{T_{SL}}$$

$$\theta_{test} = \frac{280.6 \text{ K}}{288.15 \text{ K}}$$

$$\theta_{test} = 0.97432$$

Now we can find the Mach position correction (from Equation C75)

$$\Delta M_{pc} = \frac{\Delta V_t}{a_{SL}\sqrt{\theta_{test}}}$$

$$\Delta M_{pc} = \frac{-10.3 \text{ knots}}{661.48 \text{ knots}\sqrt{0.97432}}$$

$$\Delta M_{pc} = -0.01583$$

Find the truth Mach number

Now that we know the indicated Mach number and the Mach position correction, the truth Mach number can be found from Equation D7.

$$M = M_{ic} + \Delta M_{pc}$$

$$M = 0.22256 + (-0.01583)$$

$$\Delta M_{pc} = 0.20673$$

Find the static port position error ratio ($\Delta P_p/P_s$)

From the truth Mach number, we calculate the ratio P_T/P_a

$$\frac{P_T}{P_a} = \left(1 + 0.2M^2\right)^{7/2} \qquad\qquad (M < 1) \quad (D17)$$

$$\frac{P_T}{P_a} = \left(1 + 0.2(0.20673)^2\right)^{7/2}$$

$$\frac{P_T}{P_a} = 1.03024$$

Doing the same for instrument corrected Mach number

$$\frac{P_T}{P_s} = \left(1 + 0.2M_{ic}^2\right)^{7/2} \qquad\qquad (M_{ic} < 1) \quad (D20)$$

$$\frac{P_T}{P_s} = \left(1 + 0.2(0.22256)^2\right)^{7/2}$$

$$\frac{P_T}{P_s} = 1.03510$$

The position error can then be calculated directly from these ratios by

$$\frac{\Delta P_p}{P_s} = \left(\frac{1}{\dfrac{P_T}{P_s}} - \frac{1}{\dfrac{P_T}{P_a}}\right)\frac{P_T}{P_s} \qquad\qquad (D23)$$

$$\frac{\Delta P_p}{P_s} = \left(\frac{1}{1.03510} - \frac{1}{1.03024}\right)1.03510$$

$$\frac{\Delta P_p}{P_s} = -0.00472$$

Turn Regression Data Reduction

The Turn Regression method solves for the true airspeed correction instead of solving for the true airspeed. This may not sound like a big difference, but consider this. Assume that the airspeed position correction is essentially constant over a small range, say ±2 knots. As long as the true airspeed on each leg is "constant" within ±2 knots, this method will calculate the correct true airspeed correction. The result is that this method allows more uncertainty in the airspeed input without having a significant effect on the result. Our Test Pilots do their best to fly precisely, but even the best have small variations, which they will usually blame on the atmosphere. Even so, this data reduction method is tolerant of those small errors.

Previously discussed data reduction techniques for other FTTs were designed to be accomplished with a spreadsheet, a calculator, or, if you go back far enough, a slide rule. This technique is dependent on using a statistical data analysis solver, such as available in Excel, Matlab, or many other mathematics packages. This discussion will only cover setting up the data for input into the regression routine and interpretation of the results. The specifics of running the regression routine is left as an exercise to the reader (don't you hate it when textbooks say that?).

The basic process is

        a. Correct cockpit readings for instrument errors
        b. Find the indicated Mach number
        c. Find the indicated true airspeed
        d. Set up the regression matrix
        d. Find the true airspeed error and wind velocity
        e. Find the Mach position correction

If we assume the total pressure error is zero, we can

        f. Find the position error ratio ($\Delta P_p/P_s$)

A good regression will require many lines of data, which is easy to come by for DAS data. Several lines of handheld data will work too, the more the better. For purposes of this discussion, we will only show example data for one line of data. All other lines would be processed the same way.

Indicated Airspeed (V_i)	71 knots
Indicated Altitude (H_i)	4029 feet
Indicated Temperature (T_i)	12.7 °C
GPS Ground Speed (V_g)	99 knots
GPS Ground Track (σ_g)	103°
Heading (ψ)	108.6°
Altimeter Instrument Correction (ΔH_{ic})	-20 feet
Airspeed Instrument Correction (ΔV_{ic})	+2 knots
Temperature Instrument Correction (ΔT_{ic})	-1°C (-1 K)
Temperature Recovery Factor (K_t)	1.0

Correct cockpit readings for instrument errors

The instrument corrected altitude, airspeed, and temperature are calculated by adding the instrument corrections to the indicated values.

$$H_{ic} = H_i + \Delta H_{ic} \qquad (D66)$$

$$H_{ic} = 4029 \text{ feet} + (-20 \text{ feet})$$

$$H_{ic} = 4009 \text{ feet}$$

$$V_{ic} = V_i + \Delta V_{ic} \qquad (D67)$$

$$V_{ic} = 71 \text{ knots} + (+2 \text{ knots})$$

$$V_{ic} = 73 \text{ knots}$$

$$T_{ic} = T_i + \Delta T_{ic} \qquad (C185)$$

$$T_{ic} = 12.7 \text{ °C} + (-1 \text{ °C}) + 273.15$$

$$T_{ic} = 284.85 \text{ K}$$

Find the indicated Mach number

So our next step is to determine the indicated Mach number at the test conditions. We could jump straight to the Mach meter equation with calibrated airspeed and pressure altitude, but since we will need q_{cic}/P_{SL} later, we'll calculate that first. This is the value in the middle of the calibrated airspeed equation.

$$\frac{q_{cic}}{P_{SL}} = \left(1 + 0.2\left(\frac{V_{ic}}{a_{SL}}\right)^2\right)^{7/2} - 1 \qquad (V_{ic} < a_{SL}) \quad (D12)$$

$$\frac{q_{cic}}{P_{SL}} = \left(1 + 0.2\left(\frac{73 \text{ knots}}{661.48 \text{ knots}}\right)^2\right)^{3.5} - 1$$

$$\frac{q_{cic}}{P_{SL}} = 0.008551$$

Note that because this value was calculated using V_{ic}, this is the pressure ratio seen at the airspeed indicator, and thus contains the position error. This is why the value is q_{cic}/P_{SL} and not q_c/P_{SL}.

To find the Mach number we will need q_{cic}/P_s, and to find that we need q_{cic}/P_{SL} and δ_{ic}. We'll find δ_{ic} (which also contains the position error) seen by the altimeter from the instrument corrected altitude, H_{ic}. From Equation A79

$$\delta_{ic} = (1 - 6.87559 \times 10^{-6} \, H_{ic})^{5.2559}$$

$$\delta_{ic} = (1 - 6.87559 \times 10^{-6}/\text{feet} \, (4009 \text{ feet}))^{5.2559}$$

$$\delta_{ic} = 0.86337$$

We can now find q_{cic}/P_s

$$\frac{q_{cic}}{P_s} = \frac{q_{cic}}{P_{SL}}\frac{P_{SL}}{P_s} = \frac{q_{cic}}{P_{SL}}\frac{1}{\delta_{ic}}$$

$$\frac{q_{cic}}{P_s} = (0.008551)\frac{1}{0.86337}$$

$$\frac{q_{cic}}{P_s} = 0.0099042$$

This is the number we find in the middle of the true airspeed and Mach equations. Now we can find the instrument corrected Mach number, M_{ic}, which is what a perfect Mach meter in the cockpit would have read. Note that because this Mach is calculated using numbers that contain the position error, it too contains the position error.

$$M_{ic} = \sqrt{5\left[\left(\frac{q_{cic}}{P_s}+1\right)^{2/7} - 1\right]} \qquad (D49)$$

$$M_{ic} = \sqrt{5\left[(0.0099042 + 1)^{2/7} - 1\right]}$$

$$M_{ic} = 0.11874$$

Find the Indicated True Airspeed

The Turn Regression Method requires knowing the indicated true airspeed, or the true airspeed calculated from the instrument corrected airspeed. To find the indicated true airspeed, we need to find the ambient temperature. Since we don't have the true Mach number, we will use the indicated Mach number as our best information. From Equation C187

$$T_{a_i} = \frac{T_{ic}}{1 + 0.2K_t M_{ic}^2}$$

$$T_{a_i} = \frac{284.85}{1 + 0.2(1.0)(0.11874)^2}$$

$$T_{a_i} = 284.05 \text{ K}$$

With this temperature we can calculate the indicated true airspeed (from Equations A69 and C76)

$$V_{t_i} = M_{ic}a_{SL}\sqrt{\theta}$$

$$V_{t_i} = (0.11874)(661.48 \text{ knots})\sqrt{\frac{284.05K}{288.15K}}$$

$$V_{t_i} = 78.0 \text{ knots}$$

Set up the regression matrix

As described in Appendix H, the form of the solution matrix is

$$
\begin{bmatrix} 1 & 0 & \cos\psi \\ 0 & 1 & \sin\psi \end{bmatrix}
\begin{bmatrix} V_{wn} \\ V_{we} \\ \Delta V_t \end{bmatrix}
=
\begin{bmatrix} V_g \cos\sigma_g - V_{t_i}\cos\psi \\ V_g \sin\sigma_g - V_{t_i}\sin\psi \end{bmatrix}
\tag{H8}
$$

This is the matrix for a single measurement. Each measurement will have two lines of the same form, such that for n independent measurements the A matrix will be size [2n x 3] and the C vector will be size [2n x 1]. For the example data point

$$
\begin{bmatrix} 1 & 0 & \cos(108.6) \\ 0 & 1 & \sin(108.6) \end{bmatrix}
\begin{bmatrix} V_{wn} \\ V_{we} \\ \Delta V_t \end{bmatrix}
=
\begin{bmatrix} (99)\cos(103)-(78)\cos(108.6) \\ (99)\sin(103)-(78)\sin(108.6) \end{bmatrix}
$$

$$
\begin{bmatrix} 1 & 0 & -0.31895 \\ 0 & 1 & 0.94776 \end{bmatrix}
\begin{bmatrix} V_{wn} \\ V_{we} \\ \Delta V_t \end{bmatrix}
=
\begin{bmatrix} 2.6086 \\ 22.536 \end{bmatrix}
$$

If angle of attack and bank angle are available, improve the solution by substituting ψ_{V_t} from Equation H16 for ψ in Equation H8, as shown in Equation H17.

$$
\psi_{V_t} = \psi - \alpha \sin\phi
\tag{H16}
$$

$$
\begin{bmatrix} 1 & 0 & \cos\psi_{V_t} \\ 0 & 1 & \sin\psi_{V_t} \end{bmatrix}
\begin{bmatrix} V_{wn} \\ V_{we} \\ \Delta V_t \end{bmatrix}
=
\begin{bmatrix} V_g \cos\sigma_g - V_{t_i}\cos\psi_{V_t} \\ V_g \sin\sigma_g - V_{t_i}\sin\psi_{V_t} \end{bmatrix}
\tag{H17}
$$

Find the true airspeed error and wind velocity

After setting up the regression matrix, solve for the coefficients (the b vector) in Matlab using `pinv`. The confidence intervals of the coefficients can be obtained using `regress`. Alternatively, use the regression in Excel's Data Analysis Add-in. The results will look something like this.

Regression Statistics	
Multiple R	0.988205
R Square	0.97655
Adjusted R Square	0.934674
Standard Error	2.808905
Observations	28

ANOVA

	df	SS	MS	F	Significance F
Regression	3	8214.152	2738.051	347.0304	6.83E-20
Residual	25	197.2486	7.889945		
Total	28	8411.401			

	Coefficients	Standard Error	t Stat	P-value	Lower 95%	Upper 95%
Intercept	0	#N/A	#N/A	#N/A	#N/A	#N/A
Vw_N	-2.86277	0.750764	-3.81314	0.000799	-4.40899	-1.31654
Vw_E	24.02333	0.761965	31.52811	1.19E-21	22.45404	25.59263
Del_Vt [knots]	-0.16658	0.762017	-0.2186	0.828733	-1.73598	1.402822

There are a lot of statistics here, but the key values are

Coefficient	Value	Lower Confidence Bound	Upper Confidence Bound
V_{w_n}	-2.86277	[-4.40899	-1.31654]
V_{w_e}	24.02333	[22.45404	25.59263]
ΔV_t	-0.16658	[-1.73598	1.402822]

The regression says that the expected value for the true airspeed error is -0.17 knots, with 95 percent confidence that the real value is between -1.74 knots and 1.40 knots, which is a range of ±1.57 knots. Winds with more variation and measurement errors in heading and airspeed would result in this confidence interval becoming larger. The confidence interval on the wind components will give an idea of the magnitude of the wind variation.

The ANOVA has a Significance F (sometimes called p-value) of well less than 0.05, so this model is considered significant. The significance of the wind components was good, with p-values of less than 0.05. The p-value for the true airspeed error was very much larger than 0.05, which to a statistician means that we failed to reject the null hypothesis that the value was statistically equal to zero. That's okay in this case, because the value may very well be zero. Zero is certainly in the confidence interval, and the confidence interval is reasonable small.

Find the Wind Vector (Optional)

The wind vector would be found by

$$V_w = \sqrt{V_{w_n}^2 + V_{w_e}^2} \qquad\qquad (E14)$$

$$V_w = \sqrt{(-2.86)^2 + (24.02)^2}$$

$$V_w = 24.2 \text{ knots}$$

$$\psi = \tan^{-1} \frac{V_{w_e}}{V_{w_n}} \qquad\qquad (E15)$$

$$\psi = \tan^{-1} \frac{24.02}{-2.86}$$

$$\psi = 96.8 \text{ degrees}$$

Two things to note about the calculation of the wind angle. The "y" and "x" coordinate seem to be reversed. This is because compass directions are defined differently than Cartesian coordinates. Rather than being defined counterclockwise from the horizontal (x) axis, directions are defined clockwise from the vertical (north, y) axis. Using the function ATAN2(V_{wn}, V_{we}) in Excel will return the proper direction in the proper quadrant.

Secondly, this is the direction of the wind vector, i.e. where the wind is blowing to, not from. To match the traditional method of defining wind direction as the "from" direction, simply add 180 degrees to get 276.8 degrees.

Find the Mach Position Correction

We now know the true airspeed correction, but this is not the form that we normally use position corrections. We will convert this true airspeed correction into a Mach correction. To do this, we need to know the local speed of sound at the test conditions. To find the local speed of sound, we need to know the temperature. Using the true airspeed correction we can find the truth true airspeed, and use that to find the correct ambient temperature. We will use the alternative method, which requires knowing the value of C_p for air. Various values for C_P are

$$C_p = 1005 \frac{m^2}{\sec^2 K} = 3796 \frac{knots^2}{K} = 5027 \frac{mph^2}{K} = 10814 \frac{ft^2}{\sec^2 K} = 0.24 \frac{BTU}{lbm\,^\circ R} = 186.72 \frac{ft\,lbf}{lbm\,^\circ R}$$

The truth true airspeed would be

$$V_t = V_{t_i} + \Delta V_t$$

$$V_t = 78.0 \text{ knots} + (-0.17 \text{ knots})$$

$$V_t = 77.8 \text{ knots}$$

The ambient temperature is then given by (from Equations C185 and C191)

$$T_a = T_i + \Delta T_{ic} - \frac{K_t V_t^2}{2C_p}$$

$$T_a = \left(12.7°C\right) + \left(-1°C\right) - \frac{(1.0)(77.8 \text{ knots})^2}{2\left(3796 \dfrac{\text{knots}^2}{K}\right)} + 273.15$$

$$T_a = 10.9 \ °C = 284.1 \ K$$

The test temperature ratio is given by (from Equation A69)

$$\theta_{test} = \frac{T_a}{T_{SL}}$$

$$\theta_{test} = \frac{284.1 \ K}{288.15 \ K}$$

$$\theta_{test} = 0.98577$$

Now we can find the Mach position correction (from Equation C75)

$$\Delta M_{pc} = \frac{\Delta V_t}{a_{SL}\sqrt{\theta_{test}}}$$

$$\Delta M_{pc} = \frac{-0.17 \text{ knots}}{661.48 \text{ knots}\sqrt{0.98577}}$$

$$\Delta M_{pc} = -0.000258$$

Find the truth Mach number

Now that we know the indicated Mach number and the Mach position correction, the truth Mach number can be found from Equation D7.

$$M = M_{ic} + \Delta M_{pc}$$

$$M = 0.11874 + (-0.000258)$$

$$\Delta M_{pc} = 0.11848$$

Find the static port position error ratio ($\Delta P_p / P_s$)

From the truth Mach number, we calculate the ratio P_T / P_a

$$\frac{P_T}{P_a} = \left(1 + 0.2 M^2\right)^{7/2} \qquad (M < 1) \quad (D17)$$

$$\frac{P_T}{P_a} = \left(1 + 0.2(0.11848)^2\right)^{7/2}$$

$$\frac{P_T}{P_a} = 1.00986$$

Doing the same for instrument corrected Mach number

$$\frac{P_T}{P_s} = \left(1 + 0.2 M_{ic}^2\right)^{7/2} \qquad (M_{ic} < 1) \quad (D20)$$

$$\frac{P_T}{P_s} = \left(1 + 0.2(0.11874)^2\right)^{7/2}$$

$$\frac{P_T}{P_s} = 1.00990$$

The position error can then be calculated directly from these ratios by

$$\frac{\Delta P_p}{P_s} = \left(\frac{1}{\dfrac{P_T}{P_s}} - \frac{1}{\dfrac{P_T}{P_a}} \right) \frac{P_T}{P_s} \qquad (D23)$$

$$\frac{\Delta P_p}{P_s} = \left(\frac{1}{1.00990} - \frac{1}{1.00986} \right) 1.00990$$

$$\frac{\Delta P_p}{P_s} = -0.0000396$$

Calculating Position Corrections from the Position Error Ratio

Given a position error ratio, the altitude, airspeed, and Mach position corrections can be calculated regardless of whether the position error ratio was determined from an altitude comparison method or an airspeed comparison method, if a few assumptions are made.

The Big Assumptions

To continue our analysis, we need to make a few assumptions.

   a. Total pressure error is zero

   This assumption says that all of the position error is represented by the error in measuring the ambient pressure.

   b. Same angle of attack, or sufficiently high airspeed that angle of attack changes are negligible

   The position error, represented by $\Delta P_p/P_s$, is a function of lift coefficient (a direct function of angle of attack) and Mach number. For cruise speeds and higher, the angle of attack change is very small. Ignoring angle of attack effects will introduce errors at lower speeds.

   c. Uncompensated Pitot-static probe

   Compensated Pitot-static systems may show more of a dependence on angle of attack and other factors, to the point that position error data may not generalize to a single curve. Probes mounted on the fuselage (as on the F-15) or under wings may have similar problems. Uncompensated probes mounted on nose booms are the most likely to follow the theory presented here.

General Method

Our general method will be to

   a. Find the altitude position correction
   b. Find the instrument corrected Mach number
   c. Find the Mach position correction
   d. Find the calibrated airspeed at the standard altitude for the test Mach number
   e. Find the airspeed position correction
   f. Find the Position Error Pressure Coefficient

For purposes of this discussion, consider the following test point conditions:

Instrument Corrected Altitude (H_{ic})	2465 feet
Instrument Corrected Airspeed (V_{ic})	422.5 knots

Based on data collected at these conditions, we have determined:

Position error ratio ($\Delta P_p/P_s$)	0.0073667

The relationships between our position corrections (ΔH_{pc} and ΔV_{pc}) and the position error ratio are functions of pressure altitude. Thus, to calculate ΔH_{pc} and ΔV_{pc} we must specify what pressure altitude we want these values at. This is typically referred to as the "standard altitude" since we are "standardizing" the data to that altitude. The larger the difference between the test altitude and the standard altitude, the larger the uncertainty introduced becomes.

Standard Altitude ($H_{std\ alt}$)   2300 feet

Find the Altitude Position Correction

We need to calculate the altitude position correction that would exist if the aircraft were flying at the same Mach number at the standard altitude (pressure altitude). We can find this by choosing the standard altitude and using the position error ratio (a function of Mach number and angle of attack—here we assume a negligible change in angle of attack due to the change in altitude). We start by finding the ambient pressure at the standard altitude (from Equation D10)

$$P_{a_{std\ alt}} = P_{SL}(1 - 6.87559\text{x}10^{-6}\ H_{std\ alt})^{5.2559}$$

$$P_{a_{std\ alt}} = (2116.22\ \text{lb/ft}^2)(1 - 6.87559\text{x}10^{-6}\ (2300\ \text{feet}))^{5.2559}$$

$$P_{a_{std\ alt}} = 1946.15\ \text{lb/ft}^2$$

Knowing the ambient pressure and the position error ratio, we can calculate the static pressure at this altitude (from Equation D28)

$$P_{s_{std\ alt}} = \frac{P_{a_{std\ alt}}}{1 - \dfrac{\Delta P_p}{P_s}}$$

$$P_{s_{std\ alt}} = \frac{1946.15\ \text{lb/ft}^2}{1 - 0.0073667}$$

$$P_{s_{std\ alt}} = 1960.59\ \text{lb/ft}^2$$

This is the static pressure that would be seen by the aircraft flying at the test Mach number at the standard altitude. From the static pressure we find the static pressure ratio seen at the standard altitude (from Equation D29)

$$\delta_{ic_{std\ alt}} = \frac{P_{s_{std\ alt}}}{P_{SL}}$$

$$\delta_{ic_{std\ alt}} = \frac{1960.59\ \text{lb/ft}^2}{2116.22\ \text{lb/ft}^2}$$

$$\delta_{ic_{std\ alt}} = 0.92646$$

and the static pressure altitude (from Equation D30)

$$H_{ic_{std\ alt}} = \frac{1 - 5.2559\sqrt{\delta_{ic_{std\ alt}}}}{6.87559\,x10^{-6}}$$

$$H_{ic_{std\ alt}} = \frac{1 - 5.2559\sqrt{0.92646}}{6.87559\,x10^{-6}}$$

$$H_{ic_{std\ alt}} = 2098\ feet$$

Finally, the altitude position correction for the test Mach number at the standard altitude (truth altitude, H_c, is $H_{std\ alt}$ in this case) is calculated by (from Equation D5)

$$\Delta H_{pc_{std\ alt}} = H_{std\ alt} - H_{ic_{std\ alt}}$$

$$\Delta H_{pc_{std\ alt}} = 2300\ feet - 2098\ feet$$

$$\Delta H_{pc_{std\ alt}} = 202\ feet$$

Find the instrument corrected Mach number

Before finding the Mach correction, we need to determine the instrument corrected indicated Mach number at the test conditions. This would be the Mach number that an accurate (zero instrument error) Mach meter would have shown if it were connected to the Pitot-static pressures seen at the test conditions. We could jump straight to the Mach meter equation with calibrated airspeed and pressure altitude, but since we will need q_{cic}/P_s later, we'll calculate that first. This is the value in the middle of the Mach meter equation. First we'll get q_{cic}/P_{SL} out of the test condition V_{ic} (from Equation D12)

$$\left(\frac{q_{cic}}{P_{SL}}\right)_{test} = \left(1 + 0.2\left(\frac{V_{ic}}{a_{SL}}\right)^2\right)^{7/2} - 1$$

$$\left(\frac{q_{cic}}{P_{SL}}\right)_{test} = \left(1 + 0.2\left(\frac{422.5\ knots}{661.48\ knots}\right)^2\right)^{3.5} - 1$$

$$\left(\frac{q_{cic}}{P_{SL}}\right)_{test} = 0.3159$$

Note that because this value was calculated using V_{ic}, this is the differential pressure ratio seen at the airspeed indicator, and thus contains the position error. This is why the value is q_{cic}/P_{SL} and not q_c/P_{SL}.

To find the instrument corrected indicated Mach number we will need q_{cic}/P_s, and to find that we need q_{cic}/P_{SL} and δ_{ic}. We'll find δ_{ic} (which also contains the position error) seen by the altimeter at the test conditions from the instrument corrected altitude, H_{ic}. (from Equation A79)

$$\delta_{ic_{test}} = (1 - 6.87559 \times 10^{-6} \, H_{ic})^{5.2559}$$

$$\delta_{ic_{test}} = (1 - 6.87559 \times 10^{-6}/\text{feet} \,(2465 \text{ feet}))^{5.2559}$$

$$\delta_{ic_{test}} = 0.9141$$

We can now find q_{cic}/P_s (from Equation D29)

$$\frac{q_{cic}}{P_s} = \frac{q_{cic}}{P_{SL}} \frac{P_{SL}}{P_s} = \left(\frac{q_{cic}}{P_{SL}}\right)_{test} \frac{1}{\delta_{ic\,test}}$$

$$\frac{q_{cic}}{P_s} = (0.3159)\frac{1}{0.9141}$$

$$\frac{q_{cic}}{P_s} = 0.3456$$

This is the number we find in the middle of the Mach equation. Now we can find the instrument corrected indicated Mach number, M_{ic}, which is what a perfect Mach meter in the cockpit would have read. Note that because this Mach is calculated using numbers that contain the position error, it too contains the position error. Also, because the relationship between the position error ratio and the Mach position correction is not a function of altitude, this value is valid for all altitudes.

$$M_{ic} = \sqrt{5\left[\left(\frac{q_{cic}}{P_s}+1\right)^{2/7}-1\right]} \qquad\qquad (D49)$$

$$M_{ic} = \sqrt{5\left[(0.3456+1)^{2/7}-1\right]}$$

$$M_{ic} = 0.6653$$

Find the Mach position correction

Using the position error in the form of $\Delta P_p/P_s$, we can determine q_c/P_a from q_{cic}/P_s using the following equation:

$$\frac{q_c}{P_a} = \frac{\frac{q_{cic}}{P_s}+1}{1-\frac{\Delta P_p}{P_s}} - 1 \tag{D58}$$

$$\frac{q_c}{P_a} = \frac{0.3456+1}{1-0.0073667} - 1$$

$$\frac{q_c}{P_a} = 0.3556$$

With this we can find Mach number

$$M = \sqrt{5\left(\left(\frac{q_c}{P_a}+1\right)^{2/7}-1\right)} \qquad (M<1 \text{ or } q_c/P_a < 0.89293) \tag{C117}$$

$$M = \sqrt{5\left((0.3556+1)^{2/7}-1\right)}$$

$$M = 0.6739$$

The Mach position correction would then be given by

$$\Delta M_{pc} = M - M_{ic} \tag{D7}$$

$$\Delta M_{pc} = 0.6739 - 0.6653$$

$$\Delta M_{pc} = 0.0086$$

Find the calibrated airspeed at the standard altitude for the test Mach number

Since we are finding the airspeed position corrections at the test Mach number (which is also the Mach number at the standard altitude), we must find what the airspeed for that Mach number would be at our chosen standard altitude. Again, this is the process we would use to extrapolate data to other altitudes, simply by substituting the desired altitude as the "standard" altitude. If the chosen altitude is significantly different than the test altitude, the airspeed corresponding to the test Mach number will be significantly different than the airspeed seen at the test altitude.

Since Mach number (M) can be expressed as solely a function of q_c/P_a, then the value of q_c/P_a at the new altitude will be unchanged for the same Mach number. With this value and the pressure ratio at the new altitude we can determine q_c/P_{SL}, from which we can calculate the calibrated airspeed at the new altitude for the test Mach number.

For the pressure ratio, (from Equation A79)

$$\delta_{std\ alt} = (1 - 6.87559\text{x}10^{-6}\ H_{std\ alt})^{5.2559}$$

$$\delta_{std\ alt} = (1 - 6.87559\text{x}10^{-6}/\text{feet}\ (2300\ \text{feet}))^{5.2559}$$

$$\delta_{std\ alt} = 0.9196$$

We can now find q_c/P_{SL} (from equation A70)

$$\left(\frac{q_c}{P_{SL}}\right)_{std\ alt} = \frac{q_c}{P_a}\frac{P_a}{P_{SL}} = \frac{q_c}{P_a}\delta_{std\ alt}$$

$$\left(\frac{q_c}{P_{SL}}\right)_{std\ alt} = (0.3556)(0.9196)$$

$$\left(\frac{q_c}{P_{SL}}\right)_{std\ alt} = 0.3270$$

From this we get the instrument corrected airspeed at the standard altitude. This is what the corrected instrument would have read at the same Mach number at the standard altitude. From Equation C126

$$V_{c_{std\ alt}} = a_{SL}\sqrt{5\left[\left(\left(\frac{q_c}{P_{SL}}\right)_{std\ alt}+1\right)^{2/7}-1\right]}$$

$$V_{c_{std\ alt}} = (661.48\ \text{knots})\sqrt{5\left[(0.3270+1)^{2/7}-1\right]}$$

$$V_{c_{std\ alt}} = 429\ \text{knots}$$

Find the airspeed position correction

We know the truth calibrated airspeed at the standard altitude. To find the airspeed position correction, we need to calculate the instrument corrected airspeed at the standard altitude. We can determine q_{cic}/P_{SL} from q_c/P_{SL} , $\Delta P_P/P_s$, and δ_{ic}.

$$\left(\frac{q_{cic}}{P_{SL}}\right)_{std\ alt} = \left(\frac{q_c}{P_{SL}}\right)_{std\ alt} - \frac{\Delta P_p}{P_s}\delta_{ic_{std\ alt}} \tag{D41}$$

$$\left(\frac{q_{cic}}{P_{SL}}\right)_{std\ alt} = 0.3270 - (0.0073667)(0.92646)$$

$$\left(\frac{q_{cic}}{P_{SL}}\right)_{std\ alt} = 0.3202$$

From this value we can calculate the instrument corrected airspeed at the standard altitude by (from Equation D42)

$$V_{ic_{std\,alt}} = a_{SL}\sqrt{\left[\left(\left(\frac{q_{cic}}{P_{SL}}\right)_{std\,alt} + 1\right)^{2/7} - 1\right]}$$

$$V_{ic_{std\,alt}} = (661.48\text{ knots})\sqrt{5\left[(0.3202 + 1)^{2/7} - 1\right]}$$

$$V_{ic_{std\,alt}} = 425\text{ knots}$$

Finally, the airspeed position correction is calculated by (from Equation D6)

$$\Delta V_{pc_{std\,alt}} = V_{c_{std\,alt}} - V_{ic_{std\,alt}}$$

$$\Delta V_{pc_{std\,alt}} = 429\text{ knots} - 425\text{ knots}$$

$$\Delta V_{pc_{std\,alt}} = 4\text{ knots}$$

Find the Position Error Pressure Coefficient

Sometimes the Position Error Pressure Coefficient ($\Delta P_p/q_{cic}$) is more useful than the Position Error Ratio ($\Delta P_p/P_s$). Since the Position Error Ratio is a function of Mach number, and q_{cic}/P_s (calculated above) is solely a function of Mach number, each value of $\Delta P_p/q_{cic}$ corresponds to one value of $\Delta P_p/P_s$. We can calculate it by (from Equation D77)

$$\frac{\Delta P_p}{q_{cic}} = \frac{\dfrac{\Delta P_p}{P_s}}{\dfrac{q_{cic}}{P_s}}$$

$$\frac{\Delta P_p}{q_{cic}} = \frac{0.0073667}{0.3456}$$

$$\frac{\Delta P_p}{q_{cic}} = 0.021316$$

But Sir! I'm starting with the Position Error Pressure Coefficient! How do I start?

If you are given position error expressed as $\Delta P_p/q_{cic}$ instead of $\Delta P_p/P_s$, you will need to determine M_{ic} first. Either this will be given to you or you can determine M_{ic} from V_{ic} and H_{ic} using the methods shown earlier in this section. Actually, you don't need M_{ic} so much as you need q_{cic}/P_s, which you found right before calculating M_{ic}. Using the same numbers from this section, $\Delta P_p/P_s$ would be calculated as shown:

$$\frac{\Delta P_p}{P_s} = \frac{\Delta P_p}{q_{cic}}\frac{q_{cic}}{P_s} \tag{D77}$$

$$\frac{\Delta P_p}{P_s} = (0.021316)(0.3456)$$

$$\frac{\Delta P_p}{P_s} = 0.0073668$$

which is what we started with except for round off errors.

Appendix A

Standard Atmosphere Heavy Math Section

Equation of State

The Equation of State, also known as the Perfect Gas Law or the Ideal Gas Law, can be expressed in several forms. The derivation of this equation is not presented here. The popular form used in High School Chemistry classes, where most engineers are first exposed to it, is

$$PV = NRT \tag{A1}$$

where

        P = Pressure
        V = Volume
        N = Number of molecules (moles)
        R = Gas Constant
        T = Temperature

Well, that was fine for chemists, but aero engineers aren't too interested in counting molecules, and it's tough to build a molecule counter. However, a given number of air molecules are going to have a certain mass, so the Equation of State can be re-written (with a different gas constant) as

$$PV = mRT \tag{A2}$$

where m = mass.

That's closer, but still not the parameters we were looking for. Well, mass divided by volume is density, which is something that we're looking for. Hence, the Equation of State becomes

$$P = \rho RT \tag{A3}$$

As for the gas constant, in this form of the equation, the value for R is the Specific Gas Constant. The Specific Gas Constant is related to the Universal Gas Constant (R*) by the relation

$$R = \frac{R*}{M} \tag{A4}$$

where M is the mean molecular weight of the gas. For air below an altitude of 90 kilometers

$$M = 28.9644 \, \frac{lbm}{(lb - mole)} \tag{A5}$$

where (lb-mole) is defined by Avogadro's number which states that there are 2.73179×10^{26} air molecules in a lbm (pound mass) of air. Again, Avogadro's number in Chemistry class was 6.02257×10^{23} molecules in a gram (i.e. gram-mole), which may look more familiar. (Ref 3).

Therefore, for the Universal Gas Constant

$$R* = 1545.31 \frac{ft - lbm}{(lb - mole) - °R} \tag{A6}$$

we get the Specific Gas Constant for air (converting pounds mass to slugs)

$$R = \frac{R*}{M} = \frac{1545.31 \frac{ft - lb}{(lb - mole) - °R}}{28.9644 \frac{lbm}{(lb - mole)}} * 32.1741 \frac{lbm}{slug} = 1716.6 \frac{ft - lb}{slug - °R} \tag{A7}$$

Or if we wish to use Kelvin temperature instead of Rankine, we multiply by 1.8 to get

$$R = 1716.6 \frac{ft - lb}{slug - °R} * 1.8 \frac{°R}{K} = 3089.8 \frac{ft - lb}{slug - K} \tag{A8}$$

Hydrostatic Equation

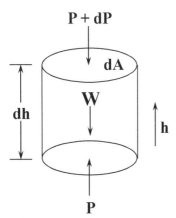

P + dP

dA

W

dh

h

P

Figure A1. Fluid Element

To develop the Hydrostatic Equation, consider a fluid element of differential size as shown in Figure A1. This element has a height of dh, and an area on the top and bottom face of dA. The element has a weight of W. This weight can be calculated as the mass (m) times the acceleration of gravity (g), or

$$W = m \, g \tag{A9}$$

Alternatively, the mass can be expressed as the density (ρ) multiplied by the volume (V), so the weight would be

$$W = \rho \, V \, g \tag{A10}$$

We can calculate the volume from our dimensions, giving us

$$W = \rho \, dA \, dh \, g \tag{A11}$$

We assume that the fluid element is at rest (hence the "static" in the name), so there are no shear forces on the fluid element. Thus, the fluid element must be held in equilibrium by pressure forces opposing the weight force. The fluid element has pressure on the top surface (P) and a slightly greater pressure (P + dP) on the bottom surface to offset the fluid element weight. There are also pressures on the side surfaces, but the resulting forces must be equal and opposite on opposing sides because the fluid element is stationary.

The difference in the pressures on the top and bottom surfaces would be

$$\Sigma F = P \, dA - (P + dP) \, dA \tag{A12}$$

which after rearranging terms and subtracting out the pressures becomes just

$$\Sigma F = - dP \, dA \tag{A13}$$

Summing the pressure and weight forces in the vertical direction gives us

$$\Sigma F = -\rho \, dA \, dh \, g - dP \, dA = 0 \tag{A14}$$

Dividing out the dA and rearranging we get the final version

$$\boxed{dP = -\rho \, g \, dh} \tag{A15}$$

Geopotential Altitude

Unfortunately we can't get our pressure profile with altitude just by integrating the hydrostatic equation to the desired altitude, like

$$\int_0^P dP = \int_0^h -\rho g \, dh \tag{A16}$$

because the density and acceleration of gravity are functions of altitude (h). To help with this problem, we would like to replace the acceleration of gravity in Equation A16 with the value of the acceleration of gravity at sea level. To do this, we take the variation out of the acceleration of gravity and put it in a new type of altitude that we call Geopotential Altitude (H), defined by

$$g \, dh = g_{SL} \, dH \tag{A17}$$

Sir Isaac Newton told us that the relationship between the acceleration of gravity at altitude and the acceleration of gravity at sea level for a single body problem is

$$g = g_{SL} \left(\frac{R_{e_{SL}}}{R_{e_{SL}} + h} \right)^2 \tag{A18}$$

where

g_{SL} = acceleration of gravity at sea level
$R_{e_{SL}}$ = radius of the earth

To get a relationship between geometric altitude and geopotential altitude, we substitute equation A18 into equation A17 to get

$$g_{SL} \left(\frac{R_{e_{SL}}}{R_{e_{SL}} + h} \right)^2 dh = g_{SL} dH \tag{A19}$$

We'll divide out the g_{SL} and swap sides to get

$$dH = \left(\frac{R_{e_{SL}}}{R_{e_{SL}} + h} \right)^2 dh \tag{A20}$$

This isn't very useful in the differential form, so we'll integrate from sea level to the altitude of interest.

$$\int_0^H dH = \int_0^h \left(\frac{R_{e_{SL}}}{R_{e_{SL}} + h} \right)^2 dh \tag{A21}$$

Since the radius of the earth is a constant (compared to altitude), we can pull it in front of the integral.

$$\int_0^H dH = \left(R_{e_{SL}} \right)^2 \int_0^h \frac{1}{\left(R_{e_{SL}} + h \right)^2} dh \tag{A22}$$

If we use the old integrating trick of considering the quantity $(R_{e_{SL}} + h)$ as the variable u, along with the resulting $du = 1$, the right hand integral becomes

$$\int u^{-2} du = -u^{-1} + \text{constant} \tag{A23}$$

Thus, equation A22 integrates to

$$H = \left(R_{e_{SL}} \right)^2 \frac{-1}{\left(R_{e_{SL}} + h \right)} \Bigg]_0^h \tag{A24}$$

Solving the definite integral

$$H = \left(R_{e_{SL}} \right)^2 \left(\frac{-1}{\left(R_{e_{SL}} + h \right)} - \frac{-1}{R_{e_{SL}}} \right) \tag{A25}$$

Add the fractions by getting a common denominator

$$H = \left(R_{e_{SL}} \right)^2 \left(\frac{-R_{e_{SL}} + \left(R_{e_{SL}} + h \right)}{R_{e_{SL}} \left(R_{e_{SL}} + h \right)} \right) \tag{A26}$$

Add $R_{e_{SL}}$ together

$$H = \left(R_{e_{SL}} \right)^2 \left(\frac{h}{R_{e_{SL}} \left(R_{e_{SL}} + h \right)} \right) \tag{A27}$$

and bring $R_{e_{SL}}$ in

$$H = \left(\frac{R_{e_{SL}} h}{\left(R_{e_{SL}} + h \right)} \right) \tag{A28}$$

or a more useable form

$$H = \left(\frac{R_{e_{SL}}}{R_{e_{SL}} + h} \right) h \qquad (A29)$$

To use geopotential altitude in the Hydrostatic equation, we simply substitute from Equation A17 into Equation A15 to get

$$dP = -\rho \, g_{SL} \, dH \qquad (A30)$$

Radius of the Earth

The radius of the earth depends on where you are and what the local elevation is. Of course, that's way more detailed than what we're looking for. What we want is the radius of the earth at sea level since we start counting altitude at sea level. Elevation makes very little difference, as even the elevation of Mount Everest adds only one tenth of a percent to the earth's radius.

People who worry about this sort of thing model the earth as an oblate spheroid, a three-dimensional surface you would get by rotating an ellipse about its minor (shorter) axis. The result is a shape like you get if you sit on an exercise ball. The spheroid definition we will use is the World Geodetic System 1984, more commonly referred to as WGS 84. This is the reference system currently used by GPS. From Reference 25, the important numbers are

Semi-major Axis (a) (radius at the equator)	6,378,137.0 meters
Semi-minor Axis (b) (radius at the poles)	6,356,752.3142 meters

The radius at a particular location is the same with longitude, but varies with latitude. For this textbook, we will use the latitude (ϕ) of Edwards AFB, 34.9 degrees. The radius of an oblate spheroid is given by (Reference 26)

$$R(\phi) = \sqrt{\frac{\left(a^2 \cos\phi\right)^2 + \left(b^2 \sin\phi\right)^2}{\left(a\cos\phi\right)^2 + \left(b\sin\phi\right)^2}} \qquad (A31)$$

For WGS-84 at 34.9 degrees latitude, the radius of the earth calculates to

$$R_{e_{SL}} = 6,371,176.179 \text{ meters}$$
$$R_{e_{SL}} = 20,902,808.99 \text{ feet}$$

Calculating the Standard Atmosphere

To calculate the pressure profile with altitude, we need to integrate the pressure change with altitude. We replaced the acceleration of gravity (varies with altitude) with the acceleration of gravity at sea level (constant) by expressing altitude in geopotential feet. We can eliminate density from the integral by dividing the Hydrostatic Equation (Equation A30) by the Equation of State (Equation A3), giving

$$\frac{dP}{P} = \frac{-\rho g_{SL} dH}{\rho RT} \qquad (A32)$$

If we divide out the density we get

$$\frac{dP}{P} = -\frac{g_{SL}}{RT}dH \tag{A33}$$

Now we have an expression that we can actually integrate. g_{SL} and R are constants, and we'll know how T varies with altitude.

Isothermal Regions

For isothermal regions, the relationship of temperature with altitude is simply

$$T = constant \tag{A34}$$

With that established, we will integrate Equation A33 starting at the base altitude (bottom of the altitude band, designated by subscript B) to the altitude of interest (no subscript). When we do that, we get

$$\int_{P_B}^{P} \frac{dP}{P} = -\frac{g_{SL}}{RT_B}\int_{H_B}^{H}dH \tag{A35}$$

These integrals are pretty straightforward, giving the definite integral

$$\ln P\big]_{P_B}^{P} = -\frac{g_{SL}}{RT_B}H\big]_{H_B}^{H} \tag{A36}$$

Substituting the limits

$$\ln P - \ln P_B = -\frac{g_{SL}}{RT_B}\left(H - H_B\right) \tag{A37}$$

Since the difference of two logarithms is the logarithm of the quotient of the arguments, or

$$\ln a - \ln b = \ln \frac{a}{b} \tag{A38}$$

we can change Equation A37 to

$$\ln \frac{P}{P_B} = -\frac{g_{SL}}{RT_B}\left(H - H_B\right) \tag{A39}$$

and since

$$e^{\ln x} = x \tag{A40}$$

we'll raise e to both sides to get

$$\boxed{\frac{P}{P_B} = e^{-\left(\frac{g_{SL}}{RT_B}\right)\left(H - H_B\right)}} \tag{A41}$$

To determine the density variation with altitude, we return to the Equation of State at the altitude of interest and at the base altitude

$$\frac{P}{P_B} = \frac{\rho RT}{\rho_B RT_B} \tag{A42}$$

and since $T = T_B$ (isothermal layer) we get

$$\frac{P}{P_B} = \frac{\rho}{\rho_B} \tag{A43}$$

Therefore

$$\boxed{\frac{\rho}{\rho_B} = e^{-\left(\frac{g_{SL}}{RT_B}\right)(H-H_B)}} \tag{A44}$$

Gradient Regions

For the gradient regions we have a different relationship between temperature and altitude. We call this relationship the temperature lapse rate and define it as

$$L = \frac{dT}{dH} = \text{constant} \tag{A45}$$

Rearranging this equation gives

$$L\,dH = dT \tag{A46}$$

Integrating from the base altitude to the altitude of interest (L is constant with altitude)

$$L\int_{H_B}^{H} dH = \int_{T_B}^{T} dT \tag{A47}$$

which becomes

$$L H]_{H_B}^{H} = T]_{T_B}^{T} \tag{A48}$$

Substituting the limits

$$L(H - H_B) = T - T_B \tag{A49}$$

Moving T_B to the other side and rearranging

$$T = T_B + L(H - H_B) \tag{A50}$$

Dividing by T_B gives our final form of the temperature profile

$$\boxed{\frac{T}{T_B} = 1 + \frac{L}{T_B}(H - H_B)} \tag{A51}$$

To find the pressure profile with altitude, we return to Equation A33

$$\frac{dP}{P} = -\frac{g_{SL}}{RT} dH \tag{A33}$$

We can rearrange Equation A45 to give us another representation of dH

$$dH = \frac{dT}{L} \tag{A52}$$

Substituting this into the pressure equation gives us

$$\frac{dP}{P} = -\frac{g_{SL}}{RT}\frac{dT}{L} \tag{A53}$$

Regrouping constants gives

$$\frac{dP}{P} = -\frac{g_{SL}}{RL}\frac{dT}{T} \tag{A54}$$

which is an equation that we can integrate

$$\int_{P_B}^{P} \frac{dP}{P} = \frac{-g_{SL}}{RL} \int_{H_B}^{H} \frac{dT}{T} \tag{A55}$$

which gives us

$$\ln P\big]_{P_B}^{P} = \frac{-g_{SL}}{RL} \ln T\big]_{T_B}^{T} \tag{A56}$$

Substituting limits

$$\ln P - \ln P_B = \frac{-g_{SL}}{RL}\left(\ln T - \ln T_B\right) \tag{A57}$$

Again since

$$\ln a - \ln b = \ln \frac{a}{b} \tag{A38}$$

we get

$$\ln \frac{P}{P_B} = \frac{-g_{SL}}{RL}\ln \frac{T}{T_B} \tag{A58}$$

Raising e to both sides to take care of the logarithms

$$e^{\left(\ln \frac{P}{P_B}\right)} = e^{\left(\frac{-g_{SL}}{RL}\ln \frac{T}{T_B}\right)} \tag{A59}$$

and remembering that

$$a^{mn} = (a^m)^n \tag{A60}$$

we get

$$e^{\left(\ln\frac{P}{P_B}\right)} = \left(e^{\left(\ln\frac{T}{T_B}\right)}\right)^{\frac{-g_{SL}}{RL}} \tag{A61}$$

which becomes

$$\frac{P}{P_B} = \left(\frac{T}{T_B}\right)^{\frac{-g_{SL}}{RL}} \tag{A62}$$

Substituting Equation A51 in Equation A62 for the temperature ratio gives

$$\boxed{\frac{P}{P_B} = \left(1 + \frac{L}{T_B}(H - H_B)\right)^{\frac{-g_{SL}}{RL}}} \tag{A63}$$

Again, returning to the equation of state, we find the density variation with altitude to be

$$\frac{P}{P_B} = \frac{\rho R T}{\rho_B R T_B} \tag{A42}$$

Dividing out the Rs and moving the temperature ratio to the other side gives

$$\frac{\rho}{\rho_B} = \frac{P}{P_B}\left(\frac{T}{T_B}\right)^{-1} \tag{A64}$$

From Equation A62 we can substitute for the pressure ratio

$$\frac{\rho}{\rho_B} = \left(\frac{T}{T_B}\right)^{\frac{-g_{SL}}{RL}}\left(\frac{T}{T_B}\right)^{-1} \tag{A65}$$

And since

$$a^m\, a^n = a^{m+n} \tag{A66}$$

we can rearrange to

$$\frac{\rho}{\rho_B} = \left(\frac{T}{T_B}\right)^{\frac{-g_{SL}}{RL} - 1} \tag{A67}$$

Substituting equation A51 for the temperature ratio gives our final version

$$\frac{\rho}{\rho_B} = \left(1 + \frac{L}{T_B}(H - H_B)\right)^{\frac{-g_{SL}}{RL} - 1} \tag{A68}$$

Temperature, Pressure, and Density Ratios

The temperature, pressure, and density ratios are defined as:

$$\theta = \frac{T}{T_{SL}} \tag{A69}$$

$$\delta = \frac{P}{P_{SL}} \tag{A70}$$

$$\sigma = \frac{\rho}{\rho_{SL}} \tag{A71}$$

Troposphere Equations

For the troposphere, the base altitude is sea level. Therefore, from Reference 3

$$T_{SL} = 288.15 \text{ K} \tag{A72}$$

$$L = -0.0019812 \text{ K/ft} \tag{A73}$$

$$g_{SL} = 32.1741 \text{ ft/sec}^2 \tag{A74}$$

$$R = 3089.8 \text{ ft-lb/slug-K} \tag{A75}$$

So

$$-\frac{L}{T_{SL}} = 6.87559 \times 10^{-6} / \text{geopotential feet} \tag{A76}$$

$$-\frac{g_{SL}}{RL} = 5.25590 \tag{A77}$$

which gives the equations

$$\theta = 1 - 6.87559 \times 10^{-6} \text{ H} \tag{A78}$$

$$\delta = (1 - 6.87559 \times 10^{-6} \text{ H})^{5.2559} \tag{A79}$$

$$\sigma = (1 - 6.87559 \times 10^{-6} \text{ H})^{4.2559} \tag{A80}$$

Stratosphere Equations

The isothermal portion of the stratosphere is defined for an altitude band from 11 kilometers to 20 kilometers (36,089.24 feet to 65,616.8 feet). In an isothermal region there is no temperature lapse rate. The base altitude is 11 kilometers. The base values for temperature, pressure, and density come from the troposphere calculations at 11 kilometers, and are

$$T_B = 216.65 \text{ K} \quad \theta_B = 0.751865 \tag{A81}$$

$$P_B = 472.679 \text{ lb/ft}^2 \quad \delta_B = 0.223360 \tag{A82}$$

$$\rho_B = 0.0007061 \text{ slug/ft}^3 \quad \sigma_B = 0.297075 \tag{A83}$$

Our equations for isothemal regions are written as ratios of the parameter to its value at the base altitude. However, it is more useful to have ratios of the parameter to the sea level value. Note that

$$\theta = \frac{T}{T_{SL}} = \frac{T_B}{T_{SL}} \frac{T}{T_B} = \theta_B \frac{T}{T_B} \tag{A84}$$

Applying this concept and inserting our constants, we get

$$\frac{-g_{SL}}{RT_B} = 4.80637 \times 10^{-5} / \text{geo ft} \tag{A85}$$

$$\boxed{\theta = 0.751865} \tag{A86}$$

$$\boxed{\delta = 0.223360 \, e^{(-4.80637 \times 10^{-5} (H - 36089.24))}} \tag{A87}$$

$$\boxed{\sigma = 0.297075 \, e^{(-4.80637 \times 10^{-5} (H - 36089.24))}} \tag{A88}$$

Comparing Water Vapor Density to Air Density

Water vapor is less dense than air. Just how much less dense can be calculated by looking at the ratio of the densities. From the Equation of State (Equation A3), we can solve for density

$$\rho = \frac{P}{RT} \tag{A89}$$

In Reference 27 we find the specific gas constant for water vapor to be

$$R_{water} = 2762 \, \frac{\text{ft} - \text{lb}}{\text{slug} - \,^{\circ}R} \tag{A90}$$

Therefore, the ratio of water vapor density to air density at the same pressure and temperature would be given by

$$\frac{\rho_{water}}{\rho_{air}} = \frac{\dfrac{P}{R_{water}\,T}}{\dfrac{P}{R_{air}\,T}} = \frac{R_{air}}{R_{water}} \tag{A91}$$

$$\frac{R_{air}}{R_{water}} = \frac{1716}{2762} = 0.62 \tag{A92}$$

which means that water vapor has a density 0.62 that of air, or 38 percent less than air.

Calculating Density of Humid Air

Table A1 Saturation Pressure of Water (Ref 27 and 28)	
Temp (°F)	Saturation Pressure (psia)
-20	0.006189
-15	0.008252
-10	0.010904
-5	0.014293
0	0.018812
5	0.024117
10	0.030993
15	0.039785
20	0.050591
25	0.063853
30	0.080553
32.018	0.08866
35	0.09992
40	0.12166
45	0.14748
50	0.17803
60	0.2563
70	0.3632
80	0.5073
90	0.6988
100	0.9503
110	1.2763
120	1.6945
130	2.225

Understanding partial pressure is the key to understanding gas mixtures, such as air and water vapor. The pressure read on an altimeter or a pressure gauge is the sum of the partial pressures of air and water vapor.

To calculate the dry air density, we must know the partial pressure of the dry air. One way to find this is to determine the partial pressure of water vapor and subtract it from the observed pressure. The temperature of the dry air and the water vapor will be the same as the observed temperature of the mixture.

For purposes of this discussion, consider the following example:

Observed Pressure Altitude (Moist):   2302 feet
Observed Temperature: 80 °F
Relative Humidity: 25 percent

Moist air will refer to the air and water vapor mixture. Dry air will refer to the air alone, and water vapor will refer to the water vapor alone.

1. Determine the saturation pressure of water vapor at the observed temperature.

This step finds the partial pressure of the water vapor assuming a totally saturated mixture. This would be when the air/water vapor mixture contains the maximum possible amount of water vapor and any additional water vapor would immediately condense out.

The saturation pressure of water vapor as a function of temperature is shown in Table A1. Note that small amounts of water vapor can still exist even below freezing temperatures.

For the example case,

$$T = 80°F \tag{A93}$$

$$P_{saturated\ water} = 0.5073\ psia \tag{A94}$$

Table A1 lists the saturation pressure of water against the saturation temperature. Tables work fine if you are calculating by hand, but if you are trying to set up a computer routine an equation is much more convenient. There are many such equations available, all of which are very close.

Generally the most popular is Tetens' expression (from Appendix G)

$$P_{water} = 6.11 * 10^{\left(\frac{7.5T}{237.3+T}\right)} \qquad T(°C) > 0 \tag{G16}$$

$$P_{water} = 6.11 * 10^{\left(\frac{9.5T}{265.5+T}\right)} \qquad T(°C) < 0 \tag{G17}$$

> Note:
> T is the Dew Point in degrees Celsius (°C)
> P_{water} is in millibars

Tetens' expression is a curve fit to experimental data, not an expression derived from first principles. As such, it is an unusual equation in that temperature is entered in Celsius, not in an absolute unit like Kelvin or Rankine. Additionally, the output unit is millibars. Conversions can be done using the values of sea level pressure

$$P_{SL} = 2116.22\ lb/ft^2 = 1013.25\ mbar$$

2. Determine the water vapor partial pressure.

Relative humidity is defined as the fraction of water vapor present in the air to the maximum possible water vapor that can exist at that temperature. The amount of water vapor present is measured by its partial pressure. The maximum possible partial pressure of water vapor is the saturation pressure for water vapor at that temperature. If the actual partial pressure of the water vapor is half of the maximum possible (saturation pressure), then the relative humidity is said to be 50 percent.

$$P_{water} = P_{saturated\ water} * Relative\ Humidity \tag{A95}$$

$$P_{water} = 0.5073\ psia * 0.25 \tag{A96}$$

$$P_{water} = 0.1268\ psia = 18.26\ lb/ft^2 \tag{A97}$$

Optional Step: Determine the Dew Point.

The Dew Point is defined as the temperature at which the air would become saturated (100 percent relative humidity) with the current amount of water vapor. In thermodynamic terms, it is the saturation temperature corresponding to the partial pressure of water vapor (Table A1). Thus, for our example

$$T_{dew} = 41\ °F \tag{A98}$$

Alternatively, the dew point can be determined by using the partial pressure of water vapor in the inverse of Tetens' expression

$$T_{dew} = \frac{237.3 \log_{10}(P_{water}) - 186.527}{8.286 - \log_{10}(P_{water})} \qquad T(^{\circ}C) > 0 \qquad (A99)$$

$$T_{dew} = \frac{265.5 \log_{10}(P_{water}) - 208.694}{10.286 - \log_{10}(P_{water})} \qquad T(^{\circ}C) < 0 \qquad (A100)$$

Note: T is the Dew Point in degrees Celsius ($^{\circ}$C), P_{water} is in millibars

Alternative method to find water vapor partial pressure.

If the dew point is known, then the partial pressure of water vapor can be determined directly by entering Table A1 with the dew point temperature, or by using the dew point temperature in Tetens' expression (Equations G16 and G17). The saturation pressure corresponding to the dew point temperature is the water vapor partial pressure.

3. Determine the moist air pressure.

The moist air pressure is determined from the observed pressure altitude.

$$\delta_{moist} = (1 - 6.87559 \times 10^{-6}\, H_c)^{5.2559} \qquad (A101)$$

$$\delta_{moist} = (1 - 6.87559 \times 10^{-6}/\text{feet} \, (2302 \text{ feet}))^{5.2559}$$

$$\delta_{moist} = 0.919566 \qquad (A102)$$

$$P_{moist} = \delta_{moist}\, P_{SL} \qquad (A103)$$

$$P_{moist} = (0.919566)(2116.22 \text{ lb/ft}^2)$$

$$P_{moist} = 1946 \text{ lb/ft}^2 \qquad (A104)$$

4. Determine the dry air pressure (partial pressure of air).

The partial pressure of air is the observed pressure minus the partial pressure of water vapor. That is

$$P_{dry} = P_{moist} - P_{water} \qquad (A105)$$

$$P_{dry} = 1946 \text{ lb/ft}^2 - 18.26 \text{ lb/ft}^2 \qquad (A106)$$

$$P_{dry} = 1928 \text{ lb/ft}^2 \qquad (A107)$$

5. Determine the dry air density.

The dry air density is important for applications such as reciprocating engine performance that depend on the amount of oxygen available. The dry air density is calculated using the partial pressure of air and the temperature of the moist air (same as the temperature of the dry air) in the Equation of State. The specific gas constant for air (1716 ft-lb/slug-°R) is used.

$$\rho_{dry} = \frac{P_{dry}}{R_{air} T} \qquad (A108)$$

$$\rho_{dry} = \frac{1928 \; lb / ft^2}{\left(1716 \dfrac{ft - lb}{slug - °R}\right)(80°F + 460)}$$

$$\rho_{dry} = 0.002081 \; slug/ft^3 \qquad (A109)$$

6. Determine the water vapor density

The water vapor density is calculated using the partial pressure of water vapor and the temperature of the moist air (same as the temperature of the water vapor) in the Equation of State. The specific gas constant for water vapor (2762 ft-lb/slug-°R) is used.

$$\rho_{water} = \frac{P_{water}}{R_{water} T} \qquad (A110)$$

$$\rho_{water} = \frac{(0.1268 \; psia)\left(144 \; psia/\left(lb / ft^2\right)\right)}{\left(2762 \dfrac{ft - lb}{slug - °R}\right)(80°F + 460)}$$

$$\rho_{water} = 1.2242 \times 10^{-5} \; slug/ft^3 \qquad (A111)$$

7. Determine moist air density

The density of the air/water vapor mixture is the sum of the densities of the dry air and the water vapor.

$$\rho_{moist} = \rho_{dry} + \rho_{water} \qquad (A112)$$

$$\rho_{moist} = 0.002081 \; slug/ft^3 + 1.2242 \times 10^{-5} \; slug/ft^3$$

$$\rho_{moist} = 0.002093 \; slug/ft^3 \qquad (A113)$$

Temperature Variations with Altitude

The standard atmosphere was calculated by solving three equations for three unknowns, namely pressure, density, and temperature. The first two equations, the Equation of State and the Hydrostatic Equation, are applicable to any ideal gas and any gas within a gravity field. In order for the Standard Atmosphere to reasonably model the actual atmosphere, the final equation needed to come from actual measurements of the atmosphere. Years of temperature measurements from weather balloons, aircraft, sounding rockets, and other sources led to a standard temperature profile as shown in Figure A2, a modification of Figure 2.2 shown earlier in this text book. The line shown in Figure A2 represents the mean value of the temperature distribution measured throughout the year at each altitude. This temperature distribution at any altitude has a very large variance, as the temperature changes greatly throughout the year with seasonal variations as well as day to day weather patterns and uneven heating from the sun. The line does not give a good representation of the actual temperature profile on any particular day, but gives a good yearly average of the temperature and a good representation of the temperature lapse rate on most days.

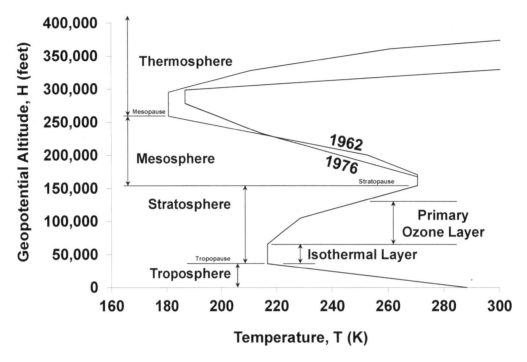

Figure A2. Temperature Profile, 1962 and 1976 Standard Atmosphere (Ref 3 and 5)

Other sections of this textbook have described how to use this temperature profile to calculate the standard atmosphere. This section endeavors to explain why this temperature profile looks like it does. The material in this section reflects contributions by Col Douglas Wickert of the USAF Academy Department of Aeronautics.

The atmosphere is divided into layers based on when the temperature lapse rate changes from negative to positive or back to negative. The lowest layer, the troposphere, has a decreasing temperature with increasing altitude. Above the troposphere, the stratosphere has increasing temperature with increasing altitude. Above the stratosphere, the mesosphere has a decreasing temperature with increasing altitude. Above the mesosphere, the thermosphere has an increasing temperature with increasing altitude. These layers can be seen in striking detail in Figure A3.

Tropospheric Cooling

Figure A4 is based on the left side of Figure I6, and shows how the solar radiation interacts with the atmosphere. The majority of the energy in solar radiation is in the Visible and Near Infrared wavelengths. The atmospheric absorption of energy in these wavelengths is minimal, as shown by the small difference in the irradiance that leaves the sun (yellow area) and what makes it to sea level (orange area). Another way of saying that the absorption is minimal is to say the atmosphere is transparent to light in these ranges. This is a good thing, because if the atmosphere was opaque to visible wavelengths it would be pretty dark on the surface of the earth and those solar panels on your roof wouldn't be making very much power.

Figure A3: Layered structure of atmosphere photographed from the International Space Station at an altitude of 183 nm. The space shuttle Endeavour (STS-130 with Terry Virts, USAFA 1989, USAF TPS 98B Test Pilot) is approaching for rendezvous and docking operations.   The troposphere (orange layer), stratosphere (white), and mesosphere (blue), and thermosphere (black) are well-defined and clearly visible. (NASA Photo)

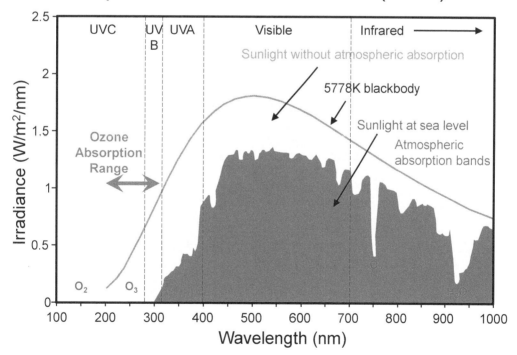

Figure A4. Spectrum of Solar Radiation (Ref 29)

Because the air is mostly transparent to a majority of the solar radiation (light), most of the light comes through the atmosphere without interacting with the air. As shown in Figure A5, a small portion of the solar radiation is absorbed by the atmosphere, mostly in the stratosphere, detailed in the next section. The remaining solar radiation arrives at the surface without heating up the air directly. Some of the incident radiation is reflected by the ground and clouds, convenient so that we can see. The remaining radiation, almost half of what arrived at the top of the atmosphere, is absorbed by the soil, water, concrete, or whatever the light falls upon, including you. The energy that is absorbed from the light is converted into kinetic energy of the molecules of the surface. That's a fancy way of saying sunlight heats up whatever it falls upon.

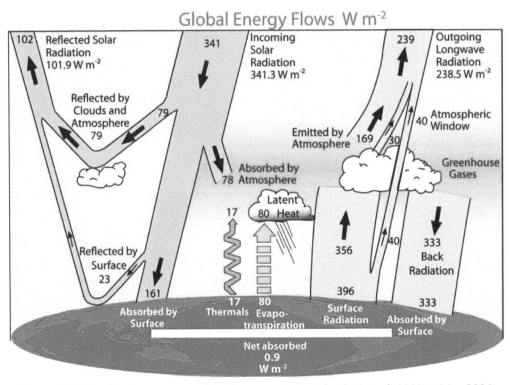

Figure A5. The global annual mean Earth's energy budget for the March 2000 to May 2004 period (W/m²). The broad arrows indicate the schematic flow of energy in proportion to their importance. (Ref 30)

The surface of the earth, now warmed by the sunlight, warms up the air next to it through conduction followed by convection, and also by radiating that energy in infrared wavelengths that are absorbed by air molecules. The air at low altitudes warms the air above it through molecular interaction and convection, commonly referred to as thermals. However, because of dry adiabatic expansion (covered in Appendix I), as the air rises, the pressure decreases and the air expands and cools at a rate of 3° C per 1000 feet of altitude gained. The sun continues to add energy to the system, so more rising air brings more energy up, warming the air more than the Dry Adiabatic Lapse Rate would suggest. Driven by this ground heating, convection, and IR radiation, the end result is that with other energy losses, the troposphere ends up on average cooling at a rate of 2°C per 1000 feet of altitude gained.

Stratospheric Heating

If you are like me, your introduction to the "Ozone Layer" was that it was something you heard about on the news that some activists were up in arms about because it had holes in it. Apparently this was bad for some reason that wasn't well explained. They went on to say that these holes were caused by chlorofluorocarbons (CFC), such as dichlorodifluoromethane (Freon 12 or R-12) that was used in our car air conditioners and other refrigeration products. Now we had to replace all of the R-12 with 1,1,1,2-Tetrafluoroethane (R-134a), which apparently was better because it didn't contain chlorine atoms. It worked like R-12, only not as well (this was only a problem when used as a direct replacement in systems designed for R-12—once refrigeration systems were designed specifically for R-134a performance was sufficient). Also we could no longer have aerosol spray cans because they were full of R-12. It seemed like the ozone layer existed just to take away our modern conveniences.

So what does this troublesome ozone layer have to do with the Standard Atmosphere? It turns out that the upper part of the stratosphere increases in temperature with increasing altitude as a result of the interaction of the ozone layer with ultraviolet light. This heating is the byproduct of the primary purpose of the ozone layer, which is to block ultraviolet light, specifically the UVC wavelengths and most of the UVB wavelengths. Shorter wavelength ultraviolet light is blocked by atmospheric nitrogen. Longer wavelength UVB light will get through to the earth's surface, where it interacts with human skin cells to produce Vitamin D, which is a good thing. However, too much of a good thing isn't, as overexposure to UVB causes sunburn and skin cancer. UVA light passes right through the ozone layer to the earth's surface. UVA is less harmful to DNA and generally does not cause skin reddening, however it can lead to long term skin damage and skin cancer.

Understanding the interaction of ultraviolet light with the ozone layer will explain the stratospheric heating phenomenon. This process was first explained by Sydney Chapman in 1930, and is commonly referred to as the "Chapman Cycle". Figure A2 shows the typical altitude range for most of the ozone layer. Figure A4 shows the wavelengths for UVC, UVB, and UVA light.

Figure A6 illustrates the Chapman Cycle, also known as the ozone-oxygen cycle.

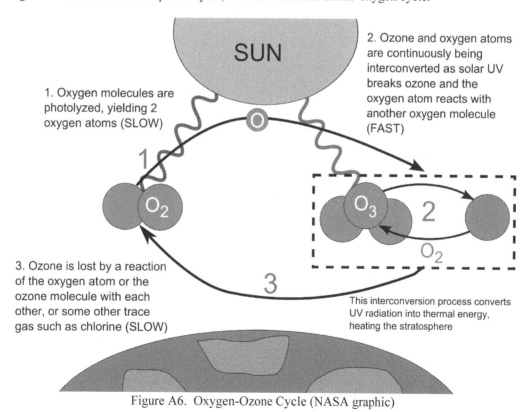

Figure A6. Oxygen-Ozone Cycle (NASA graphic)

The process is driven by photolysis, the process by which a chemical compound is broken down by collision with a photon. Quantum mechanics teaches us that atomic elements can only exist at certain discrete energy states, and for photolysis to work the impacting photon must have just the right amount of energy. The energy of a photon is inversely proportional to its wavelength, so photolysis depends on photons travelling at a particular wavelength.

The process starts when a photon of UVC light in the wavelength range of 100-200 nanometers (nm) strikes a molecule of stratospheric diatomic oxygen (O_2) and splits the molecule into two free oxygen atoms.

$$O_2 + h\nu_{(100\text{-}200\,nm)} \rightarrow 2\,O$$

Oxygen atoms don't like being alone, but since there aren't very many free oxygen atoms to bond with, the free oxygen atom is most likely to run into a diatomic oxygen molecule and bond with it, forming an ozone molecule.

$$O + O_2 \rightarrow O_3 + E_K$$

The E_K denotes the excess internal energy that was added to the free oxygen atom by the photon when the diatomic molecule was split, which is manifested after the reaction as excess kinetic energy. We recognize an increase in kinetic energy as an increase in temperature. The internal energy of the ozone molecule is less than the sum of the internal energy of a diatomic oxygen molecule and a separate free oxygen atom, so they begrudgingly stay together. The resulting ozone molecule is unstable, though in the stratosphere relatively long-lived.

Photolysis comes up again when the ozone molecule is struck with a UVC or UVB photon, which will split the ozone into diatomic oxygen and a free oxygen atom.

$$O_3 + h\nu_{(240\text{-}310\,nm)} \rightarrow O_2 + O$$

The photon has again raised the energy level of the diatomic oxygen and free oxygen atom, and the free oxygen atom will seek to lower its internal energy again by combining with another diatomic oxygen molecule to form ozone.

$$O + O_2 \rightarrow O_3 + E_K$$

The process of splitting and reforming ozone molecules happens, on a relative scale, very rapidly. Each cycle of the process absorbs the energy of an ultraviolet photon and then releases that energy as kinetic energy, raising the temperature of the gas. This absorption and release of energy occurs with no net change in the amount of ozone. Because some of the ultraviolet photons get absorbed at high altitudes, less photons make it down to lower altitudes, as shown in Figure A7. Thus the higher altitudes are warmer than the lower altitudes, resulting in the temperature lapse rate seen in Figure A2. This process is effective enough that all of the UVC radiation and most of the UVB radiation are blocked before reaching the earth's surface.

By comparison to the ozone-oxygen cycle, the splitting of diatomic oxygen happens slower, but still contributes to the heating of the stratosphere, as the high energy oxygen atoms combine with diatomic oxygen to form ozone.

So it would seem that the ozone is happy constantly breaking up and getting back together, just like a bunch of high school teenagers, absorbing and releasing energy the whole time. So where is the problem that leads to ozone depletion?

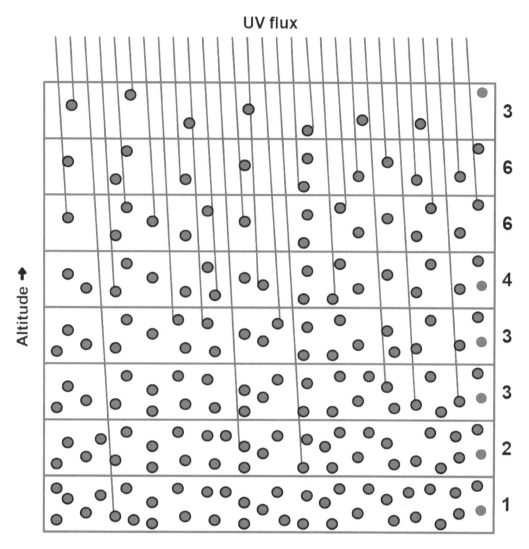

- **Density of molecules decreases with higher altitude, and abosorption is proportional to the density of the molecules and the cross-section.**

- **Greatest absorption occurs in the middle layers where the density-cross section product has become large enough for significant absorption.**

Figure A7: UV absorption increases with decreasing altitude (Ref 31)

As an ozone molecule travels around in the rarified density of the stratosphere, it will mostly bump into diatomic oxygen molecules or nitrogen molecules with no reaction other than collisions. However, the ozone molecule will occasionally bump into a free oxygen atom. The internal energy of two diatomic oxygen molecules is less than that of an ozone molecule and a free oxygen atom, so they will combine into two diatomic oxygen molecules, releasing the excess internal energy as more kinetic energy.

$$O_3 + O \rightarrow 2\,O_2 + E_K$$

For that matter, if two free oxygen atoms happen to find each other before finding a diatomic oxygen molecule, they will simply reform a diatomic oxygen molecule, again releasing their excess energy as kinetic energy.

$$O + O \rightarrow O_2 + E_K$$

Certain free radicals can catalyze the breakup of ozone back into oxygen. Some of these, such as hydroxyl (OH) and nitric oxide (NO) occur naturally in the stratosphere. Others, such as atomic chlorine (Cl) and atomic bromine (Br) arrive because of human activity.

Chlorofluorocarbons (CFC) and bromofluorocarbons are released into the troposphere. At low altitudes these compounds are stable and heavier than air. However, atmospheric mixing through thermals and wind shears can carry these molecules high into the stratosphere. Without the protection of the ozone layer at these altitudes, ultraviolet photons photolyze these molecules, releasing free chlorine atoms and free bromine atoms.

If a free chlorine atom runs into an ozone molecule, the chlorine will steal one oxygen atom to form chlorine monoxide and a diatomic oxygen molecule.

$$Cl + O_3 \rightarrow ClO + O_2 + E_K$$

The chlorine monoxide molecule floats around the stratosphere until it runs into a free oxygen atom, which steals the oxygen atom from the chlorine to form diatomic oxygen.

$$ClO + O \rightarrow Cl + O_2 + E_K$$

Thus released, the chlorine atom seeks out another ozone molecule to break down. This can happen as many as 100,000 times. Eventually the chlorine atom will run into another type of molecule, such as methane (CH_4). If this happens, the chlorine atom will be bound up into a molecule of hydrogen chloride (HCl), which can be carried downward from the stratosphere into the troposphere, where it can be washed away by rain.

Mesospheric Cooling

Continuing up in altitude into the mesosphere, the density of the oxygen molecules decreases to the point that there is not enough absorption of UV radiation to have a warming effect. There aren't enough oxygen molecules for the UV photons to run into, and if a photon happens to split an oxygen molecule, the resulting oxygen atoms are going to have a very hard time finding any other oxygen to link up with and release their energy.

However, there is another common molecule to consider that interacts with solar radiation — carbon dioxide. When I was a kid in the 70s, carbon dioxide was a gas that we exhaled and plants absorbed. Plants broke up the molecule, releasing the oxygen for us to breathe and keeping the carbon to make plant tissue. Somewhere along the way in the 21st century, carbon dioxide became better known as an evil greenhouse gas that was going to spell doom and the end of life as we know it.

How did carbon dioxide gain this evil persona? Looking at Figure A8, the red lines show the peaks of absorption by carbon dioxide at wavelengths of approximately 1900 nm, 2800 nm, 4500 nm, and 15000 nm. All of these wavelengths are in the infrared band of electromagnetic radiation. The name "greenhouse gas" came about because the Earth, having been warmed by incident solar radiation, emits radiation in the infrared bands. This infrared radiation can be absorbed by carbon dioxide molecules by changing their rotational-vibrational movements. Just as the molecule can absorb the radiation, it can also emit radiation. When the rotational-vibrational movements change back to a lower energy state a photon is released in one of these infrared wavelengths. If that photon is released in the direction of the Earth, it imparts energy back into the Earth, keeping it warm. This gives the impression of being under a giant greenhouse that keeps much of the heat from the sun trapped inside.

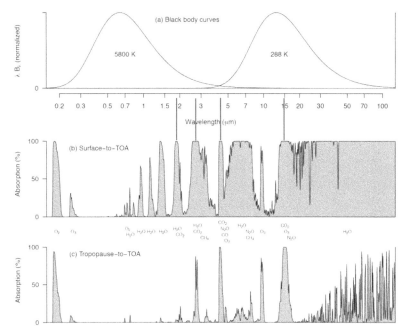

Figure 1. (a) Normalized black body curves for 5800 K (the approximate emission temperature of the Sun) and 288 K (the approximate surface temperature of the Earth). (b) Representative absorption spectrum of the Earth's atmosphere for a vertical column from the surface to space, assuming the atmosphere to be a homogeneous slab. (c) The same but for a vertical column from the tropopause (~ 11 km) to space. Spectra based on *HITRAN on the Web*; see Appendix D for details. Figure after Goody and Yung (1989, Fig. 1.1 on p. 4).

Figure A8. Atmospheric absorption spectrum (Ref 32)

However, if that same infrared photon goes to the side or up, it is likely to run into another carbon dioxide molecule and be absorbed, only to be emitted in some other random direction.

In the mesosphere, infrared radiation to be absorbed by carbon dioxide comes not only from the Earth but also directly from the sun. Because of the very low air density, any infrared photons emitted by a carbon dioxide molecule in any direction other than toward the Earth stand very little chance of finding another carbon dioxide molecule to be absorbed by, and thus will just continue on out into space. This creates a net outgoing flux of infrared radiation, taking energy away from the earth and cooling the mesosphere.

Thermospheric Heating

The top of the mesosphere is called the mesopause, and is defined as the altitude where the temperature stops decreasing. At a few kilometers above the mesopause (88.743 km geopotential altitude (90 km geometric altitude) in the 1962 US Standard Atmosphere, and at 84.852 km geopotential altitude (86 km geometric altitude) in the 1976 US Standard Atmosphere) the density of the air becomes so low that the individual molecules cannot interact with each other. The mean free path between molecular collisions becomes on the order of 1 km, which is a ridiculous distance for something as small as a molecule to travel in hopes of running into another tiny molecule. I'm told it's sort of like being in the Australian Outback (and I don't mean the Australian themed steakhouse) and looking for another person. At these altitudes, the idea of a gas acting like a continuum falls apart such that the ideal gas assumption fails.

Because of this extremely low density, the molecules stop acting like a group and start acting like individuals. The intense solar and cosmic radiation at the top of the atmosphere provide a significant boost to the kinetic energy of the few molecules in the thermosphere. These molecules get going super-fast, and the molecular-scale temperature (a measure of the average kinetic energy of a gas) in the thermosphere increases with altitude. However, man-made objects in this region would seem to be very cold, because the molecules are so scarce that the idea of "sensible temperature" (a temperature that can be sensed) is not a meaningful concept.

Isothermal Regions

You may have noticed that the transitions between atmospheric layers are modeled as isothermal (constant temperature) regions, and not as a point transition between decreasing temperature and increasing temperature. In these regions, the factors that cause cooling with altitude and the factors that cause heating with altitude interact in such a way as to create a gentle transition from one phenomena to the other. These regions are of significant size on a human scale. For instance, the transition between the cooling of the troposphere and the heating of the stratosphere in the standard atmosphere ranges from about 36,000 feet altitude to 65,000 feet altitude. In this region is most of commercial aviation up to all but the highest flying conventional aircraft and drones.

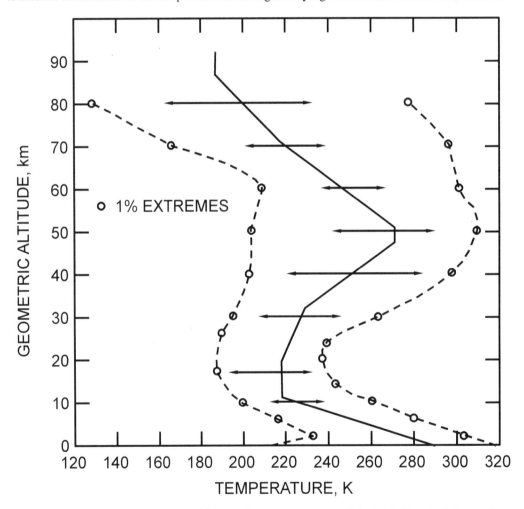

Figure A9. Range of systematic variability of temperature around the U.S. Standard Atmosphere, 1976 (Ref 5)

But is it reasonable to model these regions with a constant temperature? Remember that the standard temperature of the standard atmosphere is an overall mean value of the expected temperature distribution, which has a rather large variance. In Figure A9, lifted from Reference 5, the middle solid line shows the standard temperature profile of the 1976 U.S. Standard Atmosphere. The horizontal arrows show the lowest and highest **mean** monthly temperatures obtained for any location between the Equator and pole. That is, the arrows show how much the average temperature for any day and any location can move around for each altitude. Estimates of the one-percent **maximum** and **minimum** temperatures that occur during the warmest and coldest months, respectively, in the most extreme locations are shown by the dashed lines. With this much variation in possible temperatures and the gentle transition from cooling to heating, it is quite reasonable to represent portions of these transition areas with a constant temperature profile.

While an isothermal model may seem reasonable based on the distribution of temperatures throughout the year, how well does it model the atmosphere on any given day? Looking at Figure A10, an annotated version of Figure I10, we can see the actual temperature profile for a particular day. The air temperature is represented by the red curve and the dew point temperature is represented by the blue curve. The vertical axis shows air pressure in hectopascals (hPa, equivalent to millibars) on the left side and pressure altitude on the right side. In this Skew-T presentation, the horizontal axis represents nothing. Lines of constant temperature are plotted at approximately 45 degrees from the vertical, as highlighted by the bold red line (see Appendix I for an explanation of why these soundings are plotted in this seemingly odd manner).

As shown in the dashed green ellipses, the temperature from just above the surface up to about 35,000 feet pressure altitude cuts across the lines of constant temperature, showing a decrease in temperature with increasing altitude as expected in the troposphere. Around 35,000 feet (the actual tropopause on any given day will vary in altitude from the standard atmosphere value of 36,089 feet) the temperature curve turns to follow a line of constant temperature, showing that an isothermal model is a reasonable representation of reality in these regions.

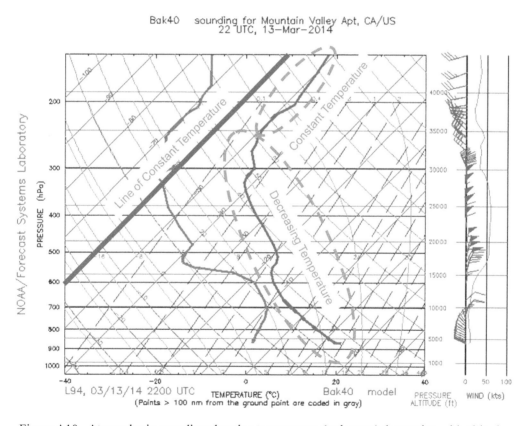

Figure A10. Atmospheric sounding showing temperature (red curve) decreasing with altitude up to 35,000 feet then maintaining a constant temperature with altitude

Appendix B

Altitude Measurement Heavy Math Section

Pressure Altitude

In Appendix A we developed the equations for the pressure ratio as

$$\delta = (1 - 6.87559 \text{x} 10^{-6} \, H)^{5.2559} \qquad \text{(troposphere)} \quad \text{(A79)}$$

$$\delta = 0.223360 \, e^{(-4.80637 \text{x} 10^{-5} \, (H - 36089.24))} \qquad \text{(stratosphere)} \quad \text{(A87)}$$

Because we are defining pressure altitude as the altitude given by the standard atmosphere for a given pressure, then it follows that we can replace the geopotential altitude (H) in these equations with pressure altitude (H_c)

$$\delta = (1 - 6.87559 \text{x} 10^{-6} \, H_c)^{5.2559} \qquad (H_c \leq 36089.24 \text{ feet}) \quad \text{(B1)}$$

$$\delta = 0.223360 \, e^{(-4.80637 \text{x} 10^{-5} \, (H_c - 36089.24))} \qquad (H_c > 36089.24 \text{ feet}) \quad \text{(B2)}$$

Note that these equations are valid for any atmosphere, not just a standard atmosphere. The pressure altitude corresponding to a pressure ratio will always be the same, regardless of the geopotential altitude that it occurs at.

(No, I don't know why pressure altitude is represented by H_c. The best guess I have is that it is sort of like "calibrated altitude" in a similar relationship to true altitude as V_c, "calibrated airspeed" is to true airspeed.)

Inverting Equations B1 and B2 by solving for H_c gives

$$H_c = \frac{1 - \sqrt[5.2559]{\delta}}{6.87559 \text{x} 10^{-6}} \qquad (H_c \leq 36089.24 \text{ feet}) \quad \text{(B3)}$$

$$H_c = \frac{\ln\left(\dfrac{\delta}{0.223360}\right)}{-4.80637 \text{x} 10^{-5}} + 36089.24 \qquad (H_c > 36089.24 \text{ feet}) \quad \text{(B4)}$$

Density Altitude

In a similar fashion, we can develop an equation for density altitude. In Appendix A we developed the equations for the density ratio as

$$\sigma = (1 - 6.87559 \text{x} 10^{-6} \, H)^{4.2559} \qquad \text{(troposphere)} \quad \text{(A80)}$$

$$\sigma = 0.297075 \, e^{(-4.80637 \text{x} 10^{-5} \, (H - 36089.24))} \qquad \text{(stratosphere)} \quad \text{(A88)}$$

Because we are defining density altitude as the altitude given by the standard atmosphere for a given density, then it follows that we can replace the geopotential altitude (H) in these equations with density altitude (H_ρ)

$$\sigma = (1 - 6.87559 \times 10^{-6} \, H_\rho)^{4.2559} \qquad (H_\rho \leq 36089.24 \text{ feet}) \quad \text{(B5)}$$

$$\sigma = 0.297075 \, e^{(-4.80637 \times 10^{-5} \, (H_\rho - 36089.24))} \qquad (H_\rho > 36089.24 \text{ feet}) \quad \text{(B6)}$$

Note that these equations are valid for any atmosphere, not just a standard atmosphere. The density altitude corresponding to a density ratio will always be the same, regardless of the geopotential altitude that it occurs at.

Inverting Equations B5 and B6 by solving for H_ρ gives

$$H_\rho = \frac{1 - \sqrt[4.2559]{\sigma}}{6.87559 \times 10^{-6}} \qquad (H_\rho \leq 36089.24 \text{ feet}) \quad \text{(B7)}$$

$$H_\rho = \frac{\ln\left(\dfrac{\sigma}{0.297075}\right)}{-4.80637 \times 10^{-5}} + 36089.24 \qquad (H_\rho > 36089.24 \text{ feet}) \quad \text{(B8)}$$

Kollsman Window Shift

The number in the Kollsman window is the pressure at sea level which would make your altimeter read field elevation at the current pressure (or pressure altitude), assuming standard sea level temperature and standard temperature lapse rate. Hence, we can figure out what the pressure ratio at sea level would be. For example, let's assume

$$\text{Altimeter Setting} = 29.82 \qquad \qquad \text{(B9)}$$

$$\delta_{\text{sea level}} = \frac{\text{Altimeter Setting}}{P_{SL}} \qquad \qquad \text{(B10)}$$

$$\delta_{\text{sea level}} = \frac{29.82}{29.92} \qquad \qquad \text{(B11)}$$

$$\delta_{\text{sea level}} = 0.9967 \qquad \qquad \text{(B12)}$$

Then by using Equation B3 we can find the amount of the shift.

$$H_c = \frac{1 - \sqrt[5.2559]{\delta_{\text{sea level}}}}{6.87559 \times 10^{-6}} \qquad \qquad \text{(B3)}$$

$$H_c = \frac{1 - \sqrt[5.2559]{0.9967}}{6.87559 \times 10^{-6}} \qquad \qquad \text{(B13)}$$

$$H_c = 93 \text{ feet} \qquad \qquad \text{(B14)}$$

Pressure Contour Shift With Temperature

Because each pressure altitude corresponds to a particular pressure, the difference between pressure altitudes is simply the difference between two pressures. The hydrostatic equation states

$$dP = -\rho\, g_{SL}\, dH \tag{A30}$$

This, of course, is a differential equation, and to be used over any sort of distance it needs to be integrated. We know that density changes with altitude, but if we can limit ourselves to small changes in altitude, we can ASSUME that the density is relatively constant. (Actually, the density will drop out in a little bit anyway). With this assumption, we can integrate Equation A30 to

$$\Delta P = -\rho\, g_{SL}\, \Delta H \tag{B15}$$

Further working with this equation, if we express altitude in terms of pressure altitude, then because pressure altitude is defined by standard day conditions, the density would be the standard day density at the pressure altitude in question, or

$$\Delta P = -\rho_{std}\, g_{SL}\, \Delta H_c \tag{B16}$$

On the other hand, if we measure the same altitude change in terms of geopotential altitude, then the density must be the test day density, or

$$\Delta P = -\rho_{test}\, g_{SL}\, \Delta H \tag{B17}$$

So when I make a climb or descent between two pressure altitudes, the change in pressure can be expressed in terms of either pressure altitude or geopotential altitude. Setting these two expressions equal we get

$$\Delta P = -\rho_{std}\, g_{SL}\, \Delta H_c = -\rho_{test}\, g_{SL}\, \Delta H \tag{B18}$$

Dropping the ΔP from the front and rearranging this equation we get

$$\frac{\Delta H}{\Delta H_c} = \frac{-\rho_{std}\ g_{SL}}{-\rho_{test}\ g_{SL}} \tag{B19}$$

From this equation, the acceleration of gravity divides out, leaving the ratio of the densities. However, we can still work with this equation to put it in more useful terms. From the Equation of State

$$P = \rho RT \tag{A3}$$

Solving for density gives

$$\rho = \frac{P}{RT} \tag{B20}$$

Substituting this relationship into Equation B19

$$\frac{\Delta H}{\Delta H_c} = \frac{\dfrac{P}{RT_{std}}}{\dfrac{P}{RT_{test}}} \tag{B21}$$

Because the expression for pressure altitude and the expression for geopotential altitude in Equation B18 are for the same location in the atmosphere, the two pressures in Equation B21 are the same. Since R is a constant, it divides out as well, leaving

$$\frac{\Delta H}{\Delta H_c} = \frac{T_{test}}{T_{std}} \tag{B22}$$

Finally, rearranging the equation into a useable form

$$\Delta H = \frac{T_{test}}{T_{std}} \Delta H_c \tag{B23}$$

Calculating Non-Standard Density

From the Equation of State

$$P = \rho R T \tag{A3}$$

we know that we can calculate density from temperature and pressure. If we divide the Equation of State by the Equation of State at sea level conditions, we get another equation

$$\frac{P}{P_{SL}} = \frac{\rho}{\rho_{SL}} \frac{R}{R} \frac{T}{T_{SL}} \tag{B24}$$

Dividing out the Rs and replacing the ratios with the standard symbols

$$\delta = \sigma\, \theta \tag{B25}$$

or solving for the density ratio

$$\sigma = \frac{\delta}{\theta} \tag{B26}$$

If needed the density can be calculated from the definition of the density ratio

$$\sigma = \frac{\rho}{\rho_{SL}} \tag{A71}$$

$$\rho = \sigma\, \rho_{SL} \tag{B27}$$

Appendix C

Airspeed, Mach, and Temperature Measurement Heavy Math Section

Dynamic Pressure

From incompressible flow, we had from Bernoulli's Equation

$$P_T = P_a + \frac{\rho V_t^2}{2} \tag{C1}$$

We could rearrange this to

$$P_T - P_a = \frac{\rho V_t^2}{2} \tag{C2}$$

From this concept came the definition of dynamic pressure, q, as

$$q = \frac{\rho V_t^2}{2} \tag{C3}$$

True Airspeed Equation

To derive the true airspeed equation, we start with the definition of enthalpy (Ref 27)

$$h = u + Pv \tag{C4}$$

where

h	Specific Enthalpy
u	Specific Internal Energy
P	Pressure
v	Specific Volume

The specific volume is merely the inverse of the density, or

$$v = \frac{1}{\rho} \tag{C5}$$

We can then take the Equation of State

$$P = \rho RT \tag{A3}$$

Rearranging would give

$$\frac{P}{\rho} = RT \tag{C6}$$

and substituting Equation C5 gives

$$Pv = RT \qquad (C7)$$

Also from Reference 27 we find that for an ideal gas (which we are assuming air to act as)

$$h = C_pT \qquad (C8)$$

$$u = C_vT \qquad (C9)$$

where

C_p Coefficient of Specific Heat at Constant Pressure
C_v Coefficient of Specific Heat at Constant Volume

Therefore, substituting Equations C8, C9, and C7 into Equation C4 we get

$$C_pT = C_vT + RT \qquad (C10)$$

Dividing out the temperatures

$$C_p = C_v + R \qquad (C11)$$

Rearrange to get

$$C_p - C_v = R \qquad (C12)$$

Divide through by C_p

$$\frac{C_p}{C_p} - \frac{C_v}{C_p} = \frac{R}{C_p} \qquad (C13)$$

The ratio of specific heats (γ) is defined as

$$\gamma = \frac{C_p}{C_v} \qquad (C14)$$

Substituting Equation C14 into Equation C13 gives

$$1 - \frac{1}{\gamma} = \frac{R}{C_p} \qquad (C15)$$

Recasting the 1 gives

$$\frac{\gamma}{\gamma} - \frac{1}{\gamma} = \frac{R}{C_p} \qquad (C16)$$

and combining

$$\frac{\gamma - 1}{\gamma} = \frac{R}{C_p} \qquad (C17)$$

Solving for C_p

$$C_p = \frac{\gamma R}{\gamma - 1} \tag{C18}$$

Now moving on to the First Law of Thermodynamics for a control volume (Ref 27)

$$\dot{W}_{in} + \dot{Q}_{in} + \dot{m}(h + ke + pe)_{in} = \dot{W}_{out} + \dot{Q}_{out} + \dot{m}(h + ke + pe)_{out} \tag{C19}$$

where

$\dot{W}_{in}, \dot{W}_{out}$	Rate of Work Interaction
$\dot{Q}_{in}, \dot{Q}_{out}$	Rate of Heat Interaction
$\dot{m}$	Mass Flow Rate
h	Specific Enthalpy
ke	Specific Kinetic Energy
pe	Specific Potential Energy

Considering the movement of a fluid element through a streamtube, we can eliminate the work interaction because no shaft work will exist in the streamtube.

ASSUME: The flow of air through the streamtube is adiabatic (no heat interactions). Actually, this is a fairly reasonable assumption.

So what do we have left of the First Law for this system?

$$\dot{m}(h + ke + pe)_{in} = \dot{m}(h + ke + pe)_{out} \tag{C20}$$

We can now divide the mass flow term out, leaving

$$(h + ke + pe)_{in} = (h + ke + pe)_{out} \tag{C21}$$

Because of the low density of air, any change in potential energy, caused by a change in elevation, will be very small compared to the changes in enthalpy and kinetic energy. Therefore, we will eliminate the potential energy terms, leaving

$$(h + ke)_{in} = (h + ke)_{out} \tag{C22}$$

Using Equation C8 and the definition of specific kinetic energy (Ref 27), Equation C22 becomes

$$C_p T_{in} + \frac{1}{2} V_{in}^2 = C_p T_{out} + \frac{1}{2} V_{out}^2 \tag{C23}$$

Now we will define our streamtube as beginning well in front of the aircraft at freestream conditions (ambient) and ending at a stagnation point (total), such as a Pitot tube. Therefore, the V_{in} would be the true airspeed, and the V_{out} would be zero.

$$C_p T_a + \frac{1}{2} V_t^2 = C_p T_T \tag{C24}$$

Solving for total temperature

$$T_T = \frac{1}{C_p}\left(C_p T_a + \frac{1}{2} V_t^2\right) \tag{C25}$$

Bring the C_p inside the parentheses to get

$$T_T = \left(T_a + \frac{V_t^2}{2C_p}\right) \tag{C26}$$

If we divide through by T_a to get a temperature ratio we get

$$\frac{T_T}{T_a} = \left(\frac{T_a}{T_a} + \frac{V_t^2}{2C_p T_a}\right) \tag{C27}$$

which reduces to

$$\frac{T_T}{T_a} = \left(1 + \frac{V_t^2}{2C_p T_a}\right) \tag{C28}$$

Substituting in Equation C18 (you wondered why we derived that…)

$$\frac{T_T}{T_a} = \left(1 + \frac{V_t^2}{2\left(\frac{\gamma R}{\gamma - 1}\right)T_a}\right) \tag{C29}$$

which can be rearranged to

$$\frac{T_T}{T_a} = \left(1 + \frac{\gamma - 1}{2}\frac{V_t^2}{\gamma R T_a}\right) \tag{C30}$$

The speed of sound is given by

$$a = \sqrt{\gamma R T_a} \tag{C31}$$

so Equation C30 becomes

$$\frac{T_T}{T_a} = \left(1 + \frac{\gamma - 1}{2}\frac{V_t^2}{a^2}\right) \tag{C32}$$

Mach Number is given by

$$M = \frac{V_t}{a} \tag{C33}$$

so Equation C32 becomes

$$\frac{T_T}{T_a} = \left(1 + \frac{\gamma - 1}{2}M^2\right) \tag{C34}$$

Note that the only major assumption made to derive Equation C34 was that the flow was adiabatic. If we further **assume** that the flow into the Pitot tube is isentropic, then we can apply the isentropic relationship (Ref 27)

$$\frac{P_2}{P_1} = \left(\frac{T_2}{T_1}\right)^{\frac{\gamma}{\gamma-1}} \tag{C35}$$

Applying Equation C35 to Equation C34 gives us

$$\frac{P_T}{P_a} = \left(1 + \frac{\gamma - 1}{2}M^2\right)^{\frac{\gamma}{\gamma-1}} \tag{C36}$$

Move the exponent to the other side

$$\left(\frac{P_T}{P_a}\right)^{\frac{\gamma-1}{\gamma}} = 1 + \frac{\gamma - 1}{2}M^2 \tag{C37}$$

Solving for Mach

$$\left(\frac{P_T}{P_a}\right)^{\frac{\gamma-1}{\gamma}} - 1 = \frac{\gamma - 1}{2}M^2 \tag{C38}$$

$$M^2 = \frac{2}{\gamma - 1}\left(\left(\frac{P_T}{P_a}\right)^{\frac{\gamma-1}{\gamma}} - 1\right) \tag{C39}$$

Using Equation C33 to get velocity (airspeed) back into the equation

$$\frac{V_t^2}{a^2} = \frac{2}{\gamma - 1}\left(\left(\frac{P_T}{P_a}\right)^{\frac{\gamma-1}{\gamma}} - 1\right) \tag{C40}$$

Isolate the velocity

$$V_t^2 = \frac{2a^2}{\gamma - 1}\left(\left(\frac{P_T}{P_a}\right)^{\frac{\gamma-1}{\gamma}} - 1\right) \tag{C41}$$

Using Equation C31

$$V_t^2 = \frac{2\gamma RT_a}{\gamma - 1}\left(\left(\frac{P_T}{P_a}\right)^{\frac{\gamma-1}{\gamma}} - 1\right) \tag{C42}$$

Replacing RT_a with its equivalent from the equation of state (Equation C6)

$$V_t^2 = \frac{2\gamma}{\gamma - 1}\frac{P_a}{\rho_a}\left(\left(\frac{P_T}{P_a}\right)^{\frac{\gamma-1}{\gamma}} - 1\right) \tag{C43}$$

Move the density term to the location we'll want it later

$$V_t^2 = \left(\frac{1}{\rho_a}\right)\frac{2\gamma}{\gamma - 1}P_a\left(\left(\frac{P_T}{P_a}\right)^{\frac{\gamma-1}{\gamma}} - 1\right) \tag{C44}$$

Because of the way our systems (airspeed indicators) are designed, along with some other conveniences down the road, we'll want to use the difference between total and ambient pressure instead of total pressure by itself. To get to this, we'll add and subtract one to the pressure ratio term.

$$V_t^2 = \left(\frac{1}{\rho_a}\right)\frac{2\gamma}{\gamma - 1}P_a\left(\left(\frac{P_T}{P_a} - \frac{P_a}{P_a} + \frac{P_a}{P_a}\right)^{\frac{\gamma-1}{\gamma}} - 1\right) \tag{C45}$$

Combining the first two fractions over a common denominator

$$V_t^2 = \left(\frac{1}{\rho_a}\right)\frac{2\gamma}{\gamma - 1}P_a\left(\left(\frac{P_T - P_a}{P_a} + 1\right)^{\frac{\gamma-1}{\gamma}} - 1\right) \tag{C46}$$

Taking the square root of both sides

$$V_t = \sqrt{\left(\frac{1}{\rho_a}\right)\frac{2\gamma}{\gamma - 1}P_a\left(\left(\frac{P_T - P_a}{P_a} + 1\right)^{\frac{\gamma-1}{\gamma}} - 1\right)} \tag{C47}$$

Using $\gamma = 1.4$ for air

$$V_t = \sqrt{\left(\frac{1}{\rho_a}\right)7P_a\left(\left(\frac{P_T - P_a}{P_a} + 1\right)^{\frac{2}{7}} - 1\right)} \tag{C48}$$

Equivalent Airspeed

Equivalent Airspeed is found by removing the dependence on ambient density and replacing it with a constant sea level density.

$$V_e = \sqrt{\left(\frac{1}{\rho_{SL}}\right) 7 P_a \left(\left(\frac{P_T - P_a}{P_a} + 1\right)^{\frac{2}{7}} - 1 \right)} \tag{C49}$$

The relationship between true and equivalent airspeed can be found using the density ratio.

$$V_e = \sqrt{\left(\frac{1}{\rho_a}\right)\left(\frac{\rho_a}{\rho_{SL}}\right) 7 P_a \left(\left(\frac{P_T - P_a}{P_a} + 1\right)^{\frac{2}{7}} - 1 \right)} \tag{C50}$$

$$V_e = \sqrt{\left(\frac{1}{\rho_a}\right)(\sigma) 7 P_a \left(\left(\frac{P_T - P_a}{P_a} + 1\right)^{\frac{2}{7}} - 1 \right)} \tag{C51}$$

$$V_e = \sqrt{\left(\frac{1}{\rho_a}\right) 7 P_a \left(\left(\frac{P_T - P_a}{P_a} + 1\right)^{\frac{2}{7}} - 1 \right)} \sqrt{\sigma} \tag{C52}$$

$$V_e = V_t \sqrt{\sigma} \tag{C53}$$

Dynamic pressure, defined as

$$q = \frac{\rho V_t^2}{2} \tag{C3}$$

can also be expressed in terms of equivalent airspeed. Rearranging Equation C53

$$V_t = \frac{V_e}{\sqrt{\sigma}} \tag{C54}$$

and substituting Equation C54 in Equation C3

$$q = \frac{\rho \left(\frac{V_e}{\sqrt{\sigma}}\right)^2}{2} \tag{C55}$$

$$q = \frac{\rho \dfrac{V_e^2}{\sigma}}{2} \tag{C56}$$

$$q = \frac{\rho\left(\frac{\rho_{SL}}{\rho}\right)V_e^2}{2} \qquad (C57)$$

$$q = \frac{\rho_{SL}V_e^2}{2} \qquad (C58)$$

So two expressions for dynamic pressure are

$$q = \frac{\rho V_t^2}{2} = \frac{\rho_{SL}V_e^2}{2} \qquad (C59)$$

Additionally, dynamic pressure can be expressed in terms of Mach number. From Equation C33 we get

$$V_t = Ma \qquad (C60)$$

Substituting in Equation C3

$$q = \frac{\rho(Ma)^2}{2} \qquad (C61)$$

Using the definition of the speed of sound (Equation C31)

$$q = \frac{\rho(\gamma RT)M^2}{2} \qquad (C62)$$

$$q = \frac{\gamma(\rho RT)M^2}{2} \qquad (C63)$$

From the Equation of State (Equation A3) we can substitute pressure to get

$$q = \frac{\gamma}{2}P_a M^2 \qquad (C64)$$

Calibrated Airspeed

Calibrated airspeed is found by replacing the ambient pressure dependence in equivalent airspeed with a constant sea level pressure.

$$V_c = \sqrt{\left(\frac{1}{\rho_{SL}}\right)7P_{SL}\left(\left(\frac{P_T - P_a}{P_{SL}}+1\right)^{\frac{2}{7}}-1\right)} \qquad (C65)$$

Differential Pressure Ratios

The one common variable between true, equivalent, and calibrated airspeed is the differential pressure. For ease of notation, we will give the differential pressure a symbol

$$q_c = P_T - P_a \qquad \text{(subsonic)} \qquad \text{(C66)}$$

If we have a way to find q_c, then we can work our way between different types of airspeed. We can also use q_c to relate airspeeds and Mach numbers. Using the isentropic relation

$$\frac{P_T}{P_a} = \left(1 + \frac{\gamma - 1}{2} M^2\right)^{\frac{\gamma}{\gamma - 1}} \qquad \text{(C36)}$$

we can subtract one from both sides

$$\frac{P_T}{P_a} - \frac{P_a}{P_a} = \left(1 + \frac{\gamma - 1}{2} M^2\right)^{\frac{\gamma}{\gamma - 1}} - 1 \qquad \text{(C67)}$$

to give

$$\frac{P_T - P_a}{P_a} = \left(1 + \frac{\gamma - 1}{2} M^2\right)^{\frac{\gamma}{\gamma - 1}} - 1 \qquad \text{(C68)}$$

Using $\gamma = 1.4$ for air, we have

$$\frac{P_T - P_a}{P_a} = \left(1 + 0.2 M^2\right)^{\frac{7}{2}} - 1 \qquad \text{(C69)}$$

and substituting Equation C66

$$\frac{q_c}{P_a} = \left(1 + 0.2 M^2\right)^{\frac{7}{2}} - 1 \qquad \text{(subsonic)} \qquad \text{(C70)}$$

Note that this relationship exists in the middle of both the true airspeed and equivalent airspeed equations.

To find q_c/P_a from equivalent airspeed, first we look at the speed of sound (Equation C31) and divide both sides by the square root of the temperature ratio

$$\frac{a}{\sqrt{\theta}} = \frac{\sqrt{\gamma R T_a}}{\sqrt{\dfrac{T_a}{T_{SL}}}} \qquad \text{(C71)}$$

$$\frac{a}{\sqrt{\theta}} = \sqrt{\gamma R T_{SL}} \qquad \text{(C72)}$$

The right hand side is just the speed of sound at sea level, so

$$\frac{a}{\sqrt{\theta}} = a_{SL} \tag{C73}$$

$$a = a_{SL}\sqrt{\theta} \tag{C74}$$

Combining with Equation C33 gives

$$M = \frac{V_t}{a_{SL}\sqrt{\theta}} \tag{C75}$$

or

$$V_t = Ma_{SL}\sqrt{\theta} \tag{C76}$$

If we go back to the relationship between true and equivalent airspeeds

$$V_e = V_t\sqrt{\sigma} \tag{C53}$$

and substitute Equation C60 we get

$$V_e = Ma\sqrt{\sigma} \tag{C77}$$

Substituting Equation C74 we get

$$V_e = Ma_{SL}\sqrt{\theta}\sqrt{\sigma} \tag{C78}$$

Substituting Equation B25 gives

$$V_e = Ma_{SL}\sqrt{\delta} \tag{C79}$$

so solving for Mach number gives

$$M = \frac{V_e}{a_{SL}\sqrt{\delta}} \tag{C80}$$

Therefore, substituting Equation C80 into Equation C70

$$\frac{q_c}{P_a} = \left(1 + 0.2\left(\frac{V_e}{a_{SL}\sqrt{\delta}}\right)^2\right)^{7/2} - 1 \tag{C81}$$

So far this discussion has been true for subsonic flight. In supersonic flight, the total pressure sensed is the total pressure behind a normal shock wave (P_T'), which is less than the freestream total pressure (P_T). From Equation 3-80 of Reference 7, we know that the relationship between the ambient pressure ahead of the shock wave (P_a) and the ambient pressure behind the shock wave (P_a') is

$$\frac{P_a'}{P_a} = \frac{1 - \gamma + 2\gamma M^2}{\gamma + 1} \tag{C82}$$

where M is the freestream Mach number. The Mach number behind the shock wave (M') is given by Equation 3-83 of Reference 7

$$M'^2 = \frac{M^2 + \dfrac{2}{\gamma - 1}}{\left(\dfrac{2\gamma}{\gamma - 1} M^2\right) - 1} \tag{C83}$$

Behind the shock, the total pressure and ambient pressure are related by the isentropic relation (Equation C36)

$$\frac{P_T'}{P_a'} = \left(1 + \frac{\gamma - 1}{2} M'^2\right)^{\frac{\gamma}{\gamma - 1}} \tag{C84}$$

To relate the total pressure behind the shock (measured in the Pitot tube) to the freestream ambient pressure (which will be recovered by some distance behind the shock), we multiply Equation C84 and Equation C82 to get

$$\frac{P_T'}{P_a} = \left(\frac{P_T'}{P_a'}\right)\left(\frac{P_a'}{P_a}\right) = \left(1 + \frac{\gamma - 1}{2} M'^2\right)^{\frac{\gamma}{\gamma - 1}} \frac{1 - \gamma + 2\gamma M^2}{\gamma + 1} \tag{C85}$$

Modifying Equation C83

$$M'^2 = \frac{M^2 + \dfrac{2}{\gamma - 1}}{\left(\dfrac{2\gamma}{\gamma - 1} M^2\right) - 1} \frac{(\gamma - 1)}{(\gamma - 1)} \tag{C86}$$

$$M'^2 = \frac{(\gamma - 1)M^2 + 2}{2\gamma M^2 - (\gamma - 1)} \tag{C87}$$

Substituting Equation C87 for M' in Equation C85

$$\frac{P_T'}{P_a} = \left(1 + \frac{\gamma - 1}{2}\left(\frac{(\gamma - 1)M^2 + 2}{2\gamma M^2 - (\gamma - 1)}\right)\right)^{\frac{\gamma}{\gamma - 1}} \frac{1 - \gamma + 2\gamma M^2}{\gamma + 1} \tag{C88}$$

$$\frac{P_T{}'}{P_a} = \left(1 + \frac{(\gamma-1)^2 M^2 + 2(\gamma-1)}{4\gamma M^2 - 2(\gamma-1)}\right)^{\frac{\gamma}{\gamma-1}} \frac{1-\gamma+2\gamma M^2}{\gamma+1} \tag{C89}$$

$$\frac{P_T{}'}{P_a} = \left(\frac{4\gamma M^2 - 2(\gamma-1)}{4\gamma M^2 - 2(\gamma-1)} + \frac{(\gamma-1)^2 M^2 + 2(\gamma-1)}{4\gamma M^2 - 2(\gamma-1)}\right)^{\frac{\gamma}{\gamma-1}} \frac{1-\gamma+2\gamma M^2}{\gamma+1} \tag{C90}$$

$$\frac{P_T{}'}{P_a} = \left(\frac{4\gamma M^2 + \gamma^2 M^2 - 2\gamma M^2 + M^2}{4\gamma M^2 - 2(\gamma-1)}\right)^{\frac{\gamma}{\gamma-1}} \frac{1-\gamma+2\gamma M^2}{\gamma+1} \tag{C91}$$

$$\frac{P_T{}'}{P_a} = \left(\frac{\gamma^2 M^2 + 2\gamma M^2 + M^2}{4\gamma M^2 - 2(\gamma-1)}\right)^{\frac{\gamma}{\gamma-1}} \frac{1-\gamma+2\gamma M^2}{\gamma+1} \tag{C92}$$

$$\frac{P_T{}'}{P_a} = \left(\frac{(\gamma+1)^2 M^2}{4\gamma M^2 - 2(\gamma-1)}\right)^{\frac{\gamma}{\gamma-1}} \frac{1-\gamma+2\gamma M^2}{\gamma+1} \tag{C93}$$

To get to q_c/P_a we subtract 1 from both sides

$$\frac{P_T{}'}{P_a} - \frac{P_a}{P_a} = \left(\frac{(\gamma+1)^2 M^2}{4\gamma M^2 - 2(\gamma-1)}\right)^{\frac{\gamma}{\gamma-1}} \frac{1-\gamma+2\gamma M^2}{\gamma+1} - 1 \tag{C94}$$

$$\frac{P_T{}'-P_a}{P_a} = \left(\frac{(\gamma+1)^2 M^2}{4\gamma M^2 - 2(\gamma-1)}\right)^{\frac{\gamma}{\gamma-1}} \frac{1-\gamma+2\gamma M^2}{\gamma+1} - 1 \tag{C95}$$

For supersonic flow, q_c is defined as

$$q_c = P_T{}' - P_a \qquad \text{(supersonic)} \tag{C96}$$

Substituting the definition of q_c and using $\gamma = 1.4$ for air

$$\frac{q_c}{P_a} = \left(\frac{(1.4+1)^2 M^2}{4(1.4)M^2 - 2(1.4-1)}\right)^{\frac{1.4}{1.4-1}} \frac{1-1.4+2(1.4)M^2}{1.4+1} - 1 \tag{C97}$$

With some clever multiplying by 1

$$\frac{q_c}{P_a} = \left(\frac{5.76 M^2}{5.6 M^2 - 0.8}\left(\frac{6.25}{6.25}\right)\right)^{\frac{1.4}{0.4}\left(\frac{5}{5}\right)}\left(\frac{-0.4+2.8 M^2}{2.4}\left(\frac{2.5}{2.5}\right)\right) - 1 \tag{C98}$$

$$\frac{q_c}{P_a} = \left(\frac{36M^2}{35M^2 - 5}\right)^{\frac{7}{2}}\left(\frac{7M^2 - 1}{6}\right) - 1 \tag{C99}$$

$$\frac{q_c}{P_a} = \left(\frac{36M^2}{5\left(7M^2 - 1\right)}\right)^{\frac{7}{2}}\left(\frac{7M^2 - 1}{6}\right) - 1 \tag{C100}$$

Combining like terms

$$\frac{q_c}{P_a} = \left(\frac{\left(36M^2\right)^{7/2}}{(5)^{7/2}\left(7M^2 - 1\right)^{5/2}}\right)\left(\frac{1}{6}\right) - 1 \tag{C101}$$

Combining constants

$$\frac{q_c}{P_a} = \frac{166.921M^7}{\left(7M^2 - 1\right)^{5/2}} - 1 \qquad \text{(supersonic)} \tag{C102}$$

Remembering that q_c in this case is the difference between the sensed total pressure (behind the normal shock wave) and the ambient pressure, reintroducing Equation C96 gives

$$\frac{P_T' - P_a}{P_a} = \frac{166.921M^7}{\left(7M^2 - 1\right)^{5/2}} - 1 \qquad \text{(supersonic)} \tag{C103}$$

Substituting Equation C80, we get the equivalent expression for equivalent airspeed

$$\frac{q_c}{P_a} = \frac{166.921\left(\frac{V_e}{a_{SL}\sqrt{\delta}}\right)^7}{\left(7\left(\frac{V_e}{a_{SL}\sqrt{\delta}}\right)^2 - 1\right)^{5/2}} - 1 \qquad \text{(supersonic)} \tag{C104}$$

If we consider the case of sea level standard day, then true airspeed is equal to calibrated airspeed and using the speed of sound at sea level, we have

$$M = \frac{V_c}{a_{SL}} \qquad \text{(at sea level)} \tag{C105}$$

Additionally the ambient pressure is equal to sea level pressure. Substituting into Equation C70 and Equation C102 we get

$$\frac{q_c}{P_{SL}} = \left(1 + 0.2\left(\frac{V_c}{a_{SL}}\right)^2\right)^{7/2} - 1 \qquad (V_c < a_{SL}) \tag{C106}$$

$$\frac{q_c}{P_{SL}} = \frac{166.921\left(\dfrac{V_c}{a_{SL}}\right)^7}{\left(7\left(\dfrac{V_c}{a_{SL}}\right)^2 - 1\right)^{5/2}} - 1 \qquad\qquad (V_c > a_{SL}) \quad (C107)$$

The interesting thing about Equations C106 and C107 is that there is no altitude dependence in either equation, so these two equations are valid at any altitude. The term q_c/P_{SL} is significant in that this is the value in the center of the calibrated airspeed equation.

The relationship between q_c/P_a and q_c/P_{SL} is given by

$$\frac{q_c}{P_a} = \frac{q_c}{P_{SL}}\frac{P_{SL}}{P_a} \qquad\qquad (C108)$$

$$\frac{q_c}{P_a} = \frac{q_c}{P_{SL}}\frac{1}{\delta} \qquad\qquad (C109)$$

or

$$\frac{q_c}{P_{SL}} = \frac{q_c}{P_a}\delta \qquad\qquad (C110)$$

Continuity Between Subsonic and Supersonic Pressures

Nature abhors a vacuum, and it doesn't tolerate discontinuities either. We can show that the differential pressure ratio q_c/P_a is continuous at $M = 1$ by showing that its value and slope are the same for both the subsonic and supersonic equations.

For the subsonic case

$$\frac{q_c}{P_a} = \left(1 + 0.2M^2\right)^{7/2} - 1 \qquad\qquad (subsonic) \quad (C70)$$

At $M = 1$

$$\frac{q_c}{P_a} = \left(1 + 0.2(1)^2\right)^{7/2} - 1 = 0.89293$$

For the supersonic case

$$\frac{q_c}{P_a} = \frac{166.921 M^7}{\left(7M^2 - 1\right)^{5/2}} - 1 \qquad\qquad (supersonic) \quad (C102)$$

At M = 1

$$\frac{q_c}{P_a} = \frac{166.921(1)^7}{\left(7(1)^2 - 1\right)^{5/2}} - 1 = 0.89293$$

The values of q_c/P_a are the same at M = 1.

Taking the derivative of the subsonic case

$$\frac{q_c}{P_a} = \left(1 + 0.2M^2\right)^{7/2} - 1 \qquad \text{(subsonic)} \quad \text{(C70)}$$

$$\frac{d\left(\frac{q_c}{P_a}\right)}{dM} = \frac{7}{2}\left(1 + 0.2M^2\right)^{5/2}(2)(0.2M) \qquad \text{(C111)}$$

At M = 1

$$\frac{d\left(\frac{q_c}{P_a}\right)}{dM} = \frac{7}{2}\left(1 + 0.2(1)^2\right)^{5/2}(2)(0.2(1)) = 2.208$$

Taking the derivative of the supersonic case

$$\frac{q_c}{P_a} = \frac{166.921M^7}{\left(7M^2 - 1\right)^{5/2}} - 1 \qquad \text{(supersonic)} \quad \text{(C102)}$$

$$\frac{d\left(\frac{q_c}{P_a}\right)}{dM} = (7)\left(166.921M^6\right)\left(7M^2 - 1\right)^{-5/2} + \left(166.921M^7\right)\left(-\frac{5}{2}\right)\left(7M^2 - 1\right)^{-7/2}(2)(7M) \qquad \text{(C112)}$$

At M = 1

$$\frac{d\left(\frac{q_c}{P_a}\right)}{dM} = (7)\left(166.921(1)^6\right)\left(7(1)^2 - 1\right)^{-5/2} + \left(166.921(1)^7\right)\left(-\frac{5}{2}\right)\left(7(1)^2 - 1\right)^{-7/2}(2)(7(1)) = 2.208$$

The values of the first derivative of q_c/P_a are the same at M = 1.

Finding Mach from Calibrated Airspeed and Pressure Altitude

We can now use calibrated airspeed to find q_c/P_{SL}. Using altitude to find δ, we can then find q_c/P_a. From this we can then find Mach number. Solving Equation C70 for Mach number:

$$\frac{q_c}{P_a} = \left(1 + 0.2M^2\right)^{7/2} - 1 \qquad \text{(subsonic)} \quad \text{(C70)}$$

Add 1 to both sides

$$\frac{q_c}{P_a} + 1 = \left(1 + 0.2M^2\right)^{7/2} \tag{C113}$$

Raise both sides to the 2/7 power

$$\left(\frac{q_c}{P_a} + 1\right)^{2/7} = 1 + 0.2M^2 \tag{C114}$$

Subtract 1 from both sides

$$\left(\frac{q_c}{P_a} + 1\right)^{2/7} - 1 = 0.2M^2 \tag{C115}$$

Multiply both sides by 5

$$5\left(\left(\frac{q_c}{P_a} + 1\right)^{2/7} - 1\right) = M^2 \tag{C116}$$

Taking the square root

$$M = \sqrt{5\left(\left(\frac{q_c}{P_a} + 1\right)^{2/7} - 1\right)} \qquad (M < 1 \text{ or } q_c/P_a < 0.89293) \tag{C117}$$

Substituting from Equations C109 and C106 into Equation C117

$$M = \sqrt{\left[5\left[\left(\frac{1}{\delta}\left\{\left[1 + 0.2\left(\frac{V_c}{a_{SL}}\right)^2\right]^{7/2} - 1\right\} + 1\right)^{2/7} - 1\right]\right]} \qquad (M < 1) \tag{C118}$$

Note that because Equations C117 and C118 were derived from the subsonic relationships, they are only valid for the subsonic case. It is possible to find values for $V_c < a_{SL}$ and pressure ratio that result in a Mach number greater than 1 using Equation C118. In those cases, the result is invalid and must be calculated a different way.

For the supersonic case, we start with Equation C102.

$$\frac{q_c}{P_a} = \frac{166.921M^7}{\left(7M^2 - 1\right)^{5/2}} - 1 \qquad (M > 1) \tag{C102}$$

Add 1 to both sides

$$\frac{q_c}{P_a} + 1 = \frac{166.921 M^7}{\left(7M^2 - 1\right)^{5/2}} \tag{C119}$$

Multiplying by a clever form of 1

$$\frac{q_c}{P_a} + 1 = \frac{166.921 M^7 \left(\dfrac{1}{7M^2}\right)^{5/2}}{\left(7M^2 - 1\right)^{5/2} \left(\dfrac{1}{7M^2}\right)^{5/2}} \tag{C120}$$

$$\frac{q_c}{P_a} + 1 = \frac{\dfrac{166.921}{7^{5/2}} \left(\dfrac{M^7}{M^5}\right)}{\left(\left(7M^2 - 1\right)\dfrac{1}{7M^2}\right)^{5/2}} \tag{C121}$$

$$\frac{q_c}{P_a} + 1 = \frac{\dfrac{166.921}{7^{5/2}} M^2}{\left(1 - \dfrac{1}{7M^2}\right)^{5/2}} \tag{C122}$$

$$M^2 = \left(\frac{q_c}{P_a} + 1\right)\left(1 - \frac{1}{7M^2}\right)^{5/2} \frac{7^{5/2}}{166.921} \tag{C123}$$

$$M = 0.881284 \sqrt{\left(\frac{q_c}{P_a} + 1\right)\left(1 - \frac{1}{7M^2}\right)^{5/2}} \qquad (M > 1 \text{ or } q_c/P_a > 0.89293) \tag{C124}$$

This is as far as we can go with this equation. Unfortunately, this is an implicit equation, since Mach number appears on both sides. Therefore it must be solved by iteration.

Using the same logic as we used to develop Equations C106 and C107, starting with Equation C117 we get an expression for calibrated airspeed less than the speed of sound at sea level

$$\frac{V_c}{a_{SL}} = \sqrt{5\left(\left(\frac{q_c}{P_{SL}} + 1\right)^{2/7} - 1\right)} \tag{C125}$$

or

$$V_c = a_{SL} \sqrt{5\left(\left(\frac{q_c}{P_{SL}} + 1\right)^{2/7} - 1\right)} \qquad \left(\frac{q_c}{P_{SL}} < 0.89293, \, V_c < a_{SL}\right) \quad \text{(C126)}$$

Substituting Equation C110

$$\frac{V_c}{a_{SL}} = \sqrt{5\left(\left(\delta\frac{q_c}{P_a} + 1\right)^{2/7} - 1\right)} \qquad \text{(C127)}$$

Substituting Equation C70 (note that because C70 is restricted to M < 1, the resulting equation is restricted to M <1)

$$\frac{V_c}{a_{SL}} = \sqrt{5\left[\left(\delta\left\{\left[1 + 0.2M^2\right]^{7/2} - 1\right\} + 1\right)^{2/7} - 1\right]} \qquad \text{(C128)}$$

$$V_c = a_{SL} \sqrt{5\left[\left(\delta\left\{\left[1 + 0.2M^2\right]^{7/2} - 1\right\} + 1\right)^{2/7} - 1\right]} \qquad (M < 1) \quad \text{(C129)}$$

For the supersonic case, we modify Equation C124 (with no altitude dependence, M > 1 becomes $V_c > a_{SL}$)

$$\frac{V_c}{a_{SL}} = 0.881284 \sqrt{\left(\frac{q_c}{P_{SL}} + 1\right)\left(1 - \frac{1}{7\left(\frac{V_c}{a_{SL}}\right)^2}\right)^{5/2}} \qquad \text{(C130)}$$

$$V_c = a_{SL} \, 0.881284 \sqrt{\left(\frac{q_c}{P_{SL}} + 1\right)\left(1 - \frac{1}{7\left(\frac{V_c}{a_{SL}}\right)^2}\right)^{5/2}} \qquad \left(\frac{q_c}{P_{SL}} > 0.89293, \, V_c > a_{SL}\right) \quad \text{(C131)}$$

Likewise for equivalent airspeed in the supersonic regime, we substitute Equation C80 in Equation C124 to get

$$\frac{V_e}{a_{SL}\sqrt{\delta}} = 0.881284 \sqrt{\left(\frac{q_c}{P_a}+1\right)\left(1-\frac{1}{7\left(\frac{V_e}{a_{SL}\sqrt{\delta}}\right)^2}\right)^{5/2}} \qquad (q_c/P_a > 0.89293) \quad \text{(C132)}$$

$$V_e = a_{SL}\, 0.881284 \sqrt{\delta\left(\frac{q_c}{P_a}+1\right)\left(1-\frac{a_{SL}^2\delta}{7V_e^2}\right)^{5/2}} \qquad (q_c/P_a > 0.89293) \quad \text{(C133)}$$

Computing f Factor and ΔV_c

f factor is typically computed for specified values of calibrated airspeed and pressure altitude. It could also be calculated for a specified value of equivalent airspeed and pressure altitude using techniques similar to those shown here.

Using the specified calibrated airspeed, calculate q_c/P_{SL} using Equation C106 or C107 as appropriate.

$$\frac{q_c}{P_{SL}} = \left(1 + 0.2\left(\frac{V_c}{a_{SL}}\right)^2\right)^{7/2} - 1 \qquad (V_c < a_{SL}) \quad \text{(C106)}$$

$$\frac{q_c}{P_{SL}} = \frac{166.921\left(\frac{V_c}{a_{SL}}\right)^7}{\left(7\left(\frac{V_c}{a_{SL}}\right)^2 - 1\right)^{5/2}} - 1 \qquad (V_c > a_{SL}) \quad \text{(C107)}$$

The pressure ratio is calculated from the specified pressure altitude using Equation B1 or B2 as appropriate.

$$\delta = (1 - 6.87559\text{x}10^{-6}\, H_c)^{5.2559} \qquad (H_c \leq 36089.24 \text{ feet}) \quad \text{(B1)}$$

$$\delta = 0.223360\, e^{(-4.80637\text{x}10^{-5}\,(H_c - 36089.24))} \qquad (H_c > 36089.24 \text{ feet}) \quad \text{(B2)}$$

Using Equation C109 to find q_c/P_a

$$\frac{q_c}{P_a} = \frac{q_c}{P_{SL}}\frac{1}{\delta} \qquad \text{(C109)}$$

we can then calculate Mach number using Equation C117 or C124 as appropriate

$$M = \sqrt{5\left(\left(\frac{q_c}{P_a}+1\right)^{2/7}-1\right)} \qquad (M < 1 \text{ or } q_c/P_a < 0.89293) \quad (C117)$$

$$M = 0.881284\sqrt{\left(\frac{q_c}{P_a}+1\right)\left(1-\frac{1}{7M^2}\right)^{5/2}} \qquad (M > 1 \text{ or } q_c/P_a > 0.89293) \quad (C124)$$

Equivalent airspeed is then calculated from Mach number using Equation C79

$$V_e = M a_{SL}\sqrt{\delta} \qquad\qquad (C79)$$

Now that the corresponding values of equivalent airspeed and calibrated airspeed are known, the f factor and ΔV_c are calculated by their definitions.

$$f = \frac{V_e}{V_c} \qquad\qquad (C134)$$

$$\Delta V_c = V_e - V_c \qquad\qquad (C135)$$

Table C1 enumerates the values of the f factor as a function of pressure altitude and calibrated airspeed. Figure C1 shows how the f factor varies with pressure altitude and calibrated airspeed.

Table C1
f factor

Pressure Altitude (ft)	Calibrated Airspeed (knots)										
	0	50	100	150	200	250	300	350	400	450	500
0	1.0000	1.0000	1.0000	1.0000	1.0000	1.0000	1.0000	1.0000	1.0000	1.0000	1.0000
5000	1.0000	0.9998	0.9994	0.9987	0.9978	0.9966	0.9952	0.9936	0.9919	0.9900	0.9881
10000	1.0000	0.9997	0.9987	0.9972	0.9950	0.9924	0.9893	0.9859	0.9822	0.9782	0.9742
15000	1.0000	0.9994	0.9978	0.9952	0.9916	0.9872	0.9822	0.9766	0.9706	0.9644	0.9580
20000	1.0000	0.9992	0.9967	0.9927	0.9874	0.9809	0.9735	0.9654	0.9569	0.9481	0.9393
25000	1.0000	0.9988	0.9953	0.9896	0.9820	0.9730	0.9629	0.9520	0.9406	0.9291	0.9193
30000	1.0000	0.9983	0.9934	0.9856	0.9754	0.9633	0.9500	0.9359	0.9215	0.9085	0.8997
35000	1.0000	0.9977	0.9910	0.9805	0.9670	0.9513	0.9343	0.9167	0.9002	0.8882	0.8813
36089	1.0000	0.9975	0.9904	0.9792	0.9649	0.9483	0.9305	0.9121	0.8955	0.8839	0.8775
40000	1.0000	0.9969	0.9879	0.9740	0.9565	0.9367	0.9157	0.8951	0.8793	0.8695	0.8648
45000	1.0000	0.9959	0.9840	0.9661	0.9441	0.9197	0.8947	0.8741	0.8606	0.8533	0.8509
50000	1.0000	0.9946	0.9792	0.9566	0.9293	0.9001	0.8734	0.8551	0.8444	0.8396	0.8393
55000	1.0000	0.9929	0.9733	0.9450	0.9122	0.8788	0.8538	0.8385	0.8306	0.8282	0.8298
60000	1.0000	0.9909	0.9661	0.9314	0.8925	0.8582	0.8365	0.8245	0.8192	0.8188	0.8220
65000	1.0000	0.9883	0.9572	0.9154	0.8713	0.8397	0.8217	0.8127	0.8098	0.8111	0.8157

Pressure Altitude (ft)	Calibrated Airspeed (knots)										
	550	600	650	661.48	700	750	800	850	900	950	1000
0	1.0000	1.0000	1.0000	1.0000	1.0000	1.0000	1.0000	1.0000	1.0000	1.0000	1.0000
5000	0.9861	0.9841	0.9822	0.9819	0.9817	0.9822	0.9831	0.9842	0.9853	0.9863	0.9873
10000	0.9700	0.9660	0.9636	0.9634	0.9636	0.9651	0.9673	0.9696	0.9718	0.9739	0.9759
15000	0.9516	0.9470	0.9452	0.9453	0.9464	0.9493	0.9528	0.9563	0.9597	0.9629	0.9658
20000	0.9322	0.9283	0.9279	0.9282	0.9305	0.9349	0.9397	0.9444	0.9489	0.9531	0.9568
25000	0.9131	0.9107	0.9119	0.9126	0.9161	0.9219	0.9281	0.9340	0.9395	0.9445	0.9490
30000	0.8951	0.8946	0.8975	0.8986	0.9034	0.9106	0.9179	0.9249	0.9313	0.9371	0.9424
35000	0.8788	0.8801	0.8848	0.8863	0.8922	0.9007	0.9091	0.9171	0.9243	0.9309	0.9367
36089	0.8755	0.8772	0.8823	0.8838	0.8899	0.8987	0.9074	0.9156	0.9230	0.9296	0.9356
40000	0.8645	0.8677	0.8739	0.8758	0.8827	0.8923	0.9018	0.9106	0.9185	0.9256	0.9320
45000	0.8525	0.8574	0.8650	0.8671	0.8750	0.8856	0.8959	0.9053	0.9138	0.9215	0.9282
50000	0.8427	0.8490	0.8578	0.8602	0.8687	0.8802	0.8911	0.9011	0.9101	0.9181	0.9252
55000	0.8346	0.8421	0.8520	0.8545	0.8637	0.8758	0.8873	0.8978	0.9072	0.9155	0.9228
60000	0.8281	0.8367	0.8473	0.8500	0.8597	0.8724	0.8843	0.8951	0.9048	0.9134	0.9210
65000	0.8229	0.8323	0.8436	0.8464	0.8565	0.8696	0.8819	0.8930	0.9030	0.9117	0.9195

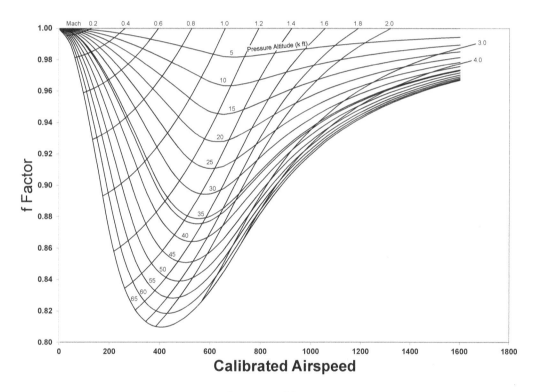

Figure C1. f factor

Table C2 enumerates the values of the ΔV_c as a function of pressure altitude and calibrated airspeed. Figure C2 shows how the ΔV_c varies with pressure altitude and calibrated airspeed.

Table C2

ΔV_c factor

Pressure Altitude (ft)	Calibrated Airspeed (knots)										
	0	50	100	150	200	250	300	350	400	450	500
0	0.0	0.0	0.0	0.0	0.0	0.0	0.0	0.0	0.0	0.0	0.0
5000	0.0	0.0	-0.1	-0.2	-0.4	-0.9	-1.4	-2.2	-3.3	-4.5	-6.0
10000	0.0	0.0	-0.1	-0.4	-1.0	-1.9	-3.2	-4.9	-7.1	-9.8	-12.9
15000	0.0	0.0	-0.2	-0.7	-1.7	-3.2	-5.3	-8.2	-11.8	-16.0	-21.0
20000	0.0	0.0	-0.3	-1.1	-2.5	-4.8	-8.0	-12.1	-17.2	-23.4	-30.4
25000	0.0	-0.1	-0.5	-1.6	-3.6	-6.7	-11.1	-16.8	-23.7	-31.9	-40.4
30000	0.0	-0.1	-0.7	-2.2	-4.9	-9.2	-15.0	-22.4	-31.4	-41.2	-50.2
35000	0.0	-0.1	-0.9	-2.9	-6.6	-12.2	-19.7	-29.1	-39.9	-50.3	-59.4
36089	0.0	-0.1	-1.0	-3.1	-7.0	-12.9	-20.8	-30.8	-41.8	-52.2	-61.3
40000	0.0	-0.2	-1.2	-3.9	-8.7	-15.8	-25.3	-36.7	-48.3	-58.7	-67.6
45000	0.0	-0.2	-1.6	-5.1	-11.2	-20.1	-31.6	-44.1	-55.8	-66.0	-74.5
50000	0.0	-0.3	-2.1	-6.5	-14.1	-25.0	-38.0	-50.7	-62.2	-72.2	-80.3
55000	0.0	-0.4	-2.7	-8.2	-17.6	-30.3	-43.9	-56.5	-67.7	-77.3	-85.1
60000	0.0	-0.5	-3.4	-10.3	-21.5	-35.4	-49.1	-61.4	-72.3	-81.5	-89.0
65000	0.0	-0.6	-4.3	-12.7	-25.7	-40.1	-53.5	-65.6	-76.1	-85.0	-92.1

Pressure Altitude (ft)	Calibrated Airspeed (knots)										
	550	600	650	661.48	700	750	800	850	900	950	1000
0	0.0	0.0	0.0	0.0	0.0	0.0	0.0	0.0	0.0	0.0	0.0
5000	-7.6	-9.6	-11.6	-11.9	-12.8	-13.4	-13.5	-13.5	-13.3	-13.0	-12.7
10000	-16.5	-20.4	-23.7	-24.2	-25.5	-26.1	-26.2	-25.9	-25.4	-24.8	-24.1
15000	-26.6	-31.8	-35.6	-36.2	-37.5	-38.0	-37.8	-37.2	-36.3	-35.3	-34.2
20000	-37.3	-43.0	-46.9	-47.5	-48.6	-48.9	-48.3	-47.2	-46.0	-44.6	-43.2
25000	-47.8	-53.6	-57.3	-57.8	-58.7	-58.5	-57.6	-56.1	-54.5	-52.7	-51.0
30000	-57.7	-63.3	-66.6	-67.1	-67.7	-67.1	-65.7	-63.8	-61.8	-59.7	-57.6
35000	-66.7	-71.9	-74.9	-75.2	-75.5	-74.5	-72.7	-70.5	-68.1	-65.7	-63.3
36089	-68.5	-73.7	-76.5	-76.8	-77.0	-76.0	-74.1	-71.8	-69.3	-66.9	-64.4
40000	-74.6	-79.4	-81.9	-82.2	-82.1	-80.7	-78.6	-76.0	-73.3	-70.7	-68.0
45000	-81.1	-85.6	-87.7	-87.9	-87.5	-85.8	-83.3	-80.5	-77.5	-74.6	-71.8
50000	-86.5	-90.6	-92.4	-92.5	-91.9	-89.9	-87.1	-84.0	-80.9	-77.8	-74.8
55000	-91.0	-94.7	-96.2	-96.2	-95.4	-93.1	-90.1	-86.9	-83.6	-80.3	-77.2
60000	-94.5	-98.0	-99.2	-99.2	-98.2	-95.7	-92.6	-89.1	-85.7	-82.3	-79.0
65000	-97.4	-100.6	-101.7	-101.6	-100.4	-97.8	-94.5	-90.9	-87.3	-83.9	-80.5

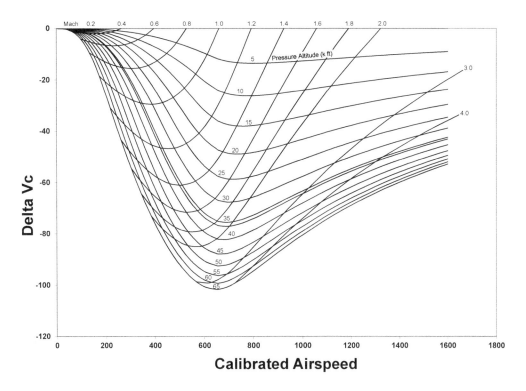

Figure C2. ΔV_c

Mach Is Mach

The catch phrase "Mach is Mach" means that for a given pressure altitude, test day Mach number is equal to standard day Mach number. This is true because true airspeed and the speed of sound vary in identical manners to changes in temperature. To see this, consider what happens to each while flying at a constant pressure altitude and constant Mach number with varying ambient air temperature.

From Equation C48

$$V_t = \sqrt{\left(\frac{1}{\rho_a}\right)7P_a\left(\left(\frac{P_T - P_a}{P_a} + 1\right)^{\frac{2}{7}} - 1\right)}$$

(C48)

or substituting q_c for P_T - P_a

$$V_t = \sqrt{\left(\frac{1}{\rho_a}\right)7P_a\left(\left(\frac{q_c}{P_a} + 1\right)^{\frac{2}{7}} - 1\right)}$$

(C136)

Because we are considering a constant pressure altitude, P_a is a constant for this analysis. Equations C70 and C102 show us that q_c/P_a is strictly a function of Mach number, so if Mach number is constant, q_c/P_a will be constant. This leaves true airspeed to vary as the square root of the inverse of the density.

$$V_t \propto \sqrt{\frac{1}{\rho_a}} \tag{C137}$$

Solving the equation of state (Equation A3) for density gives

$$\rho_a = \frac{P_a}{RT_a} \tag{C138}$$

Again, P_a is a constant for a constant pressure altitude and the gas constant (R) is just constant, so density varies as the inverse of the temperature.

$$\rho_a \propto \frac{1}{T_a} \tag{C139}$$

Substituting Equation C139 into Equation C137 gives

$$V_t \propto \sqrt{T} \tag{C140}$$

The speed of sound is defined by Equation C31

$$a = \sqrt{\gamma R T_a} \tag{C31}$$

The ratio of specific heats (γ) and the gas constant (R) are constants, so the speed of sound varies as the square root of temperature

$$a \propto \sqrt{T_a} \tag{C141}$$

Since both the speed of sound and true airspeed vary as the square root of temperature, we can say that they are proportional to each other.

$$V_t \propto a \tag{C142}$$

Thus, for different temperatures at a given pressure altitude, the true airspeed and speed of sound will change by proportional amounts such that the Mach number remains the same. Hence, Mach is Mach.

Differential Pressure and Dynamic Pressure

We can find the relationship between differential pressure and dynamic pressure by a Maclaurin series (a Taylor series expanded about x = 0) expansion of q_c. The Maclaurin series is given by (Ref 28)

$$f(x) = f(0) + \frac{f'(0)}{1!}x + \frac{f''(0)}{2!}x^2 + \frac{f'''(0)}{3!}x^3 + \frac{f^{(4)}(0)}{4!}x^4 + \dots \tag{C143}$$

For our expression for q_c we will use Equation C68, substituting q_c for $P_T - P_a$ (Equation C66)

$$\frac{q_c}{P_a} = \left(1 + \frac{\gamma-1}{2}M^2\right)^{\frac{\gamma}{\gamma-1}} - 1 \tag{C144}$$

or rearranging

$$q_c = P_a\left(\left(1+\frac{\gamma-1}{2}M^2\right)^{\frac{\gamma}{\gamma-1}} - 1\right)$$ (C145)

This is true only for the subsonic case, but that is reasonable since we will be expanding about $M^2 = 0$. The derivatives will be in terms of the independent variable M^2. We could have used M and achieved the same results, but since Mach only appears as M^2, we will use M^2 as the independent variable.

The series we will be looking for is

$$q_c = q_c(0) + \frac{1}{1!}\frac{dq_c(0)}{d(M^2)}(M^2) + \frac{1}{2!}\frac{d^2q_c(0)}{d(M^2)^2}(M^2)^2 + \frac{1}{3!}\frac{d^3q_c(0)}{d(M^2)^3}(M^2)^3 + \frac{1}{4!}\frac{d^4q_c(0)}{d(M^2)^4}(M^2)^4 + \dots$$
(C146)

For the first term at $M^2 = 0$

$$q_c(0) = P_a\left(\left(1+0.2(0)^2\right)^{7/2} - 1\right)$$ (C147)

$$q_c(0) = 0$$ (C148)

For the second term, we first differentiate the expression for q_c. Note that P_a is not a function of Mach, hence is treated as a constant.

$$\frac{dq_c}{d(M^2)} = \frac{d}{d(M^2)}\left(P_a\left(\left(1+\frac{\gamma-1}{2}M^2\right)^{\frac{\gamma}{\gamma-1}} - 1\right)\right)$$ (C149)

$$\frac{dq_c}{d(M^2)} = P_a\left(\frac{\gamma}{\gamma-1}\right)\left(1+\frac{\gamma-1}{2}M^2\right)^{\left(\frac{\gamma}{\gamma-1}-1\right)}\left(\frac{\gamma-1}{2}\right)$$ (C150)

$$\frac{dq_c}{d(M^2)} = \frac{\gamma}{2}P_a\left(1+\frac{\gamma-1}{2}M^2\right)^{\left(\frac{\gamma}{\gamma-1}-1\right)}$$ (C151)

Evaluating at $M^2 = 0$

$$\frac{dq_c(0)}{d(M^2)} = \frac{\gamma}{2}P_a\left(1+\frac{\gamma-1}{2}(0)^2\right)^{\left(\frac{\gamma}{\gamma-1}-1\right)}$$ (C152)

$$\frac{dq_c(0)}{d(M^2)} = \frac{\gamma}{2}P_a$$ (C153)

Inserting into the second term

$$\frac{1}{1!}\frac{dq_c(0)}{d(M^2)}(M^2) = \frac{1}{1}\frac{\gamma}{2}P_aM^2 \qquad (C154)$$

$$\frac{1}{1!}\frac{dq_c(0)}{d(M^2)}(M^2) = \frac{\gamma}{2}P_aM^2 \qquad (C155)$$

For the third term, we differentiate the expression for $dq_c/d(M^2)$.

$$\frac{d^2q_c}{d(M^2)^2} = \frac{d}{d(M^2)}\left(\frac{\gamma}{2}P_a\left(1+\frac{\gamma-1}{2}M^2\right)^{\left(\frac{\gamma}{\gamma-1}-1\right)}\right) \qquad (C156)$$

$$\frac{d^2q_c}{d(M^2)^2} = \frac{\gamma}{2}P_a\left(\frac{\gamma}{\gamma-1}-1\right)\left(1+\frac{\gamma-1}{2}M^2\right)^{\left(\frac{\gamma}{\gamma-1}-2\right)}\left(\frac{\gamma-1}{2}\right) \qquad (C157)$$

$$\frac{d^2q_c}{d(M^2)^2} = \frac{\gamma}{2}P_a\left(\frac{\gamma}{2}-\frac{\gamma-1}{2}\right)\left(1+\frac{\gamma-1}{2}M^2\right)^{\left(\frac{\gamma}{\gamma-1}-2\right)} \qquad (C158)$$

$$\frac{d^2q_c}{d(M^2)^2} = \frac{\gamma}{2}P_a\left(\frac{\gamma-\gamma+1}{2}\right)\left(1+\frac{\gamma-1}{2}M^2\right)^{\left(\frac{\gamma}{\gamma-1}-2\right)} \qquad (C159)$$

$$\frac{d^2q_c}{d(M^2)^2} = \frac{\gamma}{2}P_a\left(\frac{1}{2}\right)\left(1+\frac{\gamma-1}{2}M^2\right)^{\left(\frac{\gamma}{\gamma-1}-2\right)} \qquad (C160)$$

Evaluating at $M^2 = 0$

$$\frac{d^2q_c(0)}{d(M^2)^2} = \frac{\gamma}{2}P_a\left(\frac{1}{2}\right)\left(1+\frac{\gamma-1}{2}(0)^2\right)^{\left(\frac{\gamma}{\gamma-1}-2\right)} \qquad (C161)$$

$$\frac{d^2q_c(0)}{d(M^2)^2} = \frac{\gamma}{2}P_a\left(\frac{1}{2}\right)(1) \qquad (C162)$$

Inserting into the third term

$$\frac{1}{2!}\frac{d^2q_c(0)}{d(M^2)^2}(M^2)^2 = \frac{1}{2!}\frac{\gamma}{2}P_a\left(\frac{1}{2}\right)(M^2)^2 \qquad (C163)$$

$$\frac{1}{2!}\frac{d^2q_c(0)}{d\left(M^2\right)^2}\left(M^2\right)^2 = \left(\frac{\gamma}{2}P_aM^2\right)\frac{M^2}{4} \tag{C164}$$

For the fourth term, we differentiate the expression for $d^2q_c/d(M^2)^2$.

$$\frac{d^3q_c}{d\left(M^2\right)^3} = \frac{d}{d\left(M^2\right)}\left(\frac{\gamma}{2}P_a\left(\frac{1}{2}\right)\left(1+\frac{\gamma-1}{2}M^2\right)^{\left(\frac{\gamma}{\gamma-1}-2\right)}\right) \tag{C165}$$

$$\frac{d^3q_c}{d\left(M^2\right)^3} = \frac{\gamma}{2}P_a\left(\frac{1}{2}\right)\left(\frac{\gamma}{\gamma-1}-2\right)\left(1+\frac{\gamma-1}{2}M^2\right)^{\left(\frac{\gamma}{\gamma-1}-3\right)}\left(\frac{\gamma-1}{2}\right) \tag{C166}$$

$$\frac{d^3q_c}{d\left(M^2\right)^3} = \frac{\gamma}{2}P_a\left(\frac{1}{2}\right)\left(\frac{\gamma}{2}-\frac{2(\gamma-1)}{2}\right)\left(1+\frac{\gamma-1}{2}M^2\right)^{\left(\frac{\gamma}{\gamma-1}-3\right)} \tag{C167}$$

$$\frac{d^3q_c}{d\left(M^2\right)^3} = \frac{\gamma}{2}P_a\left(\frac{1}{2}\right)\left(\frac{\gamma-2\gamma+2}{2}\right)\left(1+\frac{\gamma-1}{2}M^2\right)^{\left(\frac{\gamma}{\gamma-1}-3\right)} \tag{C168}$$

$$\frac{d^3q_c}{d\left(M^2\right)^3} = \frac{\gamma}{2}P_a\left(\frac{2-\gamma}{4}\right)\left(1+\frac{\gamma-1}{2}M^2\right)^{\left(\frac{\gamma}{\gamma-1}-3\right)} \tag{C169}$$

Evaluating at $M^2 = 0$

$$\frac{d^3q_c(0)}{d\left(M^2\right)^3} = \frac{\gamma}{2}P_a\left(\frac{0.6}{4}\right)\left(1+\frac{\gamma-1}{2}(0)^2\right)^{\left(\frac{\gamma}{\gamma-1}-3\right)} \tag{C170}$$

$$\frac{d^3q_c(0)}{d\left(M^2\right)^3} = \frac{\gamma}{2}P_a\left(\frac{0.6}{4}\right)(1) \tag{C171}$$

Inserting into the fourth term

$$\frac{1}{3!}\frac{d^3q_c(0)}{d\left(M^2\right)^3}\left(M^2\right)^3 = \frac{1}{3!}\frac{\gamma}{2}P_a\left(\frac{0.6}{4}\right)\left(M^2\right)^3 \tag{C172}$$

$$\frac{1}{3!}\frac{d^3q_c(0)}{d\left(M^2\right)^3}\left(M^2\right)^3 = \left(\frac{\gamma}{2}P_aM^2\right)\frac{M^4}{40} \tag{C173}$$

For the fifth term, we differentiate the expression for $d^3q_c/d(M^2)^3$.

$$\frac{d^4q_c}{d(M^2)^4} = \frac{d}{d(M^2)}\left(\frac{\gamma}{2}P_a\left(\frac{2-\gamma}{4}\right)\left(1+\frac{\gamma-1}{2}M^2\right)^{\left(\frac{\gamma}{\gamma-1}-3\right)}\right) \qquad (C174)$$

$$\frac{d^4q_c}{d(M^2)^4} = \frac{\gamma}{2}P_a\left(\frac{2-\gamma}{4}\right)\left(\frac{\gamma}{\gamma-1}-3\right)\left(1+\frac{\gamma-1}{2}M^2\right)^{\left(\frac{\gamma}{\gamma-1}-4\right)}\left(\frac{\gamma-1}{2}\right) \qquad (C175)$$

$$\frac{d^4q_c}{d(M^2)^4} = \frac{\gamma}{2}P_a\left(\frac{2-\gamma}{4}\right)\left(\frac{\gamma}{2}-\frac{3(\gamma-1)}{2}\right)\left(1+\frac{\gamma-1}{2}M^2\right)^{\left(\frac{\gamma}{\gamma-1}-4\right)} \qquad (C176)$$

$$\frac{d^4q_c}{d(M^2)^4} = \frac{\gamma}{2}P_a\left(\frac{2-\gamma}{4}\right)\left(\frac{\gamma-3\gamma+3}{2}\right)\left(1+\frac{\gamma-1}{2}M^2\right)^{\left(\frac{\gamma}{\gamma-1}-4\right)} \qquad (C177)$$

$$\frac{d^4q_c}{d(M^2)^4} = \frac{\gamma}{2}P_a\left(\frac{2-\gamma}{4}\right)\left(\frac{3-2\gamma}{2}\right)\left(1+\frac{\gamma-1}{2}M^2\right)^{\left(\frac{\gamma}{\gamma-1}-4\right)} \qquad (C178)$$

Evaluating at $M^2 = 0$

$$\frac{d^4q_c(0)}{d(M^2)^4} = \frac{\gamma}{2}P_a\left(\frac{0.6}{4}\right)\left(\frac{0.2}{2}\right)\left(1+\frac{\gamma-1}{2}(0)^2\right)^{\left(\frac{\gamma}{\gamma-1}-4\right)} \qquad (C179)$$

$$\frac{d^4q_c(0)}{d(M^2)^4} = \frac{\gamma}{2}P_a\left(\frac{0.12}{8}\right)(1) \qquad (C180)$$

Inserting into the fifth term

$$\frac{1}{4!}\frac{d^4q_c(0)}{d(M^2)^4}(M^2)^4 = \frac{1}{4!}\frac{\gamma}{2}P_a\left(\frac{0.12}{8}\right)(M^2)^4 \qquad (C181)$$

$$\frac{1}{4!}\frac{d^4q_c(0)}{d(M^2)^4}(M^2)^4 = \left(\frac{\gamma}{2}P_a M^2\right)\frac{M^6}{1600} \qquad (C182)$$

Collecting terms back into Equation C143 we have

$$q_c = \left(\frac{\gamma}{2}P_a M^2\right)\left(1+\frac{M^2}{4}+\frac{M^4}{40}+\frac{M^6}{1600}+...\right) \qquad (C183)$$

Applying Equation C64 we get the final relationship between differential pressure and dynamic pressure

$$q_c = q\left(1 + \frac{M^2}{4} + \frac{M^4}{40} + \frac{M^6}{1600} + ...\right) \tag{C184}$$

Temperature Recovery Factor

The relationship of the total temperature to the ambient temperature is given by

$$\frac{T_T}{T_a} = \left(1 + \frac{\gamma - 1}{2}M^2\right) \tag{C34}$$

The instrument error in the temperature measuring device, as a function of indicated or ambient temperature, is used to find the instrument corrected temperature from the indicated temperature

$$T_{ic} = T_i + \Delta T_{ic} \tag{C185}$$

where

T_{ic} Instrument Corrected Temperature
T_i Indicated Temperature
ΔT_{ic} Temperature instrument correction

Sensors are not perfect, and a temperature sensor will typically only register some portion of that total temperature rise. If a sensor registers 90 per cent of the total temperature rise, then we would say that sensor has a 90 per cent recovery factor, or 0.9. The temperature recovery factor is given the symbol K_t, and Equation C34 is modified to reflect this as (using $\gamma = 1.4$ for air)

$$\frac{T_{ic}}{T_a} = 1 + 0.2K_t M^2 \tag{C186}$$

Note the change from total temperature (T_T) to instrument corrected temperature (T_{ic}), since if the recovery factor is not equal to one (1), then the measured temperature is no longer equal to the total temperature.

To find ambient temperature, we rearrange this equation to

$$T_a = \frac{T_{ic}}{1 + 0.2K_t M^2} \tag{C187}$$

To find a similar equation in terms of true airspeed instead of Mach number, we start with

$$\frac{T_T}{T_a} = \left(1 + \frac{V_t^2}{2C_p T_a}\right) \tag{C28}$$

Multiply both sides by T_a to get

$$T_T = \left(1 + \frac{V_t^2}{2C_p T_a}\right)T_a \tag{C188}$$

$$T_T = T_a + \frac{V_t^2}{2C_p} \qquad \qquad \text{(C189)}$$

Solving for T_a

$$T_a = T_T - \frac{V_t^2}{2C_p} \qquad \qquad \text{(C190)}$$

Introducing the temperature recovery factor gives

$$T_a = T_{ic} - \frac{K_t V_t^2}{2C_p} \qquad \qquad \text{(C191)}$$

$$C_p = 1005 \frac{m^2}{sec^2 \, K} = 3796 \frac{knots^2}{K} = 5027 \frac{mph^2}{K} = 10814 \frac{ft^2}{sec^2 \, K} = 0.24 \frac{BTU}{lbm \, °R} = 186.72 \frac{ft \, lbf}{lbm \, °R}$$

In order to determine the temperature recovery factor, we can rearrange Equation C186

$$\frac{T_{ic}}{T_a} - 1 = 0.2 K_t M^2 \qquad \qquad \text{(C192)}$$

$$\frac{T_{ic}}{T_a} - 1 = K_t \frac{M^2}{5} \qquad \qquad \text{(C193)}$$

If we then plot data points using $(T_{ic}/T_a - 1)$ as the "y" parameter and $(M^2/5)$ as the "x" parameter, the results should be a line with a slope of K_t. To allow for biases in the temperature measuring equipment (i.e. doesn't go to zero at zero), we have the final version of the equation

$$\frac{T_{ic}}{T_a} - 1 = K_t \frac{M^2}{5} + bias \qquad \qquad \text{(C194)}$$

Variable Temperature Recovery Factor

This section is mostly derived from Reference 33, modified to stay consistent with the nomenclature of this textbook.

The relationship between total and ambient temperature is given by Equation C34. This is the equation programmed into air data computers to calculate static air temperature (SAT) from measured temperature (T_m) values which are very close to total temperature (T_T).

If the total temperature sensor is designed such that there are no significant heat sources or thermal paths to heat sinks and such that flow over the sensing element is uniform and continuous, the sensor will indicate the adiabatic value T_{ic} very closely.

One parameter which relates T_{ic} to T_T and T_a is called the recovery factor, defined as follows:

$$K_t = \frac{T_{ic} - T_a}{T_T - T_a} \qquad \qquad \text{(C195)}$$

Some geometric shapes have constant recovery factors (e.g. the classic flat plate with airflow parallel to its surface). For sensors with a constant adiabatic recovery factor, Equations C43 and C193 combine to give Equation C186.

$$\frac{T_{ic}}{T_a} = 1 + 0.2K_t M^2 \tag{C186}$$

However, most sensors exhibit a variable recovery factor, and it is more convenient to use a recovery correction defined as

$$\eta = \frac{T_T - T_{ic}}{T_T} \tag{C196}$$

Total temperature sensors may exhibit a variable a variable η for Mach values below 1.0 but constant η for Mach values above 1.0. Even though the total temperature (T_T) in supersonic flow does not change through a shock wave, at supersonic speeds the temperature recovery characteristics of the probe may change, due to factors such as choked flow through the probe passages.

Once T_{ic} and η are known, T_T is calculated by

$$T_T = \frac{T_{ic}}{1 - \eta} \tag{C197}$$

Now that total temperature is known, the ambient temperature can be calculated by

$$T_a = \frac{T_T}{1 + 0.2M^2} \tag{C198}$$

The relationships between η and K_t are given by (using $\gamma = 1.4$ for air)

$$T_{ic} = 1 - \eta \left[1 + \frac{1}{0.2M^2} \right] \tag{C199}$$

$$\eta = \frac{(1 - K_t)0.2M^2}{1 + 0.2M^2} \tag{C200}$$

For non-adiabatic conditions, additional parameters are involved in calculating T_T and T_a.

Appendix D

Pitot-Static System Errors Heavy Math Section

Position Errors

For the purposes of this section, total pressure error and errors due to pressure lag will be assumed zero. Therefore, all errors and resulting corrections arise from the inability to accurately measure the ambient air pressure. This error is referred to as the position error and is defined as

$$\Delta P_p = P_s - P_a \tag{D1}$$

where

ΔP_p Position Error
P_s Measured Static Pressure
P_a Actual Ambient Pressure

The position error will show up as errors in the altitude, airspeed, and Mach as

$$\Delta H_p = H_{ic} - H_c \tag{D2}$$

where

ΔH_p Altitude Position Error
H_{ic} Instrument Corrected Indicated Altitude
H_c Actual Pressure Altitude

$$\Delta V_p = V_{ic} - V_c \tag{D3}$$

where

ΔV_p Airspeed Position Error
V_{ic} Instrument Corrected Indicated Airspeed
V_c Actual Calibrated Airspeed

$$\Delta M_p = M_{ic} - M \tag{D4}$$

where

ΔM_p Mach Position Error
M_{ic} Instrument Corrected Indicated Mach Number
M Actual Mach Number

It is a subtle point, but the way that errors are defined, an error must be subtracted from a measured value to calculate the corrected value. It is considered easier to work with corrections which are added to the measured value to calculate the corrected value. Hence, corrections are just negative errors. The altitude, airspeed, and Mach corrections are defined as

$$\Delta H_{pc} = H_c - H_{ic} = -\Delta H_p \tag{D5}$$

$$\Delta V_{pc} = V_c - V_{ic} = -\Delta V_p \tag{D6}$$

$$\Delta M_{pc} = M - M_{ic} = -\Delta M_p \tag{D7}$$

Note that the difference between an error and a correction is subtle, and flight test personnel will frequently say "error" when they really mean "correction." Be careful that you know what you're really talking about.

Since we know that the altitude, airspeed, and Mach position corrections are related to the position error, we need to derive the equations that characterize this relationship.

Finding Position Error Corrections

The key to characterizing position error is finding ΔP_P. We will look at methods for determining ΔP_p from a measured ΔH_{pc}, ΔV_{pc}, or ΔM_{pc}. Our primary method will be by directly calculating pressures, a method suitable for use in spreadsheets or computer programs. In the interest of historical legacy, at the end of this appendix we will also look at Taylor series expansion methods as detailed in Reference 12. Taylor series methods give a single equation method that may have been considered more suitable for use with slide rules, but introduced some error in the result.

CAUTION

> For the Pitot-statics class at the USAF Test Pilot School, use the pressure method for full credit on exams. The pressure method gives an exact answer, while the Taylor series expansion method will give an approximate answer. The Taylor series expansion methods are included for historical legacy and explanation of Herrington (Ref 12).

After determining ΔP_p, then ΔH_{pc}, ΔV_{pc}, and ΔM_{pc} can be calculated. Again, we will look at pressure methods and Taylor series expansion methods.

Finding Position Error From a Measured Altitude Position Correction

An altitude comparison method finds the altitude position correction (ΔH_{pc}) by measuring an instrument corrected altitude (H_{ic}) and comparing it to an independently measured truth pressure altitude (H_c).

By modifying Equations B1 and B2 in combination with Equation A70, we can calculate the static pressure (P_s) and ambient pressure (P_a).

$$P_s = P_{SL}(1 - 6.87559 \times 10^{-6}\, H_{ic})^{5.2559} \qquad (H_{ic} \leq 36089.24 \text{ feet}) \tag{D8}$$

$$P_s = P_{SL}\, 0.223360\, e^{(-4.80637 \times 10^{-5}\,(H_{ic} - 36089.24))} \qquad (H_{ic} > 36089.24 \text{ feet}) \tag{D9}$$

$$P_a = P_{SL}\, (1 - 6.87559 \times 10^{-6}\, H_c)^{5.2559} \qquad (H_c \leq 36089.24 \text{ feet}) \tag{D10}$$

$$P_a = P_{SL}\, 0.223360\, e^{(-4.80637 \times 10^{-5}\,(H_c - 36089.24))} \qquad (H_c > 36089.24 \text{ feet}) \tag{D11}$$

Now that we have static pressure and ambient pressure, we can find the position error from Equation D1.

$$\Delta P_p = P_s - P_a \tag{D1}$$

If we would rather have $\Delta P_p/P_s$ then simply divide ΔP_p by P_s from Equation D8 or D9.

Finding Position Error From a Measured Airspeed Position Correction

An airspeed comparison method finds the airspeed position correction (ΔV_{pc}) by measuring a instrument corrected airspeed (V_{ic}) and comparing it to an independently measured truth calibrated airspeed (V_c).

For the truth conditions, we use Equations C106 and C107

$$\frac{q_c}{P_{SL}} = \left(1+0.2\left(\frac{V_c}{a_{SL}}\right)^2\right)^{7/2} - 1 \qquad (V_c < a_{SL}) \quad (C106)$$

$$\frac{q_c}{P_{SL}} = \frac{166.921\left(\frac{V_c}{a_{SL}}\right)^7}{\left(7\left(\frac{V_c}{a_{SL}}\right)^2 - 1\right)^{5/2}} - 1 \qquad (V_c > a_{SL}) \quad (C107)$$

For the instrument corrected indicated airspeed, we find

$$\frac{q_{cic}}{P_{SL}} = \left(1+0.2\left(\frac{V_{ic}}{a_{SL}}\right)^2\right)^{7/2} - 1 \qquad (V_{ic} < a_{SL}) \quad (D12)$$

$$\frac{q_{cic}}{P_{SL}} = \frac{166.921\left(\frac{V_{ic}}{a_{SL}}\right)^7}{\left(7\left(\frac{V_{ic}}{a_{SL}}\right)^2 - 1\right)^{5/2}} - 1 \qquad (V_{ic} > a_{SL}) \quad (D13)$$

Equation C66 gives the definition of q_c

$$q_c = P_T - P_a \tag{C66}$$

Replacing the ambient pressure with the measured static pressure gives q_{cic}

$$q_{cic} = P_T - P_s \tag{D14}$$

Assuming zero total pressure error (P_T = constant), then the difference of q_c and q_{cic} is equal to ΔP_p

$$q_c - q_{cic} = (P_T - P_a) - (P_T - P_s) = P_s - P_a = \Delta P_p \qquad \text{(D15)}$$

Therefore

$$\Delta P_p = \left(\frac{q_c}{P_{SL}} - \frac{q_{cic}}{P_{SL}} \right) P_{SL} \qquad \text{(D16)}$$

If we would rather have $\Delta P_p / P_s$ then simply divide ΔP_p by P_s calculated from H_{ic} in Equation D8 or D9.

Finding Position Error From a Measured Mach Position Correction

A Mach comparison method finds the Mach position correction (ΔM_{pc}) by measuring an instrument corrected Mach number (M_{ic}) and comparing it to an independently measured truth Mach number (M).

For the subsonic truth conditions, we use Equation C36

$$\frac{P_T}{P_a} = \left(1 + \frac{\gamma - 1}{2} M^2 \right)^{\frac{\gamma}{\gamma - 1}} \qquad (M < 1) \quad \text{(C36)}$$

which using $\gamma = 1.4$ for air becomes

$$\frac{P_T}{P_a} = \left(1 + 0.2 M^2 \right)^{7/2} \qquad (M < 1) \quad \text{(D17)}$$

For the supersonic case, we start with Equation C102

$$\frac{q_c}{P_a} = \frac{166.921 M^7}{\left(7 M^2 - 1 \right)^{5/2}} - 1 \qquad (M < 1) \quad \text{(C102)}$$

To get an expression for P_T / P_a, from Equation C96

$$q_c = P_T{'} - P_a \qquad (M > 1) \quad \text{(C96)}$$

then (dropping the primed notation for total pressure)

$$\frac{q_c}{P_a} = \frac{P_T - P_a}{P_a} = \frac{P_T}{P_a} - \frac{P_a}{P_a} = \frac{P_T}{P_a} - 1 \qquad \text{(D18)}$$

Applying this to Equation C102 gives

$$\frac{P_T}{P_a} = \frac{166.921 M^7}{\left(7 M^2 - 1 \right)^{5/2}} \qquad (M > 1) \quad \text{(D19)}$$

Substituting static pressure for ambient pressure in Equations D17 and D19 gives

$$\frac{P_T}{P_s} = \left(1 + 0.2 M_{ic}^2\right)^{7/2} \qquad (M_{ic} < 1) \quad (D20)$$

$$\frac{P_T}{P_s} = \frac{166.921 M_{ic}^7}{\left(7 M_{ic}^2 - 1\right)^{5/2}} \qquad (M_{ic} > 1) \quad (D21)$$

The position error can then be calculated directly from these ratios by

$$\left(\frac{1}{\frac{P_T}{P_s}} - \frac{1}{\frac{P_T}{P_a}}\right)\frac{P_T}{P_s} = \left(\frac{P_s - P_a}{P_T}\right)\frac{P_T}{P_s} = \frac{P_s - P_a}{P_s} = \frac{\Delta P_p}{P_s} \qquad (D22)$$

or without the intervening steps

$$\frac{\Delta P_p}{P_s} = \left(\frac{1}{\frac{P_T}{P_s}} - \frac{1}{\frac{P_T}{P_a}}\right)\frac{P_T}{P_s} \qquad (D23)$$

Finding Altitude Position Correction From Position Error

Given a Position Error in the form of $\Delta P_p / P_s$ and a desired standard altitude (pressure altitude), $H_{std\ alt}$, we can find the altitude position correction, ΔH_{pc}, by first finding the ambient pressure

$$P_a = P_{SL}(1 - 6.87559 \times 10^{-6} H_{std\ alt})^{5.2559} \qquad (H_{std\ alt} \leq 36089.24 \text{ feet}) \quad (D10)$$

$$P_a = P_{SL}\ 0.223360\ e^{(-4.80637 \times 10^{-5}\ (H_{std\ alt} - 36089.24))} \qquad (H_{std\ alt} > 36089.24 \text{ feet}) \quad (D11)$$

We need to find P_s using P_a and $\Delta P_p / P_s$. To find an expression for this, start with P_s multiplied by a form of 1

$$P_s = \frac{P_a}{P_a} P_s \qquad (D24)$$

Moving P_s to the denominator of the denominator

$$P_s = \frac{P_a}{\dfrac{P_a}{P_s}} \qquad (D25)$$

Add and subtract P_s in the denominator

$$P_s = \frac{P_a}{\dfrac{P_s - P_s + P_a}{P_s}} \tag{D26}$$

Separating the denominator

$$P_s = \frac{P_a}{\dfrac{P_s}{P_s} - \dfrac{P_s - P_a}{P_s}} \tag{D27}$$

Changing to 1 and applying Equation D1

$$P_s = \frac{P_a}{1 - \dfrac{\Delta P_p}{P_s}} \tag{D28}$$

With Equation A70 we find the pressure ratio. Since we used the static pressure, we add the subscript ic to δ to indicate that this value includes the position error.

$$\delta_{ic} = \frac{P_s}{P_{SL}} \tag{D29}$$

which with Equations B3 and B4 will give the instrument corrected altitude, again using the subscript ic to indicate the value includes the position error

$$H_{ic} = \frac{1 - \sqrt[5.2559]{\delta_{ic}}}{6.87559 \times 10^{-6}} \qquad (H_{ic} \leq 36089.24 \text{ feet}) \quad (D30)$$

$$H_{ic} = \frac{\ln\left(\dfrac{\delta_{ic}}{0.223360}\right)}{-4.80637 \times 10^{-5}} + 36089.24 \qquad (H_{ic} > 36089.24 \text{ feet}) \quad (D31)$$

Finally, the altitude position correction is calculated by

$$\Delta H_{pc} = H_c - H_{ic} \tag{D5}$$

Finding Airspeed Position Correction From Position Error

Given a Position Error in the form of $\Delta P_p/P_s$, the Mach number, M, corresponding to the position error, the desired standard altitude (pressure altitude), $H_{std\ alt}$, and δ_{ic} from finding the altitude position correction above we can find the airspeed position correction, ΔV_{pc}.

From the Mach number, we find the differential pressure ratio

$$\frac{q_c}{P_a} = \left(1 + 0.2 M^2\right)^{7/2} - 1 \qquad \text{(subsonic)} \quad (C70)$$

$$\frac{q_c}{P_a} = \frac{166.921 M^7}{\left(7M^2 - 1\right)^{5/2}} - 1 \qquad \text{(supersonic)} \text{(C102)}$$

From the standard altitude we can find the pressure ratio

$$\delta = (1 - 6.87559\text{x}10^{-6}\,H_c)^{5.2559} \qquad (H_c \leq 36089.24 \text{ feet}) \text{(B1)}$$

$$\delta = 0.223360\,e^{(-4.80637\text{x}10^{-5}\,(H_c - 36089.24))} \qquad (H_c > 36089.24 \text{ feet}) \text{(B2)}$$

or in this case

$$\delta_{\text{std alt}} = (1 - 6.87559\text{x}10^{-6}\,H_{\text{std alt}})^{5.2559} \qquad (H_{\text{std alt}} \leq 36089.24 \text{ feet}) \text{(D32)}$$

$$\delta_{\text{std alt}} = 0.223360\,e^{(-4.80637\text{x}10^{-5}\,(H_{\text{std alt}} - 36089.24))} \qquad (H_{\text{std alt}} > 36089.24 \text{ feet}) \text{(D33)}$$

Working toward calibrated airspeed

$$\left(\frac{q_c}{P_{SL}}\right)_{\text{std alt}} = \frac{q_c}{P_a}\frac{P_a}{P_{SL}} = \frac{q_c}{P_a}\delta_{\text{std alt}} \tag{D34}$$

Using Equations C125 or C131

$$V_{c\text{std alt}} = a_{SL}\sqrt{5\left[\left(\left(\frac{q_c}{P_{SL}}\right)_{\text{std alt}} + 1\right)^{2/7} - 1\right]} \qquad \left(\frac{q_c}{P_{SL}} < 0.89293\right) \text{(D35)}$$

$$V_{c\text{std alt}} = a_{SL}\,0.881284\sqrt{\left(\left(\frac{q_c}{P_{SL}}\right)_{\text{std alt}} + 1\right)\left(1 - \frac{1}{7\left(\dfrac{V_{c\text{std alt}}}{a_{SL}}\right)^2}\right)^{5/2}} \qquad \left(\frac{q_c}{P_{SL}} > 0.89293\right) \text{(D36)}$$

This gives the truth calibrated airspeed at the specified Mach number and standard altitude. Next we need to determine q_{cic}/P_{SL} from the given data to determine V_{ic}.

Starting with q_{cic}/P_{SL}

$$\frac{q_{cic}}{P_{SL}} = \frac{P_T - P_s}{P_{SL}} \tag{D37}$$

Add and subtract P_a

$$\frac{q_{cic}}{P_{SL}} = \frac{P_T - P_a - P_s + P_a}{P_{SL}} \tag{D38}$$

$$\frac{q_{cic}}{P_{SL}} = \frac{P_T - P_a}{P_{SL}} - \frac{P_s - P_a}{P_{SL}} \qquad\qquad (D39)$$

Multiply second term by 1

$$\frac{q_{cic}}{P_{SL}} = \frac{P_T - P_a}{P_{SL}} - \frac{P_s - P_a}{P_s}\frac{P_s}{P_{SL}} \qquad\qquad (D40)$$

Which gives a useable expression

$$\frac{q_{cic}}{P_{SL}} = \frac{q_c}{P_{SL}} - \frac{\Delta P_p}{P_s}\delta_{ic} \qquad\qquad (D41)$$

where δ_{ic} was found by the method shown for determining the altitude position correction.

Next we calculate the instrument corrected airspeed by

$$V_{ic} = a_{SL}\sqrt{5\left[\left(\frac{q_{cic}}{P_{SL}}+1\right)^{2/7}-1\right]} \qquad \left(\frac{q_{cic}}{P_{SL}} < 0.89293\right) \quad (D42)$$

$$V_{ic} = a_{SL}\,0.881284\sqrt{\left(\frac{q_{cic}}{P_{SL}}+1\right)\left(1-\frac{1}{7\left(\dfrac{V_{ic}}{a_{SL}}\right)^2}\right)^{5/2}} \qquad \left(\frac{q_{cic}}{P_{SL}} > 0.89293\right) \quad (D43)$$

Finally, the airspeed position correction is calculated by

$$\Delta V_{pc} = V_c - V_{ic} \qquad\qquad (D6)$$

Finding Mach Position Correction From Position Error

Given a Position Error in the form of $\Delta P_p/P_s$, an instrument corrected altitude, H_{ic}, and instrument corrected airspeed, V_{ic}, we can find the Mach position correction, ΔM_{pc}.

Modifying Equations C106 and C107 for instrument corrected airspeed

$$\frac{q_{cic}}{P_{SL}} = \left(1+0.2\left(\frac{V_{ic}}{a_{SL}}\right)^2\right)^{7/2}-1 \qquad (V_{ic} < a_{SL}) \quad (D44)$$

$$\frac{q_{cic}}{P_{SL}} = \frac{166.921\left(\dfrac{V_{ic}}{a_{SL}}\right)^7}{\left(7\left(\dfrac{V_{ic}}{a_{SL}}\right)^2-1\right)^{5/2}}-1 \qquad (V_{ic} > a_{SL}) \quad (D45)$$

Likewise modifying Equations B1 and B2 for instrument corrected altitude

$$\delta_{ic} = (1 - 6.87559 \times 10^{-6}\ H_{ic})^{5.2559} \qquad (H_{ic} < 36089.24\ \text{ft}) \quad (D46)$$

$$\delta_{ic} = 0.223360\ e^{(-4.80637 \times 10^{-5}\ (H_{ic} - 36089.24))} \qquad (H_{ic} > 36089.24\ \text{ft}) \quad (D47)$$

To find M_{ic} we need q_{cic}/P_s

$$\frac{q_{cic}}{P_s} = \frac{q_{cic}}{P_{SL}} \frac{P_{SL}}{P_s} = \frac{q_{cic}}{P_{SL}} \frac{1}{\delta_{ic}} \qquad (D48)$$

The instrument corrected Mach number is then found by (from C117 or C124)

$$M_{ic} = \sqrt{5\left(\left(\frac{q_{cic}}{P_s} + 1\right)^{2/7} - 1\right)} \qquad (M_{ic} < 1 \text{ or } q_{cic}/P_s < 0.89293) \quad (D49)$$

$$M_{ic} = 0.881284\sqrt{\left(\frac{q_{cic}}{P_s} + 1\right)\left(1 - \frac{1}{7M_{ic}^2}\right)^{5/2}} \qquad (M_{ic} > 1 \text{ or } q_{cic}/P_s > 0.89293) \quad (D50)$$

Next we need an equation to determine q_c/P_a from q_{cic}/P_s and $\Delta P_p/P_s$. Starting with q_c/P_a

$$\frac{q_c}{P_a} = \frac{P_T - P_a}{P_a} \qquad (D51)$$

Splitting the fraction

$$\frac{q_c}{P_a} = \frac{P_T}{P_a} - \frac{P_a}{P_a} \qquad (D52)$$

$$\frac{q_c}{P_a} = \frac{P_T}{P_a} - 1 \qquad (D53)$$

Dividing numerator and denominator by P_s

$$\frac{q_c}{P_a} = \frac{\dfrac{P_T}{P_s}}{\dfrac{P_a}{P_s}} - 1 \qquad (D54)$$

Add and subtract values

$$\frac{q_c}{P_a} = \frac{\dfrac{P_T - P_s + P_s}{P_s}}{\dfrac{P_a - P_s + P_s}{P_s}} - 1 \qquad (D55)$$

$$\frac{q_c}{P_a} = \frac{\dfrac{P_T - P_s}{P_s} + \dfrac{P_s}{P_s}}{\dfrac{P_s}{P_s} - \dfrac{P_s - P_a}{P_s}} - 1 \tag{D56}$$

$$\frac{q_c}{P_a} = \frac{\dfrac{P_T - P_s}{P_s} + 1}{1 - \dfrac{P_s - P_a}{P_s}} - 1 \tag{D57}$$

which gives a useable equation

$$\frac{q_c}{P_a} = \frac{\dfrac{q_{cic}}{P_s} + 1}{1 - \dfrac{\Delta P_p}{P_s}} - 1 \tag{D58}$$

With this we can find Mach number

$$M = \sqrt{5\left(\left(\frac{q_c}{P_a} + 1\right)^{2/7} - 1\right)} \qquad (M < 1 \text{ or } q_c/P_a < 0.89293) \tag{C117}$$

$$M = 0.881284\sqrt{\left(\frac{q_c}{P_a} + 1\right)\left(1 - \frac{1}{7M^2}\right)^{5/2}} \qquad (M > 1 \text{ or } q_c/P_a > 0.89293) \tag{C124}$$

The Mach position correction would then be given by

$$\Delta M_{pc} = M - M_{ic} \tag{D7}$$

Alternatively, if given position error in the form of $\Delta P_p/P_s$, and a truth Mach Number, M, we would start by finding q_c/P_a

$$\frac{q_c}{P_a} = \left(1 + 0.2M^2\right)^{7/2} - 1 \qquad \text{(subsonic)} \tag{C70}$$

$$\frac{q_c}{P_a} = \frac{166.921M^7}{\left(7M^2 - 1\right)^{5/2}} - 1 \qquad \text{(supersonic)} \tag{C102}$$

Next we need an equation to determine q_{cic}/P_s from q_c/P_a and $\Delta P_p/P_s$. Starting with q_{cic}/P_s

$$\frac{q_{cic}}{P_s} = \frac{P_T - P_s}{P_s} \tag{D59}$$

Splitting the fraction

$$\frac{q_{cic}}{P_s} = \frac{P_T}{P_s} - \frac{P_s}{P_s} \qquad\qquad (D60)$$

Multiply by 1

$$\frac{q_{cic}}{P_s} = \frac{P_T}{P_s} \frac{P_a}{P_a} - 1 \qquad\qquad (D61)$$

$$\frac{q_{cic}}{P_s} = \frac{P_a}{P_s} \frac{P_T}{P_a} - 1 \qquad\qquad (D62)$$

Add and subtract

$$\frac{q_{cic}}{P_s} = \left(\frac{P_a + P_s - P_s}{P_s} \right)\left(\frac{P_T + P_a - P_a}{P_a} \right) - 1 \qquad\qquad (D63)$$

$$\frac{q_{cic}}{P_s} = \left(\frac{P_s}{P_s} - \frac{P_s - P_a}{P_s} \right)\left(\frac{P_T - P_a}{P_a} + \frac{P_a}{P_a} \right) - 1 \qquad\qquad (D64)$$

which gives a useable equation

$$\frac{q_{cic}}{P_s} = \left(1 - \frac{\Delta P_p}{P_s} \right)\left(\frac{q_c}{P_a} + 1 \right) - 1 \qquad\qquad (D65)$$

Then the instrument corrected Mach number, M_{ic}, can be determined

$$M_{ic} = \sqrt{5\left(\left(\frac{q_{cic}}{P_s} + 1 \right)^{2/7} - 1 \right)} \qquad (M_{ic} < 1 \text{ or } q_{cic}/P_s < 0.89293) \quad (D49)$$

$$M_{ic} = 0.881284 \sqrt{\left(\frac{q_{cic}}{P_s} + 1 \right)\left(1 - \frac{1}{7M_{ic}^2} \right)^{5/2}} \qquad (M_{ic} > 1 \text{ or } q_{cic}/P_s > 0.89293) \quad (D50)$$

The Mach position correction would then be given by

$$\Delta M_{pc} = M - M_{ic} \qquad\qquad (D7)$$

Applying Instrument and Position Corrections

We define the instrument corrections as the negative of the instrument errors, with the correction being added to the indicated value to give the instrument corrected value.

$$H_{ic} = H_i + \Delta H_{ic} \tag{D66}$$

$$V_{ic} = V_i + \Delta V_{ic} \tag{D67}$$

$$M_{ic} = M_i + \Delta M_{ic} \tag{D68}$$

From Equations D5 – D7, we add the position corrections to the instrument corrected values to get the position and instrument corrected values

$$H_{pc} = H_{ic} + \Delta H_{pc} \tag{D69}$$

$$V_{pc} = V_{ic} + \Delta V_{pc} \tag{D70}$$

$$M_{pc} = M_{ic} + \Delta M_{pc} \tag{D71}$$

If we assume we are only correcting for instrument error and position error, we have the following equivalencies:

$$H_c = H_{pc} + \text{residual errors} \tag{D72}$$

$$V_c = V_{pc} + \text{residual errors} \tag{D73}$$

$$M = M_{pc} + \text{residual errors} \tag{D74}$$

Position Error Ratio and Pressure Coefficient

By inspection, the relationship between the two ratios is given by

$$\frac{\Delta P_p}{P_s} = \frac{\Delta P_p}{q_{cic}} \frac{q_{cic}}{P_s} \tag{D75}$$

How do we find q_{cic}/P_s? Starting with Equation C70

$$\frac{q_c}{P_a} = \left(1 + 0.2M^2\right)^{7/2} - 1 \qquad (M < 1) \quad (C70)$$

To find the form of this equation with the position error in it, we replace ambient pressure (P_a) with static pressure (P_s). For consistency, q_c ($P_T - P_a$) must be replaced with q_{cic} ($P_T - P_s$). On the right side of the equation, the freestream Mach number (M) must be replaced with a version of the Mach number which contains the position error, namely M_{ic}. Thus, after introducing position error into Equation C70 we get

$$\frac{q_{cic}}{P_s} = \left(1 + 0.2M_{ic}^2\right)^{7/2} - 1 \qquad (M_{ic} < 1) \quad (D76)$$

Applying a similar analysis to Equation C102 gives

$$\frac{q_{cic}}{P_s} = \frac{166.921 M_{ic}^7}{\left(7M_{ic}^2 - 1\right)^{5/2}} - 1 \qquad (M_{ic} > 1) \quad (D77)$$

Position Error Ratio and Coefficient Variations

As stated elsewhere, the sensed static pressure (P_s) is generally different from the freestream ambient pressure (P_a) because the aircraft disturbs the flow field. By dimensional analysis, we can see that the factors that cause pressure changes in the flow field can be represented by shape, angle of attack (α), angle of sideslip (β), Mach number (M), Reynolds number (R_e), and the Prandtl number (P_r). We can represent this in equation form as

$$\frac{P_s}{P_a} = f_1(\text{shape}, \alpha, \beta, M, R_e, P_r) \qquad (D78)$$

By doing what engineers do best, we will **assume** away some of these effects. For a fixed static port location and fixed geometry, we can ignore the effects of shape as it will not change with changing flight conditions. Note that configuration changes, such as lowering flaps or lowering the landing gear, could change the position error through this term. For this analysis, we will assume a constant configuration.

Generally we fly in coordinated flight, so we will ignore the effects of sideslip. On a relative scale, Reynolds number effects are small compared to the other effects of changing altitude and airspeed. If we neglect heat transfer, the Prandtl number is essentially constant.

Therefore, we are left with angle of attack and Mach number as the primary factors affecting the Position Error Ratio.

$$\frac{P_s}{P_a} = f_2(\alpha, M) \qquad (D79)$$

Equation D1 shows that ΔP_p is the difference of static and freestream ambient pressure. Any relationship containing only the static pressure and the freestream pressure will be a function of the same factors shown in Equation D79, so with no loss of generality, we can say

$$\frac{P_s - P_a}{P_s} = \frac{\Delta P_p}{P_s} = f_3(\alpha, M_{ic}) \qquad (D80)$$

As shown in Equations D75 – D77, the relationship between $\Delta P_p/P_s$ and $\Delta P_p/q_{cic}$ is only a function of M_{ic}, so it follows that

$$\frac{\Delta P_p}{q_{cic}} = f_4(\alpha, M_{ic}) \qquad (D81)$$

Finally, since the lift coefficient is a function of the same parameters as the flow field, namely

$$C_L = f_5(\text{shape}, \alpha, \beta, M, R_e, P_r) \qquad (D82)$$

and using the same assumptions, we can say

$$C_{L_{ic}} = f_6(\alpha, M_{ic})$$ (D83)

So between Equation D81 and D83 we can come up with

$$\frac{\Delta P_p}{q_{cic}} = f_7(M_{ic}, C_{L_{ic}})$$ (D84)

So if we assume that lift is equal to the load factor times the weight, the lift equation gives us

$$L = nW = C_L qS$$ (D85)

and substituting Equation C64

$$nW = C_L \frac{\gamma}{2} P_a M^2 S$$ (D86)

or using the version containing the position error

$$nW = C_{L_{ic}} \frac{\gamma}{2} P_s M_{ic}^2 S$$ (D87)

Using Equation A70

$$nW = C_{L_{ic}} \frac{\gamma}{2} \delta_{ic} P_{SL} M_{ic}^2 S$$ (D88)

Solving for $C_{L_{ic}}$

$$C_{L_{ic}} = \frac{nW}{\delta_{ic}} \frac{1}{M_{ic}^2} \frac{2}{\gamma S P_{SL}}$$ (D89)

Note that the last term $(2/\gamma S P_{SL})$ is made up of constants. Using Equations D89 and D84 we can surmise

$$\frac{\Delta P_p}{q_{cic}} = f_8(M_{ic}, \frac{nW}{\delta_{ic}})$$ (D90)

Now let's look at a similar analysis in terms of airspeed. We know that angle of attack effects will be seen primarily at low Mach numbers. At high Mach numbers, even maneuvers at high load factors occur with very small changes in angle of attack from the cruise condition. At low Mach numbers, the typical Mach effects (compressibility, wave drag, etc) will not occur, so we can assume that the position error coefficient will be mostly a function of angle of attack, which we can represent with lift coefficient (Equation D84). So we have

$$C_L = \frac{2nW}{\rho V_t^2 S}$$ (D91)

or in terms of equivalent airspeed

$$C_L = \frac{2nW}{\rho_{SL} V_e^2 S} \qquad (D92)$$

For low Mach numbers, calibrated airspeed is approximately equal to equivalent airspeed, so we can say with minimal loss of accuracy

$$C_L = \frac{2nW}{\rho_{SL} V_c^2 S} \qquad (D93)$$

and after introducing position error we have

$$C_{L_{ic}} = \frac{2nW}{\rho_{SL} V_{ic}^2 S} \qquad (D94)$$

So after removing all of the constants, we have

$$\frac{\Delta P_p}{q_{cic}} = f_9\left(\frac{nW}{V_{ic}^2}\right) \qquad (D95)$$

Altitude Correction Variation With Altitude

Equation D80 tells us that position error is a function of angle of attack and Mach number. If we are at a high enough constant Mach number that angle of attack effects are negligible, then the Position Error Ratio ($\Delta P_p/P_s$) is a constant. This implies a constant ratio between the Position Error (ΔP_p) and the static pressure (P_s), which is roughly the ambient pressure (P_a), as altitude changes. However, the relationship between a change in pressure and a change in pressure altitude is not constant, but depends on the altitude. Therefore, the altitude position correction (ΔH_{pc}) should change in size with altitude for the same Position Error Ratio.

We can see this by assuming small changes and looking at the hydrostatic equation

$$dP = -\rho\, g_{SL}\, dH \qquad (A30)$$

If we change the differentials to finite differences we can get

$$P_s - P_a = -\rho\, g_{SL}\, (H_{ic} - H_c) \qquad (D96)$$

which by substituting Equations D1 and D2 becomes

$$\Delta P_p = -\rho\, g_{SL}\, \Delta H_p \qquad (D97)$$

and substituting Equation D5 gives

$$\Delta P_p = \rho\, g_{SL}\, \Delta H_{pc} \qquad (D98)$$

Divide both sides by static pressure to get the Position Error Ratio

$$\frac{\Delta P_p}{P_s} = \frac{\rho g_{SL}}{P_s} \Delta H_{pc} \qquad (D99)$$

Solving for ΔH_{pc}

$$\Delta H_{pc} = \frac{P_s}{\rho g_{SL}} \frac{\Delta P_p}{P_s} \tag{D100}$$

From the equation of state

$$P = \rho RT \tag{A3}$$

we can solve to get

$$\frac{P}{\rho} = RT \tag{D101}$$

Applying this to Equation D100 we get

$$\Delta H_{pc} = \frac{RT}{g_{SL}} \frac{\Delta P_p}{P_s} \tag{D102}$$

So if we assume that $\Delta P_p/P_s$ is a constant (that is, constant Mach and angle of attack), then the only variable on the right side of this equation is temperature. This lines up with our previous theory, as temperature is what affects the difference in geopotential altitude between two different pressures.

Finding Position Error From a Measured Altitude Position Correction, Taylor Series Expansion Method

The relationship of pressure and altitude is described by the hydrostatic equation

$$dP = -\rho\, g\, dh \tag{A15}$$

or in terms of geopotential altitude

$$dP = -\rho\, g_{SL}\, dH \tag{A30}$$

which using Equation A71 can be alternatively expressed as

$$dP = -\rho_{SL}\, \sigma\, g_{SL}\, dH \tag{D103}$$

To find the position error in terms of geopotential altitude, we must integrate this equation from the actual pressure to the indicated (instrument corrected) pressure.

$$\Delta P_p = P_s - P_a = \int_{P_a}^{P_s} dP \tag{D104}$$

$$\int_{P_a}^{P_s} dP = -g_{SL}\rho_{SL} \int_{H_c}^{H_{ic}} \sigma dH \tag{D105}$$

By Equation D5, we can replace H_c with $H_{ic} + \Delta H_{pc}$ giving

$$\int_{P_a}^{P_s} dP = -g_{SL}\rho_{SL} \int_{H_{ic}+\Delta H_{pc}}^{H_{ic}} \sigma dH \qquad (D106)$$

But how do we evaluate a function (in this case altitude) at a value of $H_{ic} + \Delta H_{pc}$? From Reference 28, we can use a Taylor Series expansion, given by

$$f(x+h) = f(x) + \frac{h}{1!}f'(x) + \frac{h^2}{2!}f''(x) + ... + \frac{h^{n-1}}{(n-1)!}f^{(n-1)}(x) + ... \qquad (D107)$$

Don't you just love this math stuff? (Note: In Reference 12, this expansion is incorrectly referred to as the Binomial Theorem)

So how do we use this? The position error would be

$$\Delta P_p = -g_{SL}\rho_{SL}\left(\int \sigma(H_{ic})dH - \int \sigma(H_{ic}+\Delta H_{pc})dH\right) \qquad (D108)$$

Using the Taylor series expansion to find the last term gives

$$\int \sigma(H_{ic}+\Delta H_{pc})dH = \int \sigma(H_{ic})dH + \frac{\Delta H_{pc}}{1!}\sigma(H_{ic}) + \frac{\Delta H_{pc}^2}{2!}\frac{d\sigma}{dH_{ic}}(H_{ic}) + ... \qquad (D109)$$

We won't go beyond these terms because we will show that any terms beyond these are insignificant. So plugging Equation D109 into D108 and subtracting out like terms, we get

$$\Delta P_p = g_{SL}\rho_{SL}\left(\frac{\Delta H_{pc}}{1!}\sigma(H_{ic}) + \frac{\Delta H_{pc}^2}{2!}\frac{d\sigma}{dH_{ic}}(H_{ic}) + ...\right) \qquad (D110)$$

We'll drop the H_{ic} and use the subscript ic to show that the values are evaluated at H_{ic}. As we'll see later, what we'll really be interested in is $\Delta P_p/P_s$. To do this, we'll divide both sides by P_s which gives

$$\frac{\Delta P_p}{P_s} = \frac{g_{SL}\rho_{SL}}{P_s}\left(\frac{\Delta H_{pc}}{1!}\sigma_{ic} + \frac{\Delta H_{pc}^2}{2!}\frac{d\sigma_{ic}}{dH_{ic}} + ...\right) \qquad (D111)$$

Then multiplying the right side by 1 in the form of P_{SL}/P_{SL} we get

$$\frac{\Delta P_p}{P_s} = \frac{g_{SL}\rho_{SL}}{P_s}\frac{P_{SL}}{P_{SL}}\left(\frac{\Delta H_{pc}}{1!}\sigma_{ic} + \frac{\Delta H_{pc}^2}{2!}\frac{d\sigma_{ic}}{dH_{ic}} + ...\right) \qquad (D112)$$

which using Equation A70 gives

$$\frac{\Delta P_p}{P_s} = \frac{g_{SL}\rho_{SL}}{P_{SL}}\left(\frac{\Delta H_{pc}}{1!}\frac{\sigma_{ic}}{\delta_{ic}} + \frac{1}{\delta_{ic}}\frac{\Delta H_{pc}^2}{2!}\frac{d\sigma_{ic}}{dH_{ic}} + ...\right) \qquad (D113)$$

Using Equation B26 we get

$$\frac{\Delta P_p}{P_s} = \frac{g_{SL}\rho_{SL}}{P_{SL}}\left(\frac{\Delta H_{pc}}{1!}\frac{1}{\theta_{ic}} + \frac{1}{\delta_{ic}}\frac{\Delta H_{pc}^2}{2!}\frac{d\sigma_{ic}}{dH_{ic}} + ...\right)$$ (D114)

Now, what about the second term? From Equation A80 we have

$$\sigma = (1 - 6.87559 \times 10^{-6}/\text{ft H})^{4.2559}$$ (A80)

Therefore, $d\sigma_{ic}/dH_{ic}$ would be

$$\frac{d\sigma_{ic}}{dH_{ic}} = (4.2559)\left(1 - 6.87559 \times 10^{-6}/\text{ft H}_{ic}\right)^{3.2559}\left(-6.87559 \times 10^{-6}/\text{ft}\right)$$ (D115)

$$\frac{d\sigma_{ic}}{dH_{ic}} = \left(-2.9261 \times 10^{-5}/\text{ft}\right)\left(1 - 6.87559 \times 10^{-6}/\text{ft H}_{ic}\right)^{3.2559}$$ (D116)

So after inserting constants from Table 1 and Equation D116 into Equation D114 the result is

$$\frac{\Delta P_p}{P_s} = 3.61371 \times 10^{-5}/\text{ft}\left(\frac{\Delta H_{pc}}{\theta_{ic}} + \frac{\Delta H_{pc}^2}{2\delta_{ic}}\left(-2.9261 \times 10^{-5}/\text{ft}\right)\left(1 - 6.87559 \times 10^{-6}/\text{ft H}_{ic}\right)^{3.2559} + ...\right)$$ (D117)

So how many terms do we need? We can compare the results of the pressure method with the results of Equation D117 using the first term and using both terms. Doing this for a range of values gives the results shown in Table D1.

TABLE D1

$\Delta P_p/P_s$ Errors From Altitude

Altitude	ΔHpc	Hic	1 term % Error	2 term % Error
0	0	0	0.00%	0.00%
	100	-100	0.15%	0.00%
	200	-200	0.29%	0.00%
	300	-300	0.44%	0.00%
	400	-400	0.58%	0.00%
	500	-500	0.73%	0.00%
	1000	-1000	1.46%	-0.01%
10000	0	10000	0.00%	0.00%
	100	9900	0.16%	0.00%
	200	9800	0.31%	0.00%
	300	9700	0.47%	0.00%
	400	9600	0.63%	0.00%
	500	9500	0.78%	0.00%
	1000	9000	1.57%	-0.01%
20000	0	20000	0.00%	0.00%
	100	19900	0.17%	0.00%
	200	19800	0.34%	0.00%
	300	19700	0.51%	0.00%
	400	19600	0.68%	0.00%
	500	19500	0.85%	0.00%
	1000	19000	1.70%	-0.02%
30000	0	30000	0.00%	0.00%
	100	29900	0.18%	0.00%
	200	29800	0.37%	0.00%
	300	29700	0.55%	0.00%
	400	29600	0.74%	0.00%
	500	29500	0.92%	-0.01%
	1000	29000	1.84%	-0.02%

Using the numbers in Table D1 we can get an idea if we need to worry about using the last term in Equation D117. As an example, MIL-P-26292C allows a maximum position error of $\Delta P_p/q_{cic}$ of 0.02 at 0.55M. At sea level this would correspond to a ΔH_{pc} of 126 feet. If this can be considered a reasonable value, let's consider what happens at a ΔH_{pc} of 300 feet, since some flight test booms may have this much error. At sea level, we would have a 0.44 percent error in calculating $\Delta P_p/P_s$, which would correspond to an error in ΔH_{pc} of 1.32 feet. This value is well within the instrument error. Even with a grossly large ΔH_{pc} of 1000 feet at sea level, a 1.46 percent error would be 14.6 feet, which is still smaller than the 20 foot increment on the altimeter face. Hence, the second term has traditionally been ignored with acceptable loss of accuracy.

Therefore, using only the first term of Equation D117 we would have

$$\frac{\Delta P_p}{P_s} = \frac{3.61371 \times 10^{-5} \, / \, \text{ft}}{\theta_{ic}} \, \Delta H_{pc} \qquad \text{(D118)}$$

> **CAUTION**
>
> For the Pitot-statics class at the USAF Test Pilot School, use the pressure method for full credit on exams. The pressure method gives an exact answer, while the Taylor series expansion method gives an approximate answer. The Taylor series expansion method is included for historical legacy and explanation of Herrington (Ref 12).

In Herrington (Ref 12), the equivalent expression to Equation D118 is given as

$$\frac{\Delta P_p}{\Delta H_{pc}} = 0.0010813 \, \sigma_s, \, \frac{"Hg}{\text{feet}} \qquad \text{(Ref 12 5.18)}$$

"where σ_s is the standard day air density ratio at H_{ic}." Let's update the notation to be consistent with the rest of this text using "ic" to identify parameters containing position error.

$$\frac{\Delta P_p}{\Delta H_{pc}} = 0.0010813 \, \frac{"Hg}{\text{feet}} \, \sigma_{ic} \qquad \text{(D119)}$$

Substituting Equation B26

$$\frac{\Delta P_p}{\Delta H_{pc}} = 0.0010813 \, \frac{"Hg}{\text{feet}} \, \frac{\delta_{ic}}{\theta_{ic}} \qquad \text{(D120)}$$

Substituting Equation A70 and rearranging

$$\frac{\Delta P_p}{\Delta H_{pc}} = \frac{0.0010813 \, \frac{"Hg}{\text{feet}}}{P_{SL}} \, \frac{P_s}{\theta_{ic}} \qquad \text{(D121)}$$

Substituting 29.92138 "Hg for P_{SL}

$$\frac{\Delta P_p}{\Delta H_{pc}} = 3.6138 \times 10^{-5} \, / \, \text{ft} \, \frac{P_s}{\theta_{ic}} \qquad \text{(D122)}$$

Swapping P_s and ΔH_{pc} to opposite sides

$$\frac{\Delta P_p}{P_s} = \frac{3.6138 \times 10^{-5} \, / \, \text{ft}}{\theta_{ic}} \, \Delta H_{pc} \qquad \text{(D123)}$$

which matches Equation D118 within round off error.

Finding Position Error From a Measured Airspeed Position Correction, Taylor Series Expansion Method

For the Taylor Series expansion method, we still start with Equations D12 and D13 as shown in the pressure method.

We know that q_{cic} occurs at V_{ic} and q_c occurs at V_c. From Equation D6 we see that

$$V_c = V_{ic} + \Delta V_{pc} \tag{D124}$$

Thus

$$\Delta P_p = q_{cic}(V_{ic} + \Delta V_{pc}) - q_{cic}(V_{ic}) \tag{D125}$$

Again using the Taylor series expansion of Equation D107, we get

$$\Delta P_p = q_{cic}\left(V_{ic}\right) + \frac{\Delta V_{pc}}{1!}\frac{dq_{cic}}{dV_{ic}} + \frac{\Delta V_{pc}^2}{2!}\frac{d^2 q_{cic}}{dV_{ic}^2} + ... - q_{cic}\left(V_{ic}\right) \tag{D126}$$

The first and last terms subtract out, so we're left with

$$\Delta P_p = \frac{\Delta V_{pc}}{1!}\frac{dq_{cic}}{dV_{ic}} + \frac{\Delta V_{pc}^2}{2!}\frac{d^2 q_{cic}}{dV_{ic}^2} + ... \tag{D127}$$

Let's work on the first term first for calibrated airspeeds below the sea level speed of sound. Rearranging Equation D12 slightly

$$q_{cic} = P_{SL}\left(1 + 0.2\left(\frac{V_{ic}}{a_{SL}}\right)^2\right)^{7/2} - P_{SL} \tag{D128}$$

Differentiating, remembering that P_{SL} is a constant, we get

$$\frac{dq_{cic}}{dV_{ic}} = \left(\frac{7}{2}\right)P_{SL}\left(1 + 0.2\left(\frac{V_{ic}}{a_{SL}}\right)^2\right)^{5/2}\left(\frac{(0.2)(2)}{a_{SL}^2}V_{ic}\right) \tag{D129}$$

Combining terms and rearranging

$$\frac{dq_{cic}}{dV_{ic}} = \frac{1.4 P_{SL}}{a_{SL}}\left(\frac{V_{ic}}{a_{SL}}\right)\left(1 + 0.2\left(\frac{V_{ic}}{a_{SL}}\right)^2\right)^{5/2} \tag{D130}$$

To get the second term in Equation D127, differentiate Equation D130 using the product rule

$$\frac{d^2 q_{cic}}{dV_{ic}^2} = \frac{1.4 P_{SL}}{a_{SL}} \left(\left(\frac{5}{2}\right) \left(\frac{V_{ic}}{a_{SL}}\right) \left(1 + 0.2 \left(\frac{V_{ic}}{a_{SL}}\right)^2\right)^{3/2} \left(\frac{(0.2)(2)}{a_{SL}^2} V_{ic}\right) + \left(1 + 0.2 \left(\frac{V_{ic}}{a_{SL}}\right)^2\right)^{5/2} \left(\frac{1}{a_{SL}}\right) \right)$$

(D131)

Continuing to combine and rearrange

$$\frac{d^2 q_{cic}}{dV_{ic}^2} = \frac{1.4 P_{SL}}{a_{SL}^2} \left(\left(\frac{V_{ic}}{a_{SL}}\right)^2 \left(1 + 0.2 \left(\frac{V_{ic}}{a_{SL}}\right)^2\right)^{3/2} + \left(1 + 0.2 \left(\frac{V_{ic}}{a_{SL}}\right)^2\right)^{5/2} \right)$$

(D132)

$$\frac{d^2 q_{cic}}{dV_{ic}^2} = \frac{1.4 P_{SL}}{a_{SL}^2} \left(\left(\frac{V_{ic}}{a_{SL}}\right)^2 \left(1 + 0.2 \left(\frac{V_{ic}}{a_{SL}}\right)^2\right)^{3/2} + \left(1 + 0.2 \left(\frac{V_{ic}}{a_{SL}}\right)^2\right)^{3/2} \left(1 + 0.2 \left(\frac{V_{ic}}{a_{SL}}\right)^2\right) \right)$$

(D133)

$$\frac{d^2 q_{cic}}{dV_{ic}^2} = \frac{1.4 P_{SL}}{a_{SL}^2} \left(\left(1 + 0.2 \left(\frac{V_{ic}}{a_{SL}}\right)^2\right)^{3/2} \left(\left(\frac{V_{ic}}{a_{SL}}\right)^2 + \left(1 + 0.2 \left(\frac{V_{ic}}{a_{SL}}\right)^2\right) \right) \right)$$

(D134)

$$\frac{d^2 q_{cic}}{dV_{ic}^2} = \frac{1.4 P_{SL}}{a_{SL}^2} \left(1 + 0.2 \left(\frac{V_{ic}}{a_{SL}}\right)^2\right)^{3/2} \left(1 + 1.2 \left(\frac{V_{ic}}{a_{SL}}\right)^2\right)$$

(D135)

Inserting Equations D130 and D135 into Equation D127 we get

$$\Delta P_p = \Delta V_{pc} \frac{1.4 P_{SL}}{a_{SL}} \left(\frac{V_{ic}}{a_{SL}}\right) \left(1 + 0.2 \left(\frac{V_{ic}}{a_{SL}}\right)^2\right)^{5/2} + \Delta V_{pc}^2 \frac{0.7 P_{SL}}{a_{SL}^2} \left(1 + 0.2 \left(\frac{V_{ic}}{a_{SL}}\right)^2\right)^{3/2} \left(1 + 1.2 \left(\frac{V_{ic}}{a_{SL}}\right)^2\right) + \dots$$

(D136)

But what we really need is $\Delta P_p / P_s$, so we will divide both sides by P_s and using Equation D29 get

$$\frac{\Delta P_p}{P_s} = \Delta V_{pc} \frac{1.4}{\delta_{ic} a_{SL}} \left(\frac{V_{ic}}{a_{SL}}\right) \left(1 + 0.2 \left(\frac{V_{ic}}{a_{SL}}\right)^2\right)^{5/2} + \Delta V_{pc}^2 \frac{0.7}{\delta_{ic} a_{SL}^2} \left(1 + 0.2 \left(\frac{V_{ic}}{a_{SL}}\right)^2\right)^{3/2} \left(1 + 1.2 \left(\frac{V_{ic}}{a_{SL}}\right)^2\right) + \dots$$

$(V_{ic} \leq a_{SL})$ (D137)

In Herrington (Ref 12), the equivalent expression to Equation D137 is given as

$$\Delta P_p = 1.4 P_{aSL} \frac{V_{ic}}{a_{SL}} \left(1 + 0.2 \left(\frac{V_{ic}}{a_{SL}}\right)^2\right)^{2.5} \frac{\Delta V_{pc}}{a_{SL}} + 0.7 P_{aSL} \left(1 + 0.2 \left(\frac{V_{ic}}{a_{SL}}\right)^2\right)^{1.5} \left(1 + 1.2 \left(\frac{V_{ic}}{a_{SL}}\right)^2\right) \left(\frac{\Delta V_{pc}}{a_{SL}}\right)^2$$

$$(V_{ic} \le a_{SL}) \qquad (\text{Ref 12 5.42})$$

"P_{aSL}" is the equivalent to "P_{SL}" as used in this text. Dividing both sides by P_s and using Equation D29

$$\frac{\Delta P_p}{P_s} = \frac{1.4}{\delta_{ic}} \frac{V_{ic}}{a_{SL}} \left(1 + 0.2 \left(\frac{V_{ic}}{a_{SL}}\right)^2\right)^{2.5} \frac{\Delta V_{pc}}{a_{SL}} + \frac{0.7}{\delta_{ic}} \left(1 + 0.2 \left(\frac{V_{ic}}{a_{SL}}\right)^2\right)^{1.5} \left(1 + 1.2 \left(\frac{V_{ic}}{a_{SL}}\right)^2\right) \left(\frac{\Delta V_{pc}}{a_{SL}}\right)^2$$

$$(V_{ic} \le a_{SL}) \qquad (\text{D138})$$

Relocating the ΔV_{pc} and a_{SL} and changing exponents to fractions

$$\frac{\Delta P_p}{P_s} = \Delta V_{pc} \frac{1.4}{\delta_{ic} a_{SL}} \left(\frac{V_{ic}}{a_{SL}}\right) \left(1 + 0.2 \left(\frac{V_{ic}}{a_{SL}}\right)^2\right)^{\frac{5}{2}} + \Delta V_{pc}^2 \frac{0.7}{\delta_{ic} a_{SL}^2} \left(1 + 0.2 \left(\frac{V_{ic}}{a_{SL}}\right)^2\right)^{\frac{3}{2}} \left(1 + 1.2 \left(\frac{V_{ic}}{a_{SL}}\right)^2\right)$$

$$(V_{ic} \le a_{SL}) \quad (\text{D137})$$

which matches Equation D137.

For calibrated airspeeds above the sea level speed of sound, we start with Equation D13 and solve for q_{cic}

$$q_{cic} = P_{SL} \frac{166.921 \left(\frac{V_{ic}}{a_{SL}}\right)^7}{\left(7 \left(\frac{V_{ic}}{a_{SL}}\right)^2 - 1\right)^{\frac{5}{2}}} - P_{SL} \qquad (\text{D139})$$

Since I could never remember the quotient rule, let's bring up the denominator so that we can differentiate by the product rule.

$$q_{cic} = P_{SL} (166.921) \left(\frac{V_{ic}}{a_{SL}}\right)^7 \left(7 \left(\frac{V_{ic}}{a_{SL}}\right)^2 - 1\right)^{-\frac{5}{2}} - P_{SL} \qquad (\text{D140})$$

Differentiating by the product rule

$$\frac{dq_{cic}}{dV_{ic}} = P_{SL} (166.921) \left(\frac{7}{a_{SL}}\right) \left(\frac{V_{ic}}{a_{SL}}\right)^6 \left(7 \left(\frac{V_{ic}}{a_{SL}}\right)^2 - 1\right)^{-\frac{5}{2}} + P_{SL} (166.921) \left(\frac{V_{ic}}{a_{SL}}\right)^7 \left(-\frac{5}{2}\right) \left(7 \left(\frac{V_{ic}}{a_{SL}}\right)^2 - 1\right)^{-\frac{7}{2}} (2) \left(\frac{7}{a_{SL}}\right) \left(\frac{V_{ic}}{a_{SL}}\right)$$

$$(\text{D141})$$

$$\frac{dq_{cic}}{dV_{ic}} = P_{SL}(166.921)\left(\frac{\left(\frac{7}{a_{SL}}\right)\left(\frac{V_{ic}}{a_{SL}}\right)^6}{\left(7\left(\frac{V_{ic}}{a_{SL}}\right)^2 - 1\right)^{5/2}} - \frac{\left(\frac{35}{a_{SL}}\right)\left(\frac{V_{ic}}{a_{SL}}\right)^8}{\left(7\left(\frac{V_{ic}}{a_{SL}}\right)^2 - 1\right)^{7/2}}\right) \tag{D142}$$

$$\frac{dq_{cic}}{dV_{ic}} = \frac{P_{SL}(166.921)}{a_{SL}}\left(\frac{7\left(\frac{V_{ic}}{a_{SL}}\right)^6\left(7\left(\frac{V_{ic}}{a_{SL}}\right)^2 - 1\right) - 35\left(\frac{V_{ic}}{a_{SL}}\right)^8}{\left(7\left(\frac{V_{ic}}{a_{SL}}\right)^2 - 1\right)^{7/2}}\right) \tag{D143}$$

$$\frac{dq_{cic}}{dV_{ic}} = \frac{P_{SL}(166.921)}{a_{SL}}\left(\frac{V_{ic}}{a_{SL}}\right)^6\left(\frac{49\left(\frac{V_{ic}}{a_{SL}}\right)^2 - 7 - 35\left(\frac{V_{ic}}{a_{SL}}\right)^2}{\left(7\left(\frac{V_{ic}}{a_{SL}}\right)^2 - 1\right)^{7/2}}\right) \tag{D144}$$

$$\frac{dq_{cic}}{dV_{ic}} = \frac{P_{SL}(166.921)(7)}{a_{SL}}\left(\frac{V_{ic}}{a_{SL}}\right)^6\frac{\left(2\left(\frac{V_{ic}}{a_{SL}}\right)^2 - 1\right)}{\left(7\left(\frac{V_{ic}}{a_{SL}}\right)^2 - 1\right)^{7/2}} \tag{D145}$$

$$\frac{dq_{cic}}{dV_{ic}} = \frac{P_{SL}(1168.447)}{a_{SL}}\left(\frac{V_{ic}}{a_{SL}}\right)^6\frac{\left(2\left(\frac{V_{ic}}{a_{SL}}\right)^2 - 1\right)}{\left(7\left(\frac{V_{ic}}{a_{SL}}\right)^2 - 1\right)^{7/2}} \tag{D146}$$

To get the second term in Equation D127, differentiate Equation D146. Rearranging for the product rule

$$\frac{dq_{cic}}{dV_{ic}} = \frac{P_{SL}(1168.447)}{a_{SL}}\left(\frac{V_{ic}}{a_{SL}}\right)^6\left(2\left(\frac{V_{ic}}{a_{SL}}\right)^2 - 1\right)\left(7\left(\frac{V_{ic}}{a_{SL}}\right)^2 - 1\right)^{-7/2} \tag{D147}$$

Now we have three factors which are functions of V_{ic}. If the product rule addresses two factors

$$\frac{d}{dx}(uv) = v\frac{du}{dx} + u\frac{dv}{dx}$$ (D148)

we can nest the product rule to give

$$\frac{d}{dx}(uvw) = vw\frac{du}{dx} + u\frac{d(vw)}{dx} = vw\frac{du}{dx} + u\left(w\frac{dv}{dx} + v\frac{dw}{dx}\right)$$ (D149)

Applying equation D149 to Equation D147 we get

$$\frac{d^2 q_{cic}}{dV_{ic}^2} = \frac{P_{SL}(1168.447)}{a_{SL}}\left(\frac{6}{a_{SL}}\left(\frac{V_{ic}}{a_{SL}}\right)^5\left(2\left(\frac{V_{ic}}{a_{SL}}\right)^2 - 1\right)\left(7\left(\frac{V_{ic}}{a_{SL}}\right)^2 - 1\right)^{-7/2}\right.$$
$$\left. + \left(\frac{V_{ic}}{a_{SL}}\right)^6\left(\frac{4}{a_{SL}}\left(\frac{V_{ic}}{a_{SL}}\right)\left(7\left(\frac{V_{ic}}{a_{SL}}\right)^2 - 1\right)^{-7/2} + \left(2\left(\frac{V_{ic}}{a_{SL}}\right)^2 - 1\right)\left(-\frac{7}{2}\right)\left(7\left(\frac{V_{ic}}{a_{SL}}\right)^2 - 1\right)^{-9/2}\left(\frac{14}{a_{SL}}\right)\left(\frac{V_{ic}}{a_{SL}}\right)\right)\right)$$ (D150)

$$\frac{d^2 q_{cic}}{dV_{ic}^2} = \frac{P_{SL}(1168.447)}{a_{SL}}\left(\frac{6\left(\frac{V_{ic}}{a_{SL}}\right)^5\left(2\left(\frac{V_{ic}}{a_{SL}}\right)^2 - 1\right)}{a_{SL}\left(7\left(\frac{V_{ic}}{a_{SL}}\right)^2 - 1\right)^{7/2}} + \frac{4\left(\frac{V_{ic}}{a_{SL}}\right)^7}{a_{SL}\left(7\left(\frac{V_{ic}}{a_{SL}}\right)^2 - 1\right)^{7/2}} - \frac{49\left(\frac{V_{ic}}{a_{SL}}\right)^7\left(2\left(\frac{V_{ic}}{a_{SL}}\right)^2 - 1\right)}{a_{SL}\left(7\left(\frac{V_{ic}}{a_{SL}}\right)^2 - 1\right)^{9/2}}\right)$$ (D151)

$$\frac{d^2 q_{cic}}{dV_{ic}^2} = \frac{P_{SL}(1168.447)}{a_{SL}^2}\left(\frac{6\left(\frac{V_{ic}}{a_{SL}}\right)^5\left(2\left(\frac{V_{ic}}{a_{SL}}\right)^2 - 1\right)\left(7\left(\frac{V_{ic}}{a_{SL}}\right)^2 - 1\right)}{\left(7\left(\frac{V_{ic}}{a_{SL}}\right)^2 - 1\right)^{9/2}}\right.$$
$$\left. + \frac{4\left(\frac{V_{ic}}{a_{SL}}\right)^7\left(7\left(\frac{V_{ic}}{a_{SL}}\right)^2 - 1\right)}{\left(7\left(\frac{V_{ic}}{a_{SL}}\right)^2 - 1\right)^{9/2}} - \frac{49\left(\frac{V_{ic}}{a_{SL}}\right)^7\left(2\left(\frac{V_{ic}}{a_{SL}}\right)^2 - 1\right)}{\left(7\left(\frac{V_{ic}}{a_{SL}}\right)^2 - 1\right)^{9/2}}\right)$$ (D152)

$$\frac{d^2 q_{cic}}{dV_{ic}^2} = \frac{P_{SL}(1168.447)}{a_{SL}^2}\left(\frac{V_{ic}}{a_{SL}}\right)^5 \left[\frac{84\left(\frac{V_{ic}}{a_{SL}}\right)^4 - 12\left(\frac{V_{ic}}{a_{SL}}\right)^2 - 42\left(\frac{V_{ic}}{a_{SL}}\right)^2 + 6 + 28\left(\frac{V_{ic}}{a_{SL}}\right)^4 - 4\left(\frac{V_{ic}}{a_{SL}}\right)^2 - 98\left(\frac{V_{ic}}{a_{SL}}\right)^4 + 49\left(\frac{V_{ic}}{a_{SL}}\right)^2}{\left(7\left(\frac{V_{ic}}{a_{SL}}\right)^2 - 1\right)^{9/2}}\right]$$

(D153)

$$\frac{d^2 q_{cic}}{dV_{ic}^2} = \frac{2P_{SL}(1168.447)}{a_{SL}^2}\left(\frac{V_{ic}}{a_{SL}}\right)^5 \left[\frac{7\left(\frac{V_{ic}}{a_{SL}}\right)^4 - \frac{9}{2}\left(\frac{V_{ic}}{a_{SL}}\right)^2 + 3}{\left(7\left(\frac{V_{ic}}{a_{SL}}\right)^2 - 1\right)^{9/2}}\right]$$

(D154)

Substituting Equations D146 and D154 into Equation D127 gives

$$\Delta P_p = \Delta V_{pc}\frac{P_{SL}(1168.447)}{a_{SL}}\left(\frac{V_{ic}}{a_{SL}}\right)^6 \frac{\left(2\left(\frac{V_{ic}}{a_{SL}}\right)^2 - 1\right)}{\left(7\left(\frac{V_{ic}}{a_{SL}}\right)^2 - 1\right)^{7/2}} + \Delta V_{pc}^2\frac{P_{SL}(1168.447)}{a_{SL}^2}\left(\frac{V_{ic}}{a_{SL}}\right)^5 \frac{\left(7\left(\frac{V_{ic}}{a_{SL}}\right)^4 - \frac{9}{2}\left(\frac{V_{ic}}{a_{SL}}\right)^2 + 3\right)}{\left(7\left(\frac{V_{ic}}{a_{SL}}\right)^2 - 1\right)^{9/2}} + \ldots$$

(D155)

Again, we are more interested in $\Delta P_p/P_s$, so we will divide both sides by P_s and using Equation D29 get

$$\frac{\Delta P_p}{P_s} = \Delta V_{pc}\frac{(1168.447)}{\delta_{ic} a_{SL}}\left(\frac{V_{ic}}{a_{SL}}\right)^6 \frac{\left(2\left(\frac{V_{ic}}{a_{SL}}\right)^2 - 1\right)}{\left(7\left(\frac{V_{ic}}{a_{SL}}\right)^2 - 1\right)^{7/2}} + \Delta V_{pc}^2\frac{(1168.447)}{\delta_{ic} a_{SL}^2}\left(\frac{V_{ic}}{a_{SL}}\right)^5 \frac{\left(7\left(\frac{V_{ic}}{a_{SL}}\right)^4 - \frac{9}{2}\left(\frac{V_{ic}}{a_{SL}}\right)^2 + 3\right)}{\left(7\left(\frac{V_{ic}}{a_{SL}}\right)^2 - 1\right)^{9/2}} + \ldots$$

$(V_{ic} \geq a_{SL})$ (D156)

In Herrington (Ref 12), the equivalent expression to Equation D156 is given as

$$\Delta P_p = 1168.45 P_{aSL}\left(\frac{V_{ic}}{a_{SL}}\right)^6 \frac{\left(2\left(\frac{V_{ic}}{a_{SL}}\right)^2 - 1\right)}{\left(7\left(\frac{V_{ic}}{a_{SL}}\right)^2 - 1\right)^{3.5}}\frac{\Delta V_{pc}}{a_{SL}} + 1168.45 P_{aSL}\left(\frac{V_{ic}}{a_{SL}}\right)^5 \frac{\left(7\left(\frac{V_{ic}}{a_{SL}}\right)^4 - 4.5\left(\frac{V_{ic}}{a_{SL}}\right)^2 + 3\right)}{\left(7\left(\frac{V_{ic}}{a_{SL}}\right)^2 - 1\right)^{4.5}}\left(\frac{\Delta V_{pc}}{a_{SL}}\right)^2$$

$(V_{ic} \geq a_{SL})$ (Ref 12 5.43)

"P_{aSL}" is the equivalent to "P_{SL}" as used in this text.

Dividing both sides by P_s and using Equation D29

$$\frac{\Delta P_p}{P_s} = \frac{1168.45}{\delta_{ic}}\left(\frac{V_{ic}}{a_{SL}}\right)^6 \frac{\left(2\left(\frac{V_{ic}}{a_{SL}}\right)^2 - 1\right)}{\left(7\left(\frac{V_{ic}}{a_{SL}}\right)^2 - 1\right)^{3.5}} \frac{\Delta V_{pc}}{a_{SL}} + \frac{1168.45}{\delta_{ic}}\left(\frac{V_{ic}}{a_{SL}}\right)^5 \frac{\left(7\left(\frac{V_{ic}}{a_{SL}}\right)^4 - 4.5\left(\frac{V_{ic}}{a_{SL}}\right)^2 + 3\right)}{\left(7\left(\frac{V_{ic}}{a_{SL}}\right)^2 - 1\right)^{4.5}}\left(\frac{\Delta V_{pc}}{a_{SL}}\right)^2$$

$$(V_{ic} \geq a_{SL}) \quad (D157)$$

Relocating the ΔV_{pc} and a_{SL}, accepting that 1168.45 is the same as 1168.447, and changing decimals to fractions

$$\frac{\Delta P_p}{P_s} = \Delta V_{pc}\frac{(1168.447)}{\delta_{ic}a_{SL}}\left(\frac{V_{ic}}{a_{SL}}\right)^6 \frac{\left(2\left(\frac{V_{ic}}{a_{SL}}\right)^2 - 1\right)}{\left(7\left(\frac{V_{ic}}{a_{SL}}\right)^2 - 1\right)^{7/2}} + \Delta V_{pc}^2\frac{(1168.447)}{\delta_{ic}a_{SL}^2}\left(\frac{V_{ic}}{a_{SL}}\right)^5 \frac{\left(7\left(\frac{V_{ic}}{a_{SL}}\right)^4 - \frac{9}{2}\left(\frac{V_{ic}}{a_{SL}}\right)^2 + 3\right)}{\left(7\left(\frac{V_{ic}}{a_{SL}}\right)^2 - 1\right)^{9/2}} + \ldots$$

$$(V_{ic} \geq a_{SL}) \quad (D156)$$

which matches Equation D156.

So again we ask, how many terms do we need? We can see what errors are involved by calculating $\Delta P_p/P_s$ directly using the pressure method for varying conditions. To calculate δ_{ic}, divide Equation D1 by P_{SL}

$$\frac{\Delta P_p}{P_{SL}} = \frac{P_s}{P_{SL}} - \frac{P_a}{P_{SL}} = \delta_{ic} - \delta \qquad (D158)$$

$$\delta_{ic} = \frac{\Delta P_p}{P_{SL}} + \delta \qquad (D159)$$

where δ is for the pressure altitude (H_c) of interest.

Doing this for a range of values gives the results shown in Table D2.

TABLE D2
$\Delta P_p/P_s$ Errors From Airspeed at Sea Level

Vc knots	ΔVpc knots	Vic knots	1 term % Error	2 term % Error
100	0	100	0	0
	10	90	-5.66%	-0.32%
	20	80	-11.81%	-0.62%
	30	70	-18.56%	-0.91%
	40	60	-26.04%	-1.18%
	50	50	-34.41%	-1.43%
300	0	300	0	0
	10	290	-3.02%	-1.04%
	20	280	-5.98%	-2.04%
	30	270	-8.88%	-3.01%
	40	260	-11.74%	-3.94%
	50	250	-14.56%	-4.83%
500	0	500	0	0
	10	490	-3.51%	-2.03%
	20	480	-6.82%	-3.95%
	30	470	-9.96%	-5.76%
	40	460	-12.93%	-7.48%
	50	450	-15.77%	-9.11%
600	0	600	0	0
	10	590	-4.08%	-2.71%
	20	580	-7.87%	-5.22%
	30	570	-11.40%	-7.57%
	40	560	-14.71%	-9.76%
	50	550	-17.82%	-11.81%
700	0	700	0	0
	10	690	-4.63%	-3.50%
	20	680	-8.94%	-6.66%
	30	670	-12.97%	-9.53%
	40	660	-16.77%	-12.12%
	50	650	-20.37%	-14.45%
800	0	800	0	0
	10	790	-5.00%	-4.22%
	20	780	-9.56%	-8.02%
	30	770	-13.73%	-11.47%
	40	760	-17.58%	-14.61%
	50	750	-21.14%	-17.47%

Calculating $\Delta P_p/P_s$ at other altitudes changes the size of the errors but not significantly. Looking at these errors, we can see that the error involved in using only the first term of the Taylor Series expansion is unacceptably large (although many people have used it for years), and even with the first two terms the error introduced by the equation is on the same order of magnitude as the uncertainty in the measurements. This problem is true for airspeeds below and above the sea level speed of sound. Reference 12 states "The resulting series may be discontinued after the second term with no loss in accuracy for $\Delta V_{pc} \leq 50$ knots." I'm not sure what standard they were using for "no loss in accuracy."

Finding Position Error From a Measured Mach Position Correction, Taylor Series Expansion Method

For the Taylor Series expansion method, we still start with Equations D20 and D21 as shown in the pressure method.

To find the relationship between ΔP_p and ΔM_{pc}, we need to find out how the static pressure varies as the Mach number varies. We know that P_s occurs at M_{ic} and P_a occurs at M. From Equation D7 we see that

$$M = M_{ic} + \Delta M_{pc} \tag{D160}$$

So if we can determine the difference $P_s - P_a$ by knowing ΔM_{pc}, we would have ΔP_p. So we will use the Taylor series expansion of Equation D107 to get

$$\Delta P_p = P_s(M_{ic}) - \left(P_s(M_{ic}) + \frac{\Delta M_{pc}}{1!}\frac{dP_s}{dM_{ic}} + \frac{\Delta M_{pc}^2}{2!}\frac{d^2 P_s}{dM_{ic}^2} + ... \right) \tag{D161}$$

The first and second terms subtract out, so we're left with

$$\Delta P_p = -\frac{\Delta M_{pc}}{1!}\frac{dP_s}{dM_{ic}} - \frac{\Delta M_{pc}^2}{2!}\frac{d^2 P_s}{dM_{ic}^2} - ... \tag{D162}$$

To find the derivatives, we need an equation for P_s in terms of M_{ic}. Rearranging Equation D20 gives (subsonic only)

$$\frac{1}{P_s} = \frac{1}{P_T}\left(1 + 0.2M_{ic}^2\right)^{7/2} \tag{D163}$$

which we can invert to

$$P_s = P_T\left(1 + 0.2M_{ic}^2\right)^{-7/2} \tag{D164}$$

Differentiating (assuming P_T = constant)

$$\frac{dP_s}{dM_{ic}} = P_T\left(-\frac{7}{2}\right)\left(1 + 0.2M_{ic}^2\right)^{-9/2}(2)(0.2M_{ic}) \tag{D165}$$

$$\frac{dP_s}{dM_{ic}} = \frac{-1.4M_{ic}}{\left(1 + 0.2M_{ic}^2\right)^{9/2}}P_T \tag{D166}$$

Since we need static pressure in the final result instead of total pressure, multiply by 1

$$\frac{dP_s}{dM_{ic}} = \frac{-1.4M_{ic}}{\left(1 + 0.2M_{ic}^2\right)^{9/2}}\frac{P_T}{P_s}P_s \tag{D167}$$

Substituting Equation D20

$$\frac{dP_s}{dM_{ic}} = \frac{-1.4M_{ic}P_s}{\left(1+0.2M_{ic}^2\right)^{9/2}}\left(1+0.2M_{ic}^2\right)^{7/2} \tag{D168}$$

$$\frac{dP_s}{dM_{ic}} = \frac{-1.4M_{ic}P_s}{\left(1+0.2M_{ic}^2\right)} \tag{D169}$$

To get the second derivative for the second term, we'll start by rearranging Equation D169

$$\frac{dP_s}{dM_{ic}} = -1.4M_{ic}P_s\left(1+0.2M_{ic}^2\right)^{-1} \tag{D170}$$

This equation has three terms that are functions of M_{ic}, so we'll differentiate using the nested product rule, as shown in Equation D149, to get

$$\frac{d^2P_s}{dM_{ic}^2} = -1.4\left(1+0.2M_{ic}^2\right)^{-1}\left(P_s + M_{ic}\frac{dP_s}{dM_{ic}}\right) + (-1.4)(M_{ic})(P_s)(-1)\left(1+0.2M_{ic}^2\right)^{-2}(2)(0.2M_{ic}) \tag{D171}$$

$$\frac{d^2P_s}{dM_{ic}^2} = \frac{-1.4P_s}{\left(1+0.2M_{ic}^2\right)} + \frac{-1.4M_{ic}}{\left(1+0.2M_{ic}^2\right)}\frac{dP_s}{dM_{ic}} + \frac{1.4(0.4)M_{ic}^2P_s}{\left(1+0.2M_{ic}^2\right)^2} \tag{D172}$$

Substituting from Equation D169

$$\frac{d^2P_s}{dM_{ic}^2} = \frac{-1.4P_s}{\left(1+0.2M_{ic}^2\right)} + \frac{-1.4M_{ic}}{\left(1+0.2M_{ic}^2\right)}\frac{-1.4M_{ic}P_s}{\left(1+0.2M_{ic}^2\right)} + \frac{1.4(0.4)M_{ic}^2P_s}{\left(1+0.2M_{ic}^2\right)^2} \tag{D173}$$

$$\frac{d^2P_s}{dM_{ic}^2} = \frac{-1.4P_s\left(1+0.2M_{ic}^2\right)}{\left(1+0.2M_{ic}^2\right)^2} + \frac{(1.4)^2M_{ic}^2P_s}{\left(1+0.2M_{ic}^2\right)^2} + \frac{1.4(0.4)M_{ic}^2P_s}{\left(1+0.2M_{ic}^2\right)^2} \tag{D174}$$

$$\frac{d^2P_s}{dM_{ic}^2} = \frac{1.4P_s\left(-1-0.2M_{ic}^2+1.4M_{ic}^2+0.4M_{ic}^2\right)}{\left(1+0.2M_{ic}^2\right)^2} \tag{D175}$$

$$\frac{d^2P_s}{dM_{ic}^2} = \frac{1.4P_s\left(-1+1.6M_{ic}^2\right)}{\left(1+0.2M_{ic}^2\right)^2} \tag{D176}$$

$$\frac{d^2P_s}{dM_{ic}^2} = \frac{-1.4P_s\left(1-1.6M_{ic}^2\right)}{\left(1+0.2M_{ic}^2\right)^2} \tag{D177}$$

Substituting Equations D169 and D177 into Equation D162,

$$\Delta P_p = -\frac{\Delta M_{pc}}{1!}\frac{-1.4M_{ic}P_s}{\left(1+0.2M_{ic}^2\right)} - \frac{\Delta M_{pc}^2}{2!}\frac{-1.4P_s\left(1-1.6M_{ic}^2\right)}{\left(1+0.2M_{ic}^2\right)^2} - \ldots \tag{D178}$$

Rearranging

$$\frac{\Delta P_p}{P_s} = \frac{1.4M_{ic}}{\left(1+0.2M_{ic}^2\right)}\Delta M_{pc} + \frac{0.7\left(1-1.6M_{ic}^2\right)}{\left(1+0.2M_{ic}^2\right)^2}\Delta M_{pc}^2 - \ldots \quad (M_{ic}<1) \tag{D179}$$

In Herrington (Ref 12), the equivalent expression to Equation D179 is given as

$$\frac{\Delta P_p}{P_s} = \frac{1.4M_{ic}\Delta M_{pc}}{\left(1+0.2M_{ic}^2\right)} + \frac{0.7\left(1-1.6M_{ic}^2\right)\Delta M_{pc}^2}{\left(1+0.2M_{ic}^2\right)^2} \quad (M_{ic}<1) \quad \text{(Ref 12 5.56)}$$

which by inspection matches Equation D179.

For the supersonic case, we start with Equation D21. To find the derivatives, we need an equation for P_s in terms of M_{ic}. Rearranging Equation D21 gives

$$\frac{1}{P_s} = \frac{1}{P_T}\frac{166.921M_{ic}^7}{\left(7M_{ic}^2-1\right)^{5/2}} \tag{D180}$$

which we can invert to

$$P_s = \frac{P_T}{166.921}\left(M_{ic}^{-7}\right)\left(7M_{ic}^2-1\right)^{5/2} \tag{D181}$$

Differentiating (assuming P_T = constant)

$$\frac{dP_s}{dM_{ic}} = \frac{P_T}{166.921}\left(-7\left(M_{ic}^{-8}\right)\left(7M_{ic}^2-1\right)^{5/2} + \left(M_{ic}^{-7}\right)\left(\frac{5}{2}\right)\left(7M_{ic}^2-1\right)^{3/2}(7)(2M_{ic})\right) \tag{D182}$$

$$\frac{dP_s}{dM_{ic}} = \frac{P_T}{166.921}\left(-7\left(M_{ic}^{-7}M_{ic}^{-1}\right)\left(7M_{ic}^2-1\right)^{5/2} + 35\left(M_{ic}^{-7}M_{ic}\right)\left(7M_{ic}^2-1\right)^{5/2}\left(7M_{ic}^2-1\right)^{-1}\right) \tag{D183}$$

$$\frac{dP_s}{dM_{ic}} = P_T\frac{\left(7M_{ic}^2-1\right)^{5/2}}{166.921M_{ic}^7}\left(\frac{-7}{M_{ic}} + \frac{35M_{ic}}{\left(7M_{ic}^2-1\right)}\right) \tag{D184}$$

Since we need static pressure in the final result instead of total pressure, multiply by 1

$$\frac{dP_s}{dM_{ic}} = \frac{P_T}{P_s}P_s\frac{\left(7M_{ic}^2-1\right)^{5/2}}{166.921M_{ic}^7}\left(\frac{-7}{M_{ic}} + \frac{35M_{ic}}{\left(7M_{ic}^2-1\right)}\right) \tag{D185}$$

Substituting Equation D21

$$\frac{dP_s}{dM_{ic}} = P_s \frac{166.921 M_{ic}^7}{\left(7M_{ic}^2 - 1\right)^{5/2}} \frac{\left(7M_{ic}^2 - 1\right)^{5/2}}{166.921 M_{ic}^7} \left(\frac{-7}{M_{ic}} + \frac{35M_{ic}}{\left(7M_{ic}^2 - 1\right)}\right) \tag{D186}$$

$$\frac{dP_s}{dM_{ic}} = P_s \left(\frac{-7\left(7M_{ic}^2 - 1\right)}{M_{ic}\left(7M_{ic}^2 - 1\right)} + \frac{35M_{ic}^2}{M_{ic}\left(7M_{ic}^2 - 1\right)}\right) \tag{D187}$$

$$\frac{dP_s}{dM_{ic}} = P_s \left(\frac{-49M_{ic}^2 + 7 + 35M_{ic}^2}{M_{ic}\left(7M_{ic}^2 - 1\right)}\right) \tag{D188}$$

$$\frac{dP_s}{dM_{ic}} = P_s \left(\frac{-14M_{ic}^2 + 7}{M_{ic}\left(7M_{ic}^2 - 1\right)}\right) \tag{D189}$$

$$\frac{dP_s}{dM_{ic}} = -\frac{7\left(2M_{ic}^2 - 1\right)}{M_{ic}\left(7M_{ic}^2 - 1\right)} P_s \tag{D190}$$

To get the second derivative for the second term, we'll start by rearranging Equation D190

$$\frac{dP_s}{dM_{ic}} = -7\left(\left(2M_{ic}^2 - 1\right)\left(P_s\right)\right)\left(\left(M_{ic}^{-1}\right)\left(7M_{ic}^2 - 1\right)^{-1}\right) \tag{D191}$$

This equation has four terms that are functions of M_{ic}, so we will nest the product rule again.

$$\frac{d^2P_s}{dM_{ic}^2} = -7\left(\left(\left(2\right)\left(2M_{ic}\right)\left(P_s\right) + \left(2M_{ic}^2 - 1\right)\frac{dP_s}{dM_{ic}}\right)\left(M_{ic}^{-1}\left(7M_{ic}^2 - 1\right)^{-1}\right) + \left(2M_{ic}^2 - 1\right)\left(P_s\right)\left(-M_{ic}^{-2}\left(7M_{ic}^2 - 1\right)^{-1} + M_{ic}^{-1}\left(-1\right)\left(7M_{ic}^2 - 1\right)^{-2}\left(2\right)\left(7M_{ic}\right)\right)\right) \tag{D192}$$

Combining terms and substituting Equation D190

$$\frac{d^2P_s}{dM_{ic}^2} = -7\left(\left(4M_{ic}P_s + \left(2M_{ic}^2 - 1\right)\left(-\frac{7\left(2M_{ic}^2 - 1\right)}{M_{ic}\left(7M_{ic}^2 - 1\right)}P_s\right)\right)\left(\frac{1}{M_{ic}\left(7M_{ic}^2 - 1\right)}\right) + \left(2M_{ic}^2 - 1\right)\left(P_s\right)\left(\frac{-1}{M_{ic}^2\left(7M_{ic}^2 - 1\right)} + \frac{-14M_{ic}}{M_{ic}\left(7M_{ic}^2 - 1\right)^2}\right)\right) \tag{D193}$$

$$\frac{d^2P_s}{dM_{ic}^2} = -7\left(\left(4M_{ic}P_s - \frac{7\left(2M_{ic}^2 - 1\right)^2}{M_{ic}\left(7M_{ic}^2 - 1\right)}P_s\right)\left(\frac{1}{M_{ic}\left(7M_{ic}^2 - 1\right)}\right) + \left(\left(2M_{ic}^2 - 1\right)\left(P_s\right)\right)\left(\frac{-\left(7M_{ic}^2 - 1\right)}{M_{ic}^2\left(7M_{ic}^2 - 1\right)^2} + \frac{-14M_{ic}^2}{M_{ic}^2\left(7M_{ic}^2 - 1\right)^2}\right)\right) \tag{D194}$$

$$\frac{d^2P_s}{dM_{ic}^2} = -7\left(\frac{4M_{ic}P_s}{M_{ic}\left(7M_{ic}^2 - 1\right)} - \frac{7\left(2M_{ic}^2 - 1\right)^2 P_s}{M_{ic}^2\left(7M_{ic}^2 - 1\right)^2} + \frac{-\left(2M_{ic}^2 - 1\right)\left(7M_{ic}^2 - 1\right)P_s + \left(2M_{ic}^2 - 1\right)\left(-14\right)\left(M_{ic}^2\right)P_s}{M_{ic}^2\left(7M_{ic}^2 - 1\right)^2}\right) \tag{D195}$$

$$\frac{d^2P_s}{dM_{ic}^2} = -7\left(\frac{4M_{ic}^2\left(7M_{ic}^2-1\right)P_s - 7\left(2M_{ic}^2-1\right)^2P_s - \left(2M_{ic}^2-1\right)\left(7M_{ic}^2-1\right)P_s + \left(-28M_{ic}^4+14M_{ic}^2\right)P_s}{M_{ic}^2\left(7M_{ic}^2-1\right)^2}\right)$$

(D196)

$$\frac{d^2P_s}{dM_{ic}^2} = \frac{-7P_s}{M_{ic}^2\left(7M_{ic}^2-1\right)^2}\left(28M_{ic}^4-4M_{ic}^2-7\left(4M_{ic}^4-4M_{ic}^2+1\right)-\left(14M_{ic}^4-2M_{ic}^2-7M_{ic}^2+1\right)-28M_{ic}^4+14M_{ic}^2\right)$$

(D197)

$$\frac{d^2P_s}{dM_{ic}^2} = \frac{-7P_s}{M_{ic}^2\left(7M_{ic}^2-1\right)^2}\left(28M_{ic}^4-4M_{ic}^2-28M_{ic}^4+28M_{ic}^2-7-14M_{ic}^4+9M_{ic}^2-1-28M_{ic}^4+14M_{ic}^2\right)$$

(D198)

$$\frac{d^2P_s}{dM_{ic}^2} = \frac{-7P_s}{M_{ic}^2\left(7M_{ic}^2-1\right)^2}\left(-42M_{ic}^4+47M_{ic}^2-8\right)$$

(D199)

$$\frac{d^2P_s}{dM_{ic}^2} = \frac{7(2)P_s\left(21M_{ic}^4-23.5M_{ic}^2+4\right)}{M_{ic}^2\left(7M_{ic}^2-1\right)^2}$$

(D200)

Substituting Equations D190 and D200 into Equation D162,

$$\Delta P_p = -\frac{\Delta M_{pc}}{1!}\frac{-7\left(2M_{ic}^2-1\right)P_s}{M_{ic}\left(7M_{ic}^2-1\right)} - \frac{\Delta M_{pc}^2}{2!}\frac{7(2)P_s\left(21M_{ic}^4-23.5M_{ic}^2+4\right)}{M_{ic}^2\left(7M_{ic}^2-1\right)^2} - \ldots$$

(D201)

Rearranging

$$\frac{\Delta P_p}{P_s} = \frac{7\left(2M_{ic}^2-1\right)}{M_{ic}\left(7M_{ic}^2-1\right)}\Delta M_{pc} - \frac{7\left(21M_{ic}^4-23.5M_{ic}^2+4\right)}{M_{ic}^2\left(7M_{ic}^2-1\right)^2}\Delta M_{pc}^2 - \ldots \qquad (M_{ic}>1) \quad \text{(D202)}$$

In Herrington (Ref 12), the equivalent expression to Equation D202 is given as

$$\frac{\Delta P_p}{P_s} = \frac{7\left(2M_{ic}^2-1\right)\Delta M_{pc}}{M_{ic}\left(7M_{ic}^2-1\right)} - \frac{7\left(21M_{ic}^4-23.5M_{ic}^2+4\right)\Delta M_{pc}^2}{M_{ic}^2\left(7M_{ic}^2-1\right)^2} \qquad (M_{ic}>1) \quad \text{(Ref 12 5.57)}$$

which by inspection matches Equation D202.

So again we ask, how many terms do we need? We can see what errors are involved by calculating $\Delta P_p/P_s$ directly using the pressure method for varying conditions.

TABLE D3
$\Delta P_p/P_s$ Errors From Mach

M	ΔM_{pc}	M_{ic}	1 Term %Error	2 Term %Error
0.2	0.001	0.199	-0.233%	0.0001%
0.4	0.001	0.399	-0.090%	0.0001%
0.6	0.001	0.599	-0.033%	0.0001%
0.8	0.001	0.799	0.001%	0.0000%
1	0.001	0.999	0.025%	0.0000%
1.2	0.001	1.199	0.067%	0.0000%
1.4	0.001	1.399	0.074%	0.0000%
1.6	0.001	1.599	0.073%	0.0000%
1.8	0.001	1.799	0.069%	0.0000%
2	0.001	1.999	0.065%	0.0000%
0.2	0.04	0.16	-10.537%	0.1328%
0.4	0.04	0.36	-3.997%	0.1240%
0.6	0.04	0.56	-1.544%	0.1042%
0.8	0.04	0.76	-0.100%	0.0787%
1	0.04	0.96	0.893%	0.0511%
1.2	0.04	1.16	2.598%	0.0132%
1.4	0.04	1.36	2.989%	-0.0521%
1.6	0.04	1.56	2.965%	-0.0654%
1.8	0.04	1.76	2.822%	-0.0639%
2	0.04	1.96	2.649%	-0.0583%

Reference 12 states that the one term solution is acceptable for values of $\Delta M_{pc} < 0.04$. As seen in Table D3, this may be true where other measurements are coarse and flight conditions are at high subsonic Mach numbers and above. The error is large at low Mach numbers. For all flight conditions, the two term solution is quite acceptable.

Finding Altitude Position Correction From Position Error, Taylor Series Expansion Method

Inverting Equation D118 gives us an equation to directly calculate the altitude position correction within the errors associated with using the Taylor Series expansion.

$$\Delta H_{pc} = \frac{\theta_{ic}}{3.61371 \times 10^{-5}/ft} \frac{\Delta P_p}{P_s}$$ (D203)

where θ_{ic} is calculated by (from Equations A78 and A86)

$$\theta_{ic} = 1 - 6.87559 \times 10^{-6} H_{ic}$$ $(H_c \leq 36089.24 \text{ feet})$ (D204)

$$\theta_{ic} = 0.751865$$ $(H_c > 36089.24 \text{ feet})$ (D205)

CAUTION

For the Pitot-statics class at the USAF Test Pilot School, use the pressure method for full credit on exams. The pressure method gives an exact answer, while the Taylor series expansion method gives an approximate answer. The Taylor series expansion method is included for historical legacy and explanation of Herrington (Ref 12).

Finding Airspeed Position Correction From Position Error, Taylor Series Expansion Method

If we only use the first term of Equation D137 ($V_{ic} \leq a_{SL}$) we can solve directly for ΔV_{pc}

$$\Delta V_{pc} = \frac{a_{SL}^2 \delta_{ic}}{1.4 V_{ic}\left(1 + 0.2\left(\frac{V_{ic}}{a_{SL}}\right)^2\right)^{5/2}} \left(\frac{\Delta P_p}{P_s}\right)$$ $(V_{ic} \leq a_{SL})$ (D206)

or for $V_{ic} > a_{SL}$ (from Equation D156)

$$\Delta V_{pc} = \frac{a_{SL}\delta_{ic}}{1168.447} \frac{\left(7\left(\frac{V_{ic}}{a_{SL}}\right)^2 - 1\right)^{7/2}}{\left(\frac{V_{ic}}{a_{SL}}\right)^6\left(2\left(\frac{V_{ic}}{a_{SL}}\right)^2 - 1\right)} \left(\frac{\Delta P_p}{P_s}\right)$$ $(V_{ic} > a_{SL})$ (D207)

CAUTION

For the Pitot-statics class at the USAF Test Pilot School, use the pressure method for full credit on exams. The pressure method gives an exact answer, while the Taylor series expansion method gives an approximate answer. The Taylor series expansion method is included for historical legacy and explanation of Herrington (Ref 12).

If we choose to use the first two terms of Equation D137, then we must solve for ΔV_{pc} using the quadratic formula, with (for $V_{ic} \leq a_{SL}$)

$$a = \frac{0.7}{\delta_{ic} a_{SL}^2} \left(1 + 0.2\left(\frac{V_{ic}}{a_{SL}}\right)^2\right)^{3/2} \left(1 + 1.2\left(\frac{V_{ic}}{a_{SL}}\right)^2\right) \qquad \text{(D208)}$$

$$b = \frac{1.4}{\delta_{ic} a_{SL}} \left(\frac{V_{ic}}{a_{SL}}\right) \left(1 + 0.2\left(\frac{V_{ic}}{a_{SL}}\right)^2\right)^{5/2} \qquad \text{(D209)}$$

$$c = -\frac{\Delta P_p}{P_s} \qquad \text{(D210)}$$

Then ΔV_{pc} is calculated by

$$\Delta V_{pc} = \frac{-b \pm \sqrt{b^2 - 4ac}}{2a} \qquad \text{(D211)}$$

As with all second order function solutions, Equation D211 will yield two solutions. The correct solution will be the value of ΔV_{pc} closest to the value obtained from Equation D206.

For $V_{ic} > a_{SL}$ we would have (from Equation D156)

$$a = \frac{(1168.447)}{\delta_{ic} a_{SL}^2} \left(\frac{V_{ic}}{a_{SL}}\right)^5 \frac{\left(7\left(\frac{V_{ic}}{a_{SL}}\right)^4 - \frac{9}{2}\left(\frac{V_{ic}}{a_{SL}}\right)^2 + 3\right)}{\left(7\left(\frac{V_{ic}}{a_{SL}}\right)^2 - 1\right)^{9/2}} \qquad \text{(D212)}$$

$$b = \frac{(1168.447)}{\delta_{ic} a_{SL}} \left(\frac{V_{ic}}{a_{SL}}\right)^6 \frac{\left(2\left(\frac{V_{ic}}{a_{SL}}\right)^2 - 1\right)}{\left(7\left(\frac{V_{ic}}{a_{SL}}\right)^2 - 1\right)^{7/2}} \qquad \text{(D213)}$$

$$c = -\frac{\Delta P_p}{P_s} \qquad \text{(D210)}$$

which would be evaluated by Equation D211. The correct solution will be the value of ΔV_{pc} closest to the value obtained from Equation D207.

Finding Mach Position Correction From Position Error, Taylor Series Expansion Method

If we only use the first term of Equation D179 ($M_{ic} \leq 1$) we can solve directly for ΔM_{pc}

$$\Delta M_{pc} = \frac{1 + 0.2M_{ic}^2}{1.4M_{ic}} \left(\frac{\Delta P_p}{P_s} \right) \qquad (M < 1) \quad (D214)$$

or for $M_{ic} > 1$ (from Equation D202)

$$\Delta M_{pc} = \frac{M_{ic}\left(7M_{ic}^2 - 1\right)}{7\left(2M_{ic}^2 - 1\right)} \left(\frac{\Delta P_p}{P_s} \right) \qquad (M > 1) \quad (D215)$$

```
┌ ■ ■ ■ ■ ■ ■ ■ ■ ■ ■ ┐
■      CAUTION       ■
└ ■ ■ ■ ■ ■ ■ ■ ■ ■ ■ ┘
```

For the Pitot-statics class at the USAF Test Pilot School, use the pressure method for full credit on exams. The pressure method gives an exact answer, while the Taylor series expansion method gives an approximate answer. The Taylor series expansion method is included for historical legacy and explanation of Herrington (Ref 12).

If we choose to use the first two terms of Equation D179, then we must solve for ΔM_{pc} using the quadratic formula, with (for $M_{ic} < 1$)

$$a = \frac{0.7\left(1 - 1.6M_{ic}^2\right)}{\left(1 + 0.2M_{ic}^2\right)^2} \qquad (D216)$$

$$b = \frac{1.4M_{ic}}{\left(1 + 0.2M_{ic}^2\right)} \qquad (D217)$$

$$c = -\frac{\Delta P_p}{P_s} \qquad (D210)$$

Then ΔM_{pc} is calculated by

$$\Delta M_{pc} = \frac{-b \pm \sqrt{b^2 - 4ac}}{2a} \qquad (D218)$$

As with all second order function solutions, Equation D218 will yield two solutions. The correct solution will be the value of ΔM_{pc} closest to the value obtained from Equation D214.

For $M_{ic} > 1$ we would have (from Equation D202)

$$a = -\frac{7\left(21M_{ic}^4 - 23.5M_{ic}^2 + 4\right)}{M_{ic}^2\left(7M_{ic}^2 - 1\right)^2} \tag{D219}$$

$$b = \frac{7\left(2M_{ic}^2 - 1\right)}{M_{ic}\left(7M_{ic}^2 - 1\right)} \tag{D220}$$

$$c = -\frac{\Delta P_p}{P_s} \tag{D210}$$

which would be evaluated by Equation D218. The correct solution will be the value of ΔV_{pc} closest to the value obtained from Equation D215.

Appendix E

Cloverleaf FTT Data Reduction Heavy Math Section

Vector Method

The Cloverleaf FTT data reduction is based on using three wind triangles to calculate the true airspeed error and the wind speed and direction. The necessary assumptions are:

1. Indicated Airspeed, and thus True Airspeed is the same on each run
2. Wind Speed and Direction are the same on each run
3. All wind is horizontal (no vertical component)

While we are mostly interested in finding the truth true airspeed, on the way to find the truth true airspeed we will also determine the wind speed and wind direction. With three unknowns, we need three equations. These "equations" are the results of flying three passes, each with its own wind triangle. Figure E1 shows the wind triangles for three passes at arbitrary headings.

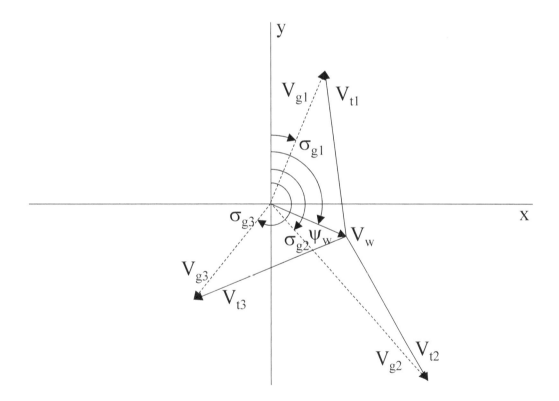

Figure E1. Wind triangles for three passes

Note that the angles are measured in same direction as headings, as if the positive y axis was North and the positive x axis was East.

To determine the wind vector, we look at Figure E2.

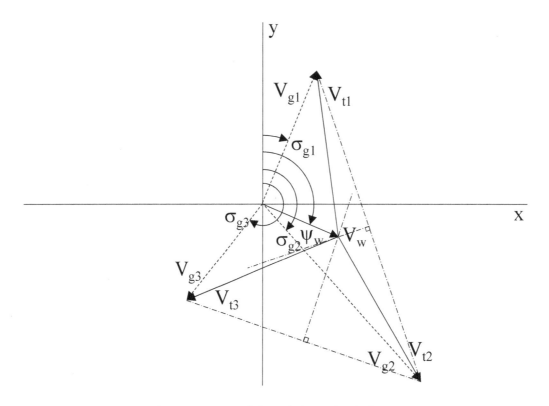

Figure E2. Determining wind speed and direction

In Figure E2, we have drawn a line segment connecting the tips of vectors V_{t1} and V_{t2}, which also connects the tips of V_{g1} and V_{g2}. Because the true airspeed was the same on legs 1 and 2 (assumed), the vectors V_{t1} and V_{t2} and the line segment connecting them form an isosceles triangle. From geometry, we know the perpendicular bisector of the side opposite the equal sides of an isosceles triangle will pass through the vertex between the equal sides (*you remembered that, right?*). Note also that this vertex is the tip of the wind vector.

The same type of triangle has been drawn between V_{t1} and V_{t3}, which is also between V_{g1} and V_{g3}. If we can find the intersection of the perpendicular bisectors, we can determine the wind vector.

To do the math, we need to convert the ground speed vectors into rectangular coordinates. For each ground speed vector, we apply

$$V_{gx} = V_g \sin \sigma_g \qquad \text{(E1)}$$

$$V_{gy} = V_g \cos \sigma_g \qquad \text{(E2)}$$

The slope of the line segment between V_{g1} and V_{g2} is given by the rise over run, or

$$\text{Slope} = \frac{V_{gy2} - V_{gy1}}{V_{gx2} - V_{gx1}} \qquad \text{(E3)}$$

which is all fine and good, but we need the slope of the perpendicular bisector.

Again, from analytic geometry, we find out that the slope of the perpendicular line is the negative inverse of the slope, or

$$\text{Slope}_\perp = -\frac{1}{\text{Slope}} \qquad (E4)$$

To find the perpendicular bisector, we need to find the midpoint of the line segment, which can be done simply by averaging the x and y values

$$\left(x_{\text{midpoint}}, y_{\text{midpoint}}\right) = \left(\frac{V_{gx1} + V_{gx2}}{2}, \frac{V_{gy1} + V_{gy2}}{2}\right) \qquad (E5)$$

Now that we know the slope of the perpendicular bisector and a point that it passes through, we can determine the equation of the perpendicular bisector. Using the slope-intercept form of a line, we have

$$y = mx + b \qquad (E6)$$

Solving for the intercept gives

$$b = y - mx \qquad (E7)$$

so the intercept of the perpendicular bisector is

$$\text{Intercept}_\perp = y_{\text{midpoint}} - \text{Slope}_\perp \left(x_{\text{midpoint}}\right) \qquad (E8)$$

This is accomplished for the line segment between V_{g1} and V_{g2} and the line segment between V_{g1} and V_{g3}. It could also be done between V_{g2} and V_{g3}, with any difference in results giving an indication of the uncertainty in the data.

With the equations of two perpendicular bisectors, we can find their intersection, which will be the tip of the wind vector. At the intersection point, the y value of both lines will be the same, so we set the two equations equal as

$$y = m_1x + b_1 = m_2x + b_2 \qquad (E9)$$

Solving for x gives

$$m_1x + b_1 - b_2 = m_2x \qquad (E10)$$

$$b_1 - b_2 = m_2x - m_1x \qquad (E11)$$

$$b_1 - b_2 = (m_2 - m_1)x \qquad (E12)$$

$$\frac{b_1 - b_2}{m_2 - m_1} = x \qquad (E13)$$

Using Equation E13, the x value of the intersection can be found, which will be V_{wx}. This x value can then be inserted in the equation for either perpendicular bisector to determine the y value of the intersection, which will be V_{wy}.

The wind speed will then be given by

$$V_w = \sqrt{V_{wx}^2 + V_{wy}^2} \qquad\qquad (E14)$$

The wind direction can be found as

$$\psi_w = \tan^{-1}\left(\frac{V_{wx}}{V_{wy}}\right) \qquad\qquad (E15)$$

Note that this returns the vector direction of the wind, that is the direction which it is going. The x value is on top instead of the y value because we are measuring angles clockwise from the y axis instead of counterclockwise from the x axis.

To determine the wind direction by the traditional definition (the direction from which it is coming), Equation E15 is modified by 180 degrees

$$\psi_w = \tan^{-1}\left(\frac{V_{wx}}{V_{wy}}\right) \pm 180^0 \qquad\qquad (E16)$$

To find the True Airspeed, we use the components of one of the true airspeed vectors, found as the difference in the components of the corresponding ground speed vector and wind vector

$$V_t = \sqrt{\left(V_{gx1} - V_{wx}\right)^2 + \left(V_{gy1} - V_{wy}\right)^2} \qquad\qquad (E17)$$

Assuming the wind was the same for each run and each run was at the same calibrated airspeed, then this will be the true airspeed for each run.

Alternate Matrix Inversion Method

The necessary assumptions for the Matrix Inversion Method are:

1. True Airspeed Error (ΔV_t) is the same on each run
2. Wind Speed and Direction are the same on each run
3. All wind is horizontal (no vertical component)

Figure E3 shows the basic wind triangle for one pass where

V_{t_i} True airspeed as calculated from the instrument corrected airspeed

ΔV_t Position error in true airspeed
V_w Wind velocity
V_g Ground velocity

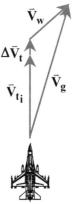

Figure E3. Basic wind triangle

The vector equation for the basic wind triangle is

$$\vec{V}_g = \vec{V}_t + \vec{V}_w \qquad (E18)$$

Breaking the true airspeed into the true airspeed calculated from the instrument corrected airspeed and the position error in true airspeed we get

$$\vec{V}_t = \vec{V}_{t_i} + \Delta\vec{V}_t \qquad (E19)$$

Substituting into Equation E18 gives

$$\vec{V}_g = \vec{V}_{t_i} + \Delta\vec{V}_t + \vec{V}_w \qquad (E20)$$

which by rearranging gives

$$\vec{V}_{t_i} + \Delta\vec{V}_t = \vec{V}_g - \vec{V}_w \qquad (E21)$$

Within this equation are three knowns and five unknowns. The known values are the magnitude of V_{ti}, the magnitude of V_g (ground speed) and the direction of V_g (ground track). The unknowns are the direction of V_{ti}, the magnitude of ΔV_t, the direction of ΔV_t, the magnitude of V_w (wind speed), and the direction of V_w (wind direction).

For three passes, we have two equations based on our assumptions. The first equation is that the error in indicated airspeed, and thus the error in true airspeed are the same on each run, even with slight variations in true airspeed between runs.

$$\Delta\vec{V}_{t_1} = \Delta\vec{V}_{t_2} = \Delta\vec{V}_{t_3} \qquad (E22)$$

The second equation is that the direction of the true airspeed error (ΔV_t) and the measured true airspeed (V_{ti}) are the same.

$$\angle\Delta\vec{V}_t = \angle\vec{V}_{t_i} \qquad (E23)$$

Thus the magnitude of each true airspeed is given by

$$V_t = V_{t_i} + \Delta V_t \qquad (E24)$$

Rearranging the basic vector equation (Equation E18)

$$\vec{V}_t = \vec{V}_g - \vec{V}_w \qquad (E25)$$

If this equation holds, then the component equations in the x and y directions must also be true. To wit

$$V_{tx} = V_{gx} - V_{wx} \qquad (E26)$$

$$V_{ty} = V_{gy} - V_{wy} \qquad (E27)$$

where the x and y subscripts denote the component in that direction.

For the ground speed vector

$$V_{gx} = V_g \sin \sigma_g \qquad\qquad (E1)$$

$$V_{gy} = V_g \cos \sigma_g \qquad\qquad (E2)$$

From our good buddy Pythagoras, we know that

$$V_t^2 = V_{tx}^2 + V_{ty}^2 \qquad\qquad (E28)$$

Substituting Equations E24, E26, and E27 into Equation E28 gives

$$(V_{t_i} + \Delta V_t)^2 = (V_{gx} - V_{wx})^2 + (V_{gy} - V_{wy})^2 \qquad\qquad (E29)$$

Multiplying out this equation gives

$$V_{t_i}^2 + 2 V_{t_i} \Delta V_t + \Delta V_t^2 = V_{gx}^2 - 2 V_{gx} V_{wx} + V_{wx}^2 + V_{gy}^2 - 2 V_{gy} V_{wy} + V_{wy}^2 \qquad (E30)$$

Collecting terms

$$(2 V_{t_i} + \Delta V_t) \Delta V_t + (2 V_{gx} - V_{wx}) V_{wx} + (2 V_{gy} - V_{wy}) V_{wy} = V_{gx}^2 + V_{gy}^2 - V_{t_i}^2 \qquad (E31)$$

Applying the Pythagorean theorem again to the ground speed components

$$(2 V_{t_i} + \Delta V_t) \Delta V_t + (2 V_{gx} - V_{wx}) V_{wx} + (2 V_{gy} - V_{wy}) V_{wy} = V_g^2 - V_{t_i}^2 \qquad (E32)$$

Applying this equation to each of the three runs

$$(2 V_{t_i 1} + \Delta V_t) \Delta V_t + (2 V_{gx1} - V_{wx}) V_{wx} + (2 V_{gy1} - V_{wy}) V_{wy} = V_{g1}^2 - V_{t_i 1}^2 \qquad (E33)$$

$$(2 V_{t_i 2} + \Delta V_t) \Delta V_t + (2 V_{gx2} - V_{wx}) V_{wx} + (2 V_{gy2} - V_{wy}) V_{wy} = V_{g2}^2 - V_{t_i 2}^2 \qquad (E34)$$

$$(2 V_{t_i 3} + \Delta V_t) \Delta V_t + (2 V_{gx3} - V_{wx}) V_{wx} + (2 V_{gy3} - V_{wy}) V_{wy} = V_{g3}^2 - V_{t_i 3}^2 \qquad (E35)$$

Eeek! Let's put that in matrix form…

$$\begin{bmatrix} 2V_{t_i 1} + \Delta V_t & 2V_{gx1} - V_{wx} & 2V_{gy1} - V_{wy} \\ 2V_{t_i 2} + \Delta V_t & 2V_{gx2} - V_{wx} & 2V_{gy2} - V_{wy} \\ 2V_{t_i 3} + \Delta V_t & 2V_{gx3} - V_{wx} & 2V_{gy3} - V_{wy} \end{bmatrix} \begin{bmatrix} \Delta V_t \\ V_{wx} \\ V_{wy} \end{bmatrix} = \begin{bmatrix} V_{g1}^2 - V_{t_i 1}^2 \\ V_{g2}^2 - V_{t_i 2}^2 \\ V_{g3}^2 - V_{t_i 3}^2 \end{bmatrix} \qquad (E36)$$

Now we just need to solve for ΔV_t, V_{wx}, and V_{wy}. The problem arises that the coefficients in the matrix are functions of the variables we are solving for. To solve for the solution vector, we have

$$[A][x] = [C] \qquad\qquad (E37)$$

$$[x] = [A]^{-1}[C] \qquad\qquad (E38)$$

Because the equations are implicit, we will solve it by iteration. You can start by assuming the zero error, zero wind case

$$\begin{bmatrix} \Delta V_t \\ V_{wx} \\ V_{wy} \end{bmatrix} = \begin{bmatrix} 0 \\ 0 \\ 0 \end{bmatrix} \tag{E39}$$

Use a spreadsheet or Matlab to invert the matrix according to Equation E38. Use the resulting solution vector to recalculate the coefficients in the matrix and repeat. Continue until the solution vector stops changing. Usually about five iterations is sufficient.

This method still gives a deterministic answer (a single answer) like the vector method, but unlike the vector method it is less sensitive to slight variations in true airspeed during data collection.

Appendix F

Finding Distances and Directions From Latitudes and Longitudes

Spherical Trigonometry

In Survey FTT data analysis it is sometimes necessary to determine the distance between two points expressed in latitude and longitude. For the distances usually involved (less than 5 nm) we could assume a flat earth, that longitude lines were parallel and figure the conversion from degrees longitude to nautical miles as a function of the latitude, but why bother when we can learn to do it with spherical trigonometry (Ref 34)? While the increase in accuracy may be small for these short distances, using spherical trigonometry has the added benefit of being useful for determining longer distances, such as how far it is from Edwards AFB to Randolph AFB in San Antonio. While you're at it, you can determine what direction to face to point at the destination.

To start this short discussion of spherical trigonometry, let's agree on some definitions. See Figure F1.

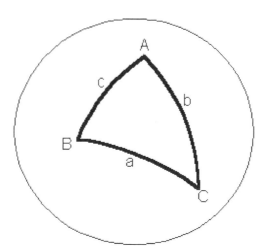

Figure F1. Triangle on a Sphere

Here we see a triangle drawn on a sphere. Each side of the triangle is an arc of a great circle, and represents the shortest distance between its endpoints. The arcs are represented by lower case letters (a, b, c). The length of each arc is represented as the size of the angle with its vertex at the center of the sphere and sides passing through the endpoints of the arc on the surface of the sphere (the angle subtended at the center of the sphere). An example of this is saying that one degree of latitude equals 60 nautical miles.

The capital letters (A, B, C) denote the angles between the sides of the triangle as measured on the surface of the sphere. Each angle is opposite the arc with the corresponding lower case letter. While it is interesting to note that the sum of A+B+C is always greater than 180 degrees (or π radians, if you prefer), it's not really that useful for the problem at hand.

Basic Relationships

The **Law of Cosines** for spherical triangles allows us to calculate the length of an arc from the lengths of the other two arcs and the opposite angle.

$$\cos a = \cos b \cos c + \sin b \sin c \cos A \qquad \text{(F1)}$$

The **Law of Sines** for spherical triangles allows us to calculate an angle if one other angle is known, and the sides opposite the known and unknown angles are known.

$$\frac{\sin a}{\sin A} = \frac{\sin b}{\sin B} = \frac{\sin c}{\sin C} \qquad \text{(F2)}$$

While we all know that the earth is an oblate spheroid (a flattened ball), we will consider it to be a perfect sphere, which will be sufficient for our purposes. Knowing that one degree of latitude equals 60 nm, we find the circumference of the earth to be

$$\text{Earth Circumference} = 360° \text{ Latitude} * 60 \text{ nm/deg} = 21{,}600 \text{ nm} \qquad \text{(F3)}$$

We will also consider both points to be located at sea level, ignoring any additional distance caused by being farther from the center of the earth of by differences in elevation. Since we are most interested in relative distances (i.e. which two points are closest), we can accept the small additional error from this simplifying assumption.

We will also assume that all vertex angles and angles subtended by the sides are less than 180°.

Distance Between Two Points

Let's say you decide that you want to travel to AFPC to check your records for the upcoming promotion board (that's what we did in the days before the Internet). You find the following coordinates for Edwards AFB and Randolph AFB:

Location	Latitude (deg min)	Longitude (deg min)	Latitude (deg)	Longitude (deg)
EDW	34° 54' N	117° 53' W	34.9°	-117.883°
RND	29° 32' N	98° 17' W	29.533°	-98.283°

Note that by convention, North latitudes and East longitudes are considered positive, and South latitudes and West Longitudes are considered negative. The minutes portion of the angles have been converted into decimal degrees by dividing by 60. This keeps the sine and cosine functions on your calculator happier.

Now we set up our triangle as shown in Figure F2.

In Figure F2, point A represents the North Pole, and the size of angle A is the difference between the longitudes.

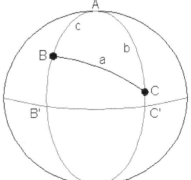

Point B is Edwards AFB, and the arc BB' is the latitude of Edwards AFB. The arc c is then equal to 90° minus the latitude of Edwards AFB.

Point C is Randolph AFB, and the arc CC' is the latitude of Randolph AFB. The arc b is then equal to 90° minus the latitude of Randolph AFB.

Figure F2. Spherical Triangle Setup

Since we want to know the length of arc a, we use the Law of Cosines to get

$$\cos a = \cos b \cos c + \sin b \sin c \cos A \tag{F1}$$

$$\cos a = \cos (90°\text{-Lat}_{RND}) \cos (90°\text{-Lat}_{EDW}) + \sin (90°\text{-Lat}_{RND}) \sin (90°\text{-Lat}_{EDW}) \cos (\text{Long}_{RND} - \text{Long}_{EDW})$$

$$\cos a = \cos (90\text{-}29.533) \cos (90\text{-}34.9) + \sin (90\text{-}29.533) \sin (90\text{-}34.9) \cos ((\text{-}98.283) - (\text{-}117.883))$$

$$\cos a = 0.95427$$

$$a = 17.394°$$

That's the size of the angle subtended at the center of the earth from Edwards AFB to Randolph AFB, but not what you thought you asked for. Since we know that 360° of arc on the surface of the earth is 21600 nm, we can get the distance from Edwards AFB to Randolph AFB by

$$\text{Dis tance} = \frac{a}{360} * \text{Circumference} \tag{F4}$$

$$\text{Dis tance} = \frac{17.394}{360} * 21600 \text{ nm}$$

$$\text{Distance} = 1043 \text{ nm}$$

Well, that's the answer we wanted, but that equation is rather painful with all of the "90 minus" stuff in it. We didn't fight to stay awake in trigonometry class just to let this sort of thing go unmodified. Digging through a bunch of dusty old notes, we find the trigonometric identities that we once had memorized

$$\cos (90 - x) = \sin x \tag{F5}$$

$$\sin (90 - x) = \cos x \tag{F6}$$

Using these identities, we can rewrite the Law of Cosines for the special case of using latitudes as

$$\cos (\text{Distance Angle}_{1\text{-}2}) = \sin (\text{Lat}_2) \sin (\text{Lat}_1) + \cos (\text{Lat}_2) \cos (\text{Lat}_1) \cos (\text{Long}_2 - \text{Long}_1) \tag{F7}$$

$$\text{Dis tance}_{1-2} = \frac{\text{Dis tance Angle}_{1-2}}{360 \text{ deg}} * 21600 \text{ nm} \tag{F8}$$

For our example, we would have

$$\cos (\text{Distance}_{EDW\text{-}RND}) = \sin (29.533) \sin (34.9) + \cos (29.533) \cos (34.9) \cos ((\text{-}98.283) - (\text{-}117.883))$$

$$\cos a = 0.95427$$

$$a = 17.394°$$

Direction to Another Point

Now let's say that we've been cleared direct from Edwards to Randolph, what True Course (TC) do we want to start on? For this we will use the Law of Sines with the arc length opposite the angle, the arc length between the points, and the angle at the North Pole. So to find angle B, we need b, a, and A. Using the Law of Sines, solving for sin B we have

$$\frac{\sin a}{\sin A} = \frac{\sin b}{\sin B} = \frac{\sin c}{\sin C} \tag{F2}$$

$$\sin B = \sin A \frac{\sin b}{\sin a}$$

Using latitudes and longitudes this would give

$$\sin B = \sin(Long_{RND} - Long_{EDW})\frac{\sin(90^\circ - Lat_{RND})}{\sin a}$$

$$\sin B = \sin((-98.283)-(-117.883))\frac{\sin(90-29.533)}{\sin 17.394}$$

$$\sin B = 0.97491$$

$$B = 77.1^\circ \text{ or } 102.9^\circ$$

Note that there will always be two possible angles for each problem. To determine which is correct, look at the relative latitudes between the points. If the destination latitude is greater than the departure latitude, the angle will be less than 90° or greater than 270° (i.e. north of east/west). If the destination latitude is less than the departure latitude, the angle will be between 90° and 270° (i.e. south of east/west). Also note that for angles between 180° and 360°, the inverse sine function on most calculators will return a negative angle (-180° to 0°). Add 360° to the possible results and apply the latitude test above to get the proper angle.

As we did before, let's apply Equation F6 to make this easier. Then we have

$$\sin(TC_{1-2}) = \sin(Long_2 - Long_1)\frac{\cos(Lat_2)}{\sin(Distance_{1-2})} \tag{F9}$$

For our example, we would have

$$\sin(TC_{1-2}) = \sin((-98.283)-(-117.883))\frac{\cos(29.533)}{\sin(17.394)}$$

$$\sin(TC_{1-2}) = 0.97491$$

$$TC_{1-2} = 77.1^\circ \text{ or } 102.9^\circ$$

Appendix G

Weather Balloon Heavy Math Section

Weather Balloons and Radiosondes

Weather balloons can be used to provide a sounding of wind, temperature, humidity, and pressure altitude level with respect to geometric altitude. It is this last bit of information that makes them useful for Pitot-static calibrations. Most aircraft can be equipped with a differential GPS or WAAS augmented GPS to give a readout of geometric altitude to go with the aircraft measurement of pressure altitude. These data could even be provided by some handheld GPS units that are WAAS capable. By consulting the weather balloon data, the truth pressure altitude for the flight geometric altitude can be found, and this truth pressure altitude can be compared to the aircraft measured pressure altitude to determine the altitude position correction.

At Edwards AFB, weather balloons are launched only by request, not on a regular time interval. The following information on weather balloons used at Edwards AFB was provided by Mr. Phil Harvey, Staff Meteorologist:

> Edwards AFB uses a Lockheed Martin LMG6 sounding system to track their LMS6 radiosonde - the instrument package (carried by a balloon rising approximately 1,000 feet per minute) - to heights of up to 100,000 feet. The LMS6 radiosonde contains a GPS receiver along with a temperature and humidity sensor. These data are transmitted every second and received by the LMG6. The LMG6 has a ground based, surveyed GPS receiver for differential GPS correction. Geometric altitude is measured directly and pressure is computed rather than measured. The pressure computations and all other meteorological computations are made with standard meteorological formulas. Preliminary data are processed in real time with final reduction occurring immediately after run termination. The minimum time between flights is two hours. Information from this service includes wind speed (Kts) and direction (true), temperature (C), dew point (C), pressure (millibars), relative humidity (%), refractive index (N), density (G/M3) and velocity of sound (Kts). All other output units or derived parameters are the responsibility of the user to compute.

> The rms altitude accuracy of GPS geometric heights, with differential correction, is approximately five (5) meters. This is somewhat better near the surface, since the surveyed geometric height of the launch point as a starting point is used for height calculations.

> The range of wind measurement is 0 to 180 m/s. The resolution is 0.1 m/s. The accuracy of wind velocity is better than +/- 0.3 m/s (RMS of magnitude of vector difference in an intercomparison between systems). The range of wind direction is 0 to 360 degrees with a minimum precision of 1 degree.

> In 2005, the World Meteorological Organization conducted a major intercomparison of GPS radiosonde systems in Mauritius. The GPS winds accuracy for all systems that used differential GPS for windfinding, with proper filtering for balloon motion, etc., were characterized as follows by WMO:

> Typical random errors in wind component [u, v] measurements for GPS radiosondes were most probably between 0.2 and 0.4 ms-1 (1 s.d.) in the troposphere and 0.3 to 0.5 ms-1 (1 s.d.) in the stratosphere.

Here is some other information regarding the LMS6 radiosonde:

Pressure (Derived from Differentially Corrected GPS Geometric Height Values)
Measuring Range: 1080 hPa to 3 hPa
Accuracy: Better than 0.5 hPa (rms)
Resolution: 0.1 hPa

Temperature Sensor
Type: Chip Thermistor
Range: -90C to +60C
Accuracy: 0.2C *
0.3C * in daylight above 20 kms
Response Time (63.2%, 6 m/s):
1000 hPa < 0.75 Secs
10 hPa < 8 Secs
Resolution: 0.1C

Humidity Sensor
Type: Capacitance
Range: 0 to 100% RH;
+45C to -60C
Accuracy: +/-5% RH * up to 20 hPa
Response Time:
1000 hPa, 6 m/s, +25C < 1.5 Secs
1000 hPa, 6 m/s, -10C < 10 Secs
1000 hPa, 6 m/s, -40C < 50 Secs
Resolution: 1% RH

Code Correlating GPS Receiver
Number of Channels: 12
Cold Start Acquisition Time: 45 Secs (nominal)
Reacquisition Time: 0.1 Secs (nominal)
Range: 0 to 100% RH;

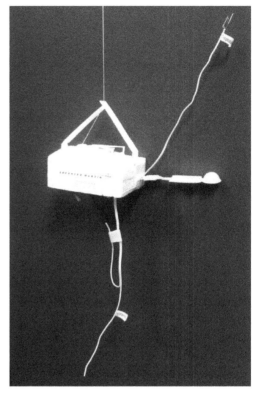

Figure G1. Radiosonde

Wait A Minute! You Don't Measure Pressure?

Yep. That's right! He said "Geometric altitude is measured directly and pressure is computed rather than measured." The instrument package in the radiosonde consists of "a GPS receiver along with a temperature and humidity sensor." Just like we did for the Standard Atmosphere (see Appendix A), the radiosonde measures a temperature profile (temperature versus geometric altitude) and then we integrate to find the pressure profile using the equation of state and hydrostatic equation.

When we did this for the Standard Atmosphere, we assumed the air was dry. Now we are dealing with the real world, and humidity is an issue we can't ignore. Additionally, the differential GPS returns altitude in geometric feet, but we need to use geopotential feet to do the integration. Yes, there's not a lot of difference between geometric and geopotential feet, but that difference accumulates to create a significant error when we integrate numerically over several hundred intervals. Fear not! The math isn't any worse than anything we've already seen in this book.

The data we will need from the radiosonde are the geometric altitude, temperature, and dewpoint. The numerical integration will be done over the intervals between data points. Where needed, the subscript "1" will denote the values at the bottom of the altitude interval, and the subscript "2" will denote the values at the top of the altitude interval.

First, we convert the geometric altitudes (h) to geopotential altitudes (H)

$$H = \left(\frac{R_{e_{SL}}}{R_{e_{SL}} + h} \right) h \tag{A29}$$

$R_{e_{SL}}$ = 20,902,808.99 ft (radius of the earth at mean sea level at 34.9° latitude)

Next we have to deal with the humidity. The problem is that the specific gas constant (R) of water is different than the specific gas constant for air. The trick to get around this is to find a "virtual temperature" which would be the temperature of a parcel of dry air that has the same density as the actual humid air at the same pressure. Starting with the Equation of State

$$P = \rho R T \tag{A3}$$

we rearrange to solve for density

$$\rho = \frac{P}{RT} \tag{G1}$$

By the concept of partial pressures, we know that the air pressure is the sum of the partial pressure of dry air and the partial pressure of the water vapor (rearrangement of Equation A105)

$$P_{moist} = P_{dry} + P_{water} \tag{G2}$$

For a parcel of air, its mass is equal to the sum of the mass of dry air and the mass of water vapor. Since these masses occupy the same volume, we can say that the overall density of the air parcel is the sum of the densities of the dry air and the water vapor.

$$\rho_{moist} = \frac{m_{dry}}{V} + \frac{m_{water}}{V} = \rho_{dry} + \rho_{water} \tag{G3}$$

Substituting equation G1 we get

$$\rho_{moist} = \frac{P_{moist}}{R_{air} T_{virtual}} = \frac{P_{dry}}{R_{air} T_{moist}} + \frac{P_{water}}{R_{water} T_{moist}} \tag{G4}$$

where the subscript "moist" refers to the humid air, "dry" refers to the air molecules in the parcel, and "water" refers to the water vapor molecules in the parcel. Note that both the dry air and water vapor are expressed at the "moist" (humid) temperature. This is because both gases are at the same temperature as the moist air. The virtual temperature will be the temperature that will calculate the proper density of the moist air while using the specific gas constant (R) for air instead of whatever specific gas constant would be appropriate for that particular mixture of air and water, which would change based on the humidity.

To begin our derivation, we factor out the moist temperature

$$\frac{P_{moist}}{R_{air} T_{virtual}} = \left(\frac{P_{dry}}{R_{air}} + \frac{P_{water}}{R_{water}} \right) \frac{1}{T_{moist}} \tag{G5}$$

and move the moist temperature to the other side

$$\frac{T_{moist}}{T_{virtual}}\frac{P_{moist}}{R_{air}} = \frac{P_{dry}}{R_{air}} + \frac{P_{water}}{R_{water}} \tag{G6}$$

Dividing through

$$\frac{T_{moist}}{T_{virtual}} = \left(\frac{P_{dry}}{R_{air}} + \frac{P_{water}}{R_{water}}\right)\frac{R_{air}}{P_{moist}} \tag{G7}$$

Combining terms on the right hand side

$$\frac{T_{moist}}{T_{virtual}} = \frac{P_{dry}}{R_{air}}\frac{R_{air}}{P_{moist}} + \frac{P_{water}}{R_{water}}\frac{R_{air}}{P_{moist}} \tag{G8}$$

Rearranging

$$\frac{T_{moist}}{T_{virtual}} = \frac{P_{dry}}{P_{moist}} + \frac{R_{air}}{R_{water}}\frac{P_{water}}{P_{moist}} \tag{G9}$$

Add and subtract P_{water}

$$\frac{T_{moist}}{T_{virtual}} = \frac{\left(P_{dry} + P_{water}\right) - P_{water}}{P_{moist}} + \frac{R_{air}}{R_{water}}\frac{P_{water}}{P_{moist}} \tag{G10}$$

Substitute Equation G2

$$\frac{T_{moist}}{T_{virtual}} = \frac{P_{moist} - P_{water}}{P_{moist}} + \frac{R_{air}}{R_{water}}\frac{P_{water}}{P_{moist}} \tag{G11}$$

Rearranging

$$\frac{T_{moist}}{T_{virtual}} = 1 - \frac{P_{water}}{P_{moist}} + \frac{R_{air}}{R_{water}}\frac{P_{water}}{P_{moist}} \tag{G12}$$

Factoring

$$\frac{T_{moist}}{T_{virtual}} = 1 - \left(1 - \frac{R_{air}}{R_{water}}\right)\frac{P_{water}}{P_{moist}} \tag{G13}$$

Solving for $T_{virtual}$

$$T_{virtual} = \frac{T_{moist}}{1 - \left(1 - \dfrac{R_{air}}{R_{water}}\right)\dfrac{P_{water}}{P_{moist}}} \tag{G14}$$

Substituting for R_{air} = 1716 ft-lb/slug-°R and R_{water} = 2762 ft-lb/slug-°R

$$T_{virtual} = \frac{T_{moist}}{1 - 0.379\dfrac{P_{water}}{P_{moist}}} \tag{G15}$$

which matches the equation provided by Phil Harvey.

To calculate the virtual temperature, T_{moist} is the measured temperature of the air. P_{moist} would be the measured pressure of the air, except that we're trying to calculate the pressure of the air. We'll come back to that in a minute.

First, we need to get a value for the vapor pressure of the water vapor (P_{water}). Table A1 lists the saturation pressure of water against the saturation temperature. Tables work fine if you are calculating by hand, but if you are trying to set up a computer routine an equation is much more convenient. According to Phil Harvey, there are many such equations available, all of which are very close. Generally the most popular is Tetens' expression

$$P_{water} = 6.11*10^{\left(\frac{7.5T}{237.3+T}\right)} \qquad T(°C) > 0 \tag{G16}$$

$$P_{water} = 6.11*10^{\left(\frac{9.5T}{265.5+T}\right)} \qquad T(°C) < 0 \tag{G17}$$

Note:
T is the Dew Point in degrees Celsius (°C)
P_{water} is in millibars (P_{SL} = 1013.25 mBar)

Tetens' expression is a curve fit to experimental data, not an expression derived from first principles. As such, it is an unusual equation in that temperature is entered in Celsius, not in an absolute unit like Kelvin or Rankine. Additionally, the output unit is millibars, which is fine in this case, because most meteorological pressure data is reported in millibars.

The final equation we need to calculate the pressures is the equation to calculate the new pressure based on the virtual temperature. The assumption we will make is that the temperature in the interval remains constant. This is quite reasonable when working with balloon data at a rate of 1Hz, which gives an interval approximately 16 feet high. Even with 100 foot data as published for balloon data this is not too rash of an assumption. We already have this equation for isothermal layers from Appendix A

$$\frac{P}{P_B} = e^{-\left(\frac{g_{SL}}{RT_B}\right)(H-H_B)} \tag{A41}$$

Expressing this equation in terms of our interval from condition 1 to 2

$$P_2 = P_1 e^{-\left(\frac{g_{SL}}{R_{air}T_{virtual}}\right)(H_2-H_1)} \tag{G18}$$

To improve our accuracy, we will use an average virtual temperature for the interval instead of the temperature at the bottom of the interval. Since we don't know the pressure at the top of the interval (that's what we're trying to calculate) we will iterate a little bit to find it.

To demonstrate the method, we will consider the following balloon data.

Bottom of Interval
Geometric Altitude (h_1)   2400 feet
Temperature (T_1)   10.1 °C
Dew Point ($T_{dp,1}$)   -6.6 °C
Pressure (P_1)   941.6313 mBar

Top of Interval
Geometric Altitude (h_2)   2500 feet
Temperature (T_2)   9.7 °C
Dew Point ($T_{dp,2}$)   -6.6 °C

First we will convert the Geometric Altitude to Geopotential Altitude.

$$H = \left(\frac{R_{eSL}}{R_{eSL} + h} \right) h \qquad (A29)$$

$$H_1 = \left(\frac{20,902,808.99 \text{ feet}}{20,902,808.99 \text{ feet} + 2400 \text{ feet}} \right) 2400$$

$$H_1 = 2399.724 \text{ feet}$$

$$H_2 = 2499.701 \text{ feet}$$

Next we find the water vapor pressure using Tetens' expression and the dew point temperatures.

$$P_{water} = 6.11 * 10^{\left(\frac{9.5T}{265.5+T} \right)} \qquad T(°C) < 0 \qquad (G17)$$

$$P_{water,1} = 6.11 * 10^{\left(\frac{9.5(-6.6)}{265.5+(-6.6)} \right)}$$

$$P_{water,1} = 3.4983 \text{ mBar}$$

$$P_{water,2} = 3.4983 \text{ mBar}$$

Calculate the virtual temperature at the bottom of the interval

$$T_{virtual} = \frac{T_{moist}}{1 - 0.379 \dfrac{P_{water}}{P_{moist}}} \qquad (G15)$$

$$T_{virtual,1} = \frac{(10.1 + 273.15)K}{1 - 0.379 \dfrac{3.4983 \text{ mBar}}{941.6313 \text{ mBar}}}$$

$$T_{virtual,1} = 283.6494 \text{ K}$$

We would do the same thing for the top of the interval, but we don't know the pressure there yet, since that's what we are trying to calculate. We'll start out assuming the virtual temperature is just equal to the measured temperature at the top of the interval.

$$T_{virtual,2} = 9.7 + 273.15$$

$$T_{virtual,2} = 282.85 \text{ K}$$

Average the virtual temperatures to get the mean virtual temperature

$$T_{mean \ virtual} = \frac{283.6494 \text{ K} + 282.85 \text{K}}{2}$$

$$T_{mean \ virtual} = 283.2497 \text{ K}$$

Before we calculate the new pressure at the top of the interval, we need a value for the acceleration of gravity (g_{SL}). Usually a nominal value of 32.2 ft/sec^2 is sufficient, but the rounding errors caused by insufficient significant digits can add up after hundreds of iterations. The acceleration of gravity is not constant everywhere, and varies with position. An approximation of the local acceleration of gravity based on latitude is given by

$$g_{SL} = \frac{980.665\left(1 - 2.6373 \times 10^{-3} \cos(2 * \text{Latitude}) + 5.9 \times 10^{-6} \cos^2(2 * \text{Latitude})\right)}{100} \quad \text{(G19)}$$

For Edwards AFB, the latitude is 34° 54.4853' or 34.908088 degrees. Inserting this value in Equation G19 gives

$$g_{SL} = 9.797733 \ \frac{m}{sec^2}$$

$$g_{SL} = 32.1448 \ \frac{ft}{sec^2}$$

which is notably different from 32.2 ft/sec^2.

Using the preliminary estimate of the virtual temperature, we calculate our first estimate of pressure at the top of the interval.

$$P_2 = P_1 e^{-\left(\frac{g_{SL}}{R_{air} T_{virtual}}\right)(H_2 - H_1)} \quad \text{(G18)}$$

$$P_2 = (941.6313 \ mBar) e^{-\left(\frac{32.1448 \ ft/sec^2}{\left(3089.8 \ ft^2/\left(sec^2 \ K\right)\right)(283.2497 K)}\right)(2499.701 \ feet - 2399.724 \ feet)}$$

$$P_2 = 938.1799 \ mBar$$

Now that we have an estimate of the pressure at the top of the interval, we can calculate the virtual temperature at the top of the interval

$$T_{virtual} = \frac{T_{moist}}{1 - 0.379 \frac{P_{water}}{P_{moist}}} \tag{G15}$$

$$T_{virtual,2} = \frac{(9.7 + 273.15)K}{1 - 0.379 \frac{3.4983 \text{ mBar}}{938.1799 \text{ mBar}}}$$

$$T_{virtual,2} = 283.2503 \text{ K}$$

Calculating a new mean virtual temperature

$$T_{mean\ virtual} = \frac{283.6494\,K + 283.2503\,K}{2}$$

$$T_{mean\ virtual} = 283.4498 \text{ K}$$

With the new mean virtual temperature, we calculate the pressure at the top of the interval

$$P_2 = P_1 e^{-\left(\frac{g_{SL}}{R_{air}T_{virtual}}\right)(H_2 - H_1)} \tag{G18}$$

$$P_2 = (941.6313 \text{ mBar})e^{-\left(\frac{32.1448 \text{ ft}/\sec^2}{\left(3089.8 \text{ ft}^2/\left(\sec^2 K\right)\right)(283.4498K)}\right)(2499.701 \text{ feet} - 2399.724 \text{ feet})}$$

$$P_2 = 938.1823 \text{ mBar}$$

We could continue the iteration, but since the only change was in the thousandth of a millibar, this is probably far enough.

To find the pressure altitude, we first find the pressure ratio

$$\delta = \frac{P}{P_{SL}} \tag{A70}$$

$$\delta = \frac{938.1823 \text{ mBar}}{1013.25 \text{ mBar}}$$

$$\delta = 0.92591$$

and then calculate pressure altitude

$$H_c = \frac{1 - \sqrt[5.2559]{\delta}}{6.87559 \times 10^{-6}} \qquad (H_c \leq 36089.24 \text{ feet}) \quad (B3)$$

$$H_c = \frac{1 - \sqrt[5.2559]{0.92591}}{6.87559 \times 10^{-6}}$$

$$H_c = 2114.514 \text{ feet}$$

Error Analysis

So just how good are these calculations? The algorithm above was used to calculate pressures for weather balloon data over Edwards AFB, using the geometric altitude (100 foot increments), temperature, and dew point. These pressures were compared to the published pressures from the weather balloon data.

Figure G2 shows the error between the calculated pressure interval and the "truth" pressure interval from the weather balloon data for each altitude increment. The average value of the error shown in Figure G2 is -0.00148 feet.

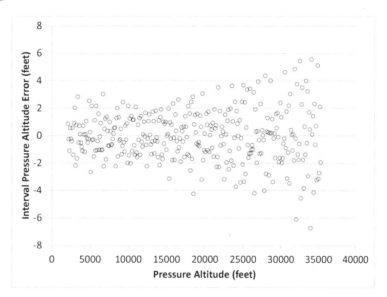

Figure G2. Interval Pressure Altitude Error

Figure G3 shows the cumulative error of the calculated Pressure Altitude compared to the "truth" pressure altitude from the weather balloon data. The cumulative error remains less than seven feet even after integrating over 34,000 feet. This is quite sufficient, since the rms altitude accuracy of the geometric altitudes from the weather balloon is approximately 5 meters, or about 16 feet.

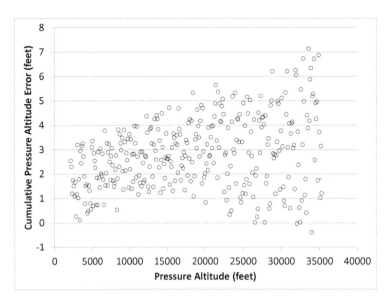

Figure G3. Cumulative Pressure Altitude Error

Appendix H

Turn Regression Heavy Math Section

Note: This appendix is essentially lifted directly from Reference 21.

Regression of Turn Data

This data reduction is motivated by Al Lawless' "Orbis Matching" technique (Reference 20) and Wayne Olson's Cloverleaf data reduction (Reference 35 and 36). By adding a single measurement, these previous iterative solutions can be replaced with a single least squares regression. Olson's method required iterations, whereas this Turn Regression technique converges in a single step; furthermore, the noise in the data is captured via confidence intervals about the solution coefficients. The Orbis and Cloverleaf techniques both solved for components of wind and determined the total velocity error; that is precisely what the Turn Regression technique provides.

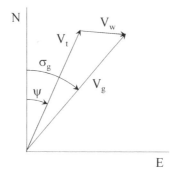

Figure H1. Velocity Vectors and Angles

The velocity vectors and angles are depicted in Figure H1. It can be seen that:

$$\vec{V}_g = \vec{V}_t + \vec{V}_w \tag{H1}$$

Heading angle, ψ, is referenced from North to the true velocity vector, $\vec{V}_t$. The track angle, σ_g, is associated with ground speed, $\vec{V}_g$, also measured from North. The vector $\vec{V}_w$ is in the direction the wind is blowing "to". Both are positive in the clockwise direction. Heading angle, ψ, is the new measurement which makes the regression possible. By separating the vectors into North, n, and East, e, components the summation creates a set of linear equations. Every data point creates two equations, one for North and one for East. All the data points create multiple equations with unknown coefficients. These coefficients are solved via least squares, or regression.

The first step is to separate the vectors into North and East components:

$$V_{g_n} = V_{t_n} + V_{w_n}$$
$$V_{g_e} = V_{t_e} + V_{w_e} \tag{H2}$$

Ground speed is measured from GPS data. The wind speed components, V_{w_n} and V_{w_e}, are unknowns. True velocity is a Pitot-static measurement, V_{t_i}, but it has an unknown correction, ΔV_t; these sum to give the truth value, V_{t_c}:

$$V_{t_c} = V_{t_i} + \Delta V_t \tag{H3}$$

Thus the components of true velocity are:

$$V_{t_n} = V_{t_c} \cos\psi = V_{t_i} \cos\psi + \Delta V_t \cos\psi \tag{H4}$$
$$V_{t_e} = V_{t_c} \sin\psi = V_{t_i} \sin\psi + \Delta V_t \sin\psi$$

Similarly, the magnitude of ground speed is V_g and the components are:

$$V_{g_n} = V_g \cos\sigma_g \tag{H5}$$
$$V_{g_e} = V_g \sin\sigma_g$$

Combining Equations H2, H4, and H5 produces:

$$V_{t_i} \cos\psi + \Delta V_t \cos\psi + V_{w_n} = V_g \cos\sigma_g \tag{H6}$$
$$V_{t_i} \sin\psi + \Delta V_t \sin\psi + V_{w_e} = V_g \sin\sigma_g$$

Next, put the unknowns V_{w_n}, V_{w_e}, and ΔV_t on the left and the measured values on the right:

$$V_{w_n} + \Delta V_t \cos\psi = V_g \cos\sigma_g - V_{t_i} \cos\psi \tag{H7}$$
$$V_{w_e} + \Delta V_t \sin\psi = V_g \sin\sigma_g - V_{t_i} \sin\psi$$

Now, the unknowns are all linear terms so Equation H7 can be rewritten in matrix form:

$$\begin{bmatrix} 1 & 0 & \cos\psi \\ 0 & 1 & \sin\psi \end{bmatrix} \begin{bmatrix} V_{w_n} \\ V_{w_e} \\ \Delta V_t \end{bmatrix} = \begin{bmatrix} V_g \cos\sigma_g - V_{t_i} \cos\psi \\ V_g \sin\sigma_g - V_{t_i} \sin\psi \end{bmatrix} \tag{H8}$$

This has the form $[A][b] = [c]$, but Equation H8 is for a single measurement. Recall a single measurement provides two components (namely North and East). During a turn multiple measurements will be recorded. If there are n independent measurements, then the [A] matrix will be size [2n x 3] and [c] will be size [2n x 1]. Thus, Equation H9 depicts the full regression matrix:

$$\begin{bmatrix} 1 & 0 & \cos\psi_1 \\ 0 & 1 & \sin\psi_1 \\ 1 & 0 & \cos\psi_2 \\ 0 & 1 & \sin\psi_2 \\ \vdots & \vdots & \vdots \\ 1 & 0 & \cos\psi_n \\ 0 & 1 & \sin\psi_n \end{bmatrix} \begin{bmatrix} V_{w_n} \\ V_{w_e} \\ \Delta V_t \end{bmatrix} = \begin{bmatrix} V_{g_1} \cos\sigma_{g_1} - V_{t_{i_1}} \cos\psi_1 \\ V_{g_1} \sin\sigma_{g_1} - V_{t_{i_1}} \sin\psi_1 \\ V_{g_2} \cos\sigma_{g_2} - V_{t_{i_2}} \cos\psi_2 \\ V_{g_2} \sin\sigma_{g_2} - V_{t_{i_2}} \sin\psi_2 \\ \vdots \\ V_{g_n} \cos\sigma_{g_n} - V_{t_{i_n}} \cos\psi_n \\ V_{g_n} \sin\sigma_{g_n} - V_{t_{i_n}} \sin\psi_n \end{bmatrix} \tag{H9}$$

Or, to be more compatible with a vector operation, in Excel or Matlab, Equation H9 can be written as:

$$
\begin{bmatrix}
1 & 0 & \cos\psi_1 \\
1 & 0 & \cos\psi_2 \\
\vdots & \vdots & \vdots \\
1 & 0 & \cos\psi_n \\
0 & 1 & \sin\psi_1 \\
0 & 1 & \sin\psi_2 \\
\vdots & \vdots & \vdots \\
0 & 1 & \sin\psi_n
\end{bmatrix}
\begin{bmatrix}
V_{w_n} \\
V_{w_e} \\
\Delta V_t
\end{bmatrix}
=
\begin{bmatrix}
V_{g_1}\cos\sigma_{g_1} - V_{t_{i_1}}\cos\psi_1 \\
V_{g_2}\cos\sigma_{g_2} - V_{t_{i_2}}\cos\psi_2 \\
\vdots \\
V_{g_n}\cos\sigma_{g_n} - V_{t_{i_n}}\cos\psi_n \\
V_{g_1}\sin\sigma_{g_1} - V_{t_{i_1}}\sin\psi_1 \\
V_{g_2}\sin\sigma_{g_2} - V_{t_{i_2}}\sin\psi_2 \\
\vdots \\
V_{g_n}\sin\sigma_{g_n} - V_{t_{i_n}}\sin\psi_n
\end{bmatrix}
\tag{H10}
$$

Which simply equals a vector version of the original Equation H8, where $\bar{1}$ and $\bar{0}$ are vectors size [n x 1].

$$
\begin{bmatrix}
\bar{1} & \bar{0} & \cos\bar{\psi} \\
\bar{0} & \bar{1} & \sin\bar{\psi}
\end{bmatrix}
\begin{bmatrix}
V_{w_n} \\
V_{w_e} \\
\Delta V_t
\end{bmatrix}
=
\begin{bmatrix}
\bar{V}_g\cos\bar{\sigma}_g - \bar{V}_{t_i}\cos\bar{\psi} \\
\bar{V}_g\sin\bar{\sigma}_g - \bar{V}_{t_i}\sin\bar{\psi}
\end{bmatrix}
\tag{H11}
$$

Notice that the coefficients in [b] are still scalars, so the full equation is still [c] = [A][b]. The solution for [b] is not unique, so the goal is to find [b] to minimize the error [c] - [A][b], which would be zero for a perfect solution. Taking the square of the error turns this into a least squares error solution, which can be solved by minimizing the cost in Equation H12 using calculus of variations.

$$
[J] = ([c] - [A][b])^T([c] - [A][b])
\tag{H12}
$$

Equation H12 can be expanded to:

$$
[J] = ([c]^T - [b]^T[A]^T)([c] - [A][b])
$$

$$
[J] = [c]^T[c] - [b]^T[A]^T[c] - [c]^T[A][b] + [b]^T[A]^T[A][b])
\tag{H13}
$$

Thus, take the partial derivative of [J] with respect to [b] and set it equal to zero to find the local extremum, e.g. minimum:

$$
\frac{\partial[J]}{\partial[b]} = 0 - [c]^T[A] - [c]^T[A] + 2[b]^T[A]^T[A]
$$

$$
\frac{\partial[J]}{\partial[b]} = -2[c]^T[A] + 2[b]^T[A]^T[A] = [\bar{0}]
\tag{H14}
$$

thus

$$
[b]^T[A]^T[A] = [c]^T[A]
$$

taking the transpose of both sides gives:

$$
[A]^T[A][b] = [A]^T[c]
$$

Then pre-multiply both sides by the inverse of $[A]^T[A]$ gives the solution to $[b]$ as:

$$[b] = ([A]^T[A])^{-1}[A]^T[c] \qquad\qquad (H15)$$

The term $([A]^T[A])^{-1}[A]^T$ is also called the "pseudoinverse" of $[A]$, and is efficiently computed in Matlab using `pinv`. The confidence intervals of the coefficients can be obtained using Matlab's `regress`, or Excel regression in the Data Analysis Add-in. The vector $[b]$ contains the desired unknowns V_{w_n}, V_{w_e}, and ΔV_t. Use measured V_{t_i}, computed ΔV_t, and Equation H3 to get V_{t_c}. Temperature is required to compute the speed of sound to convert this corrected true airspeed to Mach Number. The static pressure error ΔP_p can then be computed from this computed truth source for Mach number and the measured Mach number. Hence, this is a velocity technique for computing static pressure error ΔP_p, which is reliant on the regression described above and a temperature measurement.

Modifications for Higher Load Factors

One hidden assumption in the original data reduction is that the measured heading is equal to the direction of the component of velocity in the North-East (horizontal) plane. For aircraft operating at cruise speeds and bank angles less than 30 degrees (load factors less than 1.15g), the angle of attack is sufficiently close to zero that this assumption is valid. Reference 22 showed that because heading is measured in the body axes and velocity is measured in the stability axes (assuming no sideslip), a significant difference arises between these vectors as the angle of attack becomes significantly non-zero.

Figure H2 shows an aircraft flying at a 10 degree angle of attack. The heading is measured along the attitude vector, in this example measured by an inertial navigation system (INS), aligned with the body axes. The true airspeed vector acts along the velocity vector, aligned with the stability axes.

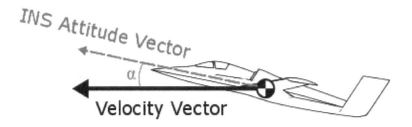

Figure H2. Heading (from Attitude Vector) in body axes, Velocity in stability axes (Ref 22)

If the aircraft is flying straight and level, as shown on the left half of Figure H3, then the velocity vector and heading are co-aligned when viewed from the North-East (or Earth horizontal) plane.

If the aircraft enters a right-hand turn at 60° bank, as shown on the right half of Figure H3, the direction of the true airspeed velocity vector would be 8.7° behind the yaw angle measured by the aircraft. This is enough to significantly affect the solution.

Aft View

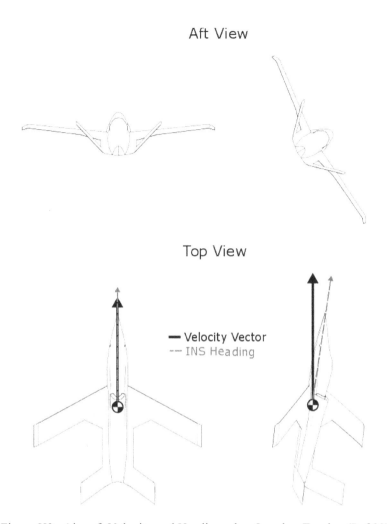

Top View

Figure H3. Aircraft Velocity and Heading when Level or Turning (Ref 22)

To determine the North-East plane direction of the velocity vector for comparison to the GPS track vector, the attitude vector (heading) must be rotated into the North-East plane. Because a level turn is assumed, the velocity vector will be in the North-East plane. Rather than do a three-dimensional coordinate transformation, the necessary transformation can be simplified to

$$\psi_{V_t} = \psi - \alpha \sin \phi \tag{H16}$$

where

ψ Heading
α Angle of Attack
ϕ Bank Angle

To account for significant angle of attack and bank angle, substitute Ψ_{V_t} from Equation H16 for Ψ in Equation H8, as shown in Equation H17.

$$\begin{bmatrix} 1 & 0 & \cos \psi_{V_t} \\ 0 & 1 & \sin \psi_{V_t} \end{bmatrix} \begin{bmatrix} V_{w_n} \\ V_{w_e} \\ \Delta V_t \end{bmatrix} = \begin{bmatrix} V_g \cos \sigma_g - V_{t_i} \cos \psi_{V_t} \\ V_g \sin \sigma_g - V_{t_i} \sin \psi_{V_t} \end{bmatrix} \tag{H17}$$

Appendix I

Soaring Weather and Air Data

Dry Adiabatic Lapse Rate

Sustained soaring flight depends on the vertical movement of air in the atmosphere, and vertical movement of air depends on the stability of the air. Stability of the atmosphere depends on buoyancy, and buoyancy depends on density. If the less dense air lies under the more dense air, buoyancy forces will force the less dense air to rise.

However, atmospheric stability is not as simple as "put the less dense air on top of the more dense air" since air density depends on pressure and temperature (Equation A3). As we showed in Chapter 2, pressure and temperature change with altitude. In the Standard Atmosphere the pressure and temperature change with altitude in a very specific way which is naturally stable. Not so much in the real world, where solar heating and other forces conspire to make the atmosphere locally unstable.

Imagine a parcel or "bubble" of air which for some reason starts to move upward. As this parcel rises, the pressure of the air surrounding the parcel decreases with altitude. The mass of air in the parcel is a constant, so to match the surrounding pressure the parcel must expand. Your buddy the Thermodynamicist reminds you that when a fixed mass of gas expands at a particular pressure, represented by Pdv, the result is known as "boundary work" (Ref 27). After all, it takes work to compress air in a bicycle pump, and that same air can do work on its environment if allowed to expand. So if our parcel of air expands, and thus is doing work on its environment, the act of doing work requires that energy is coming from somewhere. The only source of energy that the air parcel has available comes from its internal energy. Removing internal energy to do the work of expansion results in the temperature of the air parcel decreasing. What is of interest to us is the rate that temperature decreases as the parcel climbs in altitude.

Since we're talking about an exchange of energy, let's start back at the First Law of Thermodynamics for a control mass (Ref 27).

$$W_{in} + Q_{in} + m(u + ke + pe)_{in} = W_{out} + Q_{out} + m(u + ke + pe)_{out} \qquad (I1)$$

where

W_{in} , W_{out}	Work Interaction
Q_{in} , Q_{out}	Heat Interaction
m	Mass
u	Specific Internal Energy
ke	Specific Kinetic Energy
pe	Specific Potential Energy

ASSUME: The air parcel has no heat interactions with the surrounding air, which results in an adiabatic process ($Q_{in} = Q_{out}$). For a differential change in height (altitude), assume the motion (momentum) of the air is small, so that the change in kinetic energy is small compared to the other energy exchanges ($ke_{in} \approx ke_{out}$). Assume the mass of the air is small and the change in height is small such that the change in potential energy is small compared to the other energy changes ($pe_{in} \approx pe_{out}$). Any work interaction will be boundary work (no shaft work is involved).

After applying these assumptions and rearranging slightly, we get

$$-(W_{out} - W_{in}) = m(u_{out} - u_{in}) \qquad (I2)$$

Dividing by mass to deal with specific work (w)

$$-(w_{out} - w_{in}) = (u_{out} - u_{in}) \qquad (I3)$$

Changing to differential notation for differential changes

$$-dw = du \qquad (I4)$$

For an ideal gas, Reference 27 tells us that the specific internal energy can be represented as

$$u = C_v T \qquad (C9)$$

where C_v is the Coefficient of Specific Heat at Constant Volume.

As mentioned above, the only work interaction (dw) involved with this system is boundary work, expressed as Pdv. Also substituting the differential form of Equation C9 into Equation I4, we get

$$-Pdv = C_v dT \qquad (I5)$$

To differentiate the pressure-volume product, we apply the product rule

$$d(Pv) = Pdv + vdP \qquad (I6)$$

Rearranging to get an expression for Pdv

$$-Pdv = vdP - d(Pv) \qquad (I7)$$

Substituting Equation I7 into Equation I5

$$vdP - d(Pv) = C_v dT \qquad (I8)$$

The specific volume is merely the inverse of the density, or

$$v = \frac{1}{\rho} \qquad (C5)$$

and from the Equation of State

$$Pv = RT \qquad (C7)$$

Substituting Equations C5 and C7 into Equation I8

$$\frac{dP}{\rho} - d(RT) = C_v dT \qquad (I9)$$

and since R is a defined constant

$$\frac{dP}{\rho} - RdT = C_v dT \qquad (I10)$$

Combining the differential temperatures on the same side

$$\frac{dP}{\rho} = \left(C_v + R\right)dT \tag{I11}$$

and since we know for a perfect gas

$$C_p = C_v + R \tag{C11}$$

Substituting Equation C11 into Equation I11

$$\frac{dP}{\rho} = C_p dT \tag{I12}$$

Recalling the form of the Hydrostatic Equation in terms of Geopotential Altitude

$$dP = -\rho \, g_{SL} \, dH \tag{A30}$$

and rearranging

$$\frac{dP}{\rho} = -g_{SL} dH \tag{I13}$$

Substituting Equation I13 into I12

$$-g_{SL} dH = C_p dT \tag{I14}$$

Getting the differentials together

$$\frac{dT}{dH} = \frac{-g_{SL}}{C_p} \tag{I15}$$

which gives the Dry Adiabatic Lapse Rate (DALR). Lapse rate because it gives the variation of temperature with altitude for a parcel of air undergoing adiabatic expansion. Dry because we use the value of C_p for dry air.

Inserting values of

$$g_{SL} = 32.1741 \text{ ft/sec}^2 \qquad\qquad \text{(Table 1, Chapter 2)}$$

$$C_p = 1005 \frac{m^2}{sec^2 K} = 3796 \frac{knots^2}{K} = 5027 \frac{mph^2}{K} = 10814 \frac{ft^2}{sec^2 K} = 0.24 \frac{BTU}{lbm\,°R} = 186.72 \frac{ft\,lbf}{lbm\,°R}$$

we find

$$DALR = \frac{-32.1741 \frac{ft}{sec^2}}{10814 \frac{ft^2}{sec^2\,K}}$$

$$DALR = -0.00297523 \text{ K/ft} \qquad (I16)$$

which rounding to a reasonable number gives the frequently quoted -3 °C/1000 feet.

It turns out that treating the air as dry works well enough even if the air has some humidity, as long as the air parcel is not saturated (less than 100 per cent relative humidity). The mass of the water vapor is very small compared to the mass of the air. At 100 per cent humidity and 80 °F, the mass of the water vapor is only about 3 per cent the mass of the air, and even less with lower humidity. While the specific heat at constant pressure (C_p) of water differs from the C_p of air, the slight difference for such a small percentage of the total gas has such a small effect that we choose to ignore it at the level of accuracy that we need. However, when the humidity reaches 100 per cent and the water vapor starts to condense, the energy released from the latent heat of vaporization becomes very significant, but that will be covered later when we talk about moist adiabatic expansion.

Dry Adiabatic Expansion

To further investigate this idea of adiabatic expansion, let us consider the relationship for pressure change with height in regions with a linear temperature lapse rate

$$\frac{P}{P_B} = \left(\frac{T}{T_B} \right)^{\frac{-g_{SL}}{RL}} \qquad (A62)$$

To generalize the equation between any two points in the region, label the base (B) as point (1) and the point of interest as point (2).

$$\frac{P_2}{P_1} = \left(\frac{T_2}{T_1} \right)^{\frac{-g_{SL}}{RL}} \qquad (I17)$$

If we set the lapse rate (L) to the Dry Adiabatic Lapse Rate

$$L = \frac{dT}{dH} = \frac{-g_{SL}}{C_p} \qquad (I18)$$

Then the exponent of Equation I17 becomes

$$\frac{-g_{SL}}{RL} = \frac{-g_{SL}}{R} \frac{C_p}{-g_{SL}} = \frac{C_p}{R} \qquad (I19)$$

Substituting Equation I19 into I17

$$\frac{P_2}{P_1} = \left(\frac{T_2}{T_1}\right)^{\frac{C_p}{R}} \qquad\qquad (I20)$$

From Appendix C

$$\frac{\gamma - 1}{\gamma} = \frac{R}{C_p} \qquad\qquad (C17)$$

Inverting Equation C17 and substituting into Equation I20 gives

$$\frac{P_2}{P_1} = \left(\frac{T_2}{T_1}\right)^{\frac{\gamma}{\gamma-1}} \qquad\qquad (C35)$$

which was previously introduced as an isentropic relationship. Indeed, if we also assume that the adiabatic expansion of an air parcel is a reversible process, then the expansion would also be isentropic. Equation C35 is used for many isentropic processes, such as flow through an ideal turbine. Knowing the pressure and temperature at the entrance to the turbine and the pressure at the exit of the turbine, Equation C35 can be used to calculate the exit temperature of the turbine. Likewise, if the pressure and temperature of an air parcel is known at the initial altitude, and the pressure is known at the altitude to which the parcel is lifted, then Equation C35 can be used to find the temperature at the final altitude. The Dry Adiabatic Lapse Rate can tell the final temperature based on a change in altitude. Equation C35 can tell the final temperature based on a change of pressure.

Atmospheric Stability

To investigate atmospheric stability, we will first use a simple diagram of pressure altitude plotted against temperature, as shown in Figure I1. For reference, on this plot we will draw several lines with a slope of the Dry Adiabatic Lapse Rate (Equation I16), approximately -3 °C/1000 feet. Referred to as "Dry Adiabats", these lines show the path taken by a rising parcel of air as it cools by adiabatic expansion.

We have seen that an unsaturated (humidity less than 100 per cent) air parcel that is somehow lifted will undergo adiabatic expansion. If the surrounding atmosphere has an actual temperature lapse rate equal to the Dry Adiabatic Lapse Rate (represented in Figure I1 by the thick solid red line), then the air parcel will always be in thermodynamic equilibrium with the surrounding air. Having the same density as the surrounding air, no buoyant forces exist on the air parcel, and thus it will have no tendency to further rise or sink (Figure I1 dashed arrow). This atmosphere is said to have neutral stability.

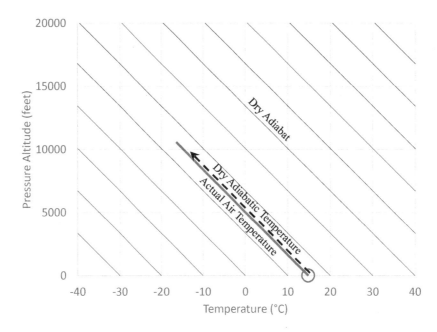

Figure I1. Neutral Atmospheric Stability

Figure I2 shows the normal lapse rate (thick solid red line) of the Standard Atmosphere in the troposphere (2 °C/1000 feet). Because the air temperature does not decrease as fast as the Dry Adiabatic Lapse Rate with increasing altitude, it is considered stable. An air parcel lifted from Sea Level (dashed arrow) will always be colder than the surrounding air as it expands adiabatically. Because the air parcel is colder and at the same pressure, its density is higher than the surrounding air and buoyant forces will push it back down. Hence, the air is content to stay where it is, and is thus considered stable. It is nice that, on "average", the atmosphere is stable. If it wasn't, it would be constantly churning up and down. There would always be turbulence, and the idea of a "smooth flight" would be unknown. While glider pilots might like that, the rest of the population would complain that "we never get to have a nice day".

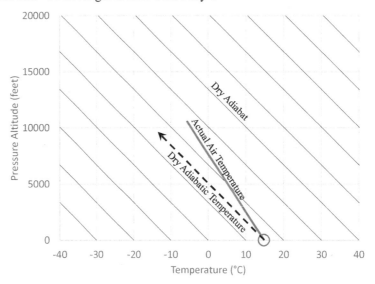

Figure I2. Standard Atmosphere (Stable)

An even more stable atmosphere can be created by a temperature inversion, as shown in Figure I3. A temperature inversion exists when the temperature on the ground is cooler than the air immediately above it. Like the case shown in Figure I2, any air parcel lifted from the ground (assumed to be a Sea Level in this example) will always be colder than the air surrounding it. Again, this means that the air parcel has a higher density than the surrounding air, and buoyant forces will push the air parcel back down from whence it came.

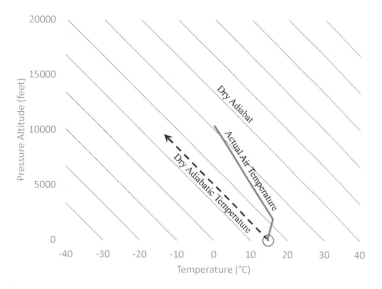

Figure I3. Temperature Inversion (Stable)

Temperature inversions are so stable that they tend to trap suspended particulates in the air, such as dust. An inversion can usually be visually identified by a layer of hazy air next to the surface which abruptly stops at the top of the inversion. The air is so stable that it is quiescent (calm winds), so there is little to no motion to disperse the suspended particulates.

So how does a temperature inversion form? A common method is through radiation. After the sun sets, the ground no longer receives solar radiation to warm it up, so it starts to cool down. The primary method the ground releases energy to cool is through emitted infrared radiation. Under cloudy or overcast skies, this infrared radiation reflects off of the clouds and right back to the ground, so little cooling takes place. If the sky is clear, the infrared radiation continues out into space and the ground cools as energy is released. If the wind is calm, then the air next to the ground will cool by contact with the colder ground. Since air insulates reasonably well, this cooling will only reach a few thousand feet or less into the atmosphere. The air next to the ground cools, but the air above remains unchanged, resulting in warmer air above colder air. Wind interferes with this cooling, as it sweeps away the air next to the cold ground and replaces it with other air before the air has a chance to cool significantly.

Figure I4 shows an unstable temperature profile. In this case, air temperature decreases faster with increasing altitude than the Dry Adiabatic Lapse Rate. Depending on how the air cooled to this condition, it might still not be moving vertically. Once a parcel of air, say at Sea Level for this example, is disturbed and started upward, it will remain warmer than the surrounding air even as it cools through adiabatic expansion. As shown in Figure I4, this parcel could continue rising as high as 12,000 feet. Because the air once started in motion will continue in motion, this air is considered unstable.

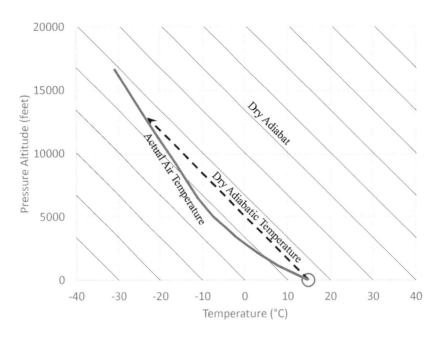

Figure I4. Unstable Temperature Profile

Frost Formation

A special form of temperature inversion leads to frost formation. The dew point is the temperature that a parcel of humid air would have to be cooled to (at constant pressure) for the water vapor in it to start condensing. That is, the temperature at which the relative humidity would be 100 percent. The frost point is similar, except that it is the temperature at which the water vapor will deposit on a surface as ice without going through the liquid phase. Of course, the frost point is only defined for sub-freezing temperatures, and is equal to the dew point when temperature is 0 °C. At colder temperatures, the frost point is always slightly warmer (less negative) than the dew point, such that frost will always form first as the air cools. This avoids violations of the Second Law of Thermodynamics, as it would be embarrassing to find liquid water on a sub-freezing surface in sub-freezing air. However, this process does have significant hysteresis. If the frost point is -5 °C, frost will not form until the surface and air have cooled to -5 °C or below. Once formed, that frost will remain until the surface and air warm above 0 °C.

Frost can be predicted to be present when the following conditions are present:

1. Air temperature below or recently below freezing
2. Dew point spread is small (relatively high humidity)
3. Calm winds
4. Clear sky

The air parcel at ground level can be disturbed and started on its upward journey by many different mechanisms, including those as simple as wind or a cold front passage. As told in Reference 37,

> These "trigger" processes can be quite pronounced or subtle in nature. As discussed last month, terrain heating can result in the movement of air up a slope resulting in the release of rising air off or near ridges or mountains. Light winds can act as a "trigger" that encourages the release of warmed air from its surface

source area. Human activity such as vehicular movement or farming operations can trigger convection. At a soaring contest some years back, a towplane was dispatched to retrieve a sailplane that reported low in altitude over a remote airstrip. The towpilot arrived while the sailplane was still struggling to stay aloft and so he landed awaiting the sailplane's expected landing. To the towpilot's amazement the sailplane climbed away to fly home as the towplane landing triggered the last thermal of the day off the airstrip.

Solar radiation can destabilize an otherwise stable atmosphere. Figure I5 shows the same standard atmosphere that was stable in Figure I2, except later in the day after the sunshine has warmed the ground (at Sea Level in this example). The ground has in turn warmed the air immediately above it, but because air is mostly an insulator, this heating does not go very high. This sets up a very unstable gradient near the ground. As demonstrated in Figure I5, if a trigger event disturbs a parcel of air at the ground and starts it rising, that parcel will continue rising to as high as 10,000 feet.

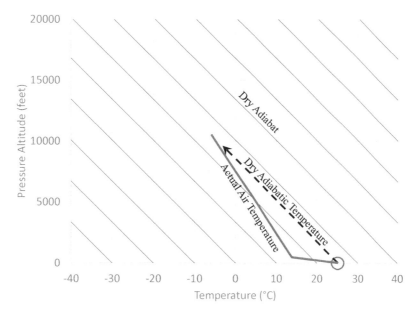

Figure I5. Standard Atmosphere With Terrestrial Heating

Figure I6 shows that the majority of the solar radiation reaches the earth in the visible wavelengths (Ref 29). Some energy does arrive in the near infrared wavelengths, but is mostly absorbed by water in the atmosphere, and the irradiance value drops off quickly with longer wavelengths. From this we can conclude that the ground will be warmed mostly by light we can see, indicating the possibility of thermals. Shadows, such as those caused by clouds obscuring the sun, indicate that thermal production is much less likely.

Strong winds also reduce thermal production as the air does not dwell long enough over the terrain to be heated. Of course, strong winds may create other forms of lift.

Spectrum of Solar Radiation (Earth)

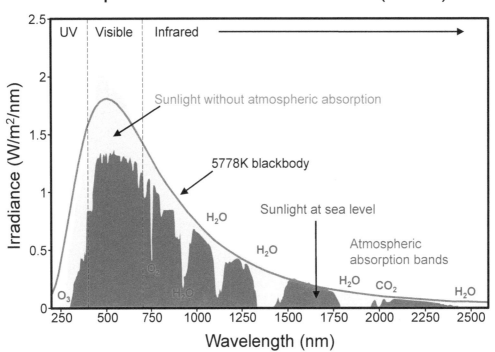

Figure I6. Spectrum of Solar Radiation (Ref 29)

Skew-T/Log-P Diagram

The presentation of temperature soundings (temperature plotted directly with altitude) as shown in Figures I1 – I5 may be intuitive, but can be improved upon to create a more information-rich depiction. Consider an actual temperature profile as shown in Figure I7. The sounding line uses a lot of the horizontal dimension showing a decrease in temperature. The angle between the lines of constant temperature (isotherms) and the dry adiabats is roughly 45 degrees (depending on the scales chosen). The angles between the sounding and the dry adiabats are small, making it difficult to determine where they actually intersect.

In 1947, N. Herlofson proposed a modification to the emagram (a log-Pressure versus temperature plot, very similar to Figures I1-I5). Instead of the isotherms being vertical, they are skewed to run at about 45 degrees from lower left to upper right, as highlighted in Figure I8. Instead of plotting altitude on the vertical axis, the air pressure is plotted on a logarithmic scale. The resulting presentation is referred to as a Skew-T/Log-P diagram. The "Skew-T" refers to the skewed isotherms, and "Log-P" refers to the presentation of pressure on the vertical scale.

This seems like a very strange way to draw a plot, so there must be a good reason for it, and indeed there is. By skewing the isotherms, the angle between the isotherms and the dry adiabats (shown highlighted in Figure I9) is opened up to an almost right angle. A further benefit is that the temperature sounding (heavy red line) is now mostly vertical instead of leaning to the left. This makes the presentation of the sounding fit better on the plot. Compare the temperature sounding shown in Figure I7 with the same temperature sounding in Figure I10.

So why Log-P for the vertical scale instead of altitude? Meteorologists created this format, so they got to say what it looked like. Meteorologists don't care so much about altitude as they do pressure, because the thermodynamic processes of weather depend much more on the local pressure of the air, and not so much on distance from the ground. However, by cleverly plotting the pressure not linearly but logarithmically, pressure altitude is presented very close to linearly on the vertical axis. Note that the vertical axis on the left side of the plot is marked as pressure in hectopascals (hPa) and the vertical axis on the right side of the plot is marked in feet of pressure altitude. Some Skew-T/Log-P presentations may use pressure units of millibars. One millibar is one hectopascal.

How does plotting pressure logarithmically produce an almost linear altitude scale? For the standard atmosphere in the troposphere, the standard temperature ratio and pressure ratio are given by

$$\theta = 1 - 6.87559 \times 10^{-6} \text{ H} \tag{A78}$$

$$\delta = (1 - 6.87559 \times 10^{-6} \text{ H})^{5.2559} \tag{A79}$$

Substituting A77 into A78 we get

$$\delta = \theta_{std}{}^{5.2559} \tag{I21}$$

Since the temperature ratio (θ) is linear with altitude, this means that the pressure ratio (δ) is an equation of the general form

$$\delta = ax^n \tag{I22}$$

which is a power law. When a power law is plotted logarithmically (logarithmic scale for input and output) the result is a line. When a power law is plotted semi-logarithmically (one linear scale and one logarithmic scale) the result is close to a line. In the case of Log-P, the pressure altitude comes out close enough to linear that it provides a visual picture that matches our idea of what altitude should look like.

For the standard atmosphere in the stratosphere, the standard pressure ratio is given by

$$\delta = 0.223360 \ e^{(-4.80637 \times 10^{-5} \ (\text{H} - 36089.24))} \tag{A87}$$

This is of the general form

$$\delta = ae^x \tag{I23}$$

which when plotted on a logarithmic scale will produce a linear pressure altitude.

Because of the skewed temperature presentation and the slight non-linearity of pressure altitude, the dry adiabats become slightly curved instead of straight as shown in Figures I1-I5.

The Skew-T/Log-P chart typically presents two soundings. The squiggly line to the right, usually shown in red, is the temperature measurement. The squiggly line to the left, usually shown in blue, is the dew point measurement, which is very useful for determining humidity and predicting cloud layers.

The Skew-T/Log-P charts shown here also present wind data on the right side. The red wind barbs show the direction and strength of the wind for each altitude (the altitude at the tip of the wind barb). A continuous blue curve next to the wind barbs shows the wind speed for each altitude.

These Skew-T/Log-P charts are readily available for you, courtesy of the United States government. Current and forecast charts are available at https://rucsoundings.noaa.gov/ for many different atmospheric models at almost any location you desire. That's a key point—the charts are not actual weather balloon data, because there are only a limited number of regular weather balloon soundings, and they are probably not at the point you are interested in. Thus, the charts are produced from model data. If you are interested in getting data from actual weather balloon soundings, those are available at http://weather.uwyo.edu/upperair/sounding.html courtesy of the University of Wyoming.

Also shown on the Skew-T/Log-P chart are the moist adiabats, highlighted in Figure I11. These differ from the dry adiabats, and show the path of adiabatic cooling for saturated air, that is air with 100 percent humidity. As we have seen earlier, a rising air parcel expands adiabatically as the pressure decreases, resulting in a temperature decrease. However, when the air parcel cools to its dew point, something else happens thermodynamically. At the dew point, the water vapor starts to condense, and in doing so releases its latent heat of vaporization. This is the energy originally used to evaporate the water (phase change from liquid to gaseous). This released energy has to go somewhere, and it goes to increasing the temperature of the air parcel. Because the temperature of the air parcel increases, its density decreases, which results in more buoyant forces pushing the air parcel upward. Because of this extra energy release, a saturated air parcel will rise a lot more than a dry (unsaturated) air parcel for the same temperature decrease. If you are thinking that this explains a lot about thunderstorm formation, you would be correct.

Inspection of the moist adiabats shows them to be quite different from the dry adiabats at warm temperatures. This difference comes from the energy release of the condensing water vapor. However, further inspection shows that below about -30 °C, the moist adiabats essentially parallel the dry adiabats. This can be explained with a look back at Table A1, which shows the saturation pressure of water as a function of temperature. Saturation pressure is directly proportional to the amount of water vapor present in saturated air. At high temperatures, air supports large amounts of water vapor, but as temperature goes down, the amount of water vapor required to reach 100 percent humidity rapidly drops off in a very non-linear fashion. Thus, at high temperatures, large amounts of energy are released from the water vapor condensation in saturated air. This explains the amount of energy present in thunderstorms, which tend to form in warm weather, not cold. Very cold saturated air has very little water vapor present in it to release energy while condensing, so the cold air ends up acting very much like dry air.

Figure I12 shows the notional path of an air parcel that reaches saturation. Initially the air parcel is unsaturated (humidity less than 100 percent), so as it rises it undergoes adiabatic expansion, cooling along the path of a dry adiabat. When the air parcel cools to the dew point, the humidity is 100 percent, and the water vapor starts to condense. The released energy heats the air, which continues to rise along the moist adiabat. While technically interesting, this is of little practical use to the soaring pilot, because once the water vapor starts condensing, clouds start to form, and inside a cloud is where few glider pilots want to be.

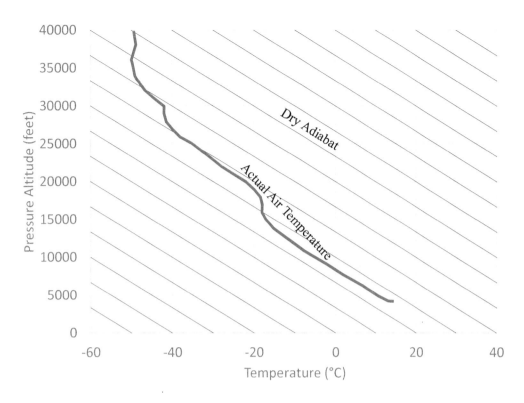

Figure I7. Temperature Profile at Mountain Valley Airport, 22 UTC, 13 March 2014

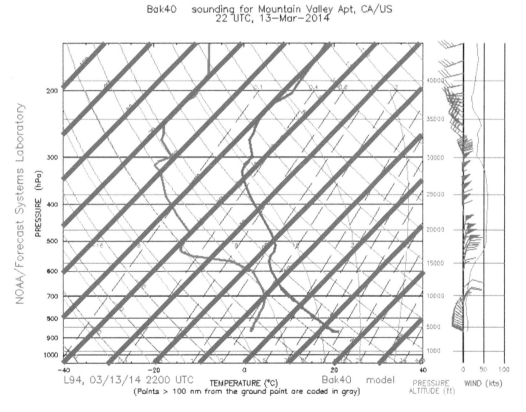

Figure I8. Skew-T/Log-P Chart With Isotherms Highlighted

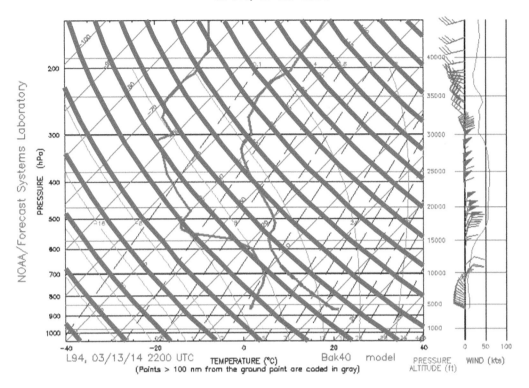

Figure I9. Skew-T/Log-P Chart With Dry Adiabats Highlighted

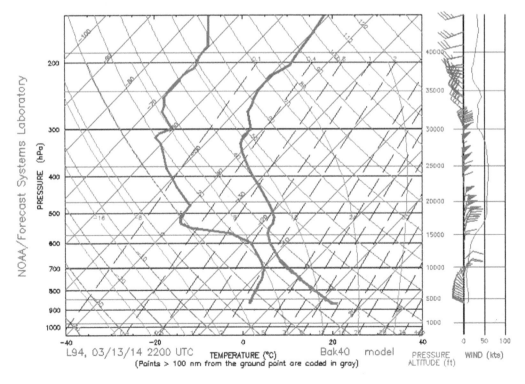

Figure I10. Skew-T/Log-P Chart for Mountain Valley Airport, 22 UTC, 13 March 2014

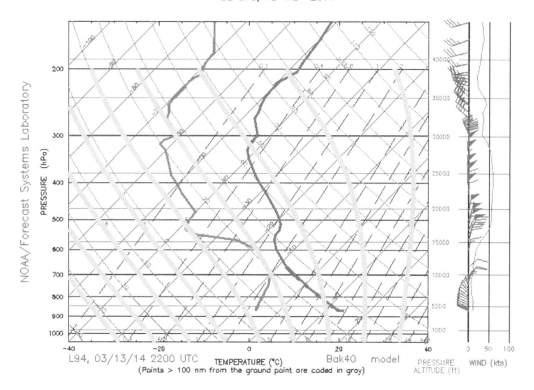

Figure I11. Skew-T/Log-P Chart With Moist Adiabats Highlighted

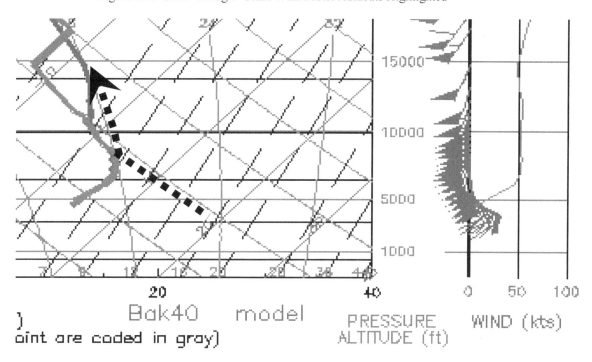

Figure I12. Path of a Rising Air Parcel That Reaches Saturation

Is It a Good Soaring Day?

Looking at the Skew-T/Log-P plots can give us insight to what sort of atmospheric stability can be expected and thus what thermal lift may be present for soaring. These example Skew-T/Log-P plots were collected over a period by Lt Col Lynn "Jinx" Gawell.

The plot shown in Figure I10 has potential for being a good soaring day. The temperature sounding below 12,000 feet pressure altitude roughly parallels the dry adiabats, indicating neutral stability. A reasonable difference between the temperature and dew point implies a sky clear of clouds. A clear sky will allow sunshine through to warm up the ground. If the ground warms up sufficiently to warm the air next to it, it will destabilize the lower atmosphere. A trigger to get the warm air parcel to start rising could easily result in that parcel continuing to rise to as high at 15,000 feet.

A typical non-aviation weather forecast will speak of clouds as clear, few, scattered, broken, or overcast, but will not specify the altitude of the base of the clouds. Looking at Figure I13, we see the dew point and temperature are equal from about 24,000 feet pressure altitude to 25,000 feet pressure altitude. When the temperature and dew point are equal, the air will be saturated and the water vapor will likely condense. Thus, in this case we would expect a high, thin layer of clouds that might block the sun from reaching the ground. Additionally the low altitudes are showing a stable slope (significantly less lapse rate than the Dry Adiabatic Lapse Rate), such that any air that was heated by the ground would probably not rise very far. Thus, few if any thermals would be expected on this day.

Figure I14 shows an even worse day. The intersection of the temperature and dew point between about 10,000 feet pressure altitude and 15,000 feet pressure altitude implies a thick band of clouds. (Theoretically the dew point can never be greater than the temperature, as this would mean a relative humidity greater than 100 percent. The portion of the dew point line to the right of the temperature line around 14,000 feet pressure altitude is an error, probably either in measurement or plotting.) Additionally, there is a strong temperature inversion near the ground, with temperature increasing about 4 °C initially, and then remaining constant for about 2,000 feet pressure altitude. The lack of sun because of the clouds, the temperature inversion, and the fairly strong low-altitude winds all point to a very low probability of thermals on this day.

In Figure I12, well, you might as well stay home. The overlapping dew point and temperature at low altitude implies fog and low clouds, so you couldn't even fly to pattern altitude. The low altitude temperature inversion is very stable and would discourage thermal production. More clouds around 17,000 feet will block even more sun. Finally, the strong winds at low altitudes will mix the air and discourage thermal production.

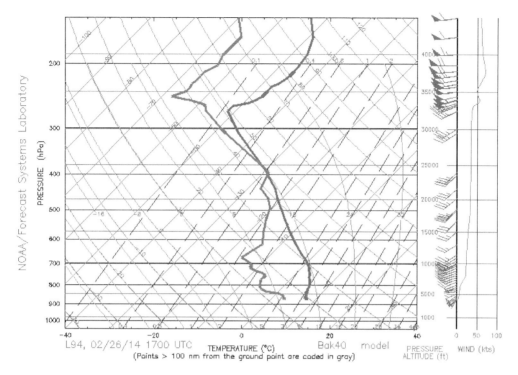

Figure I13. High Altitude Clouds

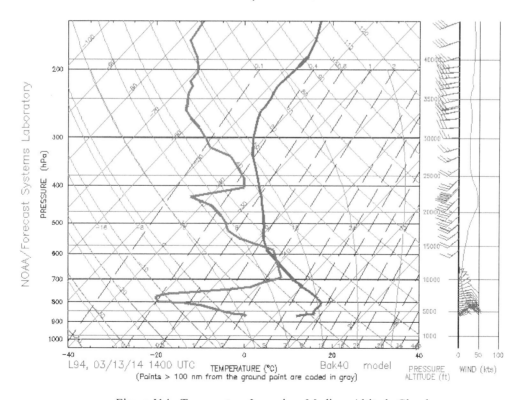

Figure I14. Temperature Inversion, Medium Altitude Clouds

Total Energy as a Guide to Atmospheric Motion

After releasing the tow rope, a glider will always descend relative to the air mass around it, overcoming aerodynamic drag by using a component of gravitational force as thrust. In a quiescent atmosphere, a glider will continue to descend until it returns to earth, where the landing gear provides the needed lift.

Glider pilots increase glider flight times by taking advantage of a non-quiescent atmosphere, exploiting the fact that air moves not only horizontally, but also vertically. By finding an air mass rising relative to the earth faster than the glider is descending relative to the air mass, the glider will actually gain altitude relative to the earth. To identify such a rising air mass, it would seem that the glider pilot would only need to note the increase of altitude on the altimeter. Better yet, the pilot can use a sensitive rate of climb instrument (usually called a variometer, see Chapter 3) to show a climb, or at least a diminished rate of descent. Some gliders are indeed set up this way, to include older trainers, such as the Schweizer SGS 2-33.

Such a system works after a fashion, but has a significant flaw. The descent or climb rate shown on the variometer accurately reflects the glider's vertical movement relative to the earth. It will show the glider descending because of normal aerodynamic drag. It will also show changes in the descent rate, or even a climb, caused by atmospheric vertical motion (lift or sink). It will also show a climb if the pilot merely pulls on the stick and climbs as airspeed decreases. Pilots frequently refer to this as "trading airspeed for altitude". Since the glider is indeed climbing relative to the earth and atmosphere, the variometer shows a climb. Glider pilots call this a "stick thermal" because the indications briefly look like you have found a thermal.

However, that's not what you as a glider pilot really want to know. You would like an instrument to show you when the air mass around the glider is rising (or falling), while ignoring any altitude changes caused by changing airspeed. Your buddy the Physics major reminds you that the interchange of altitude and airspeed can be explained as the interchange of potential and kinetic energy. Ah, yes. Energy. That always was such a useful way to explain physics.

Altitude is directly related to potential energy as

$$\text{Potential Energy} = PE = mgh \tag{I24}$$

Changing the geometric altitude (h) to geopotential altitude (H) allows us to use a constant acceleration of gravity (g_{SL})

$$PE = mg_{SL}H \tag{I25}$$

Airspeed is related to kinetic energy as

$$\text{Kinetic Energy} = KE = \frac{1}{2}mV_t^2 \tag{I26}$$

and the total energy (ignoring internal energy, which in this case will not be interacting with potential or kinetic energy) is the sum of potential energy and kinetic energy.

$$\text{Total Energy} = mg_{SL}H + \frac{1}{2}mV_t^2 \tag{I27}$$

In the Earth centered reference frame, gravity is a conservative force, and thus cannot add or extract any energy from this system. Therefore, any changes in kinetic energy solely caused by maneuvering will exactly match changes in potential energy. Aerodynamic drag is a non-conservative force which will constantly extract energy from the system. Vertical atmospheric motion creates a non-conservative force that can either add energy to the system (lift) or extract energy from the system (sink). You, the glider pilot, don't really care about the actual total energy of the system. What you care about is how it changes. You know how the aerodynamic drag extracts energy from the system. Any variation around that is either lift adding energy or sink extracting energy. If you had a system that could output the rate of energy change at any given moment, you could seek out the lift and run away from the sink.

The great thing about looking at the rate of energy change (derivative of total energy) is that it eliminates any stick thermals from our output. Because gravity is a conservative force, gains in altitude caused by losses of airspeed do not show up in the output. Only changes due to aerodynamic drag and atmospheric vertical movement show up in the output. Our challenge is to find a measurement method that measures changes in energy.

Differentiating Equation I27 gives

$$\frac{d(\text{Energy})}{dt} = mg_{SL}\frac{dH}{dt} + \frac{1}{2}m\frac{d\left(V_t^2\right)}{dt} \tag{I28}$$

Now we invoke one of those tricks that engineers do so well. Like so many other analyses, instead of thinking of the glider moving through an atmosphere frame of reference, we will focus on the air moving around the glider in a glider frame of reference. Our math major buddies tell us that these are equivalent systems.

Since the air is the object of interest, let's divide Equation I28 with a unit volume of air. This gives the convenient result of

$$\frac{1}{\text{Vol}}\frac{d(\text{Energy})}{dt} = \rho g_{SL}\frac{dH}{dt} + \frac{1}{2}\rho\frac{d\left(V_t^2\right)}{dt} \tag{I29}$$

Because we are interested in eliminating any output change caused by a "stick thermal", let's set the change in total energy to zero.

$$0 = \rho g_{SL}\frac{dH}{dt} + \frac{1}{2}\rho\frac{d\left(V_t^2\right)}{dt} \tag{I30}$$

Wait a minute, Moosebreath! Equation I30 looks strangely familiar. The first term looks like the Hydrostatic Equation (Equation A15) which would mean it was $-dP_a$. The second half looks like the derivative of dynamic pressure from Bernoulli's equation. Writing it in those terms would give

$$0 = \frac{-dP_a}{dt} + \frac{dq}{dt} \tag{I31}$$

If we integrate this equation with time, we get

$$0 = -P_a + q + C \tag{I32}$$

Aha! An integration constant! Usually we forget about those, but in this case it is important. Let's move it to the other side and call it a pressure, since everything else in the equation is a pressure.

$$P = P_a - q \tag{I33}$$

So to create our total energy measurement sensor, we need a sensor that can produce a pressure equal to the difference between the ambient pressure and the dynamic pressure.

TIME OUT! If you're like me, you get nervous whenever Bernoulli's Equation is trotted out or we start talking about dynamic pressure (q) rather than differential pressure (q_c). Bernoulli's Equation comes with a lot of assumption baggage, but in this case that's okay. We're talking about gliders, which always fly "slowly", well within the incompressible flow region. Rest securely in the knowledge that we aren't violating any important assumptions.

Venturi Total Energy Probes

So how can we build a sensor to produce the pressure given in Equation I33? One approach is to use a venturi, as shown in Figure I15. A venturi accelerates the flow through the throat, reducing its pressure below ambient. How do we design a venturi to reduce the ambient pressure precisely by a value equal to the dynamic pressure?

Going back to Bernoulli's Equation, we know that the total pressure anywhere in the flow will be constant, so we can say

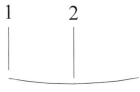

Figure I15. Total Energy Venturi

$$P_1 + q_1 = P_2 + q_2 \tag{I34}$$

Rearranging to solve for the dynamic pressure at the throat

$$q_2 = P_1 - P_2 + q_1 \tag{I35}$$

To get the desired pressure, we know from equation I33 that the pressure at station 2, where it is measured, must be equal to

$$P_2 = P_1 - q_1 \tag{I36}$$

Substituting Equation I36 into Equation I35

$$q_2 = P_1 - (P_1 - q_1) + q_1 \tag{I37}$$

which without the parentheses becomes

$$q_2 = P_1 - P_1 + q_1 + q_1 \tag{I38}$$

and thus

$$q_2 = 2q_1 \tag{I39}$$

So the venturi should be designed such that the dynamic pressure at the throat is twice that of the freestream. Breaking up the dynamic pressure into its component parts

$$\frac{\rho V_2^2}{2} = 2\frac{\rho V_1^2}{2} \tag{I40}$$

The density should remain constant since the flow is slow enough to be incompressible. Dividing out the density and the "2"

$$V_2^2 = 2V_1^2 \tag{I41}$$

Taking the square root of both sides

$$V_2 = \sqrt{2}\, V_1 \tag{I42}$$

which means that the venturi must accelerate the flow at the throat to 1.414 times the original airspeed. To find the contraction ratio necessary to do this, we use the incompressible version of the continuity equation

$$A_1 V_1 = A_2 V_2 \tag{I43}$$

which becomes

$$\frac{A_2}{A_1} = \frac{V_1}{V_2} \tag{I44}$$

Substituting Equation I42 into Equation I44

$$\frac{A_2}{A_1} = \frac{V_1}{\sqrt{2}\, V_1} \tag{I45}$$

or

$$\frac{A_2}{A_1} = \frac{1}{\sqrt{2}} \tag{I46}$$

So the area of the throat must be 0.707 times the size of the venturi entrance. To find the relationship of the radii

$$\pi r_2^2 = \frac{1}{\sqrt{2}} \pi r_1^2 \tag{I47}$$

Dividing out pi and taking the square root of both sides gives

$$r_2 = \frac{1}{\sqrt[4]{2}} r_1 \tag{I48}$$

Thus, the radius of the throat must be 0.841 times the radius of the inlet. The diameters will be of the same ratio. This ratio is shown in the venturi in Figure I15, which is a surprisingly small contraction. Figure I16 shows an actual installed total energy venturi.

Figure I16. Total Energy Venturi on a DG-1000

Tube Total Energy Probes

Another approach to creating a total energy sensor is to use a small diameter cylinder in cross flow with a small hole on the back side. One type is called a "Braunschweig Tube", which in Reference 38 was described as "the Braunschweig tube, described in Ref. 7, uses the same principles applied in developing the probes discussed in this report. However, they are more difficult to make, and were found to be more sensitive to manufacturing tolerances."

To understand how this approach works, consider the definition of the pressure coefficient (C_P) (Ref 11)

$$C_p = \frac{P - P_a}{q} \tag{I49}$$

where P is the pressure at the point of interest, which is non-dimensionalized by the ambient pressure (P_a) and the dynamic pressure (q). According to Equation I33, we want to create a pressure that is equal to the difference of the ambient pressure and the dynamic pressure. In terms of a pressure coefficient, that would look like

$$C_p = \frac{\left(P_a - q\right) - P_a}{q} \tag{I50}$$

It can be shown that this results in the simple condition of

$$C_P = -1 \tag{I51}$$

The proof is left as an exercise to the reader. (Really? Stop complaining. It's only one step, and it's hardly even algebra.)

A small cylinder at low Reynolds number in cross flow will undergo laminar separation at approximately the widest cross section (90 degrees around from the stagnation point). This separation creates a low pressure area (below ambient pressure) that decreases in pressure as the airspeed increases. See Figure I17.

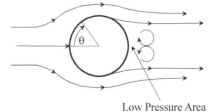

Low Pressure Area

Figure I17. Cylinder in Cross Flow

This concept was described very well in Reference 38, which is reproduced here:

> There are many aerodynamic shapes that produce pressure distributions with local pressure coefficients of -1.0, but they are often very sensitive to flow conditions or variations in angle of attack, Reynolds number, etc. For instance there may be several locations on an airfoil where $C_P = -1.0$, but the locations are likely to vary sensitively with angle of attack.
>
> A literature search of pressure distributions over various shapes indicated the possibility of using a cylinder, because the typical two-dimensional pressure distribution around a cylinder shows pressure coefficient values of -1.0 at about 55° to 60° from the stagnation point (Fig. 2 (*Figure 118 in this document*)). However, the gradient is very steep at this position and it would be necessary to locate pressure orifices quite precisely. In addition, this location would be very sensitive to variations in flow angle. What is more interesting about the pressure distributions for cylinders at relatively low Reynolds numbers is the fact that the pressure coefficients are nearly constant around the aft side of cylinders from about 100° to 180°, and for a wide range of Reynolds number are well within 10 percent of the desired $C_P = -1.0$ value.

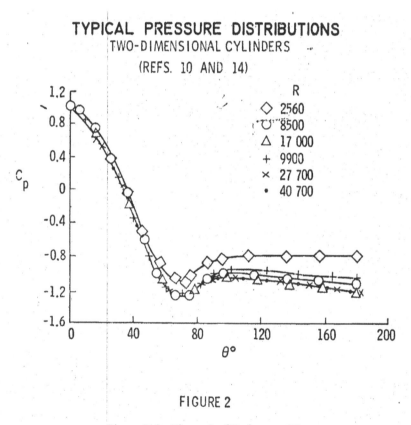

Figure I18. Figure 2 of Reference 38

After numerous wind tunnel and flight tests, Reference 38 drew the following findings and conclusions:

> The best probe configurations tested had the following characteristics:
>
> 1. Cylindrical tube, diameter of 3/16- to 1/4-inch.
> 2. Tube end squared off with very slight bevel of sharp edge.
> 3. Aft facing pressure orifice, a drilled hole about 1/3 the tube diameter (1/16- to 3/32-inch).
> 4. Center of hole located at a distance two times the tube diameter from the end of the tube (3/8- to 1/2-inch).
> 5. Probe swept forward about 20° with respect to flow direction.
> 6. Probe mounted in free-stream air, extending a minimum of 5 to 6 inches from the aircraft.
> 7. Vertical tail location good; aft fuselage acceptable.
>
> Such a probe, coupled with a good variometer in a leak-free system, should provide the following:
>
> 1. Good total energy rate information over a flight range from 40 to at least 150 mph; altitudes from sea level to at least 20,000 feet.
> 2. Insensitivities to normal yaw, pitch, and roll attitude variations.
> 3. Drag of a typical installation at 100 mph is about one-tenth of a pound.

An installed Total Energy probe is shown in Figure I19.

Figure I19. Total Energy Probe on an ASK-21

So What Exactly Is Going On Here?

After all of that math, let's come back to some concepts here. A variometer (Figure 3.7, Chapter 3) simply connected to a source of static pressure is a rate of climb indicator. The same variometer connected to a Total Energy sensor with a pressure coefficient of -1 will indicate energy being extracted from or added to "the system".

Things that extract energy from the system are aerodynamic drag and descending air currents (sink). In quiescent air at constant airspeed the variometer will show energy leaving the system as a descent rate. Sink also causes the glider to descend. In both cases, the ambient pressure increases while the dynamic pressure remains constant, hence the pressure at the Total Energy probe increases.

Things that add energy to the system are the launch system (tension on the tow rope) and ascending air currents (lift). As the glider gains altitude behind the tow plane, the variometer shows the energy entering the system as a climb rate. Atmospheric lift also causes the glider to climb. In both cases, ambient pressure decreases while dynamic pressure remains constant, hence the pressure at the Total Energy probe decreases. Additionally, energy is added to the system as the glider accelerates for takeoff. This acceleration increases the dynamic pressure, which causes the pressure at the Total Energy probe to decrease. Thus, a variometer connected to a Total Energy probe will show a climb while accelerating level for takeoff. Bet you never noticed that, huh? You were too busy paying attention to the piloting task (as you should be).

To understand the case of the stick thermal, we must first understand that in steady-state flight the pressure in the variometer system is not static pressure, but is a lower pressure, equal to the ambient pressure minus the dynamic pressure (Equation I33). This pressure drops from the ambient pressure during the takeoff run as dynamic pressure increases. If the pilot then pulls on the stick to point the nose uphill, trading airspeed for altitude, two things happen:

1. The increase in altitude decreases the ambient pressure.
2. The decrease in speed decreases the dynamic pressure.

As we have seen through the math, if the Total Energy probe operates at a pressure coefficient of -1, then the decrease in the ambient pressure will identically match the decrease in dynamic pressure, and their difference (measured at the Total Energy probe) will remain constant. Thus, the variometer should show no change during a "stick thermal".

Appendix J

Example Pitot-Static Sensor Installations

This appendix contains photographs of Pitot-static sensor (Pitot tubes, static ports) on a collection of historical aircraft. This will give the reader a background in how installations have been made in the past for evaluating new installations.

Aircraft are ordered (mostly) by their military designation.

Most of these aircraft were photographed at the Flight Test Museum at Edwards AFB and at the Pima Air Museum in Tucson AZ.

Douglas A-26 (B-26) Invader

Pitot tube near nose

Cessna A-37 Dragonfly

Flight test Pitot-static YAPS boom

Pitot tube on vertical tail

Static port on fuselage side

McDonnell ADM-20C Quail

Presumed mounting point for Pitot boom on right wingtip

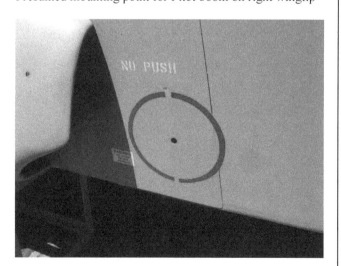

Static port on side of fuselage

Ryan AWM-34J Firebee

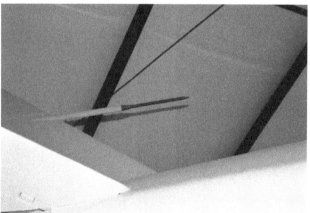

Pitot-static tube on vertical tail

Beechcraft AT-7 Navigator

Pitot tube on long strut under nose

Beech AT-11 Kansan

Pitot tube under nose

Cessna AT-17 Bobcat

Pitot-static tube under nose

Hawker Siddeley AV-8C Harrier

Pitot tube on nose boom

Static port just under canopy

Douglas B-18B Bolo

Pitot-static tube on wing

Consolidated B-24 Liberator

Pitot Tube near nosewheel

North American B-25 Mitchell

Pitot-static tube on boom on right wing

Boeing B-29 Superfortress

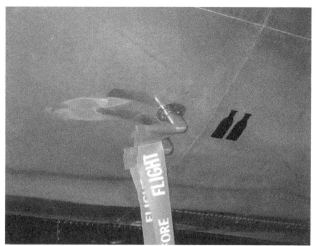

Two Pitot tubes under left nose

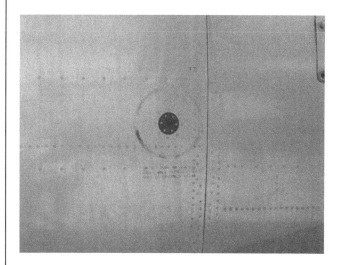

Static port on side of fuselage

Boeing B-52G Statofortress

Three Pitot tubes visible, one high, one in the middle of the picture, and one low near sensor pod

On side of fuselage, Pitot tube up high, three static ports in middle, and AOA vane low

Martin B-57E Canberra

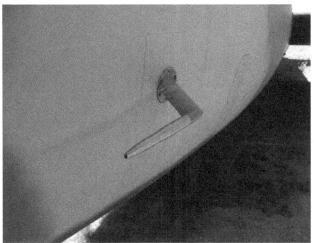

Pitot-static tube on side of fuselage

Convair B-58A Hustler

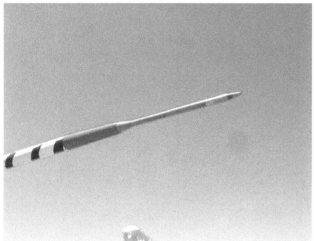

Pitot-static tube on nose boom

Vultee BT-13A Valiant

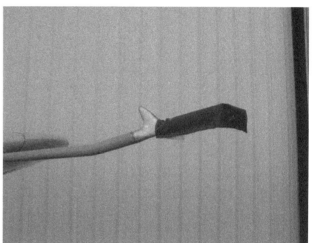

Pitot-static tube on left wing

North American BT-14 Yale

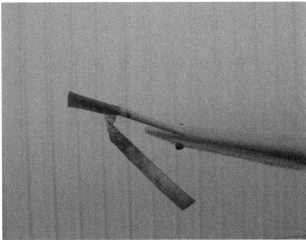

Pitot-static tube on right wing

Beech C-12C Huron

Two Pitot tubes under nose

Two static ports on aft fuselage

McDonnell Douglas C-17 Prototype (T-1)

C-17 T-1 used this flight test YAPS boom

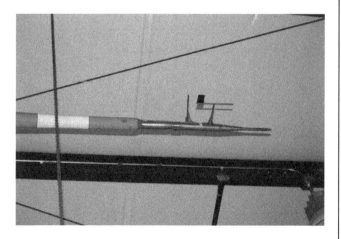

Pitot-static tube with AOA and sideslip vanes

Lockheed C-36A Electra

Two Pitot-static tubes under nose

Beech C-45J Expeditor

Two Pitot-static tubes under nose

Pitot-static tube

Curtiss C-46 Commando

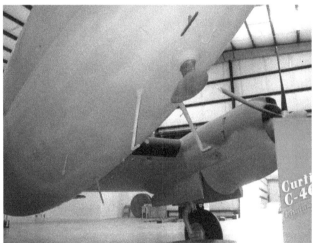

Two Pitot tubes under nose

Douglas C-47 Skytrain

Dual Pitot tubes under nose

Douglas C-54D Skymaster

Pitot tube on side of fuselage. Static port is circle in yellow stripe

Fairchild C-82A Packet

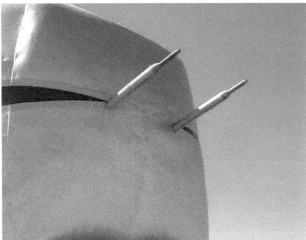

Two Pitot tubes in nose

Fairchild C-119C Flying Boxcar

Two Pitot tubes on nose

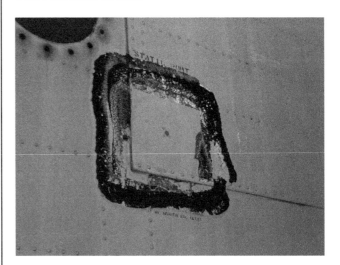

Static port on side of fuselage

Cessna C-120

Pitot tube on left wing

Fairchild C-123B Provider

Pitot tube on side of nose

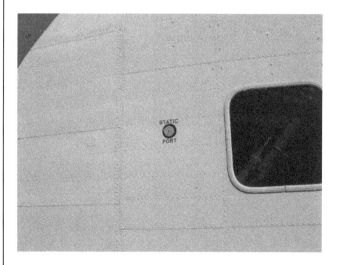

Static port on side of fuselage

Douglas C-124C Globemaster II

Lockheed C-130A Hercules

Pitot tube on side of fuselage

Pitot tube under windows

Static port in red circle left of door

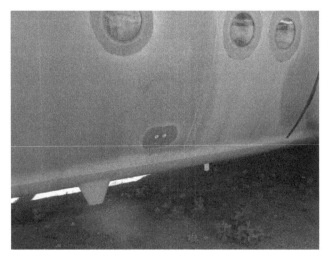

Static ports on side of fuselage

Convair C-131F Samaritan

Pitot tube on side of fuselage

Static ports on fuselage

Douglas C-133B Cargomaster

Pitot tube under nose

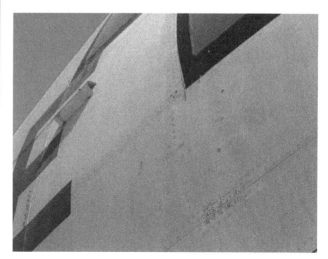

Static ports under window on fuselage

Lockheed C-140 JetStar

Pitot tube and static port on fuselage

Cessna C-150

Pitot tube under left wing

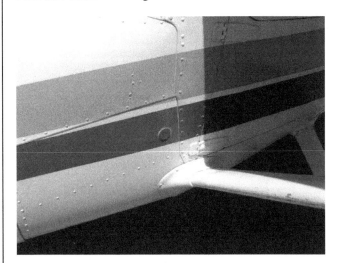

Static port on left cowl

Sikorsky CH-3

Pitot-static tubes above cockpit

Pitot-static tube

Ryan-Temco D-16 Twin Navion

Pitot tube under right wing just in front of flap

Static port on fuselage side

Boeing EB-47E Stratojet

Lockheed EC-121 Warning Star

Pitot tube on side of fuselage

Two Pitot tubes on side of fuselage. Three static ports inside red oval

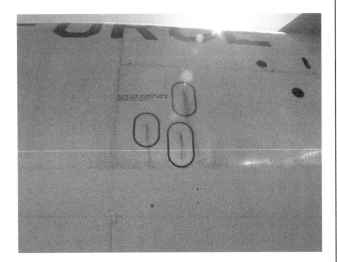

Static ports on side of fuselage

Douglas F3D-2 SkyKnight

Pitot tube in front of canopy

Static port just aft of radome

McDonnell F3H-2 Demon

Pitot tube at front of canopy

Static port on fuselage side

Additional Pitot-static tube on wing tip

McDonnell F-4C Phantom II

Pitot tube on vertical tail. Lower tube is input for flight control "q-feel" system

Static port on radome. AOA cone behind radome

McDonnell Douglas F-4E Phantom II

Pitot-static tube on nose

Note shape of compensated Pitot-static probe

Vought F4U Corsair

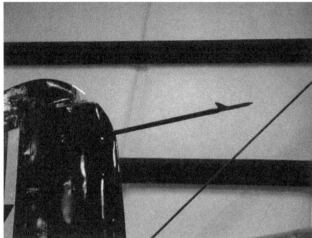

Pitot-static tube on left wing (folded)

Douglas F-6A Skyray

Pitot tube above nose

Grumman F7F Tigercat

Vought F-8A Crusader

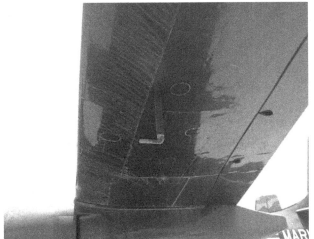

Pitot tube under left wing

Pitot tube on side of nose

Grumman F9F-4 Panther

Pitot tube under wing

Static port on side of fuselage

Grumman F9F-8 Cougar

Pitot tube under wing

Static port on side of fuselage between "star and bar" and "JET"

Grumman F-11F Tiger

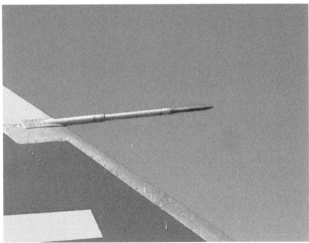

Pitot-static tube on vertical tail

McDonnell Douglas F-15 Eagle

Black cover over Pitot-static tube behind radome

General Dynamics F-16XL

McDonnell Douglas F/A-18 Hornet

Flight test YAPS boom on nose. Pitot-static tube at front is a standard F-16 Pitot-static probe.

Pitot-static tube and AOA probe on fuselage

Republic F-84C Thunderjet

Pitot tube on vertical tail

Static port on fuselage

Republic F-84F Thunderstreak

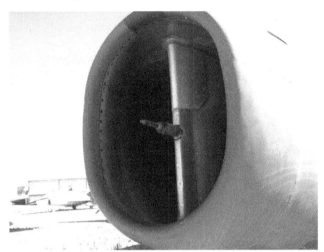

Pitot tube in inlet

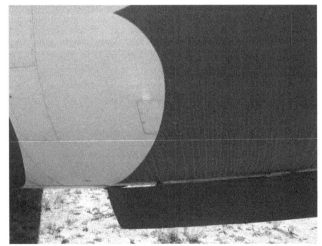

Static port on side of fuselage

North American F-86H Sabre

Pitot-static boom on right wing

North American F-86L Sabre

Pitot-static boom on right wing

Northrop F-89J Scorpion

Pitot tube on side of fuselage (over the "O") and static ports in red circle

Lockheed F-94C Starfire

Pitot tube under nose and static port on side of fuselage

North American F-100C Super Sabre

Pitot-static tube on boom under nose. Boom could fold upwards in front of inlet for protection on the ground.

McDonnell F-101B Voodoo

Pitot-static boom on nose

Lockheed F-104A Starfighter

Republic F-105 Thunderchief

Pitot-static boom on nose

Pitot-static boom on nose

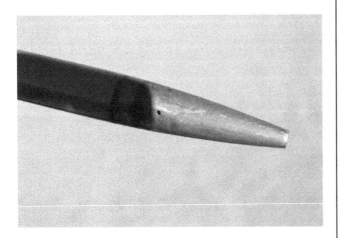

Note compensated static ports

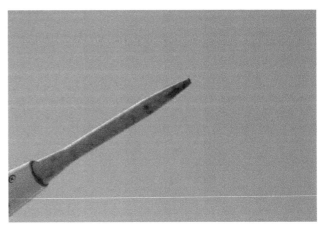

Note compensated static ports

Convair F-106B Delta Dart

Pitot-static boom on nose

General Dynamics F-111A Aardvark

Compensated Pitot-static probe on nose

Focke-Achgelis Fa 330 Bachstelze

A German gyro-kite (autogyro) towed behind a submarine to spot ships from a higher altitude

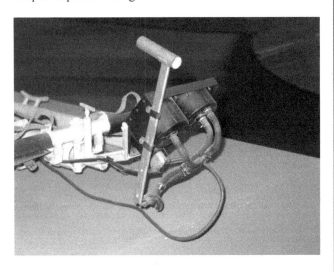

Note the simple Pitot-static tube and very short hoses for the altimeter and airspeed indicator located at the pilot's feet.

North American FJ-4B Fury

Pitot-static tube on right wingtip

Piasecki H-25 Retriever

Pitot tube under nose

Sikorsky H-37 Mojave

Pitot tubes on fuselage side

Static ports on aft fuselage

Grumman HU-16C Albatross

Grumman J4F Widgeon (Modified)

Pitot tube under left wing

Pitot-static tube on boom on right wing

Static port in blue part of bar on fuselage

Sikorsky JRS-1 (S-43)

Pitot tube above cockpit

Boeing KC-97G Stratofreighter

Pitot tube on lower fuselage near nose

Static ports on lower fuselage

Lockheed L-049 Constellation

Pitot-static tubes under nose

NASA M2-F1

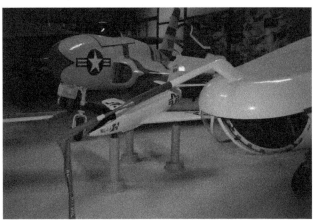

Pitot-static tube on nose

Mikoyan Gurevich MiG-15UT Midget

Pitot-static tube on boom on right wing

Mikoyan Gurevich MiG-17 Fresco

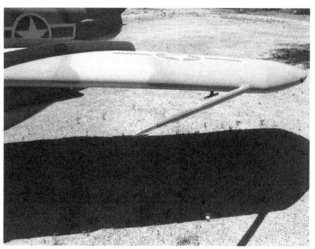

Pitot-static tube on boom on left wing

Mikoyan Gurevich MiG-21 Fishbed

Pitot-static tube over nose inlet

Aero L-39 Albatros

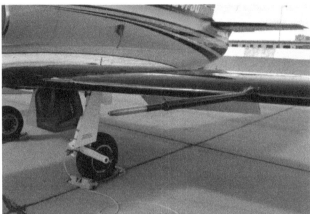

Pitot-static tube on left wing

Government Aircraft Factories N22S Nomad

Pitot tube on side of fuselage

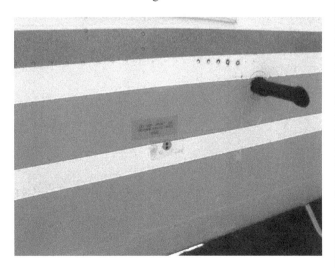

Static ports on side of fuselage

Gloster NF-11 Meteor

Pitot-static boom on left wing

Static ports are thin slots, not holes

Cessna O-2 Skymaster

Pitot tube under left wing

Grumman OV-1 Mohawk

Pitot tube on nose. Note that Pitot tube is not aligned with the horizontal, but is parallel to the surface to align with the local flow

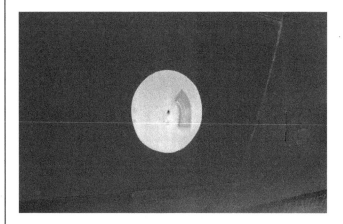

Static port on fuselage side under left window. Note compensation behind port

North American Rockwell OV-10 Bronco

Bell P-63 KingCobra

Pitot tube on nose

Pitot tube on left wing

Static port on fuselage

Lockheed P-80B Shooting Star

Pitot tube under fuselage. Static port in red circle on fuselage

Piper PA-48 Enforcer

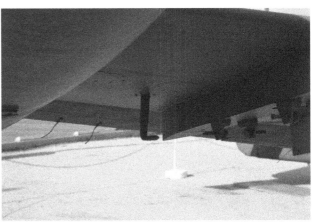

Pitot tube under right wing

Fairchild PT-19

Ryan PT-22 Recruit

Pitot tube on right wing

Pitot tube on left wing

Sikorsky R-4

Pitot-static tube on rotor mast

Martin RB-57D Canberra

Pitot tube on nose. Static port in red circle on fuselage

Sud-Aviation SE-210 Caravelle

Pitot tube on side of fuselage

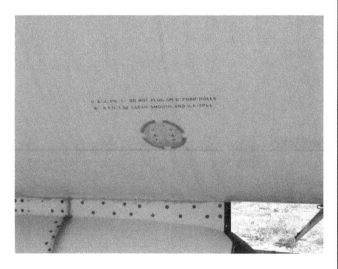

Static ports on side of fuselage

Lockheed SR-71A Blackbird

Pitot-static tube on nose. Tube on side is a four hole AOA and sideslip probe

Lockheed T-1A SeaStar

Pitot tube on strut under nose. Static ports in red circles on fuselage

North American T-6 Texan

Pitot-static tube on right wing

North American T-28B Trojan

Pitot tube on right wing

Static port on aft fuselage

Convair T-29B Flying Classroom

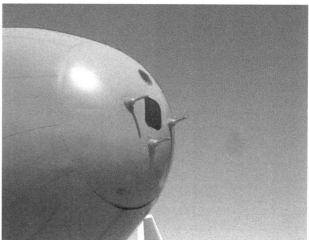

Three Pitot tubes on nose

Four static ports on side of fuselage

Lockheed T-33A Shooting Star

Cessna T-37B Tweet

Pitot tube on side of fuselage

Pitot tube on nose

Static port on nose in red circle

Static port on aft fuselage

Northrop T-38A Talon

Pitot-static tube on noseboom

AOA vane on fuselage side

This static port is part of the cabin pressurization system

North American T-39 Sabreliner

Pitot tube and static ports on left fuselage

General Motors TBM Avenger

Convair TF-102A Delta Dagger

Pitot-static boom on nose

Pitot tube on left wing (folded)

Schweizer TG-3A (SGS 2-12)

Pitot tube on nose

Taylorcraft TG-6

A WW-II training glider used to train pilots for flying the CG-4A cargo glider. It was built by removing the engine from a Taylorcraft L-2 and adding a third pilot position where the engine had been. Because of the increase in side area up front the vertical fin size was increased

Note Pitot tube above forward canopy

DeHavilland U-6 Beaver

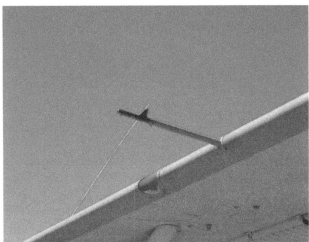

Pitot-static tube on boom on left wing

Beechcraft U-8D Twin Bonanza

Pitot tube under left wing

Static port on fuselage side

Piper U-11 Aztec

Pitot tube under left wing

Douglas VC-118 Liftmaster (DC-6)

Pitot tube and static port on left nose

Lockheed VC-121 Constellation

Two Pitot tubes on long struts under nose

Boeing VC-137 Stratoliner

Pitot tube and temperature probes

Vickers 744 Viscount

Douglas WB-66D Destroyer

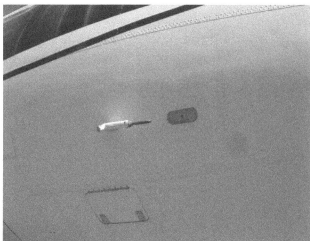

Pitot tube and static port on side of fuselage

Pitot tube in front of nose gear

Bell X-1

Northrop X-4

Pitot-static probe on nose

Pitot-static tube on nose

Pitot-static probe on each wingtip

Bensen X-25B

Wind gauges at pilot's feet used for airspeed indication

Boeing X-36

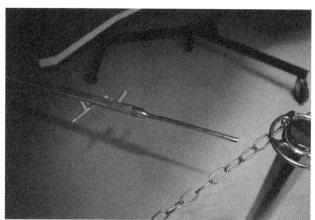

Teeny-tiny YAPS head with Pitot-static tube

Ling-Temco-Vought YA-7D Corsair II

Flight test Pitot-static probe with four hole AOA and sideslip probe

Pitot-static probes above nose

Fairchild Republic YA-10B

Pitot-static tube on right wing

Close up of Pitot-static tube

Boeing YC-14

McDonnell Douglas YC-15

Boeing YC-14 in rear

Pitot-static probes on fuselage

Pitot-static probe

Three Pitot-static tubes on side of nose, with AOA vane near bottom. Identical sensors are installed on opposite side of the fuselage

Lockheed YF-22 Raptor

Pitot-static tube on nose boom

Appendix K

Pitot-Statics Glossary

Pitot-static theory is challenging enough to understand, and it doesn't help that there are so many similar parameters with minor but important differences. These differences are typically denoted by subscripts. This glossary is provided as an easy method for tracking down the specific meaning of any symbol in this book. Symbology used in this book is consistent with the *Flight Test Engineering Handbook* (Ref 12), and thus may vary from other references.

a	speed of sound
a_{SL}	speed of sound at sea level (defined constant)
b	wingspan; intercept
C	integration constant
$^{\circ}C$	degrees Celsius (Centigrade)
$C_{L_{ic}}$	lift coefficient calculated using V_{ic}
C_p	pressure coefficient; coefficient of specific heat at constant pressure
C_v	coefficient of specific heat at constant volume
D_1	distance, first leg of speed course
D_2	distance, second leg of speed course
dA	incremental area
DALR	dry adiabatic lapse rate
dh	incremental geometric altitude
dH	incremental geopotential altitude
Distance_{1-2}	distance on spherical earth between location 1 and location 2
$\text{Distance Angle}_{1-2}$	angle between location 1 and location 2 with vertex at the center of the earth
dP	incremental pressure
dT	incremental temperature
$^{\circ}F$	degrees Fahrenheit
f	pressure correction factor (often incorrectly called the "compressibility" correction factor), $f = V_e/V_c$
g	acceleration of gravity
GS	ground speed
g_{SL}	acceleration of gravity at the sea level geopotential surface (defined constant)
H	geopotential altitude
ΔH	change in geopotential altitude
h	geometric altitude (tapeline altitude); specific enthalpy
H_B	base altitude
H_c	pressure altitude
h_{cal}	geometric (tapeline) altitude of calibrated aircraft
$H_{c_{test}}$	pressure altitude of the test aircraft
$H_{c_{tower}}$	pressure altitude measured in fly-by tower at the elevation of the grid zero line
ΔH_c	change in pressure altitude; difference in pressure altitude of test and calibrated aircraft
Δh	change in geometric (tapeline) altitude
H_i	indicated altitude
$H_{i_{cal}}$	indicated altitude of calibrated aircraft
$H_{i_{cone}}$	indicated altitude of trailing cone transducer
$H_{i_{pace}}$	indicated altitude of pace aircraft

$H_{i_{test}}$	indicated altitude of test aircraft
H_{ic}	instrument corrected altitude
$H_{ic_{pace}}$	instrument corrected altitude of pace aircraft
$H_{ic_{std\ alt}}$	instrument corrected altitude at desired standard altitude
$H_{ic_{test}}$	instrument corrected altitude of test aircraft
ΔH_{ic}	altitude instrument error correction
$\Delta H_{ic_{cal}}$	altitude instrument error correction of calibrated aircraft
$\Delta H_{ic_{cone}}$	altitude instrument error correction of trailing cone
$\Delta H_{ic_{pace}}$	altitude instrument error correction of pace aircraft
$\Delta H_{ic_{test}}$	altitude instrument error correction of test aircraft
ΔH_p	altitude position error
H_{pc}	instrument and position corrected altitude ($H_{pc} = H_c$ + residual errors)
$H_{pc_{cal}}$	instrument and position corrected altitude of calibrated aircraft
$H_{pc_{cone/bomb}}$	instrument and position corrected altitude from trailing cone or bomb
$H_{pc_{pace}}$	instrument and position corrected altitude of pace aircraft
$H_{pc_{smoke}}$	instrument and position corrected altitude of smoke trail
$H_{pc_{test}}$	instrument and position corrected altitude of test aircraft
ΔH_{pc}	altitude position correction
$\Delta H_{pc_{cal}}$	altitude position correction of calibrated aircraft
$\Delta H_{pc_{cone}}$	altitude position correction of trailing cone
$\Delta H_{pc_{pace}}$	altitude position correction of pace aircraft
$\Delta H_{pc_{std\ alt}}$	altitude position correction at desired standard altitude
$\Delta H_{pc_{test}}$	altitude position correction at test conditions
$H_{std\ alt}$	desired standard altitude
h_{test}	geometric (tapeline) altitude of test aircraft
Δh	change in geometric (tapeline) altitude
H_ρ	density altitude
K	Kelvin
KCAS	knots calibrated airspeed
KEAS	knots equivalent airspeed
KE	kinetic energy
ke	specific kinetic energy
KIAS	knots indicated airspeed
K_t	temperature recovery factor
KTAS	knots true airspeed
L	temperature lapse rate
Lat_1	Latitude of location 1
Lat_2	Latitude of location 2
$Long_1$	Longitude of location 1
$Long_2$	Longitude of location 2
M	Mach number; mean molecular weight
M'	Mach number immediately behind shock wave
m	slope; mass
m_{dry}	mass of dry air
m_{water}	mass of water vapor
$\dot{m}$	mass flow rate
M_i	indicated Mach number
M_{ic}	instrument corrected Mach number

ΔM_{ic}	Mach number instrument error correction
$M_{ic_{pace}}$	instrument corrected Mach number of pace aircraft
ΔM_p	Mach position error
M_{pc}	instrument and position corrected Mach Number ($M_{pc} = M$ + residual errors)
ΔM_{pc}	Mach number position correction
N	number of molecules (moles)
n	load factor
P	pressure
P_a	ambient pressure
P_a'	ambient pressure immediately behind shock wave
$P_{a_{std\,alt}}$	ambient pressure at desired standard altitude
P_B	pressure at base altitude
P_{dry}	partial pressure of dry air
PE	potential energy
pe	specific potential energy
P_{moist}	pressure of moist (humid) air
P_s	static pressure as measured by the static port
P_{SL}	pressure at sea level (defined constant)
$P_{s_{std\,alt}}$	static pressure at desired standard altitude
P_T	total pressure
P_T'	total pressure measured behind a normal shock wave
ΔP	change in pressure
ΔP_p	error in reading ambient pressure ($P_s - P_a$)
$\Delta P_p/P_s$	static port position error ratio
$\Delta P_p/q_{cic}$	position error pressure coefficient
P_r	Prandtl number
$P_{saturated\,water}$	saturation pressure of water vapor
P_{water}	partial pressure of water vapor
q	dynamic pressure
q_c	differential pressure ($P_T - P_a$)
q_{cic}	instrument corrected differential pressure ($P_T - P_s$)
Q_{in}	heat interaction into the system
$\dot{Q}_{in}$	rate of heat interaction into the system
Q_{out}	heat interaction out of the system
$\dot{Q}_{out}$	rate of heat interaction out of the system
R	specific gas constant for air (defined constant)
R*	universal gas constant (defined constant)
R_{air}	specific gas constant for air (defined constant)
R_{water}	specific gas constant for water vapor (defined constant)
°R	degrees Rankine
R_e	Reynolds number
$R_{e_{SL}}$	radius of the sea level geopotential surface (essentially the radius of the earth)
S	wing planform area
T	temperature
t	elapsed time over speed course
t_1	elapsed time over first leg of speed course
t_2	elapsed time over second leg of speed course
T_a	ambient temperature
T_{a_i}	ambient air temperature based on instrument corrected airspeed or instrument corrected Mach number

T_B	temperature at base altitude
T_{dew}	dew point temperature
T_i	indicated temperature
T_{ic}	instrument corrected temperature
ΔT_{ic}	temperature instrument error correction
T_{in}	temperature into the streamtube
T_{moist}	temperature of moist (humid) air
T_{out}	temperature out of the streamtube
T_{SL}	temperature at sea level (defined constant)
T_{std}	standard day temperature at a given altitude
T_T	total temperature
T_{test}	temperature at test conditions
$T_{virtual}$	virtual temperature: temperature of dry air with same density as humid air at the same pressure
u	specific internal energy
V	volume
v	specific volume
V_{aim}	aim airspeed
V_{adj}	adjusted ground speed
V_c	calibrated airspeed
ΔV_c	pressure correction factor (often incorrectly called the "compressibility" correction factor), $\Delta V_c = V_e - V_c$
$V_{c_{std\,alt}}$	calibrated airspeed at the desired standard altitude
V_e	equivalent airspeed
V_g	ground speed
V_{g_e}	ground speed, Easterly component
V_{g_n}	ground speed, Northerly component
V_{gx}	x component of ground speed
V_{gy}	y component of ground speed
V_i	indicated airspeed
$V_{i_{cal}}$	indicated airspeed of calibrated aircraft
$V_{i_{pace}}$	indicated airspeed of pace aircraft
$V_{i_{test}}$	indicated airspeed of test aircraft
V_{ic}	instrument corrected airspeed
$V_{ic_{pace}}$	instrument corrected airspeed of pace aircraft
$V_{ic_{std\,alt}}$	instrument corrected airspeed at desired standard altitude
$V_{ic_{test}}$	instrument corrected airspeed of test aircraft
ΔV_{ic}	airspeed instrument error correction
$\Delta V_{ic_{cal}}$	airspeed instrument error correction of calibrated aircraft
$\Delta V_{ic_{pace}}$	airspeed instrument error correction of pace aircraft
$\Delta V_{ic_{test}}$	airspeed instrument error correction of test aircraft
V_{in}	airspeed into streamtube
V_{out}	airspeed out of streamtube
ΔV_p	airspeed position error
V_{pc}	instrument and position corrected airspeed, calibrated airspeed ($V_{pc} = V_c$ + residual errors)
$V_{pc_{cal}}$	instrument and position corrected airspeed of calibrated aircraft
$V_{pc_{pace}}$	instrument and position corrected airspeed of pace aircraft
ΔV_{pc}	airspeed position correction
$\Delta V_{pc_{cal}}$	airspeed position correction of calibrated aircraft
$\Delta V_{pc_{pace}}$	airspeed position correction of pace aircraft

$\Delta V_{pc_{std\ alt}}$	airspeed position correction at the desired standard altitude
$\Delta V_{pc_{test}}$	airspeed position correction of test aircraft
V_t	true airspeed
ΔV_t	true airspeed error
$V_{t_{adj}}$	adjusted true airspeed
V_{t_c}	true airspeed "corrected" (sum of indicated true airspeed plus true airspeed correction
V_{t_e}	true airspeed, Easterly component
V_{t_i}	true airspeed based on instrument corrected airspeed or instrument corrected Mach number
V_{t_n}	true airspeed, Northerly component
V_w	wind speed
V_{w_e}	wind speed, Easterly component
V_{w_n}	wind speed, Northerly component
V_{wx}	wind speed, x component
V_{wy}	wind speed, y component
W	weight
W_{in}	work interaction into the system
w_{in}	specific work interaction into the system
$\dot{W}_{in}$	rate of work interaction into the system
W_{out}	work interaction out of the system
w_{out}	specific work interaction out of the system
$\dot{W}_{out}$	rate of work interaction out of the system
x	fly-by tower eyepiece to grid distance
y	fly-by tower grid division height * grid reading
z	fly-by tower eyepiece to fly-by line distance
α	angle of attack
β	sideslip
γ	ratio of specific heats, C_p/C_v, $\gamma = 1.4$ for air
δ	pressure ratio, P/P_{SL}
δ_B	pressure ratio at base altitude
δ_{ic}	pressure ratio based on instrument corrected pressure altitude, H_{ic}
$\delta_{ic_{pace}}$	pressure ratio based on instrument corrected pressure altitude, H_{ic}, of pace aircraft
$\delta_{ic_{test}}$	pressure ratio based on instrument corrected pressure altitude, H_{ic}, of test aircraft
$\delta_{sea\ level}$	pressure ratio at sea level on a non-standard day
$\delta_{std\ alt}$	pressure ratio at the chosen standard altitude
$\delta_{ic_{std\ alt}}$	pressure ratio based on instrument corrected pressure altitude, H_{ic}, at desired standard altitude
δ_{moist}	pressure ratio of moist (humid) air
η	variable temperature recovery factor
θ	temperature ratio, T/T_{SL}
θ_B	temperature ratio at base altitude
θ_{ic}	temperature ratio based on instrument corrected pressure altitude, H_{ic}
θ_{std}	standard day temperature ratio at a given altitude
$\theta_{std_{std\ alt}}$	standard day temperature ratio at the chosen standard altitude
$\theta_{std_{test\ alt}}$	standard day temperature ratio at the test altitude
θ_{test}	temperature ratio at test conditions
ν	frequency
ρ	density
ρ_a	ambient density
ρ_B	density at base altitude

ρ_{dry}	density of dry air
ρ_{moist}	density of moist (humid) air
ρ_{SL}	density at sea level
ρ_{std}	standard day density at a given altitude
ρ_{test}	density at test conditions
ρ_{water}	density of water vapor
σ	density ratio, ρ/ρ_{SL}
σ_B	density ratio at base altitude
σ_{ic}	density ratio based on instrument corrected pressure altitude, H_{ic}
σ_{std}	standard day density ratio at a given altitude
σ_g	GPS ground track
ϕ	bank angle; latitude
ψ	heading; wind direction
ψ_{rel}	wind direction relative to heading
ψ_{V_t}	direction of velocity vector in North-East (Earth horizontal) plane

References

1. McCue, J.J., Mosher, Mike, Munday, R. Brandon, *Pitot-Static Systems: Class Notes*, United States Naval Test Pilot School, Patuxent River Naval Air Station MD, December 2018.

2. Doolittle, James H., Glines, Carroll V., *I Could Never Be So Lucky Again*, Bantam Books, New York, 1991.

3. *U.S. Standard Atmosphere, 1962*, Superintendent of Documents, U.S. Government Printing Office, Washington D.C., 1962.

4. *Aeronautical Vestpocket Handbook*, United Technologies, Pratt & Whitney, August 1986

5. *U.S. Standard Atmosphere, 1976*, Superintendent of Documents, U.S. Government Printing Office, Washington D.C., 1976.

6. DoD Flight Information Publication (Enroute), *Flight Information Handbook*, National Geospatial-Intelligence Agency, St. Louis MO.

7. *Aerodynamics*, USAF Test Pilot School, Edwards AFB CA, January 2001.

8. *The Wright Story: 1903*, http://www.wrightexperience.com/edu/12_17_03/html/data_wslk.htm , 15 July 2015.

9. *Some Hints For The Use Of The APN-147/ASN-35 Doppler Navigation System*, Canadian Marconi Company, Montreal, Canada, 1963.

10. General Dynamics, Fort Worth Division, Field Service Report Number 90-02-0066.

11. Anderson, John D. Jr., *Introduction to Flight, Third Edition*, McGraw-Hill Book Company, New York, 1989.

12. Herrington, Russel M., Shoemacher, Paul E. *et al*, *Flight Test Engineering Handbook*, AF Technical Report No. 6273, Air Force Flight Test Center, Edwards AFB CA, 1966.

13. DeAnda, Albert G., *AFFTC Standard Airspeed Calibration Procedures*, AFFTC-TIH-81-5, Air Force Flight Test Center, Edwards AFB CA, 1981.

14. Anderson, John D. Jr., *Fundamentals of Aerodynamics, Fourth Edition*, McGraw-Hill Book Company, New York, 2007.

15. Webb, Lannie D. and Washington, Harold P., *Flight Calibration of Compensated and Uncompensated Pitot-Static Airspeed Probes and Application of the Probes to Supersonic Cruise Vehicles*, NASA TN D-6827, National Aeronautics and Space Administration, Washington DC, May 1972.

16. McCormick, B. W., *Aerodynamics, Aeronautics and Flight Mechanics*, Wiley, New York, 1979.

17. Hart, Ronald E., *Airspeed Calibration on a Stretch YC-141B Aircraft*, 12th Annual SFTE Symposium, Dayton OH, 16-18 September 1981.

18. Welser, Michael et al, *F-16B Pacer Aircraft Trailing Cone Length Extension Tube Investigative Study (HAVE CLETIS)*, AFFTC-TIM-07-02, Air Force Flight Test Center, Edwards AFB CA, June 2007.

19. Brown, Frank, *Determining Pitot-Static Position Error Corrections In-Ground Effect*, 412TW-TIH-16-02, Edwards AFB CA, November 2016.

20. Lawless, A., *Orbis Matching: Precision Pitot-Static Calibration*, 41st International SFTE Symposium (Training Session), Washington DC, 13-16 September 2010.

21. Jorris, T., Ramos, M., Erb, R., Woolf, R., *Statistical Pitot-static Calibration Technique using Turns and Self Survey Method*, 42nd International SFTE Symposium, Seattle WA, 8-12 August 2011.

22. Maisler, Brian, *Flight Test Results of Turning Regressions for Angle of Attack Dependent Air Data Error*, 50th International SFTE Symposium, Toulouse, France, 10-14 June 2019.

23. Jurado, J., McGehee, C., Jorris, T., Erb, R., *Statistical Pitot-Static Calibration Using Level Acceleration and Turning Acceleration Techniques*, 46th International SFTE Symposium, Lancaster CA, 14-17 September 2015.

24. Jurado, Juan D., McGehee, Clark C., *Complete Online Algorithm for Air Data System Calibration*, Journal of Aircraft 56, no. 2 (2019): 517-528.

25. *Department of Defense World Geodetic System 1984*, National Imagery and Mapping Agency TR8350.2, Third Edition, Amendment 1, 3 January 2000.

26. http://gis.stackexchange.com/questions/20200/how-do-you-compute-the-earths-radius-at-a-given-geodetic-latitude retrieved 30 April 2015.

27. Çengel, Yunus A. and Boles, Michael A., *Thermodynamics: An Engineering Approach, Second Edition*, McGraw-Hill, Inc., New York, 1994.

28. Eshbach, Ovid W. and Souders, Mott, *Handbook of Engineering Fundamentals*, John Wiley & Sons, New York, 1975.

29. Nick84 - http://commons.wikimedia.org/wiki/File:Solar_spectrum_ita.svg, CC BY-SA 3.0, https://commons.wikimedia.org/w/index.php?curid=24648395

30. Trenberth, Kevin E., Fasullo, John T., Kiehl, Jeffrey, *Earth's Global Energy Budget*, Bulletin of the American Meteorological Society, March 2009.

31. Newman, et. al., *Stratospheric Ozone: An Electronic Textbook*, Center for Coastal Physical Oceanography, Old Dominion University, (http://www.ccpo.odu.edu/SEES/ozone/oz_class.htm)

32. Goessling, H.F., Bathiany, S., *Why CO_2 Cools the Middle Atmosphere – A Consolidating Model Perspective*, Earth System Dynamics, 2016.

33. *Total Temperature Sensors*, Technical Report 5755, Revision C, Sensor Systems, Goodrich Corporation, Burnsville, MN, 1994.

34. Katsiavriades, Kryss, Spherical Trigonometry, http://www.krysstal.com/sphertrig.html

35. Olson, W. M., *Aircraft Performance Flight Testing*, AFFTC-TIH-99-01, Air Force Flight Test Center, September 2000.

36. Olson, W. M., *Air Data Calibration from Turning Flight*, Air Force Flight Test Center, 1999.

37. Gudgel, Dan, *Weather To Fly: Thermal Development*, Soaring, Soaring Society of America, August 2011.

38. Nicks, Oran W., *A Simple Total Energy Sensor*, NASA TM X-73928, National Aeronautics and Space Administration, Langley Research Center, Hampton VA, March 1976.

Milton Keynes UK
Ingram Content Group UK Ltd.
UKHW052056031123
431914UK00005B/31